Diction

D0863625

Dictionary of Counselling

Second Edition

COLIN FELTHAM
Sheffield Hallam University

and

WINDY DRYDEN
Goldsmiths College, University of London

W
WHURR PUBLISHERS
LONDON AND PHILADELPHIA

© 2004 Whurr Publishers Ltd

First Published 2004

Whurr Publishers Ltd
19b Compton Terrace, London N1 2UN, England and
325 Chestnut Street, Philadelphia PA19106, USA

British Library Cataloguing in Publication Data

A catalogue record for this book is available from the British
Library.

ISBN 1 86156 382 5

Printed and bound in the UK by Athenaeum Press Limited,
Gateshead, Tyne & Wear.

Contents

Preface to the first edition

This dictionary is intended to define the key terms and concepts used by and deemed useful to counsellors. We anticipate that it will be of interest and assistance to practising counsellors, counsellors-in-training, people who use counselling skills in their work, and members of the helping professions generally. Clients who are mystified by their counsellors' language may also find meaning in these pages. Our emphasis in selecting terms for definition has been on counselling rather than on psychotherapy, psychiatry, psychology and other related fields. We have, however, included certain significant terms from those fields. In the case of psychotherapy, the overlap with counselling terms and concepts is considerable. Existing dictionaries of psychotherapy (Walrond-Skinner, 1986; Samuels, Shorter and Plaut, 1987) and psychoanalysis (Laplanche and Pontalis, 1988; Rycroft, 1988), however, focus largely on terms derived from or closely related to psychoanalysis. Students and practitioners of humanistic, eclectic or integrative psychotherapy, therefore, may find the range of terms and concepts represented here compatible with their interests. We have included some definitions of terms from group and family therapy, but our primary focus has been on individual counselling.

While in some quarters counselling is a well-established occupation, it is broadly in a state of early evolution as a profession. Timms and Timms (1982) wryly observed that 'counselling is hard to define but there is a great deal of it about'. For non-counsellors, the very term 'counselling' is often mystifying or misunderstood: it carries the traditional meaning of advice giving, yet this is the very function that most counsellors claim not to perform. In order to address such mystification and misunderstanding, we have aimed at definitional baselines which we hope will enhance public understanding and acceptance of counselling. Unfortunately, many current dictionaries of health and social science subjects (e.g. *Concise Oxford Medical Dictionary* (1991) and the *Macmillan Dictionary of Psychology* (Sutherland, 1991)) still reinforce outdated definitions and caricatures of counselling as the giving of advice and sympathy.

We hope, on the other hand, that we have not fallen (too frequently) prey to over-esoteric definitions. In their book *Loss of the Good Authority*, Tom Pitt-Aikens and Alice Thomas Ellis write: 'definitions are, by definition, difficult. Dr Johnson, faced with the self-imposed task of defining a net, grew skittish and parodied himself: "Anything reticulated or decussated with intersections at intervals between the interstices"!' We trust that we have avoided, too, the (sometimes very real) temptation to follow the example of Sutherland, whose dictionary offers many outrageously satirical definitions of psychological terms.

In compiling this dictionary we faced certain decisions. The dictionary has benefited greatly from the suggestions and amendments (in some cases panel-beating!) of the eight consultants to this project; every entry has been checked by at least one of them. However, responsibility for the final choice of entries and the overall presentation of material is our own. We decided, for example, that we wanted to produce a practical dictionary, not an unwieldy encyclopaedia or handbook. We have therefore not included historical and biographical material. We decided, too, to aim at an accessible text offering definitions, examples and nuances, and short critical commentaries. We decided not to follow the convention of many such dictionaries, which offer references for every entry, but we have indicated a number of references for readers who may wish to pursue certain subjects further.

Because counselling is practised in such a wide variety of settings, it is impossible properly to acknowledge this contextual variety in detail (e.g. the counselling of people with learning difficulties, the counselling of torture victims, etc.) and any such omissions will, we hope, be understood as stemming from editorial necessity rather than as oversight or under-estimation of the importance of these activities. Another kind of necessary omission is detailed reference to research, particularly in the many areas of strongly divided opinion. Counselling is characterised by diverse clinical and theoretical contributions, and we have chosen to reflect this throughout in the phrases 'many counsellors believe', 'critics suggest', and so on. Readers referring to entries in the hope of finding the authoritative and definitive 'last word' on any subject should bear in mind its authors' decision to reflect the current diversity, conflicts and ambiguities of the field.

In seeking to reflect fairly the influence of the diverse models of counselling theory and practice, we have had to make decisions as to which technical terms to include and which to exclude. Many psychoanalytically derived terms are included because they are so well established and professionally influential. Certain counselling orientations, in spite of their influence, have relatively little technical language unique to them (e.g. person-centred counselling). Certain orientations generate a great deal of specialist technical language (e.g. personal construct therapy, transactional analysis and neurolinguistic programming); in such cases we have selected some of the major and most interesting terms but have had to avoid attempting to provide comprehensive coverage of each orientation. Readers with a particular need for accurate and comprehensive technical definitions of specialist terms (for example, students of transactional analysis preparing to sit examinations) are advised to consult the relevant primary specialist sources rather than relying on a dictionary of this general nature.

Finally, we fully realise the potential for development and fine-tuning in an enterprise of this kind. This dictionary inevitably reflects to some extent the views and limitations of the authors and of the period in which they write. The field of counselling and psychotherapy has been described as 'dispute-riven', and we are mindful of the advice given to Noel and Rita Timms when beginning their dictionary (Timms and Timms, 1982), which was: 'Don't attempt it'! In the rapidly evolving field of counselling, we anticipate a need for periodic revised editions of this dictionary. Your comments are therefore very welcome: please address any suggestions to us, care of the publisher.

Colin Feltham and Windy Dryden

Preface to the second edition

After a period of a decade we were finally convinced that a revision was called for. The *Dictionary* in its first edition was largely well received, in particular by students and busy practitioners. We were gratified by its translation into Japanese. We were aware that while certain terms had not changed or had changed little, others demanded revision, some (few) called for deletion, and many omissions and new terms became apparent.

This edition, then, comprises our efforts to update the counselling lexicon as authoritatively as we can. We freely admit to the difficulty of this task and the likelihood that we have missed certain terms, been swayed by our own prejudices, and exercised our selective faculties in such a way that unanimous approval cannot be guaranteed. Counselling is both a field in its own right, in its practice and academic aspects, and is also interdisciplinary; hence, borrowed terminology is quite common, and the meanings of certain terms are modified. It should be noted that attribution of all terms to their originators has not been possible and bibliographical references unfortunately cannot be comprehensive in a wide-ranging text of this kind. What we have especially striven to do in this second edition is to include terms that have arisen or gained more prominence since the publication of the first edition. These derive from the realms of professional developments (e.g. Ethical Framework, CORE), innovative models (e.g. eye movement desensitisation and reprocessing, mindfulness-based cognitive therapy), new theoretical perspectives (e.g. evolutionary psychotherapy) and topical issues (e.g. evidence-based practice).

The field has moved significantly but certainly not wholly beyond recognition in the last decade. Movement towards professionalisation has continued, a few innovative approaches have established themselves, counselling research has grown, and fruitful tensions continue between the professions of psychiatry, clinical psychology, psychotherapy, counselling and counselling psychology.

Specialist dictionaries in the field have continued to appear, such as Whurr's own dictionaries of Rational Emotive Behaviour Therapy, Person-Centred Psychology, Transactional Analysis and Personal Development. One cannot help but ironically envy the author of *The Dictionary of the Work of Wilfred Bion*, Rafael Lopez-Corvo, who in spite of a narrow remit has the distinct possibility of producing uncontested definitions. We have a very long way to go before matching the magnitude of Ray Corsini's mammoth (1156 pages) *The Dictionary of Psychology*.

But we hope the *Dictionary of Counselling* in its second edition will bring a largely accurate, updated focus to the field of counselling in the UK. And, as always, we welcome constructive comments on additions and corrections for any future edition.

Colin Feltham and Windy Dryden

Acknowledgements

We are extremely grateful to the original eight consultants to this project: Mark Aveline, Tim Bond, Petrūska Clarkson, Michael Jacobs, John Rowan, Brian Thorne, Moira Walker and Ray Woolfe. We have also been helped at various stages by Selwyn Black, Colin Brett, Brenda Clowes, Martin Cole, Emmy van Deurzen, Marie Feltham, Fay Fransella, Geoff Haines, Kirsty Hoben, Richard House, Alex Howard, Michelle Kay, James Low, Stephen Palmer, Ashfaq Qureshi, Bernard Rosen, Andrew Samuels, David Smith and Janet Symes. Our thanks are due, too, to numerous colleagues who have helped our understanding of counselling, and the language of counselling, over the years. Any errors evident here are our own responsibility.

Conventions used

Within many entries you will find certain words and phrases in small capitals. These refer to terms that can be found elsewhere in the Dictionary (cross-references), which may help to elucidate the meaning of the term you are reading about. In most cases, such cross-references are simple to identify but occasionally there is a slight variation (e.g. you will find 'person-centred counsellor' referred to under person-centred counselling). Obviously, not all those terms that do appear elsewhere can be marked as cross-references, however. Italicised words and italicised phrases represent emphasis; or subheadings within an entry; or the titles of books or journals. Where the surnames of writers on counselling and psychotherapy appear unsupported by references, this indicates the obvious person in the field (e.g. Sigmund Freud or Albert Ellis); but in cases of possible confusion about names we have made further clarifications. We have used the terms 'she', 'her', 'he' and 'his' randomly rather than resorting to more cumbersome non-sexist conventions. While abbreviations have been kept to a minimum, we have included a list of those used for readers' convenience.

Abbreviations

AA	Alcoholics Anonymous
ADD	attention-deficit disorder (or ADHD: attention-deficit hyperactivity disorder)
AIDS	acquired immune deficiency syndrome
AS	Asperger's syndrome
BACP	British Association for Counselling and Psychotherapy
BPS	British Psychological Society
CAT	cognitive analytic therapy
CBT	cognitive behaviour therapy
CFS	chronic fatigue syndrome
CMHT	community mental health team
CORE	clinical outcomes in routine evaluation
CPN	community psychiatric nurse
CSA	child sexual abuse
DSM-IV TR	*Diagnostic and Statistical Manual of Mental Disorders* (4th edition, Text Revised)
EAP	employee assistance programme
EBP	evidence-based practice
ECT	electroconvulsive therapy
EMDR	eye movement desensitisation and reprocessing
EEG	electroencephalogram
HIV	human immunodeficiency virus
ICD 10	*International Classification of (Mental and Behavioural) Disorders* (10th edition)
ISTDP	intensive short-term dynamic psychotherapy
IVF	in vitro fertilisation
LFT	low frustration tolerance
NHS	National Health Service
NLP	neurolinguistic programming
OCD	obsessive-compulsive disorder

PCA	person-centred approach
PCP	personal construct psychology
PMT/S	pre-menstrual tension/syndrome
PTSD	post-traumatic stress disorder
RC	re-evaluation counselling
REBT	rational emotive behaviour therapy
SAD	seasonal affective disorder
SFT	solution-focused therapy
SST	single session therapy
TA	transactional analysis
TLC	time-limited counselling
UKCP	United Kingdom Council for Psychotherapy
YAVIS	young, attractive, verbal, intelligent, successful

A note on relevant UK spellings

Since a great deal of American literature influences British counselling, much of it confusing to students in particular, we offer brief guidance on the following key terms:

Behaviour is correct UK spelling, e.g. *behaviour therapy* (US: *behavior*).
Person-*centred* is correct UK spelling (US: *person-centered*).
Counselling is the correct spelling in the UK, Canada and Australasia (US: *counseling*).
Practice (noun) is correct UK spelling for, e.g. 'my counselling practice'; and *practise* (verb) is correct UK spelling for, e.g. 'I *practise* as a counsellor' (US: *practice* in both cases).

ABC model used in rational emotive behaviour therapy (Dryden and Neenan, 1997) for the systematic analysis of clients' emotional and behavioural problems. A = ACTIVATING EVENT (including any interpretations of events); B = mediating evaluative beliefs; C = emotional and behavioural consequences. REBT practitioners use this system to analyse and explain to clients that their evaluative thinking about events largely dictates their feelings and actions. The ABC model is now extended to ABCDE, the D representing DISPUTING and the E the effect of practising rational thinking. (Note that the ABC sequence used in behaviour therapy, where A is antecedent, B is behaviour and C is consequence, is quite different.)

abortion counselling counselling relating to issues of pre- and post-termination of a pregnancy; not necessarily baldly referred to as abortion counselling but often a part of 'pregnancy advice and counselling'. Abortion in the UK is legal up to the twenty-fourth week of pregnancy, with the consent of two doctors. Any woman considering abortion needs access to information and support. She needs time to explore and consider the information and the implications of the decision she will reach. Abortion counselling should include all CORE CONDITIONS common to good counselling, and should help the woman to make her own decisions freely and independently. Care needs to be taken to ensure that the woman has access to all the necessary information and advice and to sound medical help. Counselling needs to provide unbiased and unprejudiced time and space to allow the individual a chance to explore her own feelings and dilemmas. This often includes the expression of loss and guilt. Problems of decisional dilemma and delayed grief are quite common. Religious opposition remains strong.

abreaction an emotional release experienced by clients either spontaneously or, more commonly, during the course of counselling and as a result of exploring concerns at some depth. Originally believed by Breuer and Freud to be the correct focus of (and main curative force in) therapy, abreaction and its attendant CATHARSIS were subsequently relegated to a position of lesser importance by many counselling theorists. However, humanistic counsellors, particularly those practising gestalt, psychodrama and primal therapy, have restored abreaction and catharsis to a position of central importance. Janov (1975) distinguishes between an abreaction and PRIMAL, arguing that the former is frequently a false and non-healing phenomenon, with more histrionic appeal than historically rooted authenticity. Others have argued that the encouragement of clients towards abreactive states is unhealthy because it tends to make them *feel*, rather than *get*, better. Counsellors working in a deliberate attempt to uncover repressed material by confrontation of defences or other means of evoking strong feelings need to provide extra safeguards for clients who undergo abreactive experiences.

absolutistic thinking the cognitive error of turning personal desires and fears into absolutes. By so doing (e.g. 'I am absolutely devastated and nothing can help') people compound their problems instead of gaining useful perspective on them.

abstinence the 'holding back' from normal social conversation and interaction that is viewed as a vital feature of PSYCHODYNAMIC COUNSELLING in particular. Sometimes misunderstood as unhelpful remoteness, the function of the 'rule of abstinence' is the promotion of self-exploration on the part of the client, as well as the creation of therapeutically optimal anxiety. Counsellor abstinence subtly refuses to contaminate clients' own internal processes, thereby promoting access to FREE ASSOCIATION and fruitful identification of deep-seated conflicts. Some research (*see* Garfield and Bergin, 1986) suggests that clients prefer a more naturalistic interaction with their counsellors than that advocated by the rule of abstinence. Abstinence also refers to the complete avoidance of alcohol or other sub-

stances by people who follow certain programmes of treatment for addiction.

acceptance an attitude of receptivity, non-judgementalism and interest. Acceptance by the counsellor of the person of the client is a central requirement for work to proceed. Acceptance is widely held to be necessary for therapeutic progress. The accepting counsellor signals his or her readiness to be with and hear the client non-judgementally, thus facilitating trust and enabling the client to make sometimes painful, embarrassing personal disclosures. A helpful distinction is sometimes made between accepting the person but not necessarily accepting certain aspects of their behaviour: neither global condemnation nor global affirmation is optimal. While an uncritical acceptance may head counselling in the direction of cosiness and COLLUSION, true but alert acceptance is a powerful therapeutic tool, as well as an essential ethical attitude. The counsellor is advised to be aware of any personal difficulties in accepting the behavioural, cultural or other differences between him- or herself and the client. Other connotations include unconditional self-acceptance, the acceptance stage of loss, and acceptance as love, forgiveness and agape.

accountability an understanding that counsellors will work professionally and will be prepared to explain their decisions if called upon to do so. In organisational contexts most counsellors are accountable for their work to line managers or to colleagues. People claiming to practise as counsellors but not belonging to any professional body are not at present legally accountable under UK law except to their clients. It is therefore in the interests of clients to use counsellors who belong to reputable organisations that require their members to be ethically accountable, to receive ongoing supervision and to have a complaints procedure.

accreditation the granting of professional status. In the UK, counselling organisations such as the British Association for Counselling and Psychotherapy have established criteria for the accreditation of counsellors, supervisors and courses based on agreed levels of training in and experience of counselling theory, skills, work with clients, and professional development. At present these are voluntary schemes, there being no statutory requirement for counsellors to demonstrate that they have received certain levels of training. *See* BACP.

accurate empathy *see* EMPATHY.

accurate symbolisation the exact word or image to describe what the client is experiencing at any given moment. Rogers (1961) noted the common sensitivity of clients to the precise fit of symbols for grasping shifting inner meanings during the processes of recalling, identifying and articulating experiences during counselling.

acquisition of disturbance the theoretical explanation given to account for how people first develop psychological problems. The term 'acquisition' implies that behaviour is learned. It is the psychological equivalent of the AETIOLOGY of physical disease but is more problematic, because the various schools of thought in counselling psychology frequently disagree about the basis of human functioning and dysfunctioning.

acting-out the client's displacement of painful or uncomfortable feelings into behaviour which both expresses these feelings in an indirect manner and denies them. This may take the form of occasional, seemingly uncontrollable outbursts of uncharacteristic behaviour or more habitual dysfunctional behaviour. Examples may include testing boundaries in counselling (such as in relation to punctuality, sullenness, violence or alcohol abuse). There is some disagreement as to how conscious and controllable such behaviour is, but there is general consensus as to its defensive and avoidant purposes. Acting-out can occur in counselling and in everyday life. A distinction is sometimes made between acting-out and 'living out' one's inner pain constructively. *See* DEFENCE MECHANISMS, GAMES, RACKETS.

activating event according to REBT theory, that which happens, is believed to have happened, or is about to happen, so as to trigger irrational beliefs which in turn lead to problematic emotions and behaviour. Many clients, particularly at the beginning of counselling, attribute their problems or entire personality structure to childhood events, past or recent trauma or anticipated undesirable events. Cognitive therapists discriminate keenly between events and interpretations made about events. *See* ABC.

active–directive methods those counselling procedures advocating a high level of counsellor activity (e.g. questioning, challenging, suggestion) and directiveness considered to be therapeutic (e.g. encouraging goalsetting, assigning homework) as well as active participation on the part of the client. The influence of Carl Rogers has generated a public perception of counselling as exclusively or predominantly

3

non-directive. Most cognitive and behavioural, as well as many humanistic, counselling models advocate active–directive methods. *See* the EGAN APPROACH, and Greenwald (1974).

active imagination *see* IMAGINATION.

active listening *see* LISTENING.

actualisation the coming to tangible, visible fruition of something previously only thought of, dreamt of, or longed for. The activity of putting plans into action. *See* SELF-ACTUALISATION.

actualising tendency according to Rogers (1961) and other humanistic counsellors, the movement towards the fulfilment of potential. Rogers believed in an innate tendency of people (and other organisms) to 'become their potential' and to 'expand, extend and mature'. This tendency is vulnerable to parental and societal distortions but is always active and can be re-nurtured. Contrast with DEFENCE MECHANISMS.

acute a psychological or emotional disturbance is described as acute when it reaches critical, debilitating or destructive proportions. Mainly a psychiatric term referring to people with distressing symptoms of recent onset, or of relatively short duration, it is also used to describe the severity of fleeting emotions, as in 'acutely embarrassed'. Contrast with CHRONIC.

Adapted Child in TRANSACTIONAL ANALYSIS THEORY the part of the functional CHILD EGO STATE and role which is concerned with behaviours of conformity to parental and social rules and demands.

adaptive flexible, responsive to changing conditions, malleable. Behaviour can be regarded as positively or negatively adaptive (maladaptive), depending on whether it is in or against the interests of the self and others. Appropriate adaptation to circumstances is a mark of maturity and is different from over-adaptation, which is usually an indication of PLACATORY BEHAVIOUR. Some critics of (non-radical forms of) counselling and psychotherapy argue that they encourage people to adapt to undesirable social norms. The term 'adaptive counselling' is sometimes used of counselling which aims to suit the client's style (*see* AUTHENTIC CHAMELEON). *See also* MALADAPTIVE.

addiction dependence, usually of a stubborn nature, on noxious substances, self-harming behaviour or persons. In the widest sense, people can be said to be addicted to any activity, including sex, work and sports. Addiction is more commonly used to refer to dependence on drug or alcohol consumption, particularly where the dependence is incessant and the effects are highly negative. Some addictions carry more stigma than others because of cultural or legal taboos. Hence, nicotine addiction, however unhealthy, carries far less stigma than addiction to illegal drugs such as heroin and cocaine. Some substances are chemically addictive; others are more psychologically addictive. The notion of the 'addictive personality' has been largely discredited and addictive behaviour is often viewed as stemming from a variety of psychological, sociological and other factors. Drug addiction is sometimes regarded as a form of PERSONALITY DISORDER and some research has investigated genetic predisposition to addiction. People addicted to alcohol or other chemical substances usually need to undergo a withdrawal programme in combination with counselling, and often need RESIDEN-

TIAL TREATMENT, intensive support, group therapy and/or behavioural regimens. Even so, such clients are usually very hard to work with, especially in acute phases of addiction, when chaotic lifestyles often include multiple dysfunctions, including deception of others. Some people hide their addictions successfully for some time and some addictions are, of course, the result of prescribed medication, most commonly in the case of TRANQUILLISERS. *See also* ALCOHOLISM, CHEMICAL DEPENDENCY, DRUG ADDICTION, MINNESOTA METHOD.

adjustment change according to circumstances or for psychological comfort or as a result of achieving psychological maturity. Like ADAPTATION, adjustment can be viewed in positive or negative terms. The term 'adjustment' has many negative connotations relating to purely external, behavioural and socially acceptable changes.

Adlerian counselling *see* INDIVIDUAL PSYCHOLOGY.

adult children of alcoholics people who suffered directly or indirectly in childhood from their parents' excessive alcohol consumption. There are thought to be recognisable signs of the effects of neglect and abuse by such parents. These can include insecurity, low self-esteem, placatory behaviour, depression, and seeking out partners who are abusive or immature. *See* CO-DEPENDENCY.

adult ego state the ego state, in TA theory, characterised by a set of feelings, attitudes and behaviour related to the here and now, to healthy adult functioning, and not being tainted by inappropriate interferences from the CHILD EGO STATE or the PARENT EGO STATE.

adult survivor someone who was abused physically, sexually or psychologically in childhood and has survived into adulthood. The long-term effects of abuse on the adult's way of life and sense of self are many and complex. Adult survivors often form support groups for those who have had similar experiences.

advanced empathy *see* EMPATHY.

advice instructions and/or information given with the intention of helping or directing. Advice giving differs from counselling in placing less emphasis on the client's own decision-making processes. While technical or urgent advice has its place both inside and outside counselling, it is considered by most (but not all) to be an ineffective means of engaging clients' own creativity and problem-solving capacities. Persistent advice giving is likely to undermine client autonomy. However, it is doubtful whether counsellors *always* refrain from offering behavioural or practical advice (if only snippets), and many counsellors work in roles where they are expected both to give advice and to counsel.

advocacy speaking on behalf of a client. Counsellors are rarely in this position, but in certain statutory or voluntary organisation settings they may be called on to make legal representation. Some clients may ask their counsellor to assist them practically or to speak or write on their behalf to local or national government welfare or housing agencies. People with serious mental health problems, learning difficulties or certain disabilities may need an advocate. Such advocacy as undertaken by a counsellor should avoid undermining the client's ability to represent, or learn to represent, himself. *See also* INNER CHILD ADVOCACY.

aetiology mainly in use in physical medicine, aetiology refers to the causation of an illness. Its relative under-use in counselling may reflect a rejection of the MEDICAL MODEL (which is incorrectly seen to be unicausal rather than multifactorial), but also reflects the multiple-model nature of counselling psychology (no consensus on causes) and the often nebulous or chronic nature of client problems. *See* ACQUISITION OF DISTURBANCE.

affect a broad term referring to feelings, emotions, mood, rather than to cognition or behaviour. In psychiatric usage, affect is viewed as disturbed in the 'affective disorders' of depression, elation and anxiety. 'Inappropriate affect' suggests that people do not feel and display those emotions commonly associated with everyday events (such as responding with laughter to a joke, with tears to bereavement). 'Lack of affect' refers to a prolonged non-expressive state and is a feature of depression.

affective bridge a statement made or action suggested by the counsellor, which seeks to demonstrate a link between a feeling currently being experienced by the client and one experienced previously. Also called *affect bridge*. This is usually a purposeful attempt to deepen the present feeling and to assist the client in accessing earlier significant feelings.

affirmation a positive attitude and statement declaring confidence in self or another and commitment to a course of action. Commonly used in the field of alcohol dependency, where the personal commitment to remaining 'dry' is crucial. Affirmation is also reinforcement or a STROKE given to another.

agenda plan or list of items to be addressed or actions to be pursued. In counselling, an agenda may refer to a particular session or to the entire course of counselling. Agendas may be formal or informal, overt (clear and fully understood) or covert (unclear, unconscious or devious), or client, counsellor or agency agendas (which should coincide, but do not always). *Hidden agendas* are undeclared intentions (for example, when a client wishes to prove how disturbed she is in order to qualify for sickness entitlement, when a counsellor wishes to test out a new theory or technique, when both collude in flirtation or avoidance). *See* GOALS.

aggression general term for attitude and behaviour that is energy directed outwards in self-protection, hostility, threat or violence. In extreme forms of individual pathology aggression may result in criminal behaviour; in moderate forms it may result in insensitivity to others' needs, indifference to the social norms of courtesy and in verbal emotional bullying. Some theorists regard aggression (rather than ASSERTIVENESS) as simply the expression of energy and as good and normal. The ability to be aggressive in certain circumstances (e.g. when protecting a child, or when competing for a job) can be seen as an important aspect of maturity. Clients exhibiting, or bringing as presenting problems, their aggression and its effects, need to be shown the differences between aggression, assertiveness and anger and their respective healthy and unhealthy expressions. *Displaced aggression* occurs when, for example, a boy cannot retaliate against a punitive father and therefore hits his younger brother or classmates. Certain environments, particularly overcrowded ones, are thought to foster aggression.

Aggression is also, empirically, an attribute of men more often than of women. *See also* PASSIVE–AGGRESSIVE, VIOLENCE.

agitation behaviour marked by unusual or prolonged restlessness. Agitation may be a symptom of anxiety or depression. The terms 'agitated depression' and 'psychomotor agitation' are found in psychiatric literature, referring to marked restlessness, irritability, hand-wringing, nihilistic delusions and other signs of disturbance; they may indicate a condition with high risk of suicide and for which psychiatric assessment is indicated.

agoraphobia anxiety in relation to open spaces (including built-up areas). Agoraphobia is usually compounded by the fear that one will inevitably become anxious in open spaces or away from the home. It is frequently a chronic condition, experienced more by women than by men, and is characterised by over-attachment to the home, low self-esteem, lack of confidence and dread of leaving the house, travelling alone or travelling beyond the immediate neighbourhood. Attempts to overcome agoraphobia without understanding the condition and how it can be dealt with may result in extreme PANIC ATTACKS and RELAPSE. Because of its self-reinforcing nature, people suffering from agoraphobia have difficulty in contacting or securing counselling help. The stigma of agoraphobia often results in the SECONDARY EMOTIONAL PROBLEMS of guilt and shame. Traditionally it has been treated with tranquillisers but these are now regarded as likely to exacerbate the problem. Research suggests that consistent EXPOSURE, supported by social and professional networks, is the most efficient treatment. Counselling can assist agoraphobic clients at critical stages of recovery. Much agoraphobia is thought to be associated with the undermining of social skills and confidence during housebound phases of child rearing or following the loss of a partner.

ahistorical models theories of counselling which place little or no significance on the contribution of the client's past to present difficulties and/or little or no weight on the power of the unearthing of past material to change the client. These models may regard memory as unreliable, people as having exaggerated views about childhood trauma or psychoanalytically derived theories of childhood development as unconvincing. It is argued that, while people have learned self-defeating behaviour in the past, it can be changed only in the present. Most COGNITIVE and BEHAVIOURAL approaches are of this kind.

AIDS counselling counselling related to the acquired immunodeficiency syndrome (AIDS). AIDS is a life-threatening (usually fatal in spite of pharmacological advances) illness, resulting from HIV (human immunodeficiency virus) infection. While much AIDS counselling involves the same core conditions and strategies as other forms of counselling, the nature of AIDS, its social ramifications and inconclusive medical research evidence, means that those working in this area usually have or need special information and additional training. It is important to be sensitive to the language used so as to avoid STIGMA and misunderstanding. There are certain risk behaviours (courting contact with known transmission routes such as anal intercourse and intravenous drug abuse) associated with HIV and AIDS, and it is inappropriate to speak of risk *groups*. Counselling in the area of AIDS spans the issues of prevention, pre- and post-HIV antibody testing, counselling people who are HIV positive (and who are either asymptomatic or becoming ill), counselling people diagnosed as having AIDS and AIDS-related conditions, counselling people with AIDS dementia, counselling at critical stages (including dying), and counselling partners, family and relatives of people with AIDS. Because a variety of professionals work in the AIDS field, the counselling offered will vary but should always be highly sensitive to the emotional, medical, social, legal and other issues involved. Because there is still no cure for AIDS and an uncertain pattern from the development of HIV infection to full-blown AIDS, many working in the field advise full exploration of anxiety-reducing methods and hope-engendering attitudes.

alcoholism the term means, or has meant, variously: an addiction to alcohol; an abuse of alcohol; a fatal disease, probably with a genetic predisposition. The last definition, although widely refuted by many researchers and counsellors, is used by Alcoholics Anonymous and by counsellors using the MINNESOTA METHOD. The term 'drink problem' is preferred by many people in order to avoid the connotation of disease. Most people accept that moderate alcohol consumption is not (for most people) problematic. Some people argue that excessive alcohol consumption and alcohol dependency is always a symptom of underlying distress or conflict but research has not validated, for example, psychoanalytic views on this. Clinical wisdom suggests that people who are denying their alcoholism or who are actively inebriated cannot be counselled usefully, but otherwise a variety of methods are used in both individual and group counselling. *See also* ADDICTION.

alienation estrangement or dissociation. Existentialist writers have argued that humans are by their nature alienated from the natural world and inevitably experience angst, anomie or existential ANXIETY. Sociologists have argued that modern urban life, the competitiveness inherent in capitalism, loss of extended families, and greater social and geographical mobility have all led to a sense of alienation in individuals. Psychologists and Marxists use the term quite differently.

alliance friendship, collaboration, rapport or agreement. Counselling and psychotherapy literature refers to social alliance, collaborative alliance, working alliance and THERAPEUTIC ALLIANCE. Used in family therapy, the term also has an ambiguous meaning suggesting the possibility of collusion.

allocation of clients assigning clients from a waiting list or immediately from intake and assessment to a suitable counsellor. Agencies operating a structured allocation system will try to allocate each client to the most appropriate counsellor (see PRESCRIPTIVE MATCHING) or simply to the next available counsellor.

all-or-nothing thinking a form of faulty information processing whereby desires and achievements are conceived of in unrealistic, absolutist terms. Reflected in irrational statements like: 'If I can't have the woman/the job I want, then life is completely meaningless', it is often a mark of depression. *See* ABSOLUTISTIC THINKING and RATIONAL EMOTIVE BEHAVIOUR THERAPY.

alter ego literally 'other self'. Its meanings are: other, lesser self or aspects of the self; dark, destructive other self or aspects of the self (as in Dr Jekyll's Mr Hyde); another person who closely resembles or complements the self. The term now has no real clinical usage.

altruism concern for others; being inclined to help others and especially to help without expectation of reward. Philosophers and social psychologists have attempted to analyse the roots of altruism and possible explanations as to why some people behave more altruistically than others. Many humanistic psychologists assert that altruism (or love) is part of human nature, while others stress that it is learned behaviour or even a DEFENCE MECHANISM. Counsellors are altruistic to the degree to which they choose a helping, other-oriented profession.

ambivalence the experience of conflicting emotions, usually towards the same object or person. In its negative sense, ambivalence is the universal problem of wavering, indecision and avoidance of commitment. Clinically, it is often expressed in the client being tentative, unpunctual, missing sessions or acting-out in other ways. A love–hate conflict with a parent may be expressed in counselling by alternating positive and negative TRANSFERENCE. Avoidance of problem-solving attitudes may indicate ambivalence towards successful counselling. In its positive sense, the ability to contain ambivalent feelings (e.g. love/hate) towards the same person is felt to be an indication of more complete human relationships. *See* APPROACH-AVOIDANCE.

amnesia loss of memory. True amnesia is largely an organic condition resulting from brain damage through accident, and most counsellors are unlikely to encounter it. Counsellors working in medical settings, especially with people suffering from head injuries, may meet people suffering from *post-traumatic amnesia*. Partial amnesia may be associated with certain kinds of drug abuse, alcoholism or electroconvulsive therapy (ECT). *Childhood amnesia* refers to the fairly commonly reported inability to recall early childhood memories and is sometimes thought to be associated with trauma and chronic defences against feeling the effects of trauma. *See* FORGETTING.

anal stage according to Freudian developmental theory, the anal stage occurs between the ages of 2 and 4 years, and is characterised by the actions of muscular control and expulsion and retention of faeces. Freud considered this stage to be significant in the formation of obsessional neuroses. Concern with defecation can be a cause of sado-masochism, pathological withholding and other disturbances. Understood as symbolic infantile gifts, faeces are sometimes also viewed as equated with money. Colloquial echoes of the anal (or anally retentive) character are found in 'tight-arsed', 'uptight' and 'tight-fisted'.

analytic third Jungian-derived concept referring to a psychic field between analyst/counsellor and analysand/client that combines the subjectivities of both parties. Also known as the interactive field, the analytic third may draw from the collective unconscious as well as from individual subjectivities. A multifaceted phenomenon, it can be deceptive in clinical practice.

analytical psychology this term is used to refer to JUNGIAN psychology and psychotherapy (hence, 'analytical psychologist' being synonymous with Jungian analyst or psychotherapist). Jung aimed to produce a psychology that included the insights of, but was wider than, that of his contemporaries Freud and Adler. Jung postulated both a personal and a COLLECTIVE UNCONSCIOUS. His psychology made ample use of various bipolar schemas, such as the anima–animus ARCHETYPE and the concept of extravert–introvert. He postulated four basic human functions: thinking, feeling, sensation and intuition. Jung gave greater weight to the importance of later life than have many other theorists, especially the search for spiritual meaning. He was concerned with psychology as teleological (relating to purpose and potential) rather than as reductionist (relating to causes and determinism) and used the term INDIVIDUATION, for example, to refer to the individual's unique psychological maturing process. Because his is a wide-ranging personality theory using aspects of psychoanalysis, psychiatry, anthropology, religion, mythology, astrology and other disciplines, analytical psychology lends itself to the notion of a 'plural psyche' (or inevitable psychological diversity) and now has at least two main schools – developmental and archetypal (Samuels, 1985). *See also* ARCHETYPE, SHADOW.

anger strong primary feeling directed against others or parts of the self. Broadly speaking, anger can encompass aspects of hostility, self-defence, protection of others and reactions against threat to self or parts of the self (e.g. cherished beliefs). Immediate and appropriate anger reactions need not be problematic, being healthy expressions and signals to others. Suppressed anger is thought to be problematic because others are denied the appropriate signals of true feeling. However, because anger is often disallowed in children by their parents, chronically suppressed anger is not uncommon and can result in personality and psychosomatic disorders. Conversely, uncontrolled and inappropriate anger can result in social problems. The identification of extremes of suppressed or uncontrollable anger, and working therapeutically to increase or modify its expression, is therefore a task in which counsellors are often engaged. *See* ANGER MANAGEMENT and RAGE.

anger management a largely cognitive-behavioural programme for understanding and controlling excessive, inappropriate anger that causes difficulties in a person's life, most notably in criminal behaviour.

anhedonia absence of pleasure or joy; inability to feel or express normal pleasure. Common in depression.

anima, animus terms used in analytical psychology to suggest a personification of the woman within the man (anima) and the man within the woman (animus). The anima and animus are representative of archetypal patterns, anima relating to imagination, fantasy and play, and animus to 'focused consciousness', authority and respect. (Anima is derived from the Latin 'soul' and animus from 'mind' or 'intellect'.) In modern usage, anima and animus refer to alternative modes of perception in both men and women.

anomalous experience external or internal events in someone's life which do not appear to fit readily into existing explanatory frameworks. Sometimes falling into psychic, parapsychological or psychiatric categories, it must also be recognised that people may sometimes have experiences that are indeed novel and non-pathological, and which may be spiritual or transpersonal. *See* Grof and Grof (1990).

anorexia nervosa an eating disorder characterised by extreme resistance to meeting one's own nutritional needs, eating being very strictly controlled while body size is usually perceived as larger than it is. 'Body mass index' is a means of calculating problematic weight loss. Often known simply as 'anorexia', it is a condition found mainly (but not exclusively) in younger women, often of high educational attainment, and mainly in Western countries. DENIAL is common in the early stages of anorexia and the stubbornness of the condition can progress to life-threatening proportions and, in the acute anorexic phase, hospitalisation may be necessary. Supportive and exploratory counselling can aid recovery and the special insights of FEMINIST COUNSELLING and therapy may be particularly helpful in addressing what is largely a woman's problem. Theories concerning the causes of anorexia abound, including those from psychoanalysis, family therapy and behaviourism. Anorexia has often been linked clinically with sexual abuse. A proportion of anorectics die (according to one survey, up to 20%), but many eventually recover spontaneously. BULIMIA NERVOSA, a variant of anorexia, is characterised by binge eating followed by purging, and is attended by secretiveness, guilt and depression. Some anorectics experience both anorectic and bulimic episodes.

anthropathology human sickness. The term suggests a species-specific property of pervasive psychological and moral malfunctioning – at individual and societal levels – that is probably impervious to counselling and psychotherapy. It connotes a kind of universal 'neurosis' rather than a degree of severity (as in PSYCHOPATHOLOGY). Similarities exist to concepts of sin, alienation, Weltschmertz, the 'pathology of normalcy' (Erich Fromm) and 'humanitis' (Saul Bellow).

antidepressant medication drugs prescribed to combat obdurate DEPRESSION. Current common antidepressants are of two main types: tricyclics and SSRIs (selective serotonin reuptake inhibitors). The drugs take some two to three weeks to take effect, often have side effects and may need to be continued for months. There has been some debate about the relative merits of counselling and MEDICATION, and the wisdom of trying to offer counselling to people receiving medication, but a common view now is that both can be used together profitably.

antidiscriminatory practice counselling practice that is informed by an awareness of, and a commitment to address, the social position and particular needs of marginalised, disadvantaged or oppressed individuals. These include ethnic minorities, disabled people, gays and lesbians, women, children, older people, and those practising different religions and identifying with different cultures and from social classes other than the middle classes from which most counsellors are likely to come. Principles of antidiscriminatory practice (also referred to as anti-oppressive practice) should permeate recruitment, training, supervision and research as well as counselling. *See* Lago and Smith (2003).

anti-future shock imagery a technique advocated by Arnold Lazarus whereby the client is taught to imagine problems arising in the future and methods for coping with them, as a kind of relapse prevention strategy or 'emotional fire drill'.

anti-psychiatry a term coined by David Cooper, but later used widely, to refer to a movement against the biomedical model of diagnosing and treating people with severe mental health problems.

antipsychotics drugs intended to reduce or eliminate clients' psychotic symptoms. These act on dopamine transmission, thus reducing elements of mental hyperactivity. Antipsychotics are sometimes referred to as typical (older) and atypical (newer) drugs. All have side effects but typical antipsychotics can affect up to 75% of clients adversely. Names include: chlorpromazine, trifluoperazine, haloperidol; amisulpride, clozapine, risperidone. Also known as major tranquillisers.

anxiety state of dysfunctional, heightened awareness of a real or imagined impending event, characterised by various symptoms: cognitively, a lack of concentration; behaviourally, avoidance of certain situations; physiologically, disturbed sleep, rapid breathing; emotionally, agitation. Anxiety is one of the most common forms of psychological disturbance. In contrast to DEPRESSION, anxiety manifests in hypervigilance and over-concern. In contrast to FEAR, anxiety is usually disproportionate to the reality of any threat. Anxiety may be stimulus specific (e.g. examination anxiety) or apparently unrelated to any recent or impending event, and may be acute (as in brief PANIC ATTACK) or persistent (as in AGORAPHOBIA). As well as resulting in acute symptoms such as hyperventilation, it may be experienced as 'free-floating'. Analyses of anxiety vary: sometimes seen as restimulation of previous experiences of being under threat, it is also viewed as a result of faulty information processing (classically, the misreading and magnifying of slight physiological changes). Each school of thought has its own approach to anxiety management or resolution and anti-anxiety medication is still used, with or without counselling support. Anxiety is also sometimes considered to be not a sign of individual pathology but a cultural norm (e.g. 'age of anxiety') or philosophical entity (e.g. existential anxiety). *See also* PHOBIA.

apathy emotional and behavioural indifference, loss of feeling and apparent inability to respond to events with a normal degree of interest and involvement. Apathy is a characteristic of DEPRESSION.

applicant a person who is applying for, or who is interested in the possibility of having, counselling. This term is more common in the USA and is hardly used in the UK, where the terms 'helpseeker' and REFERRAL can have similar meanings. It is widely acknowledged that the first counselling session should be devoted partly to mutual assessment of the likely ability of client and counsellor to work together productively. Potential clients are advised to 'shop around' for a counsellor with whom they feel comfortable and in whom they have confidence. In this sense, then, the person seeking counselling is an applicant (rather than a client) until an agreement or contract for counselling to proceed has been made.

appreciation literally, finding positive value in something or someone. Rogers spoke of PRIZING clients, meaning appreciating the unique expression of their humanity. Appreciation is also sometimes contrasted with RESENTMENT in recognition of the frequent finding that people both value certain positive attributes and dislike (or would prefer to see changed) certain perceived negative attributes in others. Appreciation is both a subjective experience and a voicing of what is appreciated. *See also* GRATITUDE.

approach-avoidance social–psychological term denoting conflict between movement towards and away from something desired. Greater proximity to the desired object increases the anxiety, leading to withdrawal; with increased distance desire returns for the object originally avoided. Such anxious behaviour can result in a prolonged impasse and poor performance.

appropriate behaviour manner of acting and relating that is considered by most people to be normal for particular circumstances. Appropriateness of behaviour is defined according to cultural norms and varies according to subjective preferences and subcultures. For example, Muslim women living in the UK would find it unacceptable to undress in front of a male doctor without the presence of a relative. The notions of gender-appropriate and age-appropriate behaviour are contentious. Counsellors are likely to weigh up any suspicions of seriously inappropriate behaviour in clients with sensitivity and due regard for their personal values, balanced against social expectations or danger of their client's courting stigma or rejection. Deliberately inappropriate behaviour can be a form of ACTING-OUT.

approval positive judgement of someone's actions. In NON-DIRECTIVE counselling approval is not considered an appropriate sentiment or attitude towards the client because it is inherently judgemental, conveying the sense that the counsellor may offer positive and negative judgement. In practice, many counsellors acknowledge that they convey approval, or conditional positive regard, consciously and unconsciously. Used judiciously as encouragement and reinforcement for progress, approval can be a useful tool.

arbitrary inference drawing highly specific conclusions from events, for which there is no objective evidence or probability. A form of FAULTY INFORMATION PROCESSING.

archetype an inherited part of the COLLECTIVE UNCONSCIOUS, which expresses itself through the lives of individuals and groups (a Jungian concept). Samuels (1985) refers to archetypes as primordial images, inherited dispositions, blueprints for psychological behaviour and portrayals of instincts. Archetypal fantasies resemble the psychoanalytic concept of unconscious phantasy. Archetypes can 'arouse affect, blind one to realities and take possession of will'. The *archetypal psychology* developed by Hillman and others stresses the centrality and irreducibility of imagery in human life, in psychology and in therapy.

arena the interpersonal context in which counselling is conceived, organised and delivered in response to certain client groups, agency restraints, clinical or ideological orientations. Arenas (treatment modalities) include individual, couple, family and group counselling. While individual counselling is by far the most common form, other arenas are well developed and many client problems may benefit from arenas offering systemic or other specialised considerations. Alternative arenas may offer more effective counselling or a kind of counselling that is more appropriate than, or helpfully complementary to, individual counselling. Some arenas offer economic advantages. Counsellors are seldom trained or qualified in more than one or two arenas and referral from one arena to another is probably considered and practised much less than might be profitable for clients.

arousal psychological and physiological state of expectancy and readiness. Level of arousal is thought to depend on several factors, including personality type (e.g. introvert/extravert), nature of stimulus and mediating cognition. Optimal arousal implies a state of alertness that equips a person well for the behaviour required of her. Over-arousal often responds well to AUTOGENIC TRAINING methods.

art therapy a therapy using painting, drawing, sculpting and other creative art forms as a way of assisting UNCONSCIOUS or emerging psychological conflicts and themes to surface. In bypassing rational processes, art therapy can access powerfully the fantasies of clients. Art therapy is often used in psychiatric settings, where its concrete, non-verbal and active character may be perceived as non-threatening, recreational or permission giving. Much art therapy stems from and works with psychodynamic and Jungian theory; while some schools are interpretive, others are firmly in the person-centred tradition. In common with play therapy, art therapy can be used productively with people, including children, who have been traumatised. The externalisation of images and CATHARSIS are often curative factors; no specific artistic skills are required of clients.

Asperger's syndrome a clinical disorder characterised by impairment in social development, communication and imagination; inability to understand nuances in, for example, jokes and interpersonal subtleties; and difficulties in understanding others' point of view and hence maintaining relationships. People with Asperger's syndrome (AS) function well or exceptionally well intellectually and may fail to be diagnosed. Preponderance of at least 4: 1 male to female ratio. AS is on the autistic spectrum. Counselling for AS should be conducted only by those with specialist knowledge.

assertiveness intentional (verbal and non-verbal) behaviour which communicates a person's wishes, preferences and boundaries. Assertiveness conveys congruently the position the person is taking. Failure to act assertively often results in submission, exploitation and RESENTMENT or in aggression, misunderstanding and negative consequences. *Assertiveness training* is a system of techniques taught to enable people to ask for what they want, complain appropriately, give positive feedback to others, stand up for themselves and, when necessary, defend themselves. Assertiveness training has been addressed particularly to women who have internalised social expectations of meekness and self-denial. Much assertiveness training entails identifying unhelpful messages and replacing them with clearer, well-projected ones, through REHEARSAL, MODELLING and experimentation. Clients may be taught assertive strategies in counselling or be referred to appropriate groups.

assessment determining a client's condition on initial presentation for counselling. Some agencies have their own standard

INTAKE INTERVIEW procedure, in which it is the responsibility of the clinician to make a formal assessment using the agency's established criteria. Psychiatric assessment procedures, for example, include biographical, medical and psychological data gathering. Where assessment is formalised it usually seeks information on the ONSET and severity of the problem, previous problems, past and present family, domestic and occupational circumstances, use and misuse of medication, physical and emotional illness and any current risk factors. Models of counselling often have their own criteria for assessment such as early childhood memories, ability to cry, coping skills, social support or ability to relate to the counsellor. Some counselling agencies have no formal assessment as an established policy or for reasons of insufficient staffing. Thus, many counsellors disapprove of the very idea of assessment, viewing it as dehumanising, leading to labelling, etc. Most counsellors probably conduct, at the very least, an intuitive assessment, and it is considered good practice to treat the first session as a form of mutual assessment of the client's and counsellor's wish and ability to work together. Assessment is also an important factor in counsellor training, whether it is self-, peer-, or tutor-assessment, and ongoing or by examination or evaluation of written work and audiotapes. See Palmer and McMahon (1997).

assimilation model a seven-stage model aiming to understand the way in which clients typically progress from, first, warding off or denying the problem, through vague awareness of the problem, insight, working through, solution and mastery.

assumption an evaluation of a situation or person, or a fixed attitude to life, that is made without full consciousness, consultation or openness to new evidence. Alternatively, an assumption may be a conscious and modifiable view. Counselling contains many assumptions – for example that most people are capable of making changes in their lives. Counselling ORIENTATIONS have different assumptions: REBT assumes that its clients have irrational beliefs which can probably be corrected; person-centred counsellors believe that their clients are fundamentally disposed to be self-actualising; psychoanalysis assumes a large measure of unconscious conflict to be present in clients; EXISTENTIAL COUNSELLING considers it vital to make clients' assumptions explicit; THERAPEUTIC ALLIANCE theory suggests that it is productive for counsellor and client to air and agree on their goals and ways of working towards them. While some counsellors tell their clients what their theoretical assumptions are, many do not. The making of an explicit CONTRACT reduces unhelpful assumptions, but is unlikely to unearth or examine the numerous and often unconscious assumptions both counsellors and clients make.

attachment strong bond with another; dependence on physical and/or emotional closeness to another. The attachment theory of Bowlby (1969) is based on observations of infants, ethology and psychoanalytic theory and suggests that babies form very strong attachments to their mothers or primary care givers in the first year of life. When such attachment is threatened or ended prematurely, infants are likely to experience ANXIETY in relation to LOSS. Early experiences of attachment, security and threats to this security form the basis of later, adult security or vulnerability to anxiety, according to Bowlby and others. This emphasis on a need for relatively consistent attachment to one person alone has been criticised from various quarters, including feminists. *See also* MATERNAL DEPRIVATION, SEPARATION ANXIETY.

attempted suicide *see* SUICIDE.

attention-deficit disorder a DSM-IVTR recognised mental health problem characterised by a marked inability to concentrate and a tendency towards hyperactivity. Associated with fidgeting, not listening, impulsivity, ADD is also known as ADHD (attention-deficit hyperactivity disorder), and begins in childhood. Often treated pharmacologically (classically, with Ritalin), ADD remains contentious as a diagnosis.

attention-giving the direction of one's perceptions towards a person or object. In counselling this means the counsellor giving her time and attention as fully as possible, implying a suspension of her own intentions, preoccupations and prejudices. Freud spoke of an 'evenly-suspended attention'. There is an argument that the counsellor's main task (at least in the more relationship-based models) is to become wholly engaged with the client. COUNTERTRANSFERENCE is often experienced as a 'disturbance in the field of attention', pointing to clinically significant material. It is widely recognised that most people have attentional deficits of some degree. Attention includes listening, observing and genuine receptivity.

attention seeking conscious or unconscious attempts to be seen and heard by others. The most common connotation of attention seeking is a negative one associated with ACTING-OUT, in which people (often disturbed children or adults with a PERSONALITY DISORDER) manipulate others, particularly carers, to pay attention to them. Such MANIPULATION can take the form of obnoxious, dramatic or persistently demanding behaviour. Suicidal gestures and self-mutilation are often described as attention seeking. The paradox of such behaviour is that it frequently drives others away. It has been suggested that attention-seeking behaviour would be better viewed as attention-*needing* behaviour, which is invariably repeating (albeit unconsciously) a chronically denied need or traumatic hurt from the past.

attitude cognitive or emotional disposition towards others, events and life; a habitual position. In common use, phrases such as 'unhelpful attitude', 'aggressive attitude' or 'pleasant attitude' suggest distinctly positive or negative dispositions. The term 'attitude problem' denotes an outlook that is unsociable or uncooperative. Attitudes encompass the ideas of WORLD VIEW, SCRIPTS and SCHEMAS. Different personality types, e.g. introverts and extraverts, are said to have fundamentally different attitudes. Attitudes can also be fleeting. The counsellor is required to have a respectful, helpful and personable attitude. The person-centred approach is sometimes said to require certain attitudes and qualities rather than skills. *See also* ASSUMPTION.

attraction pull towards another person; liking, having a positive image of or expectation about someone. Attractiveness is subjectively determined. The nature of attraction is especially significant in couple counselling, where the 'interpersonal pull' that initiated the relationship may have contained unconscious conflict patterns. Social psychologists have focused on the attraction of strangers; they have also studied cognitive, affective and behavioural aspects of attraction. Research into the role attractiveness plays in counselling suggests that the perceived attractiveness of the counsellor to the client is a significant factor in making and maintaining a THERAPEUTIC ALLIANCE. As in ordinary life, attraction between client and counsellor contains the (two-way) real and transferential tensions of affection, idealisation, misunderstanding, rejection and fantasy, and the success of counselling depends in part on the management of this tension, its interpretation, working through, or use as a learning opportunity.

attribution the ascribing of causes and qualities to events and persons. In a counselling context, attribution often refers to the manner in which clients construe experience to confirm their own negative expectations. For example, a man may attribute the fact that his new acquaintance failed to greet him this morning to her no longer liking him, or to her attempting to disguise that she likes him very much. *Attribution theory* is a complex field in social psychology concerned with common-sense explanations for events and how these are influenced by personal, situational and other variables.

auditory hallucination a delusional subjective experience of noise or voices for which there is no current external stimulus. Auditory hallucinations are the key feature of SCHIZOPHRENIA but also occur in depressive psychosis, alcoholism and amphetamine abuse. They are experienced as one's own thoughts or as the comments, accusations and commands of other people, known or unknown.

authentic chameleon a phrase coined by Lazarus to refer to the therapist's task of adapting their interpersonal style to each client in the interests of deepening rapport and securing a good working alliance. This requires the conscious use, even exaggeration if necessary, of aspects of oneself (e.g. friendliness, authority, knowledge) to help reach the client better. Critics argue that by its very nature, this 'technique' is incongruent.

authenticity human behaviour is said to be authentic when it is free from dissembling. Literally, it is a state of reliable GENUINENESS. The real self is characterised by authenticity and the false self by a lack of genuineness. While authenticity can be truly known only by the person herself, its presence can often be recognised by others. Thus, authentic gratitude is markedly different from the dutiful display of gratitude and will be experienced as such. Authenticity is also a key concept in existential therapy.

authoritarian personality a type of person who approves of harsh laws, traditional social values, repression of pleasure and who is likely to have stereotypical views on cultures and social groups to which he does not belong. Such people may have fascistic leanings and little insight or compassion, but are different from the PSYCHOPATH or SOCIOPATH in that they identify with 'society' and are likely to exercise power overtly rather than furtively, excessively or criminally.

autism a pervasive developmental disorder characterised by impairments in imagination, language and communication. Autism has a range of severity, approximately two thirds of people with autistic spectrum disorders having severe learning difficulties. Its genetically determined basis means that although some of its features may be improved – by, for example, non-verbal means such as music therapy and behavioural tasks such as social skills training – it cannot be *cured* and dramatic positive outcome claims by some child psychoanalytic psychotherapists and humanistic therapists remain contentious, with probable links to initial misdiagnosis. More common among males by at least 4:1 and a prevalence of more than 1 in 10,000 in the population. *See* ASPERGER'S SYNDROME.

autogenic training systematic training in methods designed to reduce stress. Mental imagery aimed at gaining control of autonomic arousal is taught in components, practised regularly and made part of an autosuggestion programme. *See* PROGRESSIVE RELAXATION.

automatic thoughts self-statements or 'individual instances of thought', frequently considered by clients to 'pop' into their minds and to reflect reality accurately. Cognitive therapists challenge negative automatic thoughts and hold that, although they may be habitual and rapidly processed, they can be identified, explored and altered to more accurate assessments of present realities. Automatic thoughts are particularly evident in people suffering from DEPRESSION but they are present in all emotional disorders.

autonomy literally, a state governed by its own laws. The term is central in counselling where it has the connotations of personal freedom, FREE WILL, an innate actualising tendency (*see* SELF-ACTUALISATION) and sovereignty over one's own decision-making, emotions and private behaviour. Most theories of counselling endorse the notion that humans are inherently autonomous, that they need a high level of autonomy to maintain their well-being and to flourish, and that counselling is principally concerned to help restore lost autonomy. A radical definition would have to include the right to determine one's own destiny (including 'rational suicide'), however removed such an envisaged destiny might be from consensual norms, provided that the means to achieve it do not impinge on the autonomy of others. Autonomy is enshrined in the ethics of counselling and psychotherapy owing to a faith in the original autonomy of individuals and because of the potential dangers in the counselling relationship of influencing clients in the direction of the counsellor's own values. NON-DIRECTIVE counselling is motivated by these factors. Not to be confused with egocentricity or wilfulness, autonomy is threatened not only by external forces but also by internalised forces like parental INJUNCTIONS and psychopathological constraints. Taken to the extreme, autonomy is sometimes taken to mean the supremacy of the human spirit which can transcend any suffering: this kind of definition is criticised for neglecting individual and cultural differences, and socioeconomic and educational factors (hence, 'autonomy obsession'). It must also be remembered that some clients do not see themselves as autonomous or as capable of autonomous decision-making. However, all models of counselling aim to increase client independence, growth and INDIVIDUATION.

auxiliary ego a person who acts temporarily and purposefully as either a part of another's ego or as a significant person in her life. In the latter sense, counsellors using PSYCHODRAMA may agree to role-play the way a client sees her mother, for example. More generally, an auxiliary ego is a temporarily supportive attitude on the part of the counsellor when the client needs borrowed EGO STRENGTH (see EGO-BUILDING) or when the counsellor is attempting to mobilise the client to access deeper, perhaps frightening, aspects of her experience.

availability to awareness access to the conscious mind. The term refers to material surfacing in counselling which the client is not warding off from awareness, which he can grasp, articulate and explore. It implies that some material is unavailable, unconscious, unformulated, difficult to recall or to give meaning to. In Freudian terms, available material is from the conscious and PRECONSCIOUS domains. Unless and until certain material, or certain constellations of material, are available to awareness, then premature interventions or interpretations by the counsellor may have no impact or may be perceived as persecutory.

aversion therapy behavioural treatment designed to change or eliminate certain undesired behaviour by means of coupling that behaviour with an unpleasant event or series of events. Aversion therapy has been used in attempts to change homosexual behaviour, eating disorders, alcoholism, etc. Imaginal techniques, mild electric shocks, and the administering of certain drugs (e.g. Antabuse, which induces nausea if someone who has taken it imbibes alcohol) are typical strategies. Aversion therapy alone may not effect prolonged change, and many people dispute the efficacy and ethical standing of aversion therapy. Its use has diminished in recent years.

avoidance removing; going away from; flight or escape. The word implies a non-confrontational (and therefore only partially or temporarily successful) attempt to reduce anxiety. *Avoidant behaviour* typifies anxious non-assertiveness and procrastination. According to social psychology *avoidance rituals* constitute the means by which we create and maintain desired social distances.

avoidant personality a personality type characterised by a habitual pattern of anxious distancing of himself from feared situations or people. Such people frequently exhibit fears of rejection and low self-esteem. A general category of behaviour, more in use in American than in British literature.

awareness state of consciousness, cognisance or realisation. A general term suggesting movement towards knowledge, including SELF-KNOWLEDGE, increased intuitive power, or the dimly perceived presence of something on the edge of the field of attention. Viewed by many (particularly humanistic and transpersonal) counsellors as being the end goal of the counselling process, awareness is a problematically wide and sometimes nebulous term. It includes the notion of making 'the unconscious conscious'; becoming aware of existential choices of which one was previously unaware; searching for levels of awareness such as the mystical states of mindfulness, *satori* or *samadhi*; social awareness, as explored for example in women's consciousness-raising groups, race awareness workshops and men's groups. A distinction between awareness as a predominantly cognitive, scanning, here-and-now function, and consciousness as the integrated visceral-emotional-cognitive state of a radically detraumatised person has been proposed by Janov (1975).

awfulising term coined by Ellis (*see* RATIO-NAL EMOTIVE BEHAVIOUR THERAPY) to describe a grossly exaggerated evaluation of unde-sirable events. Contrary to the kind of MAGI-CAL THINKING that says that 'everything will be fine' against all evidence, awfulising is a form of absolutist thinking which irra-tionally rates events as being more than 100% bad. Implicit in awfulising are the assumptions that things must not be the way they are and that they are not bearable as they are.

BACP British Association for Counselling and Psychotherapy, Britain's largest and most significant professional association overseeing the development of counselling. Commencing in 1970 as a charitable organisation, BACP has grown to a large membership organization with different divisions and activities. It has created categories of membership and accreditation as follows:

individual, student and organisational members: those interested and involved in counselling, who are of good standing;

accredited member: a trained and qualified counsellor who has met the requirements of training, supervised practice and CONTINUING PROFESSIONAL DEVELOPMENT (CPD);

accredited training course: a counselling course that has met requirements of course design, delivery and quality;

accredited supervisor: a counsellor supervisor who has satisfied the relevant criteria;

senior registered practitioner: a practitioner who has been accredited for at least six years and has at least 1000 hours of practice experience;

fellow: a distinguished member.

These categories sometimes offer more than one route and those involved are sub-ject to re-accreditation; criteria change periodically, and occasionally a category is suspended for review (e.g. accredited trainer at the time of writing). See www.bacp.co.uk for further details. Other counselling organisations include: COSCA (Counselling and Psychotherapy in Scotland), EAC (European Association for Counselling), IACT (Irish Association for Counselling and Therapy), and IPN (Independent Practitioners Network).

bad breast *see* GOOD BREAST.

banal script a TA concept (Steiner) referring to a negative script that, although not dramatic/tragic, produces a life that is joyless, loveless, and characterised by missed opportunities but outward normality.

basic fault term used by Balint (1968) to describe a fundamental developmental deficit resulting from a mismatch between infantile needs and maternal supply. The basic fault is considered a very early occurrence, characterised by the splitting into a REAL SELF and a false self. The term is sometimes used in a general sense to refer to clients who appear so damaged that counselling and therapy may never be able to reach or heal the damage.

BASIC ID acronym for Lazarus's (1981)

central modalities in his MULTIMODAL THERA-PY. It is a systematic approach to assessment and indication of treatment of choice. B = behaviour; A = affect; S = sensation; I = imagery; C = cognition; I = interpersonal relationships; D = drugs, lifestyle or biological factors.

befriending offering support and companionship to another, usually someone in particular need. Befriending differs from counselling in that it is usually informal, need have no explicit therapeutic aim, and has a social focus. Befrienders often address problems of isolation and loneliness, visit people in their homes, accompany them on trips, or assist those who have physical or mental health problems. The boundaries between friendship, befriending and supportive counselling sometimes are unclear to clients and not well explained by some counsellors.

beginning phase the first few sessions of counselling. The beginning phase of any counselling relationship is likely to be marked by certain factors: the level of the client's anxiety and distress; the reasons for seeking counselling at this time; his unfamiliarity with counselling and learning to trust a stranger; the telling of his story; the eliciting of goals; the counsellor and client accommodating to each other and forming a THERAPEUTIC ALLIANCE; establishing the boundaries of confidentiality, time and the professional nature of the relationship; making contracts; the testing of readiness on the part of the client and of the competence of the counsellor; diagnosis and treatment planning. (Humanistic counsellors in particular, however, regard even the first session as therapy and eschew the notion of diagnosis.) There is some research evidence

that the way the initial phase (especially the first three sessions) is handled by the counsellor is crucial to counselling continuing and having a successful outcome.

behaviour therapy all those approaches to treatment basing their understanding of human functioning and dysfunction on the basic tenets of behaviourism. According to behaviourism, only actions that are observable and measurable can be studied scientifically. Hence, only client problems which are specific, and externally observable, can be treated. Broadly speaking, behaviour therapists have denied the importance or verifiability of intrapsychic processes. Originally based on a simple model of stimulus–response (observing how the environment acts on a person and how they in turn act on it), a variety of techniques were developed, such as SYSTEMATIC DESENSITISATION, IMPLOSION, OPERANT CONDITIONING, etc. There are now numerous techniques (*see* Bellack and Hersen, 1987). Due to its stance against the validity of internal processes, classical behaviour therapy is widely criticised for ignoring the richness and influence of thinking and feeling. It is noted, however, that behaviour therapy appears to be more successful in treating some conditions (such as obsessive-compulsive disorder – *see* OBSESSION – and PANIC ATTACK) than most other therapies. COGNITIVE–BEHAVIOURAL THERAPY has grown in theory and techniques in recent years and has somewhat eclipsed purely behavioural therapy.

behavioural counselling any counselling which makes substantial use of behavioural theory or techniques (e.g. learning theory, modelling and operant conditioning). The 'task-centred casework' of some social workers is based on behavioural principles. Certain schools of therapy (e.g. reality therapy) focus on client behaviour, its consequences, and on achieving new behaviours without necessarily probing for past influences. Certain client groups (e.g. alcoholics), particularly in early stages of treatment, may require tough behavioural regimens.

'being with' refers to a quality of presence, an availability to others. Being with clients is sometimes contrasted with acting upon them or self-consciously trying to create therapeutic movement. It may also be seen as supportiveness, silent empathy, or willingness to stay with a client's times of inactivity or confusion. This relational quality is paramount in some models of counselling but is sometimes denigrated or considered insufficient by others. 'Being with' also has connotations of heightened awareness of another's presence and suffering (e.g. in working with the dying). It also has existential nuances. *See* EXISTENTIAL COUNSELLING, PRESENCE.

beliefs views or opinions, of a general, religious, philosophical, political or other nature. Examination of beliefs, their rational and irrational nature, insofar as they impinge on clients' problems and well-being, is central to COGNITIVE THERAPY and RATIONAL EMOTIVE BEHAVIOUR THERAPY. The client's personal beliefs will not necessarily come under the counsellor's scrutiny if they do not relate to problems being discussed in counselling, although classical psychoanalysis has often been inclined, for example, to regard religious beliefs as allied to fantasy. Rigidity of beliefs often indicates defensiveness, but against this must be weighed cultural factors. Belief is

probably an implicit key to success in counselling but under-researched. *See also* IRRATIONALITY, PERSONAL CONSTRUCT PSYCHOLOGY, SCHEMA.

bereavement the experience of loss, usually associated with the death of someone close, but also applying to loss through divorce, unemployment and other major life crises. Recognisable stages of bereavement reactions have been identified, which may or may not manifest sequentially (*see* Worden, 2003). These include shock, disbelief or denial, searching, anger, guilt, sadness and acceptance. Cultures differ in their expressions of GRIEF, but all regard a certain period of MOURNING and adjustment following a major loss as natural, acceptable and healthy. While a period of 6 months to 2 years is sometimes considered 'normal' for the grieving process, it is also widely acknowledged that individual differences and relationship variables will affect the depth, kind and duration of grief. It is also widely accepted that protracted mourning, which may manifest in DEPRESSION, is often a sign of continuing denial or other difficulties in adjustment. Bereavement is often compounded by real loneliness, disruption of routines and a need to learn new social skills. Some theorists regard bereavement as a recapitulation of earlier separation experiences and therefore interpret it in the light of ATTACHMENT theory. Bereavement counsellors or generalist counsellors working with clients who experience a bereavement need to be sensitive to the individual and cultural appropriateness of grief reactions, the need for support, the need for focus and active letting go, the possibilities of pathological reactions including psychosomatic and suicidal risks, social and religious supports. Counsellors sometimes encourage 'grief work' with clients who may have frozen grief reactions from recent or even distant (in time) bereavements. Invariably such work entails confrontation of the reality of loss and working through it by emotive methods.

bibliotherapy the use of (often recommended) texts as an adjunct to personal counselling: SELF-HELP literature is bibliotherapy of a kind. Some counsellors, especially the more cognitively oriented and those practising BRIEF COUNSELLING, often suggest particular books to clients as a means of accelerating understanding, supplementing work in sessions and maintaining therapeutic gains. Some NHS experiments have issued clients with prescriptions for specific books that are made available in local libraries. Clients who defensively intellectualise their problems may not be suitable candidates for bibliotherapy.

bingeing an aspect of an EATING DISORDER, in which the person craves (high-calorie) food and eats large amounts at irregular intervals. Bingeing, or binge eating, is frequently followed by self-induced vomiting and is characteristic of BULIMIA NERVOSA. The terms 'binge drinking' and 'binge spending' are also in use.

biodynamic therapy a form of therapy founded by Gerda Boyesen, based on the concept of 'life-force', or libido. Biodynamic therapy has much in common with Reichian therapy but was developed independently. Its theory includes the concepts of primary and secondary personalities, which correspond approximately with a free real self and a stifled false self. Its main therapeutic techniques are massage, somatic 'free association' and other 'body–mind' interventions.

bioenergetics a form of therapy based on BODYWORK. Developed by Lowen (1976) from the work of Wilhelm Reich, bioenergetics aims at body–mind integration through structured, largely non-verbal exercises (e.g. breathing, grounding, discharge). A particular focus is that of CHARACTER ANALYSIS based on Reich's view that defences are often, if not always, expressed bodily in the form of CHARACTER ARMOUR. Bioenergetics uses awareness of transference, and also has links with gestalt therapy and primal integration.

biofeedback information processing involving cognitive awareness of, and training in, changing aspects of physiological functioning. Biofeedback techniques often call for technical apparatus to establish, for example, baseline readings for blood pressure, EEG and heart rate. Its most common use, by behaviour therapists, is in the treatment of stress disorders (e.g. hypertension and migraine headaches). Biofeedback techniques, sometimes called 'learned autonomic control', are also associated with PROGRESSIVE RELAXATION and AUTOGENIC TRAINING.

bipolar affective disorder psychiatric classification for those conditions characterised by marked cyclical changes of mood from depression to hypomania (and mania). The best known bipolar disorder is MANIC DEPRESSION and the term 'bipolar disorder' is now commonly used instead of it.

birth order the sequence in which children are born in a family. Birth order, or 'sibling position', is considered a highly significant developmental factor in INDIVIDUAL

PSYCHOLOGY. Sequence, spacing, relationships between siblings and their formative influence received special attention from Alfred Adler and Frank Sulloway. Some research suggests that first-born children are often high achievers or very concerned with sociability and that only children often excel professionally.

birth trauma the concept, originally proposed by Rank, that birth is a traumatic event leading to later anxieties. It was given renewed prominence and supporting evidence by therapists like Janov, Lake and Feher, and obstetricians such as Leboyer, Odent and Savage. There is a difference of views as to whether birth is essentially traumatic itself or whether only violent, technologically brutalising or other unnatural birth experiences are traumatic. Janov (1975) argues broadly that the earlier the trauma, the deeper and more chronic its effects: hence, birth trauma continues, according to this view, to render the person psychologically and physiologically dysfunctional to some extent, until healed by therapeutic regression. There is disagreement as to whether clients can (or should) quickly and easily re-experience birth trauma (as with REBIRTHING techniques), or only after integrating most later traumas. There is also a 'credulity threshold': some consider traumas to go back to INTRAUTERINE EXPERIENCE (and even beyond that) while many others consider the whole concept to be fanciful or nonsensical.

bisexuality sexual attitude and behaviour which is neither exclusively heterosexual nor exclusively homosexual. Freud agreed to some extent with the view of Fliess that human beings are (somewhat) biologically bisexual, but in practice have to resolve the conflict arising from this by repressing either the masculine or feminine aspect. Jung accepted heterosexuality as the norm, viewing the masculine and feminine principles in each person as psychological ARCHETYPES rather than biological tendencies in conflict. Based on social LEARNING THEORY is the view that sexual orientation may be learned and, in a predominantly heterosexual culture, this means that homosexual and bisexual orientations are in a statistical minority. Some people are covertly bisexual, engaging in homosexual acts while maintaining a facade of pure heterosexuality. Some clients, often younger people, experience a dilemma of SEXUAL ORIENTATION, which calls for exploration in counselling. Critics of bisexual and homosexual orientations (including classical Freudians) may argue that certain stages of normal sexual development have not been completed, or that a client has over-identified with or rejected one or other parent as a model of sexual orientation, or has been traumatised sexually or formed a close same-sex relationship at a vulnerable developmental stage. Some feminists and humanistic thinkers commend an *androgynous* model of human beings (in which everyone is viewed as possessing male and female characteristics), which attempts to transcend the current conflict.

blaming attributing the causes of negative events to others. Blaming differs from the accurate attribution of responsibility in that it usually seeks to punish or denigrate and implies an unwillingness to forgive or problem-solve. A polemical subject is the weight given to the part played by their parents in clients' problems: what some view as inaccurate and unconstructive parent-blaming, others regard as correct and therapeutically necessary.

block an obstacle, more or less temporary, to therapeutic progress. A client may report having a 'block against writing reports' (which signifies resistance or procrastination), a block against exploring certain memories or images, or a block against expressing certain feelings to the counsellor. Equally, counsellors may experience blocks against understanding a client or even a client group. A block can be in the client, in the counsellor or both. *See also* IMPASSE.

body dysmorphic disorder also known as dysmorphophobia, this condition is characterised by a serious preoccupation with one's body and distorted body image, to the extent that a sufferer virtually hallucinates gross proportions and ugly features even when the reality is utterly different. Mirror checking, excessive self-grooming and seeking unnecessary surgery are also features.

body image a person's subjective perception of her or his own body, its size, shape and attractiveness. Distortions in such perceptions characterise people (usually women) who experience eating disorders such as ANOREXIA NERVOSA. The advertising industry and the media purvey certain glamorous 'norms', which serve to exacerbate self-consciousness.

body language the way in which people's feelings and thoughts express themselves, often unconsciously, through physical posture and movement. Counsellors learn by training and experience to note both gross and subtle signals given by clients' bodies and need to be aware, too, of how their own body language communicates interest or otherwise to the client. It has been claimed that much more is communicated by body language than by tone of voice or content of speech. Some models of counselling or interpersonal skills training, such as gestalt and neurolinguistic programming, make particular use of bodily cues and work with them explicitly. *See also* NON-VERBAL COMMUNICATION and VOICE QUALITY.

body therapy also known as body psychotherapy and body work (see below).

bodywork counselling or therapy which focuses on awareness of the body. Under this term come FOCUSING, REICHIAN therapy and BIOENERGETICS, as well as Rolfing and the Alexander technique. Techniques include the client's concentration on bodily sensations; encouraging clients to 'go with the body', particularly in abreactive states where convulsive movements are evident; and massage. Bodywork is used to supplement other approaches, to overcome bodily defences, to enable therapeutic REGRESSION or to overcome an impasse. Bodywork belongs in the humanistic tradition of therapy and is not in common use among general counsellors.

bond a positive mutual emotional acceptance by client and counsellor. Often an intuitive confidence in the therapeutic relationship, based on implicit assessments of compatibility of outlook, aims, experience, attraction, class, gender, race, etc. Together with GOALS and TASKS, bonds are considered in THERAPEUTIC ALLIANCE theory to be crucial determinants of successful outcome. The counsellor–client bond is not necessarily constant: it may be tested, ruptured, destroyed, repaired or strengthened.

bonding relationship forming, particularly between mother and baby. Bonding is viewed by some as a critical developmental stage, which if unsuccessful, radically affects subsequent personality development. *See* ATTACHMENT theory.

booster session formally arranged meetings between counsellor and client, some weeks or months following termination of the counselling contract, intended to review and help maintain progress, and to prevent relapse. *See* FOLLOW-UP.

borderline personality disorder the *borderline personality* is likely to be subject to mood shifts, temper tantrums or impulsivity, high suicide risk, and will use primitive defence mechanisms. One estimate is that 15% of psychiatric in-patients and 2% of the general population suffer from BPD. The meaningfulness of the term 'borderline' as anything but a general expression of clinical doubt is called into question by some counsellors. However, BPD is taken seriously and treatment success claims are made by practitioners of cognitive analytic therapy and dialectical behaviour therapy in particular.

boundaries limits set, usually by the counsellor, to aspects of behaviour within counselling, or limits which become apparent or necessary. Initial contractual boundaries include the differentiation of counselling from socialising, confidentiality, time-keeping and other practical arrangements. Both client and counsellor will realise boundaries in their work together, for example with regard to personal space and physical contact. The counsellor may need to make particular boundary decisions regarding self-disclosure, its appropriateness or otherwise in a given relationship. Boundaries also exist between supervisor and supervisee and trainer and trainee, for example, sanctions against sexual contact. It is fairly widely accepted that a necessary boundary exists between SUPERVISION and personal counselling of the supervisee, within supervision sessions. Different models and individual practitioners have different boundaries but all are subject to ethical considerations. In GESTALT, the *boundary* is a central concept, referring to the separation and meeting between person (or organism) and environment, the *contact-boundary* is the point at which active, 'creative adjustment' occurs, and gestalt counselling employs *boundary work*, which is awareness of and therapeutic focus on how clients avoid, approach and create new experience. *See also* FRAME MANAGEMENT.

brainstorming the practice of generating spontaneous ideas in response to a given subject. A creative exercise used mainly in training settings, but also by some counsellors (e.g. in the EGAN APPROACH) to develop possible solutions or alternative perspectives and to overcome obstacles. Brainstorming requires some suspension of habitual thinking patterns, and a playful attitude. Evaluation of the ideas generated follows the exercise.

breaks and holidays breaks in the continuity of counselling sessions due to planned holidays on the part of counsellor or client, or unforeseen and unavoidable breaks due to illness, accident or other events. Working with the significance of breaks is paramount in PSYCHODYNAMIC COUNSELLING in particular, because separation may be experienced and/or interpreted as charged with anxiety, feelings of betrayal, anger, and so on (*see* SEPARATION ANXIETY).

Counsellors of the brief cognitive–behavioural approaches might well suggest breaks or changes in schedule to avoid dependency and to reinforce coping skills.

brief counselling any counselling method which is of short duration by design. Because counselling is often regarded as brief by its very nature, the term 'brief counselling' is rarely used (although *see* Dryden and Feltham, 1992b). However, because certain agencies providing counselling operate under constraints of funding and time pressures, 'brief counselling' (e.g. up to six sessions) is an appropriate term. 'Brief focused counselling' is also sometimes used. *See* BRIEF THERAPY, SINGLE SESSION THERAPY.

brief therapy generic term for models of counselling and psychotherapy which specifically aim to work within a time-limited contract, using methods designed to effect rapid progress. Brief models include contracts of between 3 and 25 sessions and tend to employ active-directive methods, with an emphasis on accurate assessment, goal setting, homework, rapid formation of therapeutic alliance, confrontation of defences and discouraging of dependency. Many therapeutic systems, including psychoanalysis, began as relatively brief procedures. Certain psychoanalytic models of brief therapy aim to identify transference reactions rapidly, focusing on the nature of defences and utilising time constraints to induce anxiety for therapeutic mobilisation. COGNITIVE THERAPY and BEHAVIOUR THERAPY are intrinsically brief, focusing on problem identification, mediating beliefs and problem solving. (*See* COGNITIVE ANALYTIC THERAPY for a therapy which is specifically designed for a 16 week contract in NHS settings.) Debate on the efficacy of brief therapy centres on its claims to overcome dependency on the therapist/counsellor, and reinforcing clients' faith in their own coping capacities. Advocates of long-term therapies suggest that brief therapy suppresses symptoms and denies clients the necessary process of WORKING THROUGH. Some research findings have suggested little or no significant difference in efficacy between long and brief therapies. The term brief therapy is sometimes used synonymously with SOLUTION-FOCUSED BRIEF THERAPY. *See* INTENSIVE SHORT-TERM DYNAMIC PSYCHOTHERAPY, TIME-LIMITED THERAPY.

bulimia nervosa an eating disorder characterised by binge eating (*see* BINGEING), which can be followed by purging and vomiting. It is said that 50% of bulimics are, or have been, anorectics (*see* ANOREXIA NERVOSA). The main distinction between the two conditions is that bulimics usually maintain normal body weight and the condition is therefore often not obvious.

bullying oppression, physically aggressive or psychologically undermining behaviour, usually of one person directly by another or groups of others. Bullying used to be associated mainly with schools, as in the classical bullying of a weaker or smaller student by a stronger, bigger 'bully'. It is now recognised as an activity that can happen to adults, for example in the workplace. The psychologically damaging effects of bullying can last for years. Recovery consists in understanding, putting into perspective, and devising strategies for assertiveness and, where necessary, formal complaints. Some schools have instituted peer counselling to address bullying problems.

burnout debilitating fatigue or disillusionment experienced by members of the helping/caring professions. Burnout (sometimes called 'burnout and stress syndrome' and previously 'professional neurasthenia') is a result of a variety of factors: disillusionment, heavy case loads, insufficient support or supervision, organisational politics and pressures, being undervalued, poor pay, facing an especially demanding client group, lack of further training and development opportunities, poor balance between occupational demands and recreational and domestic life, and simply 'waning enthusiasm'. Self-care, awareness, assertiveness, stress and time management, personal therapy and good supervision are antidotes, but in some cases burnout may indicate a need for temporary withdrawal from counselling or even a change of career.

cancer counselling any counselling related to people suffering from cancer, or for their loved ones. Also known as *oncology counselling*. Counselling may be provided at various stages, from first diagnosis through developments (favourable and unfavourable) in the malignancy, response to treatment, side-effects of some treatments, changes in lifestyle, physical appearance and morale, to recovery or decline, and dying. Such counselling is provided either in medical or voluntary organisation settings and will usually overlap with information-giving. Acceptance of terminal conditions may follow initial denial and anger, and counselling may assist this process. Alternative approaches to cancer treatment have been developed, often employing transpersonal methods (*see* TRANSPERSONAL THERAPY) and radical attitude and lifestyle changes, which may aim at 'psycho-immunity' (building psychological resistance to the recurrence of cancer). Counsellors working with this client group are likely to be primarily supportive but will also help people (including family and medical staff) to confront the realities of cancer and its stigmatic associations. Some counsellors argue for this, as other serious medical conditions, to be accepted as simply another part of the whole person.

career counselling counselling addressing choice and development of occupation. Also known as careers guidance. Careers counsellors undergo specialist training equipping them with knowledge of job opportunities, employment trends and requirements for training and qualifications. Career counselling includes information giving and, often, the administering of psychometric tests to assist clients in identifying vocational strengths and weaknesses. Much of the work addresses age-specific opportunities and job market conditions. Counsellors need to be alert to sexist, racist or other inappropriate assumptions about their clients. Career counselling can utilise, for example, person-centred, psychodynamic and personal construct explorations of clients' self-characterisations and unnecessarily constrictive views of their own aims and potentials. *See also* OUTPLACEMENT COUNSELLING, REDUNDANCY COUNSELLING.

caring feeling and showing concern. The origin of the word 'care' lies in sorrow, worry, caution and concern. The *caring professions* (e.g. medicine, nursing, social work and the psychotherapies) are those whose focus is the well-being of others, and it is assumed that everyone entering or remaining in them has a caring attitude, or orientation, towards others, motivated by personal disposition, kindness, reparation needs, or religious belief. The word 'caring', however, can contain traces of paternalism and can (in its sentimental sense) undermine the goal of restoring or reinforcing clients' autonomy. The terms 'in care' and 'community care' demonstrate statutory policies of care for vulnerable citizens. Clients in counselling deserve a caring attitude from the counsellor, but one that is genuine and not presented as the sole counselling attitude or skill. See DUTY OF CARE.

case a client, or clients in couple or family counselling, as discussed with supervisors or colleagues. The term is not favoured by counsellors, having its origins in social work, psychiatry and medicine and is viewed as emphasising the problem at the expense of the person. 'Case' is also used sometimes as a synonym for 'diagnosis' (e.g. 'a case of severe depression').

case discussion method of presenting work with clients which focuses on client history, problems and dynamics. It is one model or aspect of supervision and is sometimes criticised as lacking depth or omitting actual counsellor–client dialogue in favour of the counsellor's impressions. *Case conferences*, in which counsellors are rarely involved, are multidisciplinary case discussions focusing on one client (or family) about whom a statutory decision may need to be made.

caseload the number of clients a counsellor has 'on her books' at any one time. The term is used mainly in organisational rather than private practice settings. A chronically high caseload is likely to lead to compromised effectiveness and to BURNOUT. A guideline figure for maximum caseload in a full-time counselling job is 20–25 client hours a week.

case study a written report on a completed or ongoing counselling relationship, which aims to demonstrate the client's problems, the therapeutic approach used, and reflections on success, failure and significant learning. Often required by training courses and accreditation procedures, and demanding protection of client confidentiality.

casework professional helping of clients in statutory settings (e.g. the social and probation services) which focuses on formal, face-to-face interviews. Casework may include counselling, family therapy, behavioural assignments, dealing with welfare issues, etc., but some social workers and probation officers consider their casework to be synonymous with counselling. The terms 'social work counselling/therapy' are sometimes used. With the emergence of counselling as a distinct profession, many counsellors distinguish sharply between counselling and casework on the grounds that clients in statutory settings are usually not self-referred and/or that the work involves assessment and coercion. *See* CLIENT.

catalytic counsellor interventions are described as catalytic when their purpose and/or effect is to stimulate or jolt the client into a state of fresh perspective, feeling or action. 'What if...?' questions or WORST SCENARIO images can be catalytic in challenging current self-defeating assumptions, for example.

catastrophising *see* AWFULISING.

catharsis relief from tension through crying, laughter, ABREACTION, intense physical action or vicariously through witnessing others' emotional experiences. Literally, catharsis is 'purging'. Guinagh (1987) suggests three models of catharsis: the container model (emotion is suppressed and seeks an outlet); the unfinished business model (catharsis is the urge for, and means of, completing unfinished psychological experiences); and the conflict model (emotional expression and repression of emotions are in conflict and catharsis signifies breakthrough of emotion). Catharsis commonly includes a trigger event, an emotional release, and a memory of a significant previous experience. Catharsis is viewed by some counsellors as a necessary first stage of release accompanying talking (typically, telling a life story); by some as useful primarily to overcome blocks; by some (*see* PRIMAL THERAPY and PSYCHODRAMA) as a central therapeutic task; by others still as an (often) attractive, distracting, but not ultimately therapeutic phenomenon.

cathexis originally a Freudian notion referring to the emotional investment one has in particular objects or people. Some confusion and looseness surrounds the term, due to its mistranslation and metaphorical nature. Freud viewed it as psychic energy compelling interest in people or events according to their representational meaning and power for individuals. The term has been adapted in TA theory to account specifically for the energy necessary to effect changes from one ego state to another. The cathexis school in TA specialises in treating psychotic clients. Cathexis has also been called a 'quantity of energy' and has been criticised for the quasi-biological pretensions that may have motivated Freud to coin it. *To cathect* is (often unconsciously) to invest energy and meaning in. *To decathect* is to withdraw such investment. *See also* TRANSACTIONAL ANALYSIS.

causal a level of consciousness associated with mystical experience of the pure kind, with no symbols or images. This has traditionally not been used much in counselling but Mindell (1995) and others have suggested that it can be an important resource in TRANSPERSONAL THERAPY. Instead of no-mind, the concept here is of free mind or creative mind.

chairwork a method of therapeutic ROLE PLAY in which the counsellor directs the client to imagine either significant people in his life, or parts of his own self, sitting in an empty chair in the consulting room. The client may address his remarks to the person imagined sitting in the chair and/or change chairs in order to access the imagined person's perspective on him. Many permutations on this theme are possible, and sometimes the counsellor may occupy a particular chair and take on the role of a significant person in the client's life. The purpose of chairwork (most prominently practised in GESTALT counselling) is CATHARSIS, REHEARSAL of new behaviours, and gaining new perspectives on aspects of one's behaviour and integration of different parts of oneself. Sometimes several chairs are used to represent several people or problems. Floor cushions are often used instead of chairs. *See also* ROLE REVERSAL.

chakras a set of centres in the 'subtle body' representing levels of consciousness. A term from yoga that has entered into the field of TRANSPERSONAL THERAPY.

challenging confronting a client with her

own discrepant views or feelings, or pointing out, for example, avoidance of risk or discounting of positive attributes. Judicious challenging (by immediacy, confrontation and giving feedback, for example) provides therapeutic movement. Challenging is partly synonymous with CONFRONTATION. The counsellor's failure to challenge when it is appropriate to do so is sometimes called the 'Mum effect' (Egan, 2002). The persistent challenging of defences (or 'unremitting pressure') often used in intensive short-term dynamic psychotherapy is considered by many to be excessive.

challenging behaviour a term used for some people, often children, whose persistent ACTING-OUT can only be contained by residential care, and has replaced the concept of 'maladjusted behaviour'. An aspect of conduct disorder.

change movement or transition from one state to another. Change is central to the enterprise of counselling and psychotherapy. Change usually means an improvement, although deterioration is also a change, and in reality change within counselling is usually non-linear. In counselling terms, clients have explicit or implicit change GOALS (e.g. from depression to contentment; from shyness to social ease). Perceptions and measurements of change are difficult: subjective reports from clients, and behavioural, cognitive, physiological and other criteria may all be applied. The question of *how* counselling helps people to change is a central task for researchers (*see* THERAPEUTIC FACTORS). Some counsellors insist that they will work only with clients motivated to change. Some clients believe that they intend to change but find the effort and pain too daunting. One view is that life is a process of inevitable, constant change and that NEUROSIS is resistance to this fact of life. Sometimes the term 'fundamental personality change' is used to differentiate the aims and results of PSYCHOTHERAPY from the supposedly modest aims and results of counselling. *See* STAGES OF CHANGE and SELF-CHANGE. Contrast with STASIS.

change agent anyone or anything taking part in effecting change in another. In practice it is usually associated with a facilitator in management settings.

character analysis the practice, often attributed to Reich but stemming from Freud, of observing and analysing habitual attitudes and defences (as opposed to dreams, say, or specific symptoms). 'Character' is often used of innate or chronic personality traits, and 'characterology' refers to the way in which such traits are structured. They also affect body posture and movements.

character armour REICHIAN concept that defences which protect a 'core neurosis' are embodied in physical (often sexual) inhibitions, tension, and PSYCHOSOMATIC disorders generally. Most systems of therapy using bodywork are based on such a notion.

chemical dependency term used synonymously with drug and alcohol dependency and abuse but meaning a *physical* ADDICTION to mood-altering substances. These may be legally prescribed or purchased and inadvertently or deliberately abused (e.g. minor tranquillisers, alcohol, potent glues) or illegally obtained and ingested (e.g. cocaine, heroin). In all cases there will also be psychological dependence.

Some drugs, however, produce only psychological dependence, as they are not chemically addictive.

child abuse any form of non-accidental serious physical or emotional injury of a child. Common examples of child abuse include sexual violation and beatings. Denial of basic needs for food, protection and appropriate nurturing is more usually known as child NEGLECT. Subtle examples of abuse include persistent minor beatings, humiliations, withdrawal of affection, undermining, devaluing. Counsellors frequently encounter histories of some degree of abuse. Memories of abuse are frequently repressed, but in later life can be triggered into consciousness. It is now widely acknowledged that all forms of childhood abuse have long-lasting effects into adulthood, and that it is more widespread than previously believed. Gross TRAUMA in childhood is in some ways easier to detect than slow, subtle, but still insidious forms of abuse (e.g. years of verbal humiliation). *See* Miller (1987).

child ego state one of the three structured types of ego states in TA which concerns feelings, attitudes and behaviours of the person's childhood or historical experiences. *See* ADAPTED CHILD, FREE CHILD.

child sexual abuse this term, and its abbreviated form CSA, refer to the specifically sexual abuse of children (*see* CHILD ABUSE). The incidence of CSA is considered by many to be much greater than once imagined (*see*, for example, Russell, 1983) and criticisms have been made of Freud's (and subsequently other analysts') tendencies to interpret claims of such abuse as being fantasy. *See* INCEST, RITUAL ABUSE.

childhood memories recollections of scenes from childhood by an adult. Certain therapies (e.g. INDIVIDUAL PSYCHOLOGY, PRIMAL THERAPY) regard work with childhood memories as indispensable, although some approaches focus more on imagery and REDECISION, others more on REGRESSION and DISCHARGE. Inability to access such memories is regarded variously as an indication of infantile amnesia or serious repression. The value of accessing these memories is considered to lie in the clue they hold to original, formative decisions and schemas (*see* SCHEMA), to typical emotional responses and to a limited repertoire of behaviours in adult life. Some theorists hold that such memories can be and have to be accessed in their original state, while others argue that all memory is coloured by subsequent experience and recalled selectively.

children, counselling of although not a highly developed treatment modality, there are some counsellors, particularly in schools, whose work is focused on children and, to a lesser extent, on 'whole school' issues. Traditionally, therapeutic work with children has been done by child psychoanalysts and psychotherapy following Klein, Anna Freud and Winnicott; non-directive play therapists (e.g. Axline); educational psychologists; social workers and other child guidance workers. Also much work with children takes place in FAMILY THERAPY. All such work must heed the developmental stages, ethical and legal problems inherent in work with minors, as well as preferences for non-verbal therapy. Counsellors in (early) educational settings may attempt child-centred, preventive counselling. Some schools have instituted peer counselling, particularly in response to bullying. Typical issues include: conduct problems, eating disorders, depression, parental separation and divorce, bereavement, abuse, drug problems. *See* YOUTH COUNSELLING.

choice a decision that has been, or is waiting to be, made between two or more objects or courses of action. Choice also implies some degree of FREE WILL, conscious access to decision-making processes and the ability to implement a decision. Models such as TA and Adlerian counselling claim that we make choices as children (not always the best ones) and remain dysfunctionally attached to these early choices, but we are free, particularly with therapeutic assistance, to choose anew. (*See* REDECISION.) Others argue that both childhood *and* adult choices are limited by the realities of genetics, psychopathology, age, and socioeconomic and other factors. Choices of partner and career are often very significant indicators in counselling. Counsellors sometimes speak of *choice points* within sessions or in everyday life, at which clients confront a free choice between habitual, and limited, behaviour and new avenues: 'windows of opportunity'. Choice confronts counsellors vis-à-vis ORIENTATION, clinical interventions and treatment of choice (*see* TREATMENT). There is also a spiritual view of 'choiceless awareness' in which the person transcends choices and is moved to live skilfully and non-conflictually.

chronic this term is used in contradistinction to ACUTE to denote psychiatric conditions of longstanding duration. 'Chronic schizophrenia' is an example of a non-acute condition with marked social deterioration and suggests a genetically or biologically caused and/or learned, but irreversible, MENTAL ILLNESS. The term 'chronic' is also used loosely to describe persistent states, as in 'chronic mild depression'. *See also* 'chronically endured PAIN', a concept used in CAT to 'honour' lifelong psychological suffering, in contrast to SCRIPT.

chronic fatigue syndrome (CFS) physical and mental fatigue lasting more than six months. Also known as ME, CFS is characterised by lack of energy, aches and pains, dizziness, disturbed sleep, etc. and often associated with depression. There are no drugs known to be effective with CFS itself. *Chronic fatigue* can be managed with some counselling or CBT, gradual activity, and monitoring of sleep.

clarification statement which makes information clear. Counsellors frequently seek greater clarity by reflecting clients' content, by paraphrasing or asking pertinent QUESTIONS.

classical conditioning behavioural procedure in which a desired response is solicited; for example, by pairing on a number of occasions a conditioned stimulus (e.g. an aural tone) with an unconditional stimulus (food), a dog then salivates (a conditioned response) at later presentations of the conditioned stimulus alone. The effects of extremely traumatic events such as rape have been likened to a form of classical conditioning.

classification of disorders the systematic description and categorisation of disorder (disease). All forms of physical and psychological disorder are classified for the purposes of diagnosis, prognosis, treatment and communication. In psychiatry, classification is controversial because of problems of epistemology; alleged potential

35

and actual abuse of human rights; and the totalitarian and fallible nature of such classification. Classification is sometimes referred to as 'nosology'. *See* DSM-IV TR and ICD-10.

claustrophobia fear of enclosed spaces. Speculatively, it is considered by some to be related to BIRTH TRAUMA or other neonatal traumas. It is in general use, as in 'claustrophobic relationship', signifying undesirably close, symbiotic or demanding partnerships.

client one who engages the services of a counsellor. In counselling preference is given to the term 'client' over that of PATIENT, which is used in psychoanalysis, some analytically oriented therapies and psychiatric treatment. 'Client' attempts to respect the autonomy of the person in counselling or therapy and suggests a more egalitarian relationship than that of the therapist–patient dyad. (Some writers argue that 'patient' is the more honest, accurate, containing, and less euphemistic term.) 'Client' is also intended to overcome connotations of sickness and is promoted particularly by humanistic counsellors and the ethos of PERSONAL GROWTH. Rogers (1961) is especially responsible for promotion of the term in his CLIENT-CENTRED THERAPY (although *see* PERSON-CENTRED COUNSELLING). Some critics dislike the fixed-role connotations of 'client' and use the terms 'counsellee' or 'helpee', meaning the person who is in the temporary functional position of receiving counselling or help. *See also* CONSUMER, USER.

client-centred therapy Carl Rogers' (1961) original model of counselling and therapy, which placed emphasis on the client's autonomy, innate trustworthiness, tendency towards SELF-ACTUALISATION and the role of the counsellor as providing the climate in which therapy would naturally occur. The term 'client-centred' replaced NON-DIRECTIVE and client-centred therapy is now more often referred to as PERSON-CENTRED COUNSELLING or the person-centred approach.

client–counsellor match the notion that compatibility of any client and her counsellor is a significant factor in determining a good OUTCOME. Common variables of the client–counsellor match (or fit) are age, gender, race, socioeconomic status, personality and perceived values. *See also* PRESCRIPTIVE MATCHING, THERAPEUTIC ALLIANCE.

client group a relatively homogeneous group of people identified as the main recipients of a counsellor's or counselling agency's services. Alternatively, a group of people perceived as sharing a common experience or problem. Client groups may be said to include children, adults, older people; disabled people, students, women; people with AIDS, people diagnosed as depressed, anxious, obsessive–compulsive; and so on. For many client groups, specialist training or knowledge is required of counsellors.

climate-setting the purposeful creation of an atmosphere conducive to progress in counselling. It is generally agreed by counsellors that the CORE CONDITIONS of genuineness, empathy and unconditional positive regard are necessary in the building of such a climate. It is also widely acknowledged that good counselling work is unlikely to be achieved without attention being paid to the emotional climate in which the client is received, especially in the beginning phase. Therapists working within some psychodynamic and psychoanalytic traditions may use a different approach to climate-setting in which they abstain from self-disclosure in order to create the conditions in which negative transferences are more likely to become manifest and the focus for exploration.

clinical relating, literally, to the 'sick bed'. The term has both precise and general meanings. It can also have a derogatory meaning, referring to a person or setting that is cold, unemotional and unwelcoming. The term is often avoided by counsellors since it is perceived as belonging to the medical model. The term 'clinical' is also used to distinguish this aspect from other parts of a practitioner's or agency's work (e.g. clinical supervision as opposed to managerial supervision).

clinical accountability the notion that what is done in relation to a client by a professional in the counselling/therapy field is a responsible act or set of actions that can be attributed to that professional individual and potentially (negatively) lead to sanctions in cases of negligence or misjudgement. The term was debated particularly in the late 1990s in relation to the 'Anthony Smith' case, in which both the counsellor and supervisor came under scrutiny. The prevalent view is that accountability is probably shared but its weight depends on the parties involved, agency setting, profession, and theoretical orientation.

clinical affiliate a term used by some EAP providers to refer to counsellors and other allied professionals.

clinical audit systematic monitoring of clinical procedures and outcomes. Now routine in NHS settings, audit may be carried out by counting, for example, appropriate referrals but also by setting targets for reductions in inappropriate referrals.

clinical chaos a theory of chaos, complexity and non-linear dynamics supporting the perceived reality that much counselling/therapy does not proceed smoothly, 'by the book', but in an unpredictable fashion. Chamberlain and Butz (1998) argue that chaos theory principles of sensitive dependence on initial conditions, 'strange attractors', uncertainty, dissipative structures and bifurcations can be fruitfully applied to clinical work.

clinical counselling although used rarely, this is employed, for example, in some medical settings such as HIV and AIDS clinics.

clinical depression connotes a DEPRESSION severe enough to warrant medical attention and treatment, i.e. major depression rather than mild depression.

clinical excellence a health philosophy aspiring to the highest possible standards of care and treatment. Emanating from the NHS and focusing initially on physical medicine, clinical excellence also has implications for evidence-based practice in counselling.

clinical psychology is an applied branch of PSYCHOLOGY and clinical psychologists work in hospital and clinic settings, often cognitive-behaviourally but also psychodynamically and with other therapeutic models. Clinical psychologists have a first degree in psychology, or equivalent (and increasingly a doctorate), as well as further training, are members of the BPS, and may specialise in certain conditions, groups or tasks, such as assessment, eating disorders, PTSD, elderly people, etc.

clinical strategy usually synonymous with a treatment plan (*see* TREATMENT).

clinical theology therapeutic approach pioneered by Lake (1966) that attempts to combine Christian insights with innovative, eclectic, and primal theories and practices. Clinical theology (at one time under Lake's leadership) concentrated much of its work on intrauterine and birth experiences, identifying the sources of much later life experience and symbolism with suffering in 'constricted confusion' in the womb. Prenatal distress could be gradually discharged and/or integrated into awareness. Lake originally used LSD and special breathing techniques in order to access primal pain (*see* PRIMAL THERAPY), but like other practitioners abandoned these in favour of simpler methods. Clients in this kind of counselling or therapy are also considered 'souls in travail'.

closed question *see* QUESTIONS.

coaching the teaching, often in one-to-one situations, of skills by modelling, problem-solving and counselling. Coaching overlaps with, but departs from, the non-directive and often open-ended model of much counselling. Coaching is used particularly in performance professions (e.g. sports, arts, and management) and employs insights from the psychology of counselling and therapy (e.g. self-talk). 'Experiential transfer' refers to direct teaching from experience and is similar to the social skills models of behaviour therapy. The terms coaching and mentoring are sometimes used interchangeably.

co-counselling the counselling of peers by each other, as opposed to one-way, professional counselling. Various schools of co-counselling have evolved from Jackins' (1965) original RE-EVALUATION COUNSELLING model. 'Co-counselling' refers to a specialised method of peer counselling (a central method of which is emotional DISCHARGE), variants of this such as John Heron's model, and any form of peer counselling. Each kind rests on the concept of the client and counsellor assuming temporary functional roles, which are alternated by agreement. Co-counselling is preferred by some people on economic grounds (no payment need be involved) and by others on political grounds (it has a democratic ethos and society-changing potential, and can avoid professional hierarchies). Critics suggest that it lacks appropriate rigour and adequate containment and cannot replace professional counselling and therapy.

code of ethics and practice a document composed by a professional body which sets out what are considered to be good, normative standards of counselling practice, and what are areas of concern and prohibition. All practising counsellors and therapists should observe such a code, which offers minimal protection, at least, to consumers. Breaches of any such code, depending on their seriousness and consequences, should be the subject of a recognised COMPLAINTS PROCEDURE. The BACP originally published such codes for counsellors, supervisors and trainers before moving to its ETHICAL FRAMEWORK. *See also* ETHICS.

co-dependency a partnership in which each person, consciously or unconsciously, supports or encourages an unhealthy habit in the other. One or both may be dependent on drugs, alcohol, over-eating or other dysfunctional behaviours. Co-dependency is a collusive syndrome, complicated by the partners' emotional dependency on each other. It has been called 'one addiction feeding another'. Critics of the term suggest that it can be used of any relationship that contains any degree of dependency.

co-facilitator one who leads, with another, a counselling, therapy or personal growth group. A co-facilitator may be an assistant (learning to facilitate) or a colleague of equal status. The term is comparable with 'co-therapist' and 'co-leader', but 'co-facilitator' is likely to be used more in humanistic therapies. The function, often, is to act as an observer and to consult with the leader in order to provide balanced perception of events, and greater safety. *See* FACILITATE.

cognition *see* THINKING.

cognitive analytic therapy a brief therapy devised by Ryle (1990) representing an integration of OBJECT RELATIONS theory, PERSONAL CONSTRUCT theory and aspects of BEHAVIOUR THERAPY and COGNITIVE THERAPY. CAT is a highly structured form of therapy and counselling, which places much emphasis on assessment, client activity, homework, self-monitoring, continuous evaluation of progress and discouragement of dependency. Following the client's completion of the 'psychotherapy file' and the identification of TRAPS, DILEMMAS and SNAGS, the counsellor draws up a written reformulation that serves as the basis for goal setting and insight. Various written and diagrammatic means are used to focus on 'target problems' and their resolution. Ryle commends working with transference, but also views CAT as open to technical eclecticism.

cognitive–behavioural therapy (CBT) an umbrella term for those approaches based on, related to, or developing from BEHAVIOUR THERAPY and COGNITIVE THERAPY. Under this description are often included problem-solving therapy, self-management therapy,

COGNITIVE THERAPY, RATIONAL EMOTIVE BEHAVIOUR THERAPY and STRESS INOCULATION TRAINING. The core concept of cognitive-behavioural therapy (CBT) or counselling is that beliefs about events in our lives are open to examination and change, and that changing beliefs result in greater control of our lives and reduction in dysfunctional behaviour. A hallmark of all these approaches is their clinical insistence on changing behaviour through the inter-relationship of cognition and behaviour. This distinguishes them from radical behaviourism, which tends to deny the role of mediating thought processes in psychological problems. Criticised by many as ignoring the 'whole person' (especially the deeper feelings, and childhood) CBT has a good record with anxieties, phobias, depression and social problems. Also termed 'cognitive behaviour therapy'.

cognitive dissonance a term coined by Festinger to describe the phenomenon of two conflicting beliefs co-existing in the same person, who then usually feels bound to engage in cognitive dissonance reduction strategies (similar to self-deceit).

cognitive error an incidence of FAULTY INFORMATION PROCESSING.

cognitive humanistic therapy a therapeutic model proposed by Nelson-Jones which honours the best in each of these two approaches.

cognitive restructuring alternative term for the general philosophy and strategy of CBT in seeking to identify unhelpful thinking and replace it with rational, constructive thoughts.

cognitive therapy the model of therapy originated by Beck (1979) which identifies cognitions (or thought processes) as the most significant factor in psychological disturbance and its treatment. Based on COLLABORATIVE EMPIRICISM, cognitive therapy seeks to identify specific instances and general patterns of faulty information processing. Originally used to treat depression, it is now applied widely to other conditions. As in REBT, a core concept is that thinking is a central part of experience and that AUTOMATIC THOUGHTS need to be analysed into their habitual, non-empirical, and modifiable components. Clients learn to re-examine such thoughts and to test their effects against empirical evidence in behavioural assignments in everyday life. Cognitive therapy begins with identifying, and then goes on to change, dysfunctional schemas in the latter part of the therapy. It is generally a short-term approach, but longer therapy takes place with clients with so-called personality disorders. It is not necessarily, as critics suggest, limited to problem solving, because it can be adopted as an empirical attitude to life and personal growth. *See also* COGNITIVE TRIAD, RATIONAL EMOTIVE BEHAVIOUR THERAPY and SCHEMA.

cognitive triad a concept used in cognitive therapy to explain depressive and anxious thought patterns. The negative cognitive triad characterising depression is: negative view of self, of the world, and of the future. The anxiogenic (anxiety-creating or anxiety-maintaining) cognitive triad is characterised by view of self as vulnerable, of the world as threatening, and of the future as unpredictable.

cohesion a term used largely of the phenomenon in groups of the bonding of participants in beneficial and purposeful ways.

collaborative empiricism client and counsellor examining evidence, together, of events in the client's life and the functional and dysfunctional attributions made in regard to them. The term is used in COGNITIVE THERAPY to underline its scientific method and to counteract misconceptions of therapy being done to people.

collective unconscious a term used in ANALYTICAL PSYCHOLOGY to refer to the dimension of psychic reality that is shared by all human beings, is prior to the personal unconscious, and contains the ARCHETYPES. The collective unconscious is sometimes understood as Jungian 'territory', with the personal unconscious being Freudian. It has been called the 'unfalsified voice of nature' and is characterised by mythological imagery and 'intrinsic polarities'. Some Jungians, however, argue that the collective and personal unconscious overlap or interweave, rather than exclude each other. *See* UNCONSCIOUS.

colloquial terms language, initiated by some clients, that may be slang, emotive and close to everyday experience. Because of the intimate (and often emotional) nature of counselling and the counsellor's attempt to remain in the FRAME OF REFERENCE of the client, colloquial terms may frequently be used. Examples include 'pissed off' (angry), 'screwed up' (confused, distressed), 'fucked up' (damaged), 'my shit/stuff/baggage' (my material, or unfinished business), 'gutted' (devastated). *See also* PROFANITY IN COUNSELLING.

collusion literally, playing a game together. In a counselling context it refers to the counsellor's participation in, and therefore reinforcement of, the client's self-defeating behaviour, irrational thoughts or avoidance strategies. Collusion may occur where the counsellor lacks the experience to identify it, is unknowingly seduced into it by the client, shares and has not personally resolved some of the same problems as the client, or fails to confront signs of it sufficiently early and allows a culture of cosy agreement to be established. In itself collusion is countertherapeutic, but if identified and worked with it can hasten progress. Collusion can operate on many levels, including the client colluding with the counsellor's neurosis. One aim of SUPERVISION is to identify and confront counsellor–client collusion.

collusive fit a term used sometimes in couple counselling of relationships based on certain unhealthy, co-dependent reasons for the partners to be attracted to each other.

commitment loyal adherence to an attitude, policy, relationship or course of action. Sufficient commitment is needed from clients for the hard work, confrontation of defences, risk-taking and pain that counselling often entails. This can be reflected in regularly keeping appointments and arriving on time. Equally, counsellors and therapists need a commitment to their clients and to ensuring and maintaining standards. The concept of commitment is also important in couple counselling and the term 'commitment-phobic' is sometimes used to connote resistance. *See also* STAGES OF CHANGE.

communication the transmission of information (which may be factual, verbal, precise; emotional, non-verbal, general). Communication is central to counselling, which is why training in counselling skills focuses on accurate listening to and reflecting back of a client's content and feeling, and awareness of manifest and covert content and process. Effective communication is clearly expressed and emotionally open. Experienced counsellors are aware of nuances of communication relating to the HERE AND NOW and the THERE AND THEN, and of the appropriateness of responding to different aspects of the client's experience. The term 'communication skills' is sometimes used synonymously with counselling skills and is found particularly in health and medical psychology literature.

communicative approach a form of psychoanalytic therapy, developed by Langs, which emphasises the role of the client's unconscious perception of therapist activity. According to Langs, clients are highly sensitive to therapists' intentions and skills and seek to monitor and correct interventions by presenting unconscious commentaries about the therapist, her work, and the therapeutic relationship. Communicative psychotherapy claims that therapists can act 'madly' and that clients unconsciously strive to correct and even heal them. The only techniques regarded as permissible are interpretation, silence, and frame management (the establishing and keeping of strict boundaries). Critics suggest that the communicative approach is inflexible and mechanistic. *See* Smith (1991).

community meeting the coming together of trainees and tutors on a counselling course in order to discuss matters not addressed elsewhere, to air grievances, celebrate progress and facilitate cohesion. Community meetings are also used in therapeutic communities.

community mental health team a multidisciplinary team made up of community psychiatric nurses, social workers, applied social workers, occupational therapists, clinical psychologists, psychiatrists and support workers, that takes referrals, makes assessments and delivers treatments in a particular area. Often known as CMHT.

community psychiatric nurse (CPN) a qualified mental health nurse, part of a CMHT (see above), who is based in the community. CPNs mainly take referrals from GPs but also from psychiatrists, health visitors, district nurses, counsellors and others. CPNs work in primary care (treating anxiety, depression, social phobia, etc.), enduring mentally ill (EMI), and elderly, teams. They can give depot injections but cannot 'section' people; a large part of their role is assessment. While a few are counselling trained and in dual roles, most have no counselling training.

comorbidity a term in (mainly US) psychiatric usage referring to the co-existence of two or more diagnosable mental health problems or disorders in the same client, e.g. depression and addiction or severe mental illness and drug addiction. While some practitioners argue that these may stem from a single source such as early childhood deprivation, others caution that each condition may require quite separate treatment. More commonly known in the UK as *dual diagnosis*.

compassion and pity, are often dismissed as relevant to counselling and psychotherapy, being considered as akin to SYMPATHY and lacking the discipline of EMPATHY. But Buddhism has compassion as one of its cornerstones and some commentators suggest that, along with kindness, love, forgiveness, etc., it is an overlooked value.

compassion fatigue specifically, the con-

dition of secondary traumatic stress disorder suffered by those treating victims of PTSD; generally, any helper who eventually becomes 'burnt-out' by lengthy caring commitments.

compassionate nihilism a fellow-feeling and philosophy of affectionate concern resting on no overriding belief but simply on an emotional recognition of fellow sufferers in an ultimately indifferent universe.

compensation a defence mechanism whereby someone seeks to overcome personal deficiencies by behaving or fantasising in contradiction to the realities of her personality or situation. Adler's definition differed from Freud's in focusing specifically on inferiority feelings and the attempt made in various ways to compensate for them.

complaints procedure clearly and publicly stated means whereby dissatisfied or aggrieved clients of counsellors can present their case systematically and have it heard and assessed according to the principles of the professional organisation concerned, and which is backed up by possible sanctions against errant counsellors. Complaints can also apply to counsellor trainers and others.

complex a term of psychoanalytic origin referring to a cluster of emotionally loaded meanings and experiences. Complexes were considered to be rooted in childhood development and to be both conscious and unconscious. In spite of the well-known examples of OEDIPUS COMPLEX and castration complex, Freud came to avoid the term 'complex' because it became popularised to the point of meaninglessness and misuse (e.g. 'inferiority complex' referring to anyone exhibiting self-doubt). The idea of complexes was important to

Jung, who referred to them as 'splinter psyches' which could be either positive or negative.

complex trauma a suggested alternative conception of PTSD as a 'spectrum of conditions' rather than a single disorder.

compliance *see* PLACATORY BEHAVIOUR. Client compliance is a term found mainly in American literature referring to the expectation that the client should acquiesce in and co-operate with the treatment plan devised by or in conjunction with the therapist, client non-compliance therefore being regarded as a significant cause of therapeutic failure.

compulsion irrational urge to act in a particular, often repetitive and ritualistic, way. Such behaviour is often coupled with obsessional preoccupations (ruminations), as in obsessive–compulsive disorder (*see* OBSESSION), but compulsions represent the more active (though equally distressing) part of the condition. Examples of compulsions include checking locks and electrical appliances, ritualistic counting, hoarding. *Obsessive-compulsive disorder* is characterised by PERFECTIONISM, intolerance of uncertainty, excessive activity, dominance and emotional impoverishment. Many people suffer from minor, subclinical compulsions. The TREATMENT OF CHOICE is behaviour therapy or appropriate medication. Supportive counselling and self-help groups can assist.

computer-assisted therapy any counselling/therapy utilising computer packages. A client may be referred to an online facility to assist them in working through a CBT programme for depression, for example.

conceptualisation the client's and/or counsellor's view of the client's problem, what it comprises, whence it may derive, and what may be the best means of attempting to resolve it. *Case conceptualisation* is the term sometimes used of the counsellor's assessment, hypothesis and planning for a client.

conciliation counselling counselling specifically in circumstances of impending or established marital breakdown or workplace conflict. Conciliation – sometimes known as or overlapping with mediation – may be offered by court officials (probation officers) or independent counsellors or mediation workers. Conciliation implies the possibility of reconciliation, whereas mediation often means the arbitration of a third party where conciliation is deemed unlikely. Emotional, practical and legal matters require settlement with the assistance of a neutral, informed third party. Since established families may be involved, it is necessary to decide on ongoing arrangements and to separate these from psychological problems. Means used may include family therapy, and techniques of conflict management, reframing, negotiation and task-setting.

concreteness the quality of SPECIFICITY. Clients are encouraged to become progressively concrete in the way they relate their stories (with facts and attendant feelings) in order to identify problem areas and to erode defensive vagueness. A vital skill for counsellors in certain approaches is to be able to elicit clear and specific statements and goals. Signs of tentative concreteness (e.g. facial expression at emotive moments) can be identified and reflected. Clients who persistently avoid being concrete may be too afraid, too damaged, or may have a preference for therapeutic models which work slowly, for example with symbolism.

condensation the process of joining and converting many different feelings and thoughts into a single image, in dreams, puns and other expressions of symbolisation.

conditioning originally a behavioural term which also has the general meaning of imposing or eliciting new and durable (although not necessarily desirable) behaviour and attitudes. See CLASSICAL CONDITIONING, OPERANT CONDITIONING and SHAPING.

conditions of worth the terms on which one receives approval from significant others. 'Conditions of worth' is a central concept in PERSON-CENTRED COUNSELLING, explaining one of the factors underlying clients' acquisition of disturbance. When children realise that they are not unconditionally loved, but must earn approval by being and doing (to some extent) what their parents want, they tend to adopt, progressively, an external LOCUS OF EVALUATION (e.g. 'I am only good when I am thin' or 'I'm only as good as my next exam result'). Such an attitude may become persistent in adult life, alienating the person from her organismic self.

confabulation the act, conscious or unconscious, of inventing details of memory about oneself, where true memories are lost (and the person may invent them out of embarrassment). It typically occurs in brain damage secondary to alcoholism.

confession disclosure of something which is likely to incriminate, or make vulnerable, the person disclosing. In a religious context, confession is the acknowledgement of sins. In a counselling context, examples of confession might be that the client had lied in a previous session with his counsellor about some aspect of his life or the client has never told anyone before about his voyeuristic tendencies. Psychologically, confession has a cathartic property. The potency of certain group approaches to the treatment of addictions (*see* MINNESOTA METHOD) is partly based on the dynamics of confession. Some people suffering from obsessive–compulsive disorder (*see* OBSESSION) confess to crimes or sins that they have not committed.

confidentiality the understanding that the fact and content of counselling is private, confined to the counsellor–client relationship. Confidentiality is a *sine qua non* of counselling, both to provide a climate of TRUST and self-disclosure and to protect the client's rights. However, this must be considered an idealistic view of confidentiality, as there are compelling exceptions: discussion of cases with supervisors (including supervision groups and in some cases line managers); cases of extreme concern, relating to possible self-harm or harm to others, including child abuse; an obligation to surrender information to a court of law if called upon to do so. It is good practice at the beginning of counselling to strive for active agreement with clients about the realistic and acceptable extent of confidentiality. In the event of any of the above exceptions, it is good practice to ask the client's permission to consult with other concerned professionals. Occasionally it may become necessary to act when permission is denied. Depending on their accountability and ethos, agencies may have different boundaries in respect to confidentiality.

configurational analysis a term used originally by Erickson and developed by others to refer to the multiple phenomena (e.g. memories, schemas, defences) that create various states of mind and shifts between states of mind. It is used in assessment for some brief therapy and resembles some TA procedures.

conflict discrepancy between two or more beliefs or feelings within a person, between personal wishes or needs and external reality, between two or more people. Conflicts may be conscious or unconscious. Unconscious conflict results from developmental disturbances and their repression, and Freud and others view civilisation as inherently conflict-making (although not necessarily neurosis-making, because conscious overriding of one part of a conflict by another, internally, is a healthy adaptation). Conflict in one form or another is at the heart of all clients' problems, in individual and couple counselling. The terms *conflict resolution* and *conflict management* refer to specific programmes designed to help change a conflict situation between couples or groups of people.

confluence the over-identification, or merging, of an individual with a partner, or aspect of the environment, temporarily or chronically. Confluence may be benign, as in aspects of empathy in the clinical situation or creative absorption in the arts. Examples of confluence witnessed by the counsellor are likely to be dysfunctional. Confluence has been called 'dysfunctional closeness' (Clarkson, 1989) and suggests a difficulty in making or maintaining appropriate BOUNDARIES. Mainly a GESTALT concept.

confrontation the act and skill of presenting facts or feelings to clients that are at variance with their own. Recognised by Truax and Carkhuff (1965) as one of the essential qualities of effective counselling, confrontation (in mild or strong forms) usually emerges after the establishment of interpersonal bonds. Some approaches (e.g. REBT, gestalt, intensive short-term dynamic psychotherapy, Minnesota method) are, however, far more confrontational than others, and work with some client groups (e.g. alcoholics and addicts) often *begins* with confrontation of self-defeating habits including DENIAL and MANIPULATION. The purposes of confrontation are to challenge blind spots, to identify strengths, to arrest denial, procrastination, and further self-sabotaging behaviour. Confrontation aims for alliance with the healthy part of the client, which, in the act of coming for counselling, signals his ability to confront parts of himself.

confusion a mental state in which thoughts and feelings are in disarray and the person may act out of character or inappropriately. Mild and temporary confusion in turmoil is a common experience. Serious *confusional states* are often associated with dementia, epilepsy, alcoholism, etc. Clients in counselling or therapy may become confused as a defence against painful memories or against a need to change. They may also become confused as a result of REGRESSION, especially if a piece of regressive work is left incomplete.

congruence GENUINENESS, honesty exhibited by the counsellor as an essential part of her person and her work; likewise, the genuineness of the client. Congruence has long been regarded as an essential quality in the counsellor, since clients are sensitive to insincere or role-bound behaviour and are unlikely to be helped by counsellors who model a false self or defensive style. Congruence implies that the counsellor is in touch with her thoughts and feelings, voices them when it is perceived to be helpful, and that her body language mirrors her statements. It demands spontaneity, risk taking and, paradoxically, judgement as to how freely the counsellor expresses herself. Congruence is a key feature of PERSON-CENTRED COUNSELLING in particular. *See* INCONGRUENCE.

conjoint therapy any therapy or counselling involving two or more clients seen simultaneously. The 'conjoint' refers to clients and should not be confused with either 'co-therapist' or 'co-facilitator'.

consciousness awareness, wakefulness; the sum of all personal feelings, thoughts and perceptions. Consciousness is often used synonymously with AWARENESS although some writers claim a distinction. Psychoanalytic theory dwelled on the UNCONSCIOUS (and the PRECONSCIOUS) to the extent that the *conscious* part of the mind (identified with the activities of the ego) was, arguably, devalued. Radical behaviourists deny the possibility of studying 'consciousness' scientifically because of its subjective nature. Cognitive therapists harness and promote the power of the rational, conscious mind in therapy. Humanistic and transpersonal counsellors, generally speaking, seek for greater than (that which is accepted as) 'normal' consciousness. Some neuropsychologists have attempted to show the physiological bases of consciousness. The *stream of consciousness* consists of all those thoughts, images and memories that fill the everyday mind.

consciousness raising mainly understood as the activity of people grouping together for mutual education, support and (often) political activism, especially in the areas of feminism and anti-racism.

consequences results which follow from actions. The idea that a client's actions (including passivity) have an impact on the world is a key educational element in counselling, whether or not a particular model conveys the notion overtly. In REBT, clients are explicitly taught the ABC sequence, where the C is initially believed to be the consequence (emotional and/or behavioural) of an event but which, the therapist demonstrates, is actually a consequence of the client's mediating belief. A goal of REBT and many other approaches to counselling is to show the client that she is an agent of change rather than a victim of consequences.

constancy a term referring both to the importance of the (psychodynamic) counsellor's reliable presence and CONTAINMENT, and (as *constancy principle*) to the Freudian view of the psyche's attempt to achieve a level of constancy between the differing demands of id and superego.

constructionist social constructionism argues, in contrast to *constructivist* philosophy and narrative therapy, that 'experience is socially constructed' and must be understood as part of the client's reality, while constructivist approaches are concerned with the ways in which clients build their own stories and how these are then subject to change.

constructive alternativism the term used by George Kelly to describe his philosophy of PERSONAL CONSTRUCT PSYCHOLOGY. At its simplest it means that we can always interpret events in different ways and that in being open to alternative constructions we are open to changes from dysfunctional behaviour to functional behaviour and to avenues of PERSONAL GROWTH that we had assumed were closed to us.

consultant one who has expertise and is called upon by individuals or organisations to advise accordingly. In a counselling context, consultants will advise on the setting up of counselling services, standards of practice, requirements regarding training and qualifications, and specialist areas such as disability issues, HIV and AIDS or stress management. Psychoanalysts and some psychotherapists, who are not required to receive ongoing supervision, may occasionally confer with a consultant (senior colleague) regarding particular clients. A *consultant psychotherapist* is a senior practitioner in a health authority setting who is often also a psychiatrist.

consultative a model of counselling, supervision or training which is based on co-operative alliance rather than on hierarchical authority is said to be consultative. 'Consultative supervision' is the most common usage.

consulting room designated room for formally seeing clients. Used by some private psychiatrists and psychotherapists; counsellors are more likely to refer to 'counselling room' or office, as appropriate. Private practitioners are advised to provide separate, private accommodation for their counselling work, for the sake of confidentiality and in order to avoid any intrusion (including the telephone). Considerations of privacy, comfort, ambience, suitability to reflection, anonymity, insurance, etc. are all pertinent. Some counsellors

regard the room as a 'sacred space' or sanctuary (also known in Jungian terms as 'temenos').

consumer one who is a user or purchaser of a service or product. While not used greatly in counselling (the term 'client' is usually preferred), it is a reminder that clients are entitled to consumer rights and protection. In recent years some consumers or ex-clients have written critical accounts of their counselling or therapy. The 'community care' movement emphasises such rights; in this context *consumerism* advocates that people with mental health problems or learning disabilities should be given access to funds or decision-making rights in relation to purchasing services.

contact literally, being in touch with. Contact is primarily a GESTALT concept (or experience) and is made between the person and his environment. Psychopathology may be seen as a disturbance of contact, for example withdrawal from contact with the world (of people, work, nature) and health as re-embracing the world. Contact may be painful or blissful but in either case it is a being in touch with reality. *Final contact* (in gestalt) means a complete act of contact (e.g. sexual, aesthetic or cathartic), which in its very fullness effects personal change (i.e. is therapeutic).

containment psychodynamic concept referring to the counsellor's act and attitude of therapeutic receptivity, consistency, intuitive forbearance and responsiveness. The term is associated mainly with Bion and Winnicott and echoes the maternal capacity to take in both the good and bad behaviour of the child and to respond from the position of a mature caretaker with responsibility for assisting with development. It is sometimes said of people whose behaviour is chaotic that containment, even though it may show no immediate results, is a necessary first therapeutic step. The term also echoes that of 'holding' in the sense of therapeutically containing someone's destructiveness and preventing it from spilling into everyday life.

content the details discussed in a counselling session; the MATERIAL brought up by the client. Often contrasted with PROCESS (the way in which the material and the relationship are handled by counsellor and client) content includes the client's report on her life history, present circumstances, problems, preoccupations, plans and aspirations. Too great a concentration on MANIFEST CONTENT suggests repression of LATENT CONTENT or conscious avoidance of painful material. The skill of the counsellor is to be alert to, and reflect, underlying feelings as well as verbal content.

contextual modular therapy a time-limited therapy (six sessions) with predetermined programmes for addressing common conditions (e.g. couple problems, depression, anxiety, etc.) and with each module of six sessions dedicated to a specific problem.

contextual variables see SOCIAL CONTEXTS OF COUNSELLING.

continuing professional development (CPD) that aspect of counselling training expected to continue after initial training and for the duration of a counsellor's practice. CPD requirements, common to many professions, now form a major component of BACP accreditation and re-accreditation. CPD typically consists of attendance at further courses, workshops, conferences and professional activities.

contract an agreement made between client and counsellor as to the work to be undertaken together. Usually by the end of the first session, some sort of contract will be made concerning: practical arrangements, times, fees, confidentiality, goals, etc. A *contract to counsel* distinguishes the counselling relationship from other (e.g. social) kinds of relationship. Some counsellors (*see* Stewart, 1989) distinguish between *business contracts* (payments, times, missed appointments, number of sessions, etc.) and *therapeutic contracts* (the problem to be addressed, treatment plan, model to be used, homework, etc.). Contracts are often reviewed, and the term *contract husbandry* has been used to refer to contract maintenance and renegotiation. Holmes and Lindley (1989) refer to an 'evolving contract' which is responsive to what emerges for both client and counsellor within counselling. Some counsellors dislike the legalistic connotations of the term 'contract' and prefer 'agreement' or 'understanding'. *See* WRITTEN CONTRACT. *See* Sills (1998).

contraindication clinical evidence that a certain course of treatment is likely not to be in the client's interests. For example, tranquillisers may be contraindicated in the case of a client who is likely to overdose; psychoanalysis may be contraindicated for clients with severe phobias or obsessional rituals.

control theory theory behind Glasser's (1984) reality therapy. Glasser contends that people always have control over their own lives and always make the best choices that they are aware of. When they are taught in REALITY THERAPY that their current choices are not the best ones they can make, they can control their behaviour increasingly in accordance with their picture of where they want to go. Control of need-satisfying choices includes, in Glasser's view, control of actions, thinking, feeling and physiology. When Glasser talks of control, he intends it in the sense of steering rather than suppression.

controlling behaviour general description of acts and attitudes which seek to suppress, manipulate or limit the freedom of others. Controlling behaviour is a characteristic of people dominated by the PARENT EGO STATE or AUTHORITARIAN PERSONALITY, may be situation-specific or generalised, and may be learned (imitatory) or defensive.

conversational model approach to psychotherapy and counselling formulated by Hobson (1985) which places emphasis on problem-solving through intimate dialogue. Hobson advocates a practice of therapy based on an I–THOU relationship, with techniques viewed as important but secondary. Key features are negotiation, HERE AND NOW awareness, sharing hypotheses, exploring feelings, metaphors and symbolism. The conversational model is a synthesis of many strands including concepts from ANALYTICAL PSYCHOLOGY and the study of audiotaped interviews.

conversion hysteria Freudian explanation for the manner in which a psychological conflict manifests in external symptoms (e.g. psychosomatic disorders). Such conversions of affect into physical problems may include actual illness or ('hysterical') delusions of illness or incapacity.

coping skills various cognitive, behavioural and affective attitudes and strategies demonstrating an ability to manage problems in living. *Coping* implies a certain level of difficulty or adversity which is overcome or negotiated adequately and is an index of mental health. Inability to cope, temporarily or for an extended period, may be a symptom of depression, anxiety or other disorders, may indicate a recent trauma, or may suggest certain learning deficits. An example of a specific coping skill is breathing exercises, which aid some anxious clients. Cognitive and behavioural counsellors explicitly teach coping skills. Some critics argue that this practice ignores or suppresses underlying dynamics. Behaviour therapists distinguish between coping and mastery skills, and it is thought that on counselling courses, trainees may benefit from demonstrations of the former by their trainers, because the latter may too easily be deskilling.

cop-out colloquial term used to denote avoidance of risk-taking, confrontation, or ownership of feelings or actions, and heard more in certain group settings than in dyadic counselling (e.g. in some encounter groups and in certain drug dependency treatment programmes).

CORE Clinical Outcomes in Routine Evaluation. A system of standardised quality evaluation of counselling procedures and results administered by questionnaire to clients, psychological therapists and counsellors. Piloted extensively from the 1990s in the NHS and elsewhere, it has been used as a screening tool and measurement for global distress.

core competencies a term used to suggest that there are, in the emergent profession of counselling, identifiable and indispensable skills and levels of those skills. Counsellors should be able to understand and

49

utilise the CORE CONDITIONS and CORE SKILLS and to demonstrate comfortable ability to make and be able to explain interventions and therapeutic structuring. There are also competencies associated with supervision and training. Some writers analyse all such competencies as falling into a spectrum of conscious and unconscious competency and incompetency. Such competencies can also be identified and, some argue, measured in other, counselling-related disciplines (e.g. teaching).

core conditions those attitudes and skills considered necessary for effective counselling. Classically, these are: EMPATHY, UNCONDITIONAL POSITIVE REGARD and CONGRUENCE (three of Rogers' original six conditions). Most counsellors accept that these are necessary qualities (and most counselling training seeks to foster them) but there is a debate as to their sufficiency. Person-centred counsellors (*see* PERSON-CENTRED COUNSELLING) hold that these core conditions in themselves (and their being communicated to clients) are sufficient to facilitate therapeutic progress. This view rests on the belief that the relationship between client and counsellor (or between person and person) is the central (if not exclusive) agency of therapy and the USE OF SELF is therefore the focus for training.

core skills those skills considered essential to good counselling practice. As well as the skills associated with empathy, unconditional positive regard and congruence, it is recognised that counsellors do well to have the skills associated with CONFRONTATION, CONCRETENESS and IMMEDIACY. Counsellor self-disclosure is sometimes considered a core skill. The boundaries between counselling skills in general, communication and interviewing skills, microskills (*see* MICROCOUNSELLING SKILLS) and social skills (*see* SOCIAL SKILLS TRAINING) are not clear. However, all professional counsellors are expected to be able to communicate empathy, for example, using empathic responses including reflection of feeling and content, appropriate paraphrasing and clarifying. Similarly, it is an expectation that counsellors will have a fairly high level of awareness of (their own and their clients') body language and proximics (factors of personal space preferences and meanings). The skills involved in structuring a counselling session are also vital. Beyond the CORE CONDITIONS there is no real consensus as to core skills across models of counselling.

core theoretical model the central identified theoretical affiliation of a counselling training course. The BACP insists that courses seeking its accreditation are designed around a clearly identified, coherent core theoretical model (e.g. person-centred, psychodynamic, integrative) and that this model should permeate the course in its theoretical, skills, personal development and supervised practice elements. There has been much debate about the wisdom or otherwise of this mandate.

corrective emotional experience the notion that clients (particularly in psychodynamic counselling) undergo positive affective change by virtue of their good RELATIONSHIP with the counsellor. The term was coined by Alexander. At its simplest, the concept is that clients whose experience of being parented has been unhappy or inadequate, receive a form of therapeutic reparenting from counsellors which is potent enough to substantially heal past hurts. Clients who feel *heard, held* and *helped* may be said to have such a corrective emotional experience. While many psychodynamic and person-centred counsellors accept this as part of the healing dynamic, others give different explanations for the change process, and still others are critical that it de-emphasises the roles of negative transference and non-relationship factors (e.g. cognitive techniques).

counsellee *see* CLIENT.

counselling this term has a variety of meanings (and many of them are problematic), so a core definition is given here, followed by others.

Counselling is a principled relationship characterised by the application of one or more psychological theories and a recognised set of communication skills, modified by experience, intuition and other interpersonal factors, to clients' intimate concerns, problems or aspirations. Its predominant ethos is one of facilitation rather than of advice giving or coercion. It may be of very brief or long duration, take place in an organisational or private practice setting and may or may not overlap with practical, medical and other matters of personal welfare.

The definition of counselling given by the British Association for Counselling (1985) was:

'...people become engaged in counselling when a person, occupying regularly or temporarily the role of counsellor offers or agrees explicitly to offer time, attention and respect to another person or persons temporarily in the role of client. The task of counselling is to give the client an opportunity to explore, discover and clarify ways of living more resourcefully and toward greater well-being.'

In addition, counselling may be considered to 'facilitate the client's work in ways which respect the client's values, personal resources and capacity for self-determination'; counselling is distinguished from situations in which COUNSELLING SKILLS are used 'when both the user and the recipient explicitly agree to enter into a counselling relationship' (BAC, 1990).

Counselling is, then, both a distinctive activity undertaken by people agreeing to occupy the roles of counsellor and client (*see*, for example, CO-COUNSELLING) and it is an emergent profession. It is the activity conducted by members of that profession and by trained volunteers. It is a service sought by people in distress or in some degree of confusion who wish to discuss and resolve these states in a relationship which is more disciplined and confidential than friendship, and perhaps less stigmatising than helping relationships offered in traditional medical or psychiatric settings. The counselling process can involve many different experiences, for example developmental issues, critical decision-making, painful confrontation of self-defeating patterns of feelings, thoughts and behaviour; or acknowledgement of painful life events. According to the American Counseling Association (1992), 'those who work in the counseling and human development field recognise that *all* people routinely need help and advisement as they experience the normal stages and transitions of life'.

There are many schools of counselling but all share respect for the client's autonomy. Counselling is usually conducted on a

'1 hour a week' basis. Individual adult counselling is the most common form but couple, family and group counselling are also practised. Counselling aims to promote healthy functioning as well as having a problem-solving focus.

Counselling has traditionally been understood as advice giving (*see* ADVICE) and although professional counsellors seek to disown this association in favour of a 'helping people to help themselves' ethos, the former has some popular persistence. This is no doubt reinforced by the coupling of counselling with guidance in some course settings and descriptions.

Information-giving counselling is the combined activity of transmitting sensitive information and assisting the client to digest and explore the impact and implications of the information. Many medical and careers agencies may have staff in this position, and their job titles and qualifications often reflect the occupational structure of the agency rather than any background requiring counselling training.

Psychotherapeutic counselling. While this term itself is rarely used, it refers here to the problem of the 'counselling–psychotherapy interface'. A commonly suggested discrimination is that counselling concerns itself with presenting problems and their resolution, that it is of relatively short duration and does not deal with TRANSFERENCE, while PSYCHOTHERAPY is concerned with the whole structure of the personality, actively works with transference, operates at profound levels, attempts to alter personality structure and/or adaptive ability and takes some considerable time. However, many commentators believe that the overlaps are so

numerous that no meaningful difference exists. Brief psychotherapy can be shorter than some counselling, and some counselling can be more personality changing than some psychotherapy. Confusion regarding these terms probably has more to do with tradition and investments in training and status than with actual observation of what transpires within counselling sessions. Halmos (1981) uses the word 'counselling' as an umbrella term for all psychological helping professions, including psychoanalysis. Some practitioners and clients use the term 'therapy' in preference to either counselling or psychotherapy. The terms 'psychological counselling', 'therapeutic counselling' and 'psychological therapy' are also sometimes used.

The term 'counselling' is also used in diverse commercial settings. There are so-called financial counsellors, debt counsellors, mortgage counsellors, and so on. The terms 'beauty counselling', 'leisure counselling', etc., are also found. In the opinion of most mainstream personal counsellors, such usage is incorrect and/or unfortunate, but no one yet has any proprietary rights over the words 'counselling' or 'counsellor' (but see STATUTORY REGULATION). The clinical psychologist Oliver James (1998: 360) gives a deliberately distorted definition of a counsellor as 'someone nice to talk to who won't make a lot of value judgements'. See Feltham (1995) for various terminological arguments and Feltham and Horton (2000) for further contextual illustrations of counselling.

counselling as an academic subject counselling is a legitimately autonomous subject, although its closest links are with psychology. It is variously located in departments of education, psychology, social work, life-long learning, etc. It is delivered at both undergraduate and postgraduate levels, usually has high tutor-contact hours (for the purposes of feedback on skills practice) and is usually part-time, with fees self-funded by students. A common route is from Certificate in Counselling Skills to Diploma in Counselling, MA Counselling, and options such as Certificate or Diploma in Supervision. Some training takes place in independent training institutions, with some such courses being validated by universities. It is still a relatively new subject, with small student groups. A great deal of its literature base is American, as are the founders of many models of counselling and therapy. Its research base is growing. See TRAINING (COURSE ACCREDITATION).

counselling as a career counselling has roots in the voluntary sector and much counselling is still unpaid or low-paid. There is a relatively small proportion of full-time careers in further and higher education (see STUDENT COUNSELLING) and in large organisations (see EMPLOYEE ASSISTANCE PROGRAMME). There is an increasing volume of work in the NHS (see PRIMARY CARE COUNSELLING), although much of this is part-time. Many counsellors have a part-time PRIVATE PRACTICE. Counselling can be characterised as a part-time or portfolio career, many counsellors working in counselling-related roles as well, and elsewhere. Most counsellors are of mature age, with counselling being their second or third career.

counselling psychology that branch of psychology which studies, researches and applies its findings to the practice of counselling. It includes, in its broadest sense, all counselling and psychotherapy theory. A *counselling psychologist* has a qualification in psychology and counselling psychologists practise as counsellors, organisational consultants or in other roles. The British Psychological Society (BPS) has a qualification in counselling psychology, the framework for which requires competence in a number of arenas.

counselling skills all those communication skills that are used as a basis for counselling practice or are used in other helping professions. Counselling skills include the CORE CONDITIONS, core skills and microskills. It is recognised that some are common to good interpersonal skills and some are found in counselling-related jobs in particular (e.g. nursing and teaching). A distinction is usually made between the use of counselling skills in these and informal settings, and the use of counselling skills in formal, structured and purposeful counselling sessions by trained counsellors. Another distinction is made between general communication skills and skills used in specific caring/helping roles, which are informed by the values of counselling.

counselling studies the term is often used to denote an academic course (e.g. MA) in counselling that does not include any substantial training in counselling skills, being instead theoretical and sometimes taking students from other fields. The term is also used more broadly and aspirationally for an ambitious new interdisciplinary subject incorporating sources and kinds of suffering, meaning seeking, etc. (Feltham, 2001).

counsellor one who practises any form of counselling. Its primary meaning is a *trained and professional* provider of personal counselling. However, many people consider themselves to be acting as counsellors as part of their work (e.g. nurses or psychologists) and may not have had counselling training. None the less, the term 'counsellor' as a job title is slowly achieving a distinct identity: under current British law, however, no one can yet (in 2004) be prevented from describing herself or himself as a counsellor or psychotherapist. The terms 'senior counsellor' and 'principal counsellor' are found in some organisations with a well-established counselling service. The term 'counsellor-in-training' is often used synonymously with 'trainee counsellor'. *See* COUNSELLING, GENERALIST COUNSELLOR, SPECIALIST COUNSELLOR and VOLUNTEER COUNSELLOR.

counsellor in training this term, often used synonymously with trainee counsellor, refers to anyone who is still in the initial, pre-qualified stages of training; usually, on a Diploma course. The term is especially important in PLACEMENTS, where clients have a right to know the level of competency of their counsellor. It is also recognised however that all counsellors are always engaged in CONTINUING PROFESSIONAL DEVELOPMENT. *See also* READINESS TO PRACTISE.

countdown the practice, in some brief therapy and counselling, of reminding the client formally how many sessions have gone by and how many remain, according to the agreed contract.

counterdependency *see* DEPENDENCE.

counterphobic a term describing the behaviour and dynamics of someone who persistently confronts situations of which she is afraid. Such behaviour is a DEFENCE MECHANISM rather than a concerted effort to overcome phobias; a superficial demonstration of fearlessness that often hides profound inner anxiety.

countertransference the TRANSFERENCE feelings and responses of the counsellor towards the client. Originally considered as an obstacle to psychoanalysts working effectively, and an indication of their need for further personal analysis, countertransference came to be appreciated not only negatively as the possible intrusion of the analyst's material, but also positively as potentially offering valuable information about the client. By a 'disturbance in the field of attention' counsellors are alerted to significant, unconsciously transmitted client dynamics. Countertransference may be conscious or unconscious. Counsellors sometimes experience physically the effect of unconscious client material (sometimes called 'embodied countertransference'). Rowan (1998) lists seven kinds of countertransference: defensive; aim-attachment; transferential; reactive; induced; identification; and displaced. While many counsellors do not work intentionally with a transference–countertransference model, all need to be aware of such dynamics, and SUPERVISION is often aimed at helping to identify both the positive and negative aspects of a counsellor's countertransference relationship to the client.

couple counselling the counselling of partners in which the relationship, its dynamics, difficulties and future, is the focus. The term has gained currency since it does not (like 'marital counselling') assume heterosexual or marital status. (It is, however, based on a Western, dyadic model, not on models of relationship in which there are multiple partners.) Many models can be applied in couple counselling but probably the most commonly used are the psychodynamic, person-centred, behavioural and systemic. While many of the same skills are used as in individual counselling, the counsellor has in addition the tasks of time and conflict management, and interactional focus. She must also maintain a high level of empathic symmetry (*see* EMPATHY) and awareness of triadic dynamics. Couple counselling is often a form of brief counselling because it is problem-focused and because it often involves particular decisions. Also rendered as 'couples counselling' and 'relationship counselling'. *See* ARENA, CONCILIATION COUNSELLING, PSYCHOSEXUAL THERAPY, UNILATERAL COUPLE COUNSELLING.

covert non-overt, hidden or intrapsychic. There are various covert therapeutic procedures (which are known as covert because they are practised in imagination). *Covert conditioning* includes covert desensitisation, extinction, reinforcement and modelling. These often involve exercises in imagination which allow the client to rehearse desired behaviour with accompanying aversive, supportive or other self-instructions.

creative-expressive therapies all those approaches to counselling and therapy utilising non-verbal means of working, e.g. art therapy, dance and movement therapy, psychodrama; as well as the use of these methods within traditional, conversation-based therapy. Some 'traditional' approaches integrate creative-expressive techniques.

crisis counselling counselling offered at the time of a crisis or disaster, enabling survival of the immediate crisis, an opportunity to explore factors contributing to it and possible consequences. Counselling itself is sometimes wrongly caricatured as dealing only with crisis situations. *See* POST-TRAUMATIC STRESS DISORDER.

crisis intervention the application of therapeutic and/or practical methods of assistance to someone undergoing an acutely difficult time. Crisis intervention may be offered by social workers or other professionals and may contain elements of 'emotional first aid', BEFRIENDING or supportive psychotherapy (*see* SUPPORT). There is also a school of thought which suggests that crisis can be used effectively as a key to profound change, often by following the client through the immediate crisis into catharsis and subsequent WORKING THROUGH. Sometimes counselling is dismissed as a kind of crisis intervention, or problem-solving with no lasting meaning. However, there is some evidence that counselling offered soon after a crisis may have a good outcome. *See* POST-TRAUMATIC STRESS DISORDER.

critical incident debriefing a procedure often delivered by those attending a major traumatic incident (e.g. road traffic accident, railway disaster, mass shooting). Delivered often to groups of those affected, CID happens relatively soon after the incident, allows for emotional ventilation, story telling, education, solidarity, and hopefully prevention of the worst effects of PTSD.

Critical Parent that functional subdivision of the PARENT EGO STATE in TA which is characterised by controlling and critical behaviour and attitudes. When someone copies the critical behaviour of his parents (learned in childhood) he is said to be 'in critical parent'. There are both positive and negative aspects of the critical (or controlling) parent.

critical psychology a movement of radical psychologists aiming to make the practice of psychology more relevant to communities, more politically responsive, etc. Seeks especially to honour feminist thought, multicultural realities, local needs and conditions.

critiques of counselling any analysis of counselling which is not necessarily or wholly favourable. Such critiques include: that counselling is superficial, that it plasters over deeper problems, that it ignores the question of SOCIAL CONTEXTS, that there is no real evidence that it works, that it is divided by schools of thought, that its practitioners are often abusive in both gross and subtle ways to clients, that it is driven more by the vanity and status-seeking of its practitioners than by a dispassionate search for best solutions to people's emotional problems. *See* Dryden and Feltham (1992a).

cross-cultural counselling all forms of counselling which take seriously the reality of multicultural factors in society and the largely hidden ethnocentrism in any society and its institutions; any counselling involving two or more parties from different cultures, ethnicities, language groups. Counselling aims to be empathic on a personal level but it is questioned to what extent in the UK a predominantly white profession such as counselling can enter the experience of people from other cultures and races. In addition to any personal distress, people living in predominantly white countries, who are identifiably of another culture or race, routinely suffer discrimination, stereotyping and racial harassment which compound their difficulties. Counselling may well be understood differently by people from non-white, non-Christian cultures. Both individually and organisationally, therefore, it behoves counsellors to strive to offer ethnically sensitive counselling, where necessary changing the forms in which it is offered or ensuring, for example, that counselling is offered in other languages. Some black people argue that all black people should be counselled by black people only, but others assert that the choice of the counsellor is entirely a matter for each black client. All counsellors need to be aware, through training and personal reflection, of the factors involved in counselling across cultural assumptions and sensitivities. Cross-cultural counselling is also referred to (not with exactitude but pragmatically) as multicultural or transcultural counselling and is not confined to issues of black and white relationships. Cross-cultural counselling is not synonymous with anti-racist counselling (*see* RACISM). *See* Palmer (2002).

crying the expression of feelings (e.g. of loss, sadness, agony or joy) through tears. Crying, weeping, sobbing and howling are common phenomena in the more experiential therapies and are sometimes regarded as a royal road to and index of mental health. Whereas a high level of consensus exists that crying is a necessary and appropriate grief reaction, its general therapeutic value is disputed or minimised by some practitioners. Clients who report crying frequently without knowing why are likely to need some structured exploration in counselling rather than encouragement to cry. It is of significance that women, children and people from some cultures cry more readily, openly or deeply than most men. Counsellors often debate the merits and demerits of

TOUCHING or holding clients who are crying. Most counsellors probably do not themselves cry during their counselling work, although *see* Mearns and Thorne (1999).

cultural trauma the experience of trauma suffered by a group of people exposed to enslavement, genocide, colonisation or similar cultural shock, displacement, etc.

cure the healing or mending of an illness or disturbance. The concept of cure in counselling and psychotherapy has been largely avoided or dismissed. Terms like 'goal-attainment' or 'significant improvement' are often preferred. This is because psychological problems are frequently multifaceted and a 'cure' tends to imply freedom from all or most suffering. It is also because most counsellors prefer to avoid medical concepts. A notable exception is Janov (1975) who describes PRIMAL THERAPY as 'the cure for neurosis'.

cyclical psychodynamics a term used by Wachtel for his integration of psychodynamic and behavioural aspects of therapy, for example linking client insights with possible new behavioural opportunities and pointing out the psychodynamic meaning of in-session (transferential) behaviour.

cyclothymic a cyclothymic personality is one characterised by mood swings, most commonly from depression to elation. It is also a term applied to consistent cyclical alteration in mood and implies a less extreme disturbance than MANIC DEPRESSION. The distinction between cyclothymia and cyclothymic personality is a fine one.

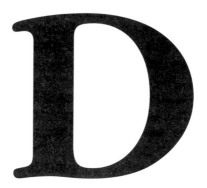

damning attitude and/or vocalisation attributing extreme blame, with contempt, hatred and dismissiveness. REBT points out that damning is unrealistic (because no one is totally damnable), unhelpful (because it blames rather than problem-solves) and inaccurate (because it condemns whole people rather than giving feedback on aspects of their behaviour).

dangerous severe personality disorder (DSPD) a proposed psychiatric classification for people with psychopathic tendency towards serious violence and sexual offences who, deemed to be a menace to society regardless of criminal record, should be detained in high security centres. Contentious legislation in process considers such individuals (perhaps a total of 2 500 in the UK, 98% male) untreatable, having no sense of guilt. But DIALECTICAL BEHAVIOUR THERAPY has been used with some of this group. Proposals are contentious because they ignore civil rights, politicise popular fears about 'madmen' and fail to take into account possible reasons for such people not responding to the treatment given them. *See* PERSONALITY DISORDER.

daydreaming preoccupation with internal images of wish-fulfilment, including mod-est and grandiose self-rewards, compensations for suffering, romantic encounters, revenge on enemies and escape from responsibilities. Generally a flight from reality, daydreaming can be turned to advantage by identifying its more attainable objects and coupling these with realistic GOAL SETTING and analysis of DEFICITS. A *directed daydream* is a therapeutic exercise utilising VISUALISATION TECHNIQUES.

death the cessation of all vital life processes. Its importance in counselling is, broadly speaking, twofold. Any bereavement involves either actual death or similar loss and gives rise to painful feelings which seek resolution. Because everyone dies, the sense of mortality is embedded in everyone, but is understood or interpreted differentially. EXISTENTIAL COUNSELLING makes a central reality of death (or mortality) and the meaning of life derived from it. Some forms of BRIEF THERAPY dwell on the parallel between mortality and time limits in therapy. Some humanistic and transpersonal approaches attempt to address the reality of death squarely and even joyfully, working with dying clients to achieve acceptance of it. Death is viewed as a finality, gateway or transition in different religions and cultures. Counsellors working with very elderly clients or with clients who have a terminal illness work constantly within an awareness of death.

death imprint intrusive images of death or threatened death following catastrophic incidents such as bombing. The difficulty of assimilating the reality of such an experience leads to high anxiety among survivors of traumatic incidents.

death instinct a controversial term proposed by Freud to account for all drives in human beings which are self-destructive, self-denying or resistant to hedonistic drives. It is the opposite of LIBIDO and is also called THANATOS. The death drive is the movement of the organism towards the state of non-being from which it originally came. Most of Freud's followers rejected his view of the death drive, although it was very important in Klein's work. A *death wish* (the term is in popular usage) is characterised by behaviour that is clearly self-destructive and related to REPETITION COMPULSION.

debt counselling advising and assisting people who are in financial difficulties. Debt counsellors offer help with budgeting, information and advice regarding how to approach credit companies, banks, etc., and on legal rights. Debt counselling has little in common with mainstream personal counselling ('debt guidance' might be a more appropriate term). *See* MONEY.

decision-making the processing of information leading to choices. Any decision entails some commitment to certain courses of action and a forgoing of others. Counsellors are continually faced with CHOICE in their moment-to-moment work. Perhaps the most crucial are those microdecisions

during sessions which influence the client and her progress in both minute and gross positive and negative ways. The counsellor is also frequently engaged in enabling the client to make her own decisions by reinforcing her autonomy, clarifying uncertainties and confronting evasions. Balance sheets of pros and cons of choices are sometimes used. Counsellors' ethical decision-making has received great attention in the 1990s and early 2000s. *See* THERAPIST/COUNSELLOR INTENTIONS.

decompensation characterised by regression, decompensation follows the dysfunctioning of defence mechanisms in which underlying conflicts or problems surface.

deeper potentials areas of hitherto unexpressed or not fully expressed affective experience within the person, and which the counsellor aims to elicit, and help the client to realise, in EXPERIENTIAL PSYCHOTHERAPY.

defence mechanism a concept from psychoanalysis denoting the warding off of anxiety from the ego by various means. Defence mechanisms keep painful or unacceptable experience away from the conscious mind by repression, which is consignment to the unconscious. DENIAL, DISPLACEMENT, IDEALISATION, PROJECTION, REACTION FORMATION and SPLITTING are common examples of defence mechanisms. Healthy self-protectiveness differs from the actions of a defence mechanism in that the latter is unconscious and (usually) no longer appropriate. Recognition of, respect for and interpretation of defences are important aspects of psychodynamic counselling.

defensive style the characteristic manner in which someone defends himself from psychological hurt. 'Characterology' is a term sometimes used to refer to fixed defensive styles. *Defensiveness* refers to an attitude of denial. Defensive body posture (e.g. tightly folded arms) is particularly unhelpful in counsellors.

deficit a lack or deficiency in certain behaviours. It refers to an experiential or learning gap (e.g. a social skill that has never been learned in the normal process of growing up) and stands in contrast to PSYCHOPATHOLOGY. (It is not a 'character defect' or flaw.) Behaviour therapists distinguish between skill and performance deficits, the latter being the failure to implement a behaviour, the former an ignorance of how to perform it. Maslow spoke of *deficiency motivation*, referring to the tendency people have to strive to make up for such gaps.

delayed adolescence the notion that when the developmental stage of adolescence is bypassed or not satisfactorily negotiated, it may erupt in later life and demand attention. It is characterised by a crisis of identity, insecurity and rebellion against norms of behaviour.

delayed grief reaction *see* BEREAVEMENT.

delayed PTSD symptoms of PTSD arising at least six months after the relevant incident and often lasting for years.

deliberate self-harm physical violence against the self. The most common kinds are cutting and burning the body, and can be associated with experience of abuse in childhood. Hatred and abuse become internalised. Overdosing on drugs, head banging and recurrent 'accidents' may also fall into this description. Hospital Accident and Emergency departments see many such cases. *See* SELF-MUTILATION.

delusion in psychiatric usage, a false interpretation of events that is at odds with a consensual interpretation of the same events and not amenable to change through logic. In its looser, general sense, a delusion may be equated with a cognitive error (e.g. personalisation): a client may be 'deluded' as to how good he is at a certain task. A delusion reaches psychotic proportions (*see* PSYCHOSIS) when the client's perceptions are characterised by persistent or recurrent HALLUCINATIONS. PARANOIA is characterised by delusions of persecution. Most hardened *delusional systems* are intransigent, i.e. are not vulnerable to modification by the pressures of reality.

demanding the attitude and act of commanding and insisting that life events go the way one wishes them to. It is pointed out in REBT that when people demand, rather than prefer, they are thinking and behaving irrationally. (There is no evidence that things absolutely should be other than the way they are.) Demands can be made on self, others and life conditions in general. *See also* MUSTURBATION.

denial refusal to accept (usually painful) realities. Denial is a common part of the reaction to unexpectedly bad news (e.g. death of a loved one or hearing one's HIV antibody test result confirmed as positive). Other denials in counselling occur when clients cannot or will not accept evidence that contradicts their self-image (e.g. their assumption that they have nothing but goodwill towards a parent) or their refusal to accept that they have a serious problem (e.g. alcohol abuse). Understood psychoanalytically, denial is a common DEFENCE MECHANISM to ward off painful intrapsychic conflicts.

dependence reliance on, need for, others, objects or activities outside ourselves.

Children are vitally dependent on adult caretakers for food, shelter, safety and socialisation. The point in their maturational process at which children cease to be genuinely physically and psychologically dependent on adults is debated. Some adults exhibit age-inappropriate dependent behaviour and appear not to have fully made this transition. The *dependent personality* is characterised by anachronistic traits of helplessness, neediness and failure to attain adult maturity. Dependency in group therapy is seen in the 'basic assumption behaviour' (Bion) of group members who passively and angrily expect to be led or nurtured. *Counterdependency* is the inauthentic denial of actual dependency feelings and the pretence of independence or acting-out of rebellion. A judiciously encouraged therapeutic dependence is characteristic of psychoanalysis and related psychotherapy, in order to elicit and work through transference feelings. Critics of long-term models of therapy claim that clients frequently become unhealthily and untherapeutically dependent on therapy and therapists.

depersonalisation loss of the sense of being the person one usually is, characterised by an unnerving sense of unreality. In this state the person's body may feel as if it does not belong to her, or that the person is outside themselves in the role of onlooker. It is often found in association with DEREALISATION.

depression a short-lived mood or chronic condition characterised by hopelessness, apathy, meaninglessness, withdrawal, low self-esteem, sadness. Depression, in its various forms, is the most common kind of psychological disturbance. Depressed affect reveals itself in sadness or dejection; depressed cognitions include a negative evaluation of one's self, the world and one's future (*see* COGNITIVE TRIAD); depressed behaviour includes lethargy, isolation and disturbed eating and sleeping patterns. Psychiatrists have suggested that there is an *endogenous depression* which is based on a constitutional predisposition, and a *reactive depression* (or *exogenous depression*) which results from life events such as LOSS. (POSTNATAL DEPRESSION is sometimes viewed in this light, although other interpretations exist.) A major depressive episode can become a PSYCHOSIS. *Agitated depression* is characterised by restlessness, despair and nihilistic delusions; there is a high risk of suicide if untreated. Various aetiologies of depression are offered: psychodynamically, suppressed anger or unexpressed grief are seen as causative factors. It may be seen as a developmental problem indicating a need for regressive therapy. It is viewed by cognitive therapists as the result of *depressogenic thinking*, with treatment lying in the gradual adoption of a more empirical, logical and functional attitude towards everyday events. There is an argument that life itself is depressing and that the depressed person is more in touch with reality than others. Women have been diagnosed more often than men as depressed. Depression has many varieties and degrees of severity, and so can be treated by different approaches. The RELATIONSHIP offered in counselling, along with strategies for coping and gradually re-evaluating self-image, is frequently beneficial.

depressive position KLEINIAN concept referring to a developmental stage (from about the age of three months onwards) in

OBJECT RELATIONS, in which the infant comes to perceive the mother as a good *and* a bad 'object' and feels concerned and guilty lest his sadistic feelings have damaged her. Following on from the OBJECT RELATIONS view, the depressive position enables the infant to defend against his sadistic impulses by inhibiting them and to internalise mother as a whole (rather than part) object.

depth psychology broad term covering psychoanalysis, analytical psychology (and possibly other models) and referring to psychological explanations which concentrate on unconscious factors.

derealisation a subjective sense of the world being unreal. It often occurs with DEPERSONALISATION; it may occur in severe or psychotic depression but is also a feature of anxiety states.

derepression term used by Davanloo to refer to the practice of vigorous challenging of defences, enlisting the client's (often unconscious) healthy energy directed against repression, and achieving fairly rapid change, in INTENSIVE SHORT-TERM DYNAMIC PSYCHOTHERAPY (ISTDP).

desensitisation any means of reducing anxiety responses but especially those approaches using a step-by-step method, as compared with FLOODING. Although most commonly associated with behaviour therapy, most counselling approaches probably contain elements of planned, incidental or covert desensitisation. *See* SYSTEMATIC DESENSITISATION, IN VIVO DESENSITISATION.

deskilled a counsellor is said to be or to feel deskilled when her usual repertoire of professional skills seems to fail her or when these skills are dismissed as not being relevant to the tasks of helping. Counsellors and other helping professionals some-

times report feeling deskilled after insensitive management or supervision of their work, following a break from their work, or when comparing themselves negatively with the apparently brilliant performances of charismatic colleagues. Counsellors responding to disasters have sometimes reported feeling dramatically deskilled in the face of enormous human suffering.

destructive feelings unhelpfully negative, angry, hateful, vengeful or nihilistic forms of affect. Freud used the concept of a destructive instinct which differed from the death instinct in being externally directed. Destructive feelings may lead to overt anger or aggression. Such feelings range from minor, fleeting fantasies of hitting people or objects to smashing property. They therefore range from 'normal' to chronic or acute pathological phenomena. Analytical psychology views such feelings as part of the SHADOW which, if owned, will not progress to destructive behaviour. See Fromm (1973).

deterioration worsening of client's condition during the course of counselling. Deterioration can refer to worsening as a result of poor counselling or to worsening in spite of good counselling (but usually refers to the former). Not to be confused with therapeutic REGRESSION or temporary RELAPSE, deterioration is an observable, prolonged negative condition. Some research claims to identify factors contributing to deterioration.

determinism philosophical view that events unfold according to previous causes, allowing for little or no notion of FREE WILL. Freudian thought is often said to be deterministic because it posits certain instincts and a sense of the inevitability of human fate. Behaviourism is deterministic in the sense that human actions are viewed as mechanistic responses to stimuli. Genetic and sociobiological determinism have gained some ascendancy in the 1990s and early 2000s (see EVOLUTIONARY PSY-CHOTHERAPY). The distinction is sometimes made between 'unidirectional' and 'recip-rocal' determinism, the latter implying a *cycle* of determinants. There is little room for classical determinism in counselling, which rests on notions of AUTONOMY, hope and change. Empirically, however, many would agree that people are neither fully determined nor fully free.

detoxification the processes involved in the transition of a person addicted to alcohol or drugs from an intoxicated ('poisoned') state to a relatively healthy state. A severely addicted person would normally undergo withdrawal in hospital where they would receive nursing and medical care. The withdrawal phase is unpleasant and potentially lethal. Detoxification is a prelude to primary treatment for alcoholism or drug addiction, including or followed by counselling. Commonly known as 'detox'.

development an unfolding, progression or growth. All human beings develop throughout life, experiencing greater and lesser obstacles, catalysts and nurturants along the way. Clinically, development connotes a significant change during the course of counselling, fortuitously or as a result of counselling. The concept has general applications, overlapping with personal growth, change and maturational processes. *See also* DEVELOPMENTAL STAGES, PERSONAL DEVELOPMENT GROUP.

developmental dyssynchrony being 'off course' developmentally. Budman and Gurman (1988) consider it crucial that counsellors working with time-limited contracts attempt to identify issues of not being 'on time' with respect to 'normal' developmental expectations.

developmental stages the concept referring to chronological and psychologically significant markers of maturation between birth and death. The term 'lifespan development' is sometimes used. Freud's schema includes the oral, anal and genital stages, followed by latency, adolescence and maturity. Melanie Klein identified a PARANOID–SCHIZOID POSITION followed by a DEPRESSIVE POSITION. Jung's model, basically a simple one, stressed the importance of midlife and later life stages. Erikson (1959) proposed eight stages involving issues of 'basic trust vs mistrust' through autonomy, initiative, industry and identity to intimacy, generativity and integrity, with each stage involving a different goal for personal development. Other theorists include intrauterine development on the one hand and transpersonal experience and posthumous survival on the other.

developmentally needed relationship therapeutic stage recognising the importance and conscious choice of the counsellor to meet a developmental deficit in certain clients. Compare with CORRECTIVE EMOTIONAL EXPERIENCE.

deviancy antisocial or eccentric behaviour. Deviancy is a problematic term because it is predicated on the concept of normality (*see* NORMAL). In its narrow sense, deviancy refers to criminal behaviour, including criminal sexual deviancy (e.g. paedophilia). More broadly it can refer to the behaviour and status of people on the margins of society, including those who are (or are classified as) mentally ill, criminal, alcoholic, itinerant, etc. Whether accepting deviant status or not, such people may seek, or be forced by law or circumstances to receive, some form of psychological attention, classification or help; or incarceration. These client groups will usually receive the attention of statutory professionals and where help is offered it may well be a form of counselling. (The term 'counselling' in such contexts is, however, problematic.) *See* CASEWORK, OFFENDER COUNSELLING.

diagnosis identification of a particular illness, neurosis or psychological disturbance. Ideally it refers to a discrete disease process with known aetiology and prognosis. Diagnosis implies the ability to discriminate between one category of disturbance and another and among degrees of severity; it also implies an ability to decide on a TREATMENT OF CHOICE and to predict the untreated course of the disease. Essentially a medical and psychiatric aid to communication, diagnosis is not favoured by most counsellors because of the danger of pre-emptive labelling (and thereby stigmatising and dehumanising), the fallibility (and arguably the redundancy) of diagnosis, and because most counsellors have no medical or psychiatric training. Preferred concepts are WORKING HYPOTHESIS or case conceptualisation. The term *transitive diagnosis* is used in personal construct psychology to denote an attempt to help the client plan a new future. Some models of counselling (e.g. TA) employ what is, in effect, a microdiagnostic focus, aiming to identify and change pathological units of behaviour. *See also* ASSESSMENT, DSM-IV TR, ICD 10.

diagnostic overshadowing the tendency to perceive a client's presenting problem in terms of an existing diagnosis, particularly unhelpfully – for example, in the case of someone with a learning difficulty being regarded as experiencing emotional troubles *because* of their learning difficulty instead of other factors common to us all.

dialectical behaviour therapy a distinctive approach to therapy (mainly with clients diagnosed as having borderline personality disorder) based on biosocial theory. Created by Linehan, DBT argues that clients have done and do their best in an 'invalidating environment'. Their typically emotionally unstable behaviour, including suicidal tendencies, is treated with respect. 'Reciprocal communication' and 'irreverent communication' is used along with a focus on mindfulness, interpersonal skills training, distress tolerance training, and individual and group therapy.

dialogical psychotherapy a form of therapy based on belief in the centrality of the human encounter, particularly that understanding proposed by Buber (see I–THOU). Dialogical psychotherapy also contains several variants, some of which include family and transgenerational approaches.

dialogue discussion between two people. Much, if not most, counselling involves dialogue. The term also connotes a certain quality of relationship, shared truthfulness and discovery. Some models of counselling utilise a dialogue between parts of the (client's) self, in imaginative exercises, on paper, or in CHAIRWORK. Mahrer (1996) de-emphasises the usefulness of dialogue, arguing that it creates distracting role-relationships between counsellor and client (with the real task being to encourage the client to enter his own experiential world ever more deeply). *See also* I –THOU, CONVERSATIONAL MODEL, SOCRATIC DIALOGUE.

diary keeping the recording of personal events or reflections on a daily or occasional basis. It is common practice for cognitive–behavioural counsellors to ask clients to monitor their behaviour as part of a HOMEWORK assignment. Sometimes purpose-designed forms are issued for this task. Diary keeping encourages clients to take an active role in their therapy, serves to encourage specificity, and provides baseline measurements for clients to observe and acknowledge progress.

dichotomous thinking form of faulty information processing. *See* DILEMMAS.

dilemmas conflicts between courses of action or feelings and thoughts. In CAT, dilemmas represent the core dichotomies in which clients perceive themselves placed. A common dilemma is 'I have to keep my feelings bottled up, otherwise things will get out of control'. People who chronically, inaccurately and unhelpfully polarise their experiences may be helped to see more choices and experience subtler nuances in their lives.

directed daydream *See* DAYDREAMING.

directive guiding, prescriptive or controlling behaviour. Counsellor behaviour is sometimes criticised as (overly) 'directive' when it loses sight of the client's AUTONOMY or abuses the power of the counsellor. Some misunderstanding of the term exists because of the strong influence of Rogers' original emphasis on 'non-directive' therapy. It is important to distinguish between intentional and unintentional directive counselling. *See* ACTIVE–DIRECTIVE METHODS.

disability awareness consciousness-raising in relation to physical and sensory impairments. Sensitivity to disability issues is important for counsellors for several reasons. The enabling or empowering ethos of counselling (*see* EMPOWERMENT) means that both counsellors and clients who have disabilities should have their needs and sensitivities fully considered. Disabled people are in danger of being perceived as less than fully human or stereotyped; in fact their disability may have no bearing on their work and has none on their worth. Disabilities include mobility difficulties through loss or dysfunctioning of parts of the body or damage to the central nervous system, blindness or partial-sightedness, and deafness or hearing problems. Help for people with disabilities includes (depending on the setting) improved physical access, signing interpreters, escorts, Braille transcriptions, audiotapes, large print books and materials, etc. In some cases specialist counselling may be required.

disaster counselling any counselling of the victims of (usually large-scale) accidents, criminal acts, war, or natural catastrophes. Survivors of such occurrences frequently suffer from POST-TRAUMATIC STRESS DISORDER, including delayed grief reactions, numbness, guilt, flashbacks, etc. Rapid responses to the (direct and indirect) victims of disaster have become better coordinated, and needs better understood, in recent years. By definition, disaster counsellors need to be available at short notice, and sensitive to the complexities of sudden bereavements in often horrifying conditions. There are few 'disaster counsellors' as such (most such rapid-response counselling is offered by social workers or volunteers) but training in counselling in the context of disasters has been developed. *See* SURVIVOR GUILT.

discharge expression or unleashing of emotion. *See* ABREACTION, CATHARSIS.

disclosure revealing information. Technically, everything a client says about herself is disclosure, but the word refers specifically to information previously withheld or out of awareness. A disclosure can have the character of CONFESSION or of a less dramatic indication of trust in the counsellor and the counselling process. *See also* SELF-DISCLOSURE.

discomfort anxiety a term used in REBT to describe emotional disturbances relating to people's irrational beliefs (*see* IRRATIONALITY) that life must be comfortable and that instances of discomfort are awful or unbearable. Compare ego anxiety (*see* EGO).

discounting avoiding in oneself the means and information to solve problems. Discounting is a concept of TA, and it is claimed that clients' internal discounting can be detected in various forms of passivity, body language and, for example, incomplete sentences. Discounts are blind spots which reveal themselves in some forms of incongruity, which may be confronted or dealt with therapeutically by the counsellor. The *discount matrix* is a systematic means of identifying how, and with what intensity, people minimise the significance of parts of themselves, others and the environment.

displacement a defence mechanism whereby affect is directed from one object to another. The relationship towards one person or object is shifted to another in order to lessen anxiety and maintain repression of unconscious conflict, and to protect the original object from ambivalent feelings.

dispositional assessment a kind of assessment of clients focusing on their attitude towards therapy and their ability to work within an intense relationship, in contrast with diagnostic assessment.

disputing systematic debate with a client initiated by a counsellor in order to expose faulty logic, to demonstrate the implications of holding irrational beliefs and to suggest alternative ways of construing events. Used principally in REBT (*see also* ABC), disputing has a philosophical lineage but is criticised by many counsellors for its directiveness and apparent indifference to subtle intrapsychic factors. In practice, disputing is a special skill, demanding sensitivity, creativity and persistence and is best done socratically (*see* SOCRATIC DIALOGUE).

distress emotional upset. The term is used in a general sense to refer to misery and unhappiness. It is used to refer to acute unhappiness, as in 'he was distressed to hear of the death of his friend'. *Mental distress* is sometimes used in preference to 'mental illness'. *Psychic distress* or *psychological distress* are sometimes used synonymously with acute neurotic or reactive states. In RE-EVALUATION COUNSELLING a *distress pattern* is the way in which somebody's lifelong painful experiences are expressed. *Eating distress* refers to the experience of a serious eating disorder. Sometimes distress is regarded as synonymous with extreme agitation, anxiety, crying or other vivid expression of pain.

divided self the notion that people suffering from extremes of mental distress experience tension between a real and a false self in response to and as a defence against a hostile environment. The term was popularised by the existentialist psychiatrist R.D. Laing and also applies to the common human experience of ALIENATION.

DNA (did not attend) *see* MISSED SESSIONS.

doorknob effect the observation that clients sometimes disclose significant material just as they are about to leave the session, i.e. with their hand on the doorknob, when it may feel safe to utter the hitherto unsafe.

double-bind contradictory information or injunctions and the experience of confusion resulting from them. The term has been used in an attempt to offer a theory of social causation of SCHIZOPHRENIA: children or adolescents whose parents or caretakers bombard them with paradoxical demands lose the ability to maintain or develop a strong enough personal identity to function normally. Instead, they may introject parental voices and/or act in paradoxical ways.

drama triangle *see* KARPMAN TRIANGLE.

dramatherapy a form of group psychotherapy using dramatic techniques, differing from PSYCHODRAMA in certain conventions and in its emphasis on within-group relationships rather than on the outside world. Dramatherapy fosters a group momentum which in turn stimulates individual change through role-play and catharsis.

dreams nocturnal, unconscious processes usually characterised by visual imagery. Dreams often have a surrealistic quality but are sometimes readily understandable. Freud and many later psychoanalysts and analytical psychologists consider dreams to be a 'royal road to the unconscious' (and hence to 'cure') because they are created below the level of defences and represent conflicts and clues to interpretation. *Dream analysis* or *interpretation* seeks to decode the SYMBOLISM and latent content in dreams. *Dream work* is the activity involved in processing dream imagery. Dreams are viewed (depending on the counselling model) as forms of wish-fulfilment, as condensed representations of conflict and resolution, as residues of daytime UNFINISHED BUSINESS, as contact with the COLLECTIVE UNCONSCIOUS, as anticipatory. As they are largely unconscious, dreams do not figure large in the work of behavioural and cognitive counsellors, although potentially they can be used to demonstrate cognitive errors like irrational demands. *Dream recall* is the ability to remember narrative and detail of dreams and poor or absent recall is believed by some counsellors to indicate strong repressive tendencies.

drink problem a term used by some people in preference to alcoholism and to denote behaviour characterised by alcohol abuse that is not very severe.

drive motivation or instinct. Freudian theory has it that drives (or instincts) are biologically determined forms of energy seeking satisfaction. Freud's later theory posited two primary drives: life and death (Eros and Thanatos). Freud at one point considered the instincts or drives for sex and self-preservation to be in opposition to each other. OBJECT RELATIONS theorists challenged the emphasis on drives and elevated the concept of the early infant–mother relationship. Many counsellors, particularly of a humanistic orientation, de-emphasise sexual and other drives, preferring a holistic, and far less predetermined, view of human motivation.

drivers observable, second-by-second behaviours which, according to TA theory, reveal and reinforce a person's SCRIPT process. These are finite behaviours recognisable in words, gestures, posture, and so on. There are five drivers: 'Be perfect'; 'Please others'; 'Try hard'; 'Be strong'; 'Hurry up'. It is thought that most people have a *primary driver* and some may have two main drivers, but not usually more.

drug addiction chemical and/or psychological dependence on organic or manufactured mood-altering substances. *See* ADDICTION. The terms 'substance abuse/misuse' and 'drug dependency' are also used. Illegal drugs commonly abused are: cannabis, cocaine, heroin, lysergic acid diethylamide (LSD), ecstasy, etc. and the effects sought are relaxation, stimulation, euphoria and hallucinations. Benzodiazepines, which are minor TRANQUILLISERS (e.g. diazepam), are also commonly misused or, although used in good faith, may lead to addiction. Chronic smoking constitutes an addiction to nicotine. Addiction is a stubborn behaviour to change, and often requires different approaches at different stages of change and relapse. See SUBSTANCE MISUSE.

DSM-IV TR *The Diagnostic and Statistical Manual of Mental Disorders (4th Edition, Text Revised)* of the American Psychiatric Association (2000) is an exhaustive attempt (listing approximately 340 disorders) to classify all varieties of psychiatric or psychological disturbances, thus providing a common language for DIAGNOSIS, TREATMENT PLANNING and professional dialogue. It is updated every few years. Despite its strengths, critics argue that many of its categories are spurious, ever-shifting, or dehumanising.

duty of care derived from the law of tort, as applied to counsellors, this suggests that they should refrain from unethical and exploitative behaviour towards clients, seek informed consent for what they do, work within their trained limits, desist from harming the client and from giving poor advice, and so on. All employers owe a duty of care to their employees and many 'stress cases' have been brought on grounds of failure to show a duty of care by protecting against unwarranted stress. *See* Jenkins (1997).

dyad two people in relation to each other. Most counselling is *dyadic* in that it involves a counsellor and a client. Counselling training makes much use of dyadic exercises.

dynamic psychological phenomena characterised by the interaction between different unconscious processes are described as dynamic. Freud's explanation of mental events departed from other static theories, and emphasised this movement of the psyche. The terms *dynamic psychology, dynamic psychiatry* and *dynamic psychotherapy* carry this meaning. *See* PSYCHODYNAMIC.

dysfunction psychological impairment, enduring or otherwise. Behaviour is said to be dysfunctional when it is not in the interests of the person concerned. In the context of personal growth all obstacles to self-actualisation may be said to be dysfunctional. Some people believe the term 'dysfunctional' to be judgemental or dehumanising.

dysmorphophobia *see* BODY DYSMORPHIC DISORDER.

eating disorder a psychological disturbance characterised by distorted attitudes to and behaviour associated with eating. Eating disorders affect women more than men. Such women are abnormally preoccupied with food, weight and body size. Eating disorders include ANOREXIA NERVOSA and BULIMIA NERVOSA, compulsive eating and dietary chaos syndrome. Problems associated with food intake increased during the 1990s and 2000s. *See* OBESITY.

eclecticism any combining of approaches and/or techniques from different models of counselling. The strength of eclecticism is that different components can be applied to different clients' needs. In practice many, if not most, practitioners are to some extent eclectic. There are many forms of eclecticism. *Technical eclecticism* refers to the judicious use of techniques (e.g. chairwork or visualisation) with different clients or with the same client at different times, in the interests of the client's progress. Lazarus (1981) is the foremost proponent of this practice. *Theoretically consistent eclecticism* is the use of diverse techniques by counsellors who remain committed to one theoretical approach. Although counselling practice moves in the direction of greater eclecticism, it has been criticised as a 'mish-mash' (Eysenck) and as possibly leading to greater confusion. Effective eclectic practice requires high levels of new technical skills from counsellors. The work of Egan (*see* EGAN APPROACH) has been referred to as *developmental* (or *systematic*) *eclecticism* because it derives from a variety of theories and conceives of consistent helpfulness as based on the systematic use of certain strategies. *See* INTEGRATION.

edge of awareness a concept taken from Gendlin's focusing and significant in person-centred counselling, referring to material that the client is not quite conscious of but the counsellor may be. *See* AWARENESS.

education literally 'leading out'. Education means both the facilitation of personal potential and the presenting of culturally valued knowledge. Counselling education in the UK is normally subsumed under TRAINING. Some counselling takes place in educational settings (*see* STUDENT COUNSELLING). Some writers stress the psychoeducational aspects of counselling, referring to its preventive potential and its passing on of coping, thinking and interpersonal skills.

effect size *see* RESEARCH.

effectiveness the power to make changes or achieve desired results. Also sometimes called EFFICACY, the subject of the effectiveness of counselling and psychotherapy is large and contentious. Does counselling effect what it sets out to achieve, or not? Various researchers, most notably Eysenck, have claimed that counselling (or psychotherapy) is no more effective than placebo treatment or than no treatment. This is debated but findings, although broadly positive, are not wholly conclusive. Even when it is agreed that counselling is effective, it is often difficult to demonstrate *how* it is effective. Effectiveness research focuses on 'real world' settings such as a busy counselling agency. *See also* OUTCOME, POTENCY, RESEARCH.

efficacy refers to (a) research carried out in strictly controlled conditions, such as a randomised controlled trial (contrasted with EFFECTIVENESS research); (b) the power to carry out intentions and effect desired lifestyles, as in self-efficacy.

Egan approach Gerard Egan's (2002) work attempts to distil lessons from various approaches into a systematic 'problem-management model'. This is a three-stage model: 'identifying and clarifying problem situations and unused opportunities; developing a preferred scenario; formulating strategies and plans'. Egan integrates the relationship attitudes and communications skills needed for effective counselling, and adds emphasis on GOAL SETTING, LEVERAGE and action. Egan has called his approach a developmental or systematic ECLECTICISM. It is taught on many counselling skills courses.

ego the conscious and reasoning aspect of the mind. The Latinate term is the translation of Freud's term, 'Ich' ('I'). Freud believed the ego emerged from the ID and had to mediate between the id and the external world as a reality-testing function (*see* REALITY TESTING). It mediates between the unconscious and the conscious, although it is also partially unconscious. It has defensive and developmental functions. A 'weak ego' implies psychological vulnerability and a 'strong ego' maturity. (The 'ego' of popular usage – i.e. connoting pride and grandiosity – has distorted the meaning.) *Ego-syntonic* describes those behaviours and feelings that are consistent with the self-image. *Ego-dystonic* refers to behaviours felt to be inconsistent with or alien to the self. *Ego anxiety* (from REBT) stems from demands upon oneself (e.g. to be competent) and consequent global negative self-rating, which leads to psychological disturbances. An *ego ideal* is an image of what the self wishes to become, closely linked to the superego. *See also* OBSERVING EGO.

ego-building refers to the therapeutic restoration of mature strength (*ego strength*) and the ability to withstand life pressures.

ego psychology refers to theoretical developments in psychoanalysis centring on the ego (and stands in contrast to object relations theory).

ego state a concept used in TA to refer to a 'consistent pattern of feeling and experience directly related to a corresponding consistent pattern of behaviour' (Berne). TA has three categories of ego state: PARENT, ADULT and CHILD. These differ from the superego, ego and id of Freudian theory (*see* Stewart and Joines, 1987). TA counsellors perform a 'structural analysis', which enables them to make accurate observations of shifts between ego states. At any one time a person will be 'in child', 'in parent' or 'in adult'. (These are then said to have executive power over other ego states.) These are also broken down into further roles (e.g. free child and adapted child).

egocentric behaviour is said to be egocentric when it is constantly focused on the self and on the needs of the self rather than of others. Egocentricity is characterised by immaturity and insensitivity to others.

elegant solution a means of solving a problem that is optimally satisfying logically and empirically. The term is used in REBT when a client has changed irrational to rational beliefs and these changes have been integrated sufficiently into the person's belief system to affect the client's feelings and behaviour.

eliciting drawing something out from someone. Eliciting is the skill of subtly prompting and encouraging clients in a bid to jog thoughts and feelings and call forth significant material. *See* QUESTIONS.

email counselling counselling by electronic means. Some growth in this took place in the late 1990s and it seems set to expand if problems of confidentiality can be addressed. Some clients prefer its privacy, easy access and ability to use from home, but some counsellors lament its undermining of the importance of the relationship. In different variants, also known as online and cyber therapy/counselling.

embarrassment The subjective feeling of acute self-consciousness which may be perceptible in the person's blushing or other gestures. Associated with shyness (a trait), embarrassment (a state) may be viewed as a mixture of ego anxiety and discomfort anxiety.

emergency appointment facility for a client to be seen by a counsellor with little or no waiting. Some agencies operate a system whereby emergency time slots allow for this.

emotion feeling, affect, excitation. Commonly recognised emotions are love, joy, fear, sadness and anger. The term 'emotion' is used imprecisely and usually synonymously with FEELINGS (although some writers distinguish between feelings as experienced and emotions as exhibited, or vice versa). There is a 'normal' range of emotions, which only become problematic when they are exaggerated or out of control (as in the 'affective disorders'). Counselling theories do not agree on what constitutes healthy emotions. The humanistic therapies often endeavour to help clients release suppressed emotion. The so-called 'hydraulic model' of emotion views the suppression of emotions as dangerous and counselling as a process of necessary release. Psychologists and physiologists have analysed the components of emotion into arousal, learned responses, cognitive appraisal and other factors. 'Emotional' sometimes has the negative connotation of 'over-emotional'. *Emotional vocabulary* is sometimes used to describe the range of emotions a client displays or is aware of. *Emotive* refers to the excitation or calling forth of emotion. The meaning and acceptability of emotions varies across cultures.

emotional dysregulation high emotional vulnerability and inability to regulate one's emotions, as characteristic of borderline personality disorder and treated by dialectical behaviour therapy.

emotional intelligence a term popularised by Goleman (1995) to refer to the domain of emotional self-knowledge, management of emotions, motivation, recognition of emotion in others and handling relationships. The concept achieved popularity in the 1990s and was used in educational and commercial settings in both specific training programmes and as a recommended general ethos. The concept links with emotional literacy and affective learning, creative and spiritual domains, and is something of a counterfoil to the assumptive primacy of IQ. *See also* MULTIPLE INTELLIGENCES.

empathy the attitude and skill of following, grasping and understanding as fully as possible the client's subjective experience as if from the perspective of the client himself. In addition, it is the communication to the client that the counsellor is experientially alongside him and that she is sensitively striving to understand what he is feeling or struggling to articulate. It is not identifying with the client, offering sympathy, pre-empting his own understanding of himself or silently assuming that she understands him (false empathy). *Basic empathy* is the ability to be in touch with and communicate one's understanding of the contents of the client's experience. *Accurate empathy* refers to the precise identification of what the client means and feels from moment to moment. *Advanced empathy* is the skill of perceiving and communicating one's understanding of what the client intends but does not say; the ability to sense half-hidden meanings and to voice them for the client, thus moving counselling forward. Empathy has been called 'vicarious introspection' (Kohut). It is recognised as a core condition in counselling. *Philosophical empathy* is the counsellor's act of understanding the client's core belief systems and helping him to bring these into explicit awareness for evaluation. *Empathic symmetry* is the balance of empathy necessary in the arena of couple counselling. Regarded by many (especially person-centred) counsellors as the cornerstone of counselling, there is some debate about the limits of empathy's helpfulness and the danger of its inducing dependence.

employee assistance programme (EAP) a structured provision of counselling and other welfare services to the employees of an organisation. EAP models differ in scope and kind. Some are offered in-house by company employees, others are bought in from specialist EAP providers. Some EAPs offer extensive telephone and face-to-face personal counselling, advice on financial, health, legal and other matters, and are available to all staff and their families. Others offer more limited or targeted help (e.g. stress or redundancy counselling). Most EAPs offer time-limited counselling. Companies installing an EAP are motivated by humanitarian and/or corporate efficiency concerns (many EAP providers claim to save their clients money by reducing absenteeism, sick leave, accidents at work, staff turnover, etc.), by concerns about potential litigation, or in some cases by specific occupational hazards: some American insurance companies demand that employers provide EAPs before they will agree to insurance cover.

employee counselling any counselling offered and delivered to people working in an organisation, with the dual aims of addressing employees' well-being issues and improving corporate efficiency. *See* EMPLOYEE ASSISTANCE PROGRAMME.

empowerment helping another to redis-cover her own resources. Almost synony-mous with ENABLING but perhaps with a greater association with social and politi-cal realities, empowerment is a key con-cept in feminist counselling. *Empowering psychotherapy* is also a term used by Robert Langs.

empty chair *see* CHAIRWORK.

enabling restoring to people confidence in their own autonomy and personal power. Enabling is a key concept in counselling because it affirms the value and self-direct-edness of people and is a reminder that counselling and other helping activities run a risk of undermining and disabling people. When helpers impose their own views on clients rather than elicit and rein-force their self-directedness, enabling becomes disabling. Note that the term *enabler* has been used in the field of alco-holism to refer to a friend, relative or helper of the alcoholic who consciously or inadvertently colludes with her alcoholic behaviour and tries to rescue her from its consequences.

encounter meeting or confrontation of two people. Also important are encounter groups. The following types of encounter group need to be distinguished from each other. *Basic encounter* was devised by Carl Rogers, and adopts his person-centred method. Participants usually sit on chairs throughout and there is little or no physical interaction. *Open encounter*, developed by Will Schutz, is more body-oriented and intensive. It can take the form of a marathon, lasting 30 hours or more. The leader is much more active and does not take words very seriously; it is the energy behind the words or actions that matters.

There is a general emphasis on natural flow rather than neurotic control, and the leader has many techniques at her disposal in order to achieve this. Most of the work is concerned with the individual's internal conflict resolution. People generally feel very intimate after taking part in an open encounter group, because they have been through a lot together. *Synanon encounter* is used in residential communities for the ex-addict and ex-convict. The essence of this approach is the direct aggressive con-frontation of one group member by several others, including the leader. This kind of approach is now little used or respected. A *microlab* is a series of exercises suggested by a group leader in order to bring out cer-tain issues, such as mutual trust, which may be important to members of the group.

encouragement siding with and reinforcing the client in his own motivation and progress. While a person-centred approach does not overtly and directively offer approval to clients, it clearly offers implicit encouragement to an undistorted self-actu-alising tendency within clients. Adlerian counsellors explicitly endorse the use of encouragement. PROMPTING is sometimes called *minimal encouragement* (e.g. head-nods and 'uh-huh' utterances) and such actions on the part of the counsellor are important ingredients in forming an alliance and stimulating HOPE.

endings the final phase of counselling rela-tionships. Endings in counselling have sig-nificance for various reasons. An ending should coincide with the resolution of the client's specific problems and therefore mark a successful conclusion but this does not always happen and an ending may be premature, unplanned and unsatisfactory;

a successful conclusion will be mutually decided, timely and satisfying. TIME-LIMITED THERAPY and BRIEF THERAPY models will have had an end in sight from the beginning; other counselling contracts expire when the client *feels* the time is right. Some counsellors prefer a planned ending in order to work through the feelings attached to endings, and to review progress, and will make this clear to clients. Psychodynamically oriented counsellors would be particularly aware of the possibility of themes of separation and loss that can be triggered by endings.

endogenous depression *see* DEPRESSION.

endurance persistence. In a counselling context the concepts of endurance of symptoms and of change are both important. The endurance of symptoms generally indicates a lengthier therapy and the endurance of change indicates a successful OUTCOME.

environmental factors any and all external phenomena which impinge on the client in her everyday life. These may include: housing conditions, personal economics, personal relationships, family system, access to community resources. *See also* SOCIAL CONTEXTS OF COUNSELLING, EXTRA-THERAPEUTIC FACTORS.

envy covetousness; the desire for what others have or the wish to be like them. Envy is a central concept in KLEINIAN therapy. Klein considered envy an 'oral–sadistic and anal–sadistic expression of destructive impulses'. It is an 'angry feeling' which originates in early infancy in relation to the breast (the mother is the powerful giver of food and nurturance, over which the baby has no power). It is related to guilt in that the baby comes to realise that she has harboured anger towards her mother. It contrasts with GRATITUDE and admiration in lacking the generosity of those feelings. Unconscious envy often manifests in adult life in begrudging others' happiness, and in the defences of idealisation and devaluation. Envy is distinct from JEALOUSY, which always involves *three* people. *Penis envy* is the Freudian concept according to which women and boys feel inadequate and/or threatened by the genital power of adult males; this view has been criticised as absurdly phallocentric. *Womb envy* is said to represent men's feelings of inadequacy at not having the ability to carry and give birth to babies.

epidemiology the discipline dedicated (in this context) to understanding the 'frequency and distribution of mental disorders or psychological distress in a population'. For example, it strives to gather statistical data on the incidence of depression in the UK; it may specify factors relating to age, gender, marital status, etc. Epidemiology of mental distress is relatively young in the UK but aims to suggest needs for assessment and treatment. Counselling and counselling training appear only very loosely related to any established epidemiological studies.

eros Freudian concept of the 'life instinct', a drive towards propagation and survival. Jung's concept of Eros has a greater flavour of passivity and relatedness. The term 'eros' is sometimes used to convey a drive towards fulfilment and wholeness. Its 'erotic' (sexual) connotations are limited.

erotic transference *see* TRANSFERENCE.

errors mistakes made by the counsellor during counselling. Counsellor errors include misdiagnosis, countertransference entanglements, inappropriate interventions. Errors are not always serious and can actually help clients to realise that making mistakes is not ego shattering. Clients cannot, strictly speaking, make errors in counselling, although *see* FREUDIAN SLIP.

escape hatch means whereby the client (as construed in TA theory) may sabotage her counselling and successful living. The main escape hatches are considered to be killing self or others, harming self or others, and mental illness. Others include accidents and psychosomatic disorders. A major (usually initial) task of the TA counsellor is to ask the client to commit herself to closing the escape hatches, either in a time-limited sense or forever, and from a fully congruent adult ego state.

Ethical Framework the BACP's revised ethical 'code' (2002), fully titled *Ethical Framework for Good Practice in Counselling and Psychotherapy*. This replaced previous professional ethical codes and placed more emphasis on moral philosophical principles (values, principles, personal moral qualities), standards of practice, etc. It emphasises the principles of fidelity (honouring the trust placed in the counsellor), autonomy (respecting client self-determination), beneficence (commitment to client well-being), non-maleficence (avoiding harm), justice (fairness and impartiality).

ethical mindfulness an attitude to counselling that incorporates an ethical outlook as a central, guiding component.

ethics the system of values and prohibitions by which (in this case) the profession of counselling is disciplined. Professional ethics include such considerations as responsibility, competence and confidentiality. The former BAC CODE OF ETHICS AND PRACTICE established firm boundaries regarding professional conduct: it is unethical, for example, to practise counselling without regular supervision or to engage in sexual acts with clients. Professional ethics generally do not cover areas of social and theoretical ethics, but may well be informed by them. *See* ETHICAL FRAMEWORK.

evaluation assessment of the professionalism and efficacy of a counsellor's work. Once trained, there is no obligation for a counsellor's work to be formally evaluated at all, although supervision provides continuous *monitoring*. Accreditation systems aim to establish a periodic evaluation process (and *see* ETHICAL FRAMEWORK). Ideally, counsellors should attempt to evaluate their own work, for example by tape recordings and comparisons between earlier and later work, by exposing their work in supervision, by asking for feedback from clients. *See* ASSESSMENT and CORE.

evidence-based practice (EBP) counselling (or other) practice taking seriously and basing decisions on rigorous research into which treatments are effective for which conditions (see Rowland and Goss, 2000). Originating in physical medicine, EBP advocates are in philosophical and professional opposition to psychological therapies that appear to be practised on the basis of faith or enthusiasm alone. Also known (especially in the US) as empirically supported therapy, EBP is associated with a growing body of research findings that claim to indicate preferential treatments for defined clinical problems (e.g. cognitive–behavioural therapy for anxiety). EBP has been criticized for relying on EFFICACY research, hence supporting those short-term therapeutic models that lend themselves to measurement. A case for qualitative research methods and PRACTICE-BASED EVIDENCE has been made against EBP.

evil an immoral act or acts carried out with total disregard for the suffering caused to others. Alternatively (in some theologies) a metaphysical force encouraging human beings to perform evil deeds. In a predominantly non-religious society the concept of evil may be given less credence. However, some totally destructive behaviour (such as ruthless violence, including rape) is sometimes considered to be beyond any psychological explanation and therefore to warrant the description of 'evil'. Many consider a 'psychology of evil' to be long overdue. Many regard paedophilia as a question of evil rather than psychopathology.

evolutionary psychotherapy any form of psychological therapy resting theoretically on Darwinian or sociobiological explanatory principles. Stevens and Price (2000) propose an evolutionary aetiology of mental disorders including depression, anxiety, phobias, obsessions, eating disorders, personality disorders, schizophrenia, etc., using plausible links to concepts of human adaptation and survival in primitive conditions. Attachment and rank are major concepts here. Evolutionary psychotherapy can be adapted to Jungian, cognitive, psychoanalytic and other models and its strength is generally explanatory rather than predictive or 'curative'. Opponents are wary of its apparent closeness to theories of sociobiological and genetic DETERMINISM.

exaggeration enlarging on how good or bad something is, or simply enlarging an aspect of behaviour. As a dysfunction, exaggeration is seen in AWFULISING or maximisation, in which people overstate how bad an event is. As a therapeutic intervention, exaggeration is used in gestalt therapy where, for example, the client may be asked to repeat and enlarge on a gesture (in order to discover the feeling beneath it), or in RE-EVALUATION COUNSELLING where the 'client' may be asked to say something repeatedly, and louder, for the same reasons.

exceptions instances in a client's life when their problems do not arise. This is a solution-focused therapy technique aiming to challenge clients' tendency to indulge in problem-saturated accounts (or in REBT terms to 'awfulise') and to build on the client's experience of 'the good times' or times when the client has been successful in any way, especially in overcoming their own problems. In other words, they have the capacity for creating solutions.

exhibitionism form of sexual and/or criminal deviancy in which someone compulsively displays his body or part of his body (often the penis) to others (usually women). The term *exhibitionist* is used loosely of people who behave in a manner designed to attract attention.

existential counselling an approach to counselling informed by writers from the philosophical perspective of phenomenology and existentialism. Existentialism holds broadly that life has no essential (given) meaning: any MEANING has to be found or created. People have free will and face the challenge of thinking, deciding and acting responsibly for themselves within the boundaries and context of a given situation. Existential counselling involves making sense of life through a personal WORLD VIEW, clarification of personal values, authenticity, individual creativity, will, commitment and risk-taking; through acceptance of mortality and willingness to face one's life and life problems. In practice, there are many different styles of existential counselling, from the intellectually oriented to the (experiential) existential-humanistic model of Mahrer. *See* van Deurzen (2000).

expectations anticipated futures or aspects of the future. Clients inevitably have expectations of counselling (i.e. anticipations or preferences) and these may or may not match reality. Where expectations cannot be realised, it is important that the client should be helped to revise them. Where expectations are within the realms of the possible, it is useful to elicit them and help the client to form explicit GOALS. The counsellor has a contract with the client, has intentions and perhaps a treatment plan, but guards against having *personal* expectations of the client. *See* COUNTERTRANSFERENCE. Some consider 'expectation' to be a vague word as it can mean anticipation, preference and demand.

experience consciousness of events; subjective knowledge of and inferences from the reality of the world in which one lives. To 'fully experience' implies optimal ability to be affectively, cognitively, sensuously, spiritually and behaviourally engaged in life events (*see* CONTACT). Experience connotes, also, individual (owned) sensations and responses, so that some counsellors may say, for example, 'I experience you as terrified', rather than 'You are terrified'. The counsellor's experience of the client may be offered in the form of feedback and sometimes with IMMEDIACY. The client's experience of the counsellor and of the counselling process is an important factor in determining a satisfactory outcome.

Professional experience refers to length of practice and to mastery. Research into the differences between experienced and inexperienced counsellors is not conclusive, although it appears that more experienced counsellors may be more active in their sessions. *Experiential* exercises are distinguished from didactic learning on training courses. *See also* EXPERIENTIAL PSYCHOTHERAPY, PEAK EXPERIENCE.

experiential psychotherapy any approach to therapy or counselling which centres on the subjective feelings of the client and works experientially with those feelings. Mahrer (1996) is the chief proponent of the theory and method, which builds on the work of Rogers and Gendlin. Experiential psychotherapy is a humanistic–existentialist therapy. Clients are encouraged to enter fully into their feelings, however frightening, obscure or hateful, for example, and to allow themselves to be at one with these (previously warded off) experiences. The process of therapy gradually takes the client back into earlier experiences and scenes, but also uses the energy of these experiences to project a taste for new, challenging experiences in the future. It is an interesting peculiarity of Mahrer's method that he is seated parallel to his client, with closed eyes, in order to co-access the client's experiencing and to prompt them further into it. There is also a healthy person-centred/experiential tradition.

exploration an open investigation in order to gather information, to establish the client's concerns and priorities and to examine expectations of the relationship with the counsellor; exploration is also the client's (counsellor-assisted) self-exploration. Often the beginning phase of counselling is characterised by an exploratory process. Much of PERSON-CENTRED COUNSELLING might be described as exploratory in intent but this does not prevent person-centred counsellors and their clients from formulating specific goals when these are appropriate.

exposure behavioural term referring to therapeutic methods which require the client to confront his known phobic situation. This may involve actual confrontation (e.g. going directly into an open space in order to conquer agoraphobia) or imaginal confrontation (eliciting the fearful feelings in imagination while in the consulting room). Some counsellors consider exposure more successful with PHOBIA than other methods, including SYSTEMATIC DESENSITISATION. Exposure is usually graded.

expression the manner in which each client articulates thoughts and feelings, either verbally or non-verbally. Styles of expression vary from individual to individual and are influenced by personality, psychopathology, social learning, cultural and other factors. *Facial expression* is a major indication of a person's inner experiencing or ego state.

expressive making feelings clearly known to others. Some models of counselling are more expressive in nature than others (e.g. psychodrama and gestalt). *Expressive–supportive* therapy is any therapy encouraging the release of feelings while offering containment at the same time. This may be particularly appropriate in crisis work.

extra-therapeutic factors term denoting all those conditions in the client's life which act on her and on her therapeutic progress independently of the counsellor, for better or worse. Often, good rela-

tionships outside counselling heal people or abet their counselling, intentionally or not. Job promotions and generally good fortune can greatly improve someone's life. According to one study, extra-therapeutic factors may account for 40% of outcome variance. Conversely, ill fortune, accidents, divorce, etc. can be depressogenic and can lead to relapse. *See also* LIFE EVENTS.

extraversion an aspect of behaviour characterised by an enduring preference for outwardness and personal relationships (in contrast with the preference for introspection, privacy, etc. of introversion – *see* INTROVERT). Jung is usually credited with originating the concept within his 'psychological types'. It has been used and developed by others, including the behaviourist Eysenck. It is claimed by some that all human beings are fundamentally either extraverted or introverted. The implications are that people will manifest psychological disturbances differentially and may well require different counselling methods to take account of their outward or inward orientation.

eye contact the client and counsellor looking at each other. Eye contact is significant and highly variable. Its forms include: almost total avoidance, quick glances, calculating looks, socially 'normal' looking, hostile 'eyeballing', gazes full of hope or erotic transference, penetrating, searching looks. Each of these carries nuances of feeling and meaning and the counsellor is advised to be aware of their variety and uses. The eye contact from counsellor to client should preferably be neither avoidant nor over-intrusive, but alert and inviting. In some cultures direct eye contact is considered rude. Classical psychoanalysts, seated behind their patients, can obviously make little, if any, use of observation of eye contact. This is also true of Mahrer (1996) whose experiential psychotherapy is conducted with eyes closed throughout. *Eye movements* are thought by some (e.g. in TA or NLP) to contain precise clues to a client's state of mind.

eye movement desensitisation and reprocessing a form of treatment devised by Shapiro, initially for PTSD symptoms, relying on 'accelerated information-processing' effected by the therapist's finger movements and the client's visual recall of traumatic scenes. It has been extended to other uses and makes large claims to rapid successes, although evidence is mixed. Commonly known as EMDR.

face-to-face interpersonal work conducted between two people when both are physically present in the same room. Some counselling-related professions (e.g. youthwork) use 'face-to-face' and 'one-to-one' to denote meetings for counselling as distinct from more informal contact or group or business meetings. Counsellors working in EAPs and other settings may distinguish between face-to-face and telephone counselling.

facilitate to enable to happen or to make possible non-coercively. The word is used in counselling (particularly PERSON-CENTRED COUNSELLING) to differentiate between a minimally directive style of counselling or of working in groups, and a directive, prescriptive or controlling one. A *facilitator* is usually a group leader who helps to provide a learning climate rather than setting her own agenda. Someone is *facilitative* when she empathically senses needs in others and sensitively invites them to make them known and to explore them. Facilitation is a style of encouraging learning that places greater reliance on a genuine inner desire to learn than on the exercise of coercion or authority.

factitious disorder DSM-IV TR-recognised mental health problem characterised by a person presenting with feigned or artificially induced symptoms of a psychological or physical nature, or both. Factitious disorder differs from malingering in its motives, which revolve around assuming a sick role, sometimes even to the point of seeking and receiving unnecessary surgery.

failure lack of success; not achieving targets. Clients sometimes describe themselves as failures if they have LOW SELF-ESTEEM, but they can be helped to specify in which areas of their life they have not reached their goals, rather than condemning themselves in inaccurate, global, negative terms. Counselling is said to fail when clients drop out prematurely or, after persisting with counselling, do not achieve their goals, or significant improvements. Such failure may be related to a variety of factors, including poor client–counsellor match, inaccurate assessment, unskilful counselling, client resistance or unreadiness (*see* STAGES OF CHANGE). Also known as NEGATIVE OUTCOME (Mays and Franks, 1985).

faith an attitude of belief, trust or devotion. Some counsellors bring a specific religious faith or focus to their work (*see* PASTORAL COUNSELLING). Halmos (1981) claimed that all helping professionals implicitly have faith in the healing power of human relationships. It is sometimes claimed that success in counselling and psychotherapy rests on the faith the client has in the process: this can be interpreted as TRUST leading to greater openness and learning, or alternatively as 'blind faith' in the expertness of professionals, with any success dependent on a PLACEBO effect. Halmos and others criticise the 'scientific' posture of some counsellors, arguing instead that counselling is an act of faith and love.

false empathy *see* EMPATHY.

false memory syndrome (FMS) a critical view of clients' memories of strongly negative memories (particularly of childhood sexual abuse), arguing that certain therapists (and writers of self-help manuals) suggest and 'implant' memories of events that did not actually happen. Since many such memories have led to accusations and criminal charges against parents, FMS represents a counter-accusational force, and indeed a number of clients have retracted their accusations. Many psychologists concur that memory is susceptible to distortion and are wary of the extent to which accusations of childhood sexual abuse are made (as well as BIRTH TRAUMA). The British False Memory Society champions this cause. *See also* RECOVERED MEMORY MOVEMENT.

false self term describing a defensive persona, adopted from early infancy in response to a perceived maternal inadequacy or other environmental threats. The concept is derived from Winnicott but widely used and sometimes referred to as an 'unreal self' or 'phoniness'. It can be argued that we all have, to some degree, a false self or socialised persona which protects us from a harsh society. A pathological false self, however, is likely to render the person both socially and psychologically dysfunctional.

family counselling any counselling which takes the family, or part of the family, as its client. 'Family counselling' is not a term that is used much; historically FAMILY THERAPY has taken the family as client. Some schools of counselling, however (e.g. INDIVIDUAL PSYCHOLOGY or Adlerian counselling), have a distinctive approach to family problems and argue that all counselling is implicitly family counselling.

family therapy the arena of therapy which is devoted to the treatment of a family system rather than its individual members. There are various models of family therapy, including the psychoanalytic, behavioural, systemic and structural; some focus on family subsystems (e.g. the direct parents) but all regard the interpersonal dynamics within the family as more important than individual intrapsychic factors. Family therapy can be a highly direct, catalytic method of therapy. It requires specific training and (probably) few counsellors are equipped to practise it. (*See* Street and Dryden, 1988.)

fantasy the word has at least two meanings in the counselling context:

1. A distorted perception of or flight from reality, for example into reassuring, 'fairy-tale' images, which compensate the person for present suffering or help him to avoid it, but sometimes into painful fantasies which reflect fears and anxieties or unconscious assumptions.

2. A positive, non-pathological property of the human mind; an exercise in imagination.

Jungian thinkers often regard fantasy as the 'poetic basis of mind' and as more primitive and potent than many other faculties. This distinction is sometimes marked by the use of the spelling *phantasy* for the former kind. Segal (1985) uses the word phantasy to refer to everyday constructs or interpretations of the world around us. 'Fantasy' is sometimes used mundanely in the phrase 'My fantasy is that...', which is often synonymous with a pictorial conceptualisation. *See also* GUIDED FANTASY, PHANTASY.

father the male parent. The part played by fathers in individuals' psychological development has been restored within analytical psychology and feminist thought. Traditionally fathers have been, or have been represented as, remote, unemotional, rational, authoritarian figures, involved more with work than with relationships. Feminists have urged greater participation from men in child rearing and domestic activity, predicting that this may profoundly affect future attitudes. It is debated whether fathers can provide nurturance equal to the mother. Winnicott viewed the father as an essential part of the NURSING TRIAD, providing protection to mother and child. *Father figure* refers to a tendency or need in some people to become attached to men in order to feel protected or chastised. *See also* PATRIARCHY.

faulty information processing making cognitive inferences from experience that are unwarranted or inaccurate. Faulty information processing is characterised by 'private logic' and a non-empirical attitude. All counselling theories carry some explicit or implicit notion of faulty information processing, but cognitive-behavioural therapy is the most explicit.

Examples include PERSONALISATION and SELECTIVE ABSTRACTION. The most extreme form of faulty information processing is found in SCHIZOPHRENIA.

fear a state of AROUSAL coupled with a cognitive appraisal of an event or object as threatening. Fear is an adaptive response to a real danger (e.g. being confronted by a gun) but less adaptive in response to non-life-threatening situations. Such (latter) fears are better termed ANXIETIES and PHOBIAS, which are maladaptive chronic response patterns. Someone who has a fear of flying may confuse the *possibility* with the probability of dying. A woman's fear of being out alone at night may represent a realistic assessment of danger and a pragmatic avoidance of such a situation. It is sometimes said that fear is stimulus-specific and anxiety more generalised. *Phrenophobia* is the fear of fear, an agitated kind of SECONDARY EMOTIONAL PROBLEM. Fear can be extreme, as in terror and panic (*see* PANIC ATTACK), or mild.

feedback giving data, often personal impressions, to someone on their performance or interpersonal style. Some counsellors employ an empirical, HERE AND NOW and I–THOU method of sensitising clients to how they are perceived, thus inviting ongoing reappraisal of self-image and personal constructs. Feedback is implicit in GENUINENESS, IMMEDIACY and CONFRONTATION. Some counsellors regularly invite feedback from clients on their experiences of the counselling process. Ideally, feedback should be an integral and constructive part of all counselling training and supervision.

feeding psychological feeding is a metaphor for supplying the client with the nurturing that she may previously have been denied.

Feeding is a psychoanalytic and specifically Winnicottian concept which views early feeding and nursing experiences as crucial to development: the intuitive nurturance, or failure to nurture (or the baby's perception of such failure), influences later developments in relating to others generally. Some counsellors see their more supportive and interpretative function as a kind of feeding of the client. In some forms of regressive therapy (*see* REPARENTING) clients are actually fed from a bottle by the therapist.

feelings affect, emotion. The word is commonly used as a synonym for EMOTIONS. All counsellors recognise the importance of being sensitive to, and reflecting on, clients' feelings as well as the content of their talk. Some writers (e.g. Janov, 1975) suggest that feelings are truer, deeper experiences than emotional displays. The primary feelings are, perhaps, anger, sadness and joy. There is an ongoing debate as to whether feelings or thoughts are more primary and responsible for dysfunctional behaviour, and also as to whether they are simultaneous processes. In general terms, the more humanistic therapies (*see* HUMANISTIC PSYCHOLOGY) focus on feelings much more than do psychoanalysis or CBT. It has been noted that clients can sometimes feel, as distinct from *getting*, better; however, they can also appear better even though their bodies do not feel (or are not) better (according to Janov). Some writers consider GUILT to be a feeling, but others consider it more properly to be a cognitive appraisal. Feelings are often associated with the 'feminine' aspects of life, like relationships and aesthetics. 'Hurt feelings' suggest either a form of irrational belief (*see* IRRATIONALITY) ('people should not say,

do unfair things to me') or natural human sensitivity.

fees payments made by clients for counselling. There are no direct financial transactions in NHS and some other agencies, but all counsellors in PRIVATE PRACTICE must determine and charge a (usually hourly) fee. Level of fee is determined by the market rate, counsellor location and reputation. There is no objective evidence for the view that clients appreciate counselling more or have more successful outcomes when paying rather than receiving a free service, but many counsellors do argue such a case. *See also* MONEY, SLIDING SCALE.

felt sense term coined by Gendlin (1978) referring to delicate, precise awareness, as registered by subtle bodily sensations, of the nature and avenue for resolution of problems. Using the technique of FOCUSING, people can become finely attuned to where, when and how they feel disturbed. This awareness can be used to access underlying factors and to effect a form of biofeedback self-help. Mahrer (1996) refers to the felt sense as a 'feelinged attentional centre' to accentuate its present-tense quality in the session.

feminist counselling any counselling centrally informed by feminist thought. There is no *one* model of feminist counselling. Feminism broadly argues that most contemporary cultures are profoundly patriarchal (*see* PATRIARCHY), and are thereby oppressive to women. Feminist counselling essentially acknowledges the power and influence of the political and structural on the lives of women. It seeks to explore the interface between the individual's psychology and history, and her external world, and attempts to unravel and acknowledge their respective influences. Feminist counselling aims to empower. It can incorporate a variety of counselling techniques and methods, depending on the theoretical stance of the practitioner. This can include consciousness raising and assertiveness training and may incorporate a psychodynamic stance. Feminist counsellors believe women should have a real choice as to the gender of their counsellor, and some feel strongly that women counsellors are most appropriate for a woman client. *See* SEXISM. *See* Walker (1990).

fifty-minute hour the traditional, and still typical, designation of 50 minutes of working time in each session. Derived from psychoanalysis, this convention is pragmatic, allowing the counsellor or therapist to see clients at hourly intervals with short breaks in between. *See* SESSION.

fight or flight behaviour characterised by internal conflict in which someone, faced with an objectively or subjectively frightening stimulus, typically chooses either to escape or to confront. Phobic experiences are often characterised by such a choice. It should not be assumed that the 'fight' option is necessarily the better one, since some people characteristically seek defensively to disguise their anxiety by confronting challenges counterphobically, without actually resolving them.

final contact *see* contact

firing order the sequence of reactions to stimuli. According to Lazarus (1981) we may respond to a relevant stimulus first by a sensation, followed by a cognition, then imagery, behavioural and interpersonal reactions. The multimodal therapist believes it is important to be aware of these, to cue in when possible and to utilise such knowledge to track and influence clients.

five relationships framework an understanding of the therapeutic relationship proposed by Clarkson, comprising the following: the working alliance; the transferential/countertransferential relationship; the developmentally needed/reparative relationship; the person-to-person/real relationship; the transpersonal relationship. These are viewed as overlapping states. While each kind of relationship can be attributed to certain models of therapy, the overall framework is intended to assist integrative practice.

fixation dysfunctional attachment to a particular object or person. Originally a Freudian concept, clients are said to be fixated (e.g. orally fixated) if part of their development is arrested by inadequate or excessive stimulation. Fixation has been used in reference to sexual preoccupations but is now used generally and imprecisely to refer to any excessive and self-defeating preoccupation.

fixed role therapy a method, forming part of Kelly's (1955) PERSONAL CONSTRUCT PSYCHOLOGY, which encourages clients systematically to explore alternative ways of behaving. It is based on an initial SELF-CHARACTERISATION exercise, which is then modified in the direction of a desired alternative, promoting 'the art of being different'.

flashbacks involuntary visual memories of (usually distressing) scenes. Flashbacks are associated with POST-TRAUMATIC STRESS DISORDER and are considered to represent the full impact of an original trauma attempting to assert itself and to break through defences against memory and working through. Overwhelming trauma may be automatically screened from conscious awareness at the time of the experience itself, but achieve partial awareness at various times later. People who have experienced armed combat, for example, may later hear the sounds of gunfire, helicopters, etc.; because these memories are cut off from awareness, they may emerge randomly and have a psychotic or disturbing flavour. Drug abuse (particularly of LSD) can also lead to disturbing flashback experiences.

flexibility adaptability; capability of modified responses to new situations. Personal flexibility is an essential quality in counsellors, who need to be able and willing to accept other people (including those whose values and customs are very different from their own) and to respond therapeutically. Flexibility does not mean that counsellors neutrally adapt to everything in the client without clinical consideration.

flight into health a possible defensive reaction to counselling, whereby the client prematurely declares herself to be 'cured' or in no need of further help, or states that she feels wonderful, or simply withdraws from counselling and tells herself that she has no need of it. Of psychoanalytic origin, the term implies that symptomatic relief does not constitute true mental health, and that such relief can often represent an avoidance of deeper and more painful material. Flight into health is a contentious concept, since a client's self-determination must be respected above the idea of the counsellor knowing better than the client what her inner state truly is. Some clients in fact receive the level of help they want in a short time. Conversely, some clients no doubt consciously or unconsciously seek to escape from counselling or from a particular counsellor by declaring themselves as being well and in no further need of counselling.

flight into history a defensive reaction against the pain or embarrassment that some clients are faced with when confronted with challenges in counselling or in everyday life. Some clients are apt to describe their past easily and endlessly and may do this rather than dealing with issues in the present (whether in the counselling session or in present relationships or situations).

flight into illness psychoanalytic concept whereby a person seeks escape from the pressures of relationships and unacceptable feelings by developing neurotic or PSYCHOSOMATIC symptoms.

flooding the behavioural intervention of exposing clients to the very objects or situations of which they are afraid. The original intention of flooding was to bring the client and what he was afraid of closer and closer together so that he would become habituated to the object of his fear and thereby lose the fear. While there is evidence that for some phobic clients (*see* PHOBIA) nothing but such exposure methods are effective, caution must be exercised when considering this intervention. Some writers regard flooding as synonymous with IMPLOSION therapy, which deliberately sets out to increase anxiety levels, but Bellack and Hersen (1987) insist on distinguishing between them. Other methods are similar in character to flooding but have different rationales (e.g. the shame-attacking exercises of rational emotive behavioural therapy). Flooding is one form of EXPOSURE.

focal therapy a particular form of psychoanalytic therapy which seeks to focus on an identified conflict, its interpretation and resolution, and which lends itself to brief treatment. *See* BRIEF THERAPY.

focusing a technique promoted by Gendlin (1978) which introduces the client to a method of becoming intimately and accurately aware of subtle bodily cues associated with particular life problems or repressed experiences. Also known as focusing-oriented psychotherapy. Clients following instructions on focusing learn to recognise, and utilise for change, these idiosyncratic sensations. Focusing can be used within any eclectic approach (e.g. Lazarus, 1981) but is derived from the person-centred approach and forms a part of Mahrer's (1989) EXPERIENTIAL PSYCHOTHERAPY. *See* FELT SENSE.

folie à deux literally, the foolishness of two people, this term refers to a shared delusion. In the extreme, both people may believe in the same psychotic ideas (although it is often the case that one of the pair tends to be the 'initiator'). More loosely, but inaccurately, the term refers to any CO-DEPENDENCY syndrome, in which both partners neurotically 'feed' each other's self-defeating behaviour.

follow-up any counselling session which is arranged at some distance in time from the main series of counselling sessions, and whose purpose is to evaluate the maintenance of therapeutic gains or to offer reinforcement. Follow-up sessions are usually scheduled some 3, 4 or 6 months from the original counselling although yearly follow-ups are also occasionally considered. Commonly used in COGNITIVE ANALYTIC THERAPY and TWO PLUS ONE APPROACH. *See* BOOSTER SESSIONS, EVALUATION.

force field analysis a method of examining the client's resources and sources of resistance in any given problematic situation. Force field analysis was devised by the social psychologist Lewin and is used both in organisational development work and in individual counselling. The method consists of encouraging clients to analyse what positive motivations they have, as against any self-sabotaging motivations. The emphasis is on weakening the negatives rather than strengthening the positives.

forgetting failing to recall. Psychodynamic counsellors place particular emphasis on the likely unconscious purposes of forgetting, arguing that people defend against internal conflict by repressing painful memories. Forgetting names and significant childhood memories, or forgetting to attend a counselling session, are instances of defensive forgetting; such forgetting may also have the quality of ACTING-OUT. Repeated forgetfulness on the part of clients is likely to be regarded by most counsellors as a sign of avoidance or resistance. Counsellors should, however, bear in mind possible individual differences with regard to recall, and also organic factors, particularly when working with older clients. *See* AMNESIA.

forgiveness the willingness to lay aside resentment, hostility, bitterness and other negative attitudes towards those who have caused pain or harm to oneself. Forgiveness is a central ethical principle in the Christian religion. Willingness to feel and act benignly towards people who may have harmed us has the psychological power of removing or alleviating RESENTMENT, thus leaving us free from preoccupation with attributing blame and seeking revenge. Many counsellors believe that adults can fully flourish only when they are able to forgive their parents (or other significant people) the (perceived) harm they have done to them. It is debated, however, to what extent it is possible or even desirable for victims of traumatic crime or violence (e.g. child sexual abuse, rape, aggravated burglary) to forgive perpetrators. The forgiveness of oneself, however, for unsavoury past behaviour is generally believed to be an essential requirement for positive mental health.

formative having to do with crucial developmental phases (*see* DEVELOPMENT). The importance of 'the formative years of a child' is a concept shared by most but not all theories of counselling psychology. 'Formative' tends to imply a certain sense of DETERMINISM, but some counsellors think of the person as being self-creating rather than following any necessary developmental path. The concept of the formative is also used in relation to the development of a counsellor and her professional skills. There is the known 'formative influence' of certain tutors, for example. Some supervisors regard counselling supervision as having a partly formative function (along with the restorative and normative functions).

forming in groups the initial stage in the life of a group convened for therapeutic purposes. This stage is often characterised by group members struggling for direction, experiencing dependency and testing BOUNDARIES. Group dynamics is often said to be characterised by the processes of forming, storming, norming and performing. Following the initial stage of forming, members experience and exhibit conflict between each other in the storming stage; the norming stage is charac-

terised by group cohesion and a readiness for intimacy and exploration; in the performing stage the group concentrates on tasks, having resolved many of the processes that inhibit its full potential for therapeutic effect.

frame management a term used in the communicative approach to therapy, which refers to the importance of the therapist's establishing and maintaining strict limits. Elements of the 'secure frame' include therapist neutrality (or abstinence) and anonymity; no physical contact; consistency of meeting place, time and fee. A 'deviant frame' is considered to break some or all of such conditions, to fail to 'hold' the client and to expose the 'madness' of the therapist. While very few counsellors or therapists adhere to such rigorous conditions, most recognise the significance of mutually agreed-upon boundaries and contracts.

frame of reference the typical way in which someone makes sense of his world, according to his own experiences, values, culture, and so on. In counselling it is considered highly important that counsellors are able to grasp, understand and accept the frame of reference of their clients and to work within it empathically. Each individual's frame of reference as it applies to each unit of experience is idiosyncratic, and the counsellor must be alert to this. 'Frame of reference' also implies typical linguistic nuances used by clients. There is a further distinction between internal and external frames of reference: in the former, people have their own, well-defined means of construing events; in the latter, people have a tendency to refer to outside sources, particularly parents or parent-figures, for confirmation. The necessity of working within the client's frame of reference is sometimes wrongly understood or wrongly taught to mean that counsellors must never venture an opinion of their own or attempt an intervention which has not already been invited by the client.

free association the psychoanalytic method of asking the client to express, uncensored, all thoughts, feelings and images which enter his stream of consciousness within the therapeutic session. In practice, free association will be composed of recent events, associated memories, imagination, wordplay, and so on. Freud came to value free association, in preference to hypnosis and other methods, as a way into the client's inner world. True free association implies that the client is willing and able to suspend the everyday practice of selecting material that is socially acceptable. The purpose of encouraging free association is to welcome all data which might shed light on the client's neurosis, with the likelihood being that uncensored thoughts in particular will have a certain potency and meaning. In practice, Freud acknowledged that it is rare that any client's 'free association' is actually free from censorship (that is, not selective). Those points at which free association stops are often significant, potentially demonstrating resistance to particular thoughts and feelings which may therefore be of special importance.

Free Child the functional EGO STATE (or role) in which (according to TA theory) the person thinks, feels and behaves as she would have done as a spontaneous child. There is thought to be at least some element of the 'free child' in everyone, however damaged they have been by adverse events in child-hood and after. The free child is likely to laugh, cry and respond to life generally without inhibitions. A balance between ego states is desirable for adult functioning, and the goal is not that clients should be always or frequently in their free child, but should have access to it. The free child is the converse of the ADAPTED CHILD and has both positive and negative attributes (inappropriately uninhibited behaviour as an adult, for example, is not in the best interests of clients).

free-floating anxiety that kind or quality of anxiety which appears to arise for no obvious reason and may have a particularly menacing subjective feeling, as in generalised anxiety disorder. *See* ANXIETY.

free will philosophically and theologically derived term for the capacity of the human being to transcend her conditioning and to practise self-determination. It is a basic assumption in counselling that people have (at least a high degree of) free will, which is implied in AUTONOMY. It is also a universal observation that people often either use their free will unwisely, destructively or immorally, or that it is perhaps contaminated by hidden factors (unconscious DETERMINISM). Willpower is often considered insufficient for personal change and the widespread need for helping services implies that free will is problematic. Some models of counselling (e.g. gestalt and TA) argue that we are clearly responsible for all our actions and capable of change by insight and REDECISION. Others (e.g. primal therapy) argue that what we have suffered in childhood has largely robbed us of genuine freedom of choice. Wood (1983) argues that therapy itself promotes irresponsibility and de-emphasises moral courage, effort and self-help.

frequency of sessions the spacing of meetings between client and counsellor. The normal frequency of counselling is weekly. However, in cases of crisis or other exceptional circumstances, counsellors will sometimes see clients more frequently. For practical or financial reasons, some clients are seen fortnightly, or at other intervals, and it is fairly common for counsellors to suggest staggered or tapered endings to withdraw clients gradually from dependence on counselling. Psychotherapists often see clients two or three times a week, and psychoanalysts may see their patients four or five times a week. This latter frequency reflects not the severity of clients' problems, but the therapeutic intention of analysts to foster and work through intense transference feelings.

Freudian the adjective attributing to Sigmund Freud and his followers those theories and practices he developed or which are perceived as attributable to him. The term 'Freudian therapy' is sometimes used synonymously with PSYCHOANALYSIS or psychoanalytically oriented psychotherapy. Freudian varieties of therapy and counselling are based on the concepts of the unconscious, transference, repression, the Oedipus complex and other phenomena. Within the mainstream of psychoanalytic thought, classical Freudian doctrine is distinguished from both the KLEINIAN and the 'middle school' (or 'independent' tradition), with Freud having placed more emphasis on internal drives and conflicts than on internal relationships. Freud is often spoken of, too, as one of the triad of Freud, Adler and Jung, the last two, after initially following Freud, having founded individual psychology and analytical psy-

chology respectively. In popular thought, 'Freudian' is often taken to be synonymous with a sexually focused analysis of human problems.

Freudian slip popular term for the involuntary expression of some otherwise repressed, unacceptable thought or intention *see* PARAPRAXIS.

frustration the experience of being thwarted or defeated. As many commentators have pointed out, life is intrinsically frustrating, because it does not invariably (or even often) yield to our individual preferences. Frustration is sometimes distinguished from deprivation to point up the subjective or intentional nature of the former. According to REBT, disappointment at not having one's goals met is a rational response, whereas a state of angry agitation, often characterised by regressive tantrums, is irrational. It is believed by some that a certain degree of frustration is character building. Sexual frustration has been considered by some theorists (e.g. Reich) to be intrinsically unhealthy. *See* LOW FRUSTRATION TOLERANCE.

fully functioning person originally a Rogerian concept of optimal functioning, it is to some extent preserved as an aspiration but also criticised for being too individualistic and unattainable.

functioning coping, performing one's everyday tasks adequately. It is important for counsellors to consider whether their clients are functioning well enough, and in an adult manner, in their everyday lives, to be able to take responsibility for their own welfare. Also, clients whose levels of functioning are severely impaired (e.g. a complete inability to work or to relate to people) are unlikely to benefit from counselling and may need a referral to a day centre, psychiatric or other facility. *Optimal* functioning (at the other end of the spectrum) implies that a person is liberated from neurosis and able to avail herself of most of her talents and potential: the FULLY FUNCTIONING PERSON.

gambling betting, risking of one's money. Although many people gamble fairly innocuously, some clients are addicted to a gambling habit, and may lose much or all of their money and other possessions. Extreme forms of gambling are often considered an addiction and many people derive aid from self-help organisations like Gamblers Anonymous. Gambling is also sometimes associated with HYPOMANIA. (It is sometimes referred to as an 'impulse control disorder'.) It can take various forms, from betting on horse races to feeding 'fruit machines'. Problematic gambling is an irrational and stubborn behaviour which purely 'talking treatment' is unlikely to change (although psychoanalytic theorists sometimes interpret it as a frenzied bid for love).

games inauthentic encounters between people which are characterised by unconscious and repetitive behaviour. A game is a concept from transactional analysis and is roughly equivalent to ACTING-OUT. Typically, people involved in games are not in an adult ego state; they 'find themselves' helplessly replaying part of their experience as a child with unconsciously consenting others. It is only towards the end of or after a game that they become uncom-

fortably aware of what has happened, and they then experience racket feelings (*see* RACKET SYSTEMS). The KARPMAN TRIANGLE is a means of analysing games into Persecutor, Rescuer or Victim parts. Behaviour which has the quality of inauthenticity is sometimes described as 'gamey'.

gay and lesbian affirmative therapy any form of psychological therapy that, as well as not pathologising homosexuality, actively seeks to accept and encourage the sexuality of gay and lesbian people; promoting real equality and resources for the gay and lesbian community and challenging all forms of subtle HOMOPHOBIA.

gay issues any matters relating to homosexuality and problems perceived as belonging to being gay. The homosexual community draws attention to those aspects of being gay in a predominantly (and oppressively) heterosexual society. Gay issues which are pertinent to counselling may include the general need for political and psychological awareness of the position of gays in society, the fear experienced by many young people of 'coming out' (publicly admitting to being homosexual), victimisation of gay people (being discriminated against in the job market or suffering 'queer bashing'), having to live with a sense of shame, isolated from rejecting parents and others; not having normal feelings of bereavement respected when a loved one dies, etc.

gender the sex-distinguishing category to which everyone belongs by virtue of biological determination. This view has been challenged in that the degree to which we are behaviourally and stereotypically male or female is now more open to question. For example, transsexuals claim to be psychologically other than the gender to which biology consigns them. (The term *gender dysphoria* is sometimes used by transsexuals.) Some feminists and sociologists argue that much behaviour is interchangeable and learnt, rather than inherently gender-specific. Others argue that there are innate male and female behavioural characteristics. In counselling, a client's choice regarding the gender of the counsellor should be respected.

generalisation the term as used in counselling has two meanings:

1. People are said to generalise defensively when they avoid specific feelings or statements.
2. What clients learn in counselling is intended to be generalised to a variety of situations. Thus, for example, if a client learns that she need not be afraid of her mother or her boss, she may learn to generalise that she need not be afraid of anyone who is not physically harmful. At the conceptual level, if she learns to dispute her irrational thinking in one problem situation, she can generalise it to others. *See also* OVER-GENERALISATION.

generalised anxiety disorder excessive worry, restlessness, irritability, tension,

sleep disturbance and fatigue that persist for at least six months and appear to have no particular trigger.

generalist counsellor a counsellor who works with clients whose concerns span a wide variety of symptoms or conditions. In practice, generalist (or generic) counsellors are probably in the majority. The term 'generalist counsellor' is also used to refer to practitioners whose training has grounded them in core skills and conditions but who practise no specific counselling orientation.

genetic counselling giving information to people which is based on an understanding of heredity and risk factors, often in circumstances where that information is likely to have serious implications for individuals or their prospective or actual children; giving clients an opportunity to explore such implications using counselling skills. Genetic counselling mainly takes place in medical settings and may be offered by various professionals. It should include an awareness on the part of the professional of the emotional consequences of distressing news for clients; counsellors need to be aware of possible misconceptions held by clients, as well as clients' tendency towards self-blame. There are relatively few 'genetic counsellors' as such, rather medical professionals who impart genetic information as part of their work, but specific training for genetic counselling at Masters level is now available. Relevant conditions may include some cancers, sickle cell anaemia, hydrocephalus, Down's syndrome, haemophilia, etc.

genital stage a stage of development representing the capability of full sexual relationships with others. In Freudian thought there is a stage of male (phallic) sexuality before the genital stage is reached in adolescence, but Klein and Erikson, among others, have different emphases. Actual adolescent genitality is considered to be anticipated by earlier, infantile sexual development.

genogram a diagrammatic representation by clients of the past and present members of their family. Genograms are used in individual, couple and family counselling when there are complex relationships involved and when it is considered useful to map these clearly. Constructing a genogram is an exercise in its own right, but can be used as a means of accessing feelings about family relationships and events. It is sometimes set as a homework assignment. *Genosociograms* are used by practitioners of TRANSGENERATIONAL PSYCHOTHERAPY.

genuineness a quality of authentic, unaffected being in relationship to others. Genuineness (Rogers also called it 'congruence' and 'realness') is regarded as a CORE CONDITION in counselling, because it serves to model self-acceptance and to challenge the idea that others' norms of behaviour have any superiority. Rogers regarded full genuineness as an *awareness* of one's experiencing and the *communication* of that awareness to others. Genuineness is not synonymous with thoughtless impulsivity; it is an appropriate freedom to be oneself as a counsellor in the counselling session. In practice, counsellors often choose specific moments in which to demonstrate their genuineness, for example by disclosing a strong feeling about the client for therapeutic purposes. Obstacles to counsellor genuineness include: the counsellor's personal patholo-

gy, which may need attention in personal counselling; the counsellor's performance anxiety, whereby she stresses the 'doing to' aspects of counselling over the 'being with' aspects; or simply a lack of practice and awareness, which can be improved in personal development groups. Person-centred counsellors place much more emphasis on genuineness than most other counsellors and stress the importance of being in touch at all times with the flow of experience even if the counsellor gives no overt expression to what is being experienced.

gestalt therapy/counselling a distinctive method of counselling and therapy initiated by Fritz and Laura Perls, which emphasises immediacy, experiencing and personal responsibility. Perls developed Gestalt therapy from psychoanalysis and used psychodramatic techniques to focus fully on the client's behaviour (verbal, nonverbal, emotional, intellectual and physical) within the session. Gestalt aims at heightened awareness of behaviour and facilitating conscious choices and responsive living. It may have a HERE AND NOW focus, facilitated by a very active counsellor. Clients may be asked to perform CHAIRWORK, an exercise which heightens awareness of incomplete experiences and often produces cathartic release. Clients are often encouraged to engage in dialogues between one part of themselves and another, the aim being to clarify incomplete understanding and to enable integration. The gestalt stress on responsibility means that clients may be asked to consider how they give themselves headaches, for example, or other psychosomatic escapes from responsibility. Gestalt therapists and counsellors are sometimes called *gestaltists*, and distinct pieces of gestalt work are called *gestalten*.

gifts unsolicited presents from the client to the counsellor (or more rarely from counsellor to client). Gifts are sometimes proffered in addition to payments or in lieu of payment where a service is free. They are more commonly presented at the end of a counselling relationship to signify gratitude. However, gifts are sometimes used by clients to ward off feelings of guilt or to compromise the counsellor, and because of this some counsellors refuse to accept such gifts as a matter of policy. Because a fee is a legitimate gift in exchange for which the counsellor also gives her expertise, the counselling relationship has been called a 'gift-relationship'.

global statements pronouncements made by clients, often about themselves, which have a sweeping and inaccurate character. Examples are: 'I always get things wrong' or 'Everything she does is perfect'. Such statements, instances of FAULTY INFORMATION PROCESSING, fail to take into account any nuances and confirm clients' unrealistic assessment of circumstances. People who are depressed commonly claim, for example, that they enjoy 'nothing at all' but when probed may realise that there are at least some enjoyable moments or aspects in their lives. *Global self-rating* describes the way in which clients specifically judge themselves, absolutistically, as entirely bad, stupid, ugly, etc.

goal setting the deliberate practice of identifying with clients empirical and achievable objectives. These may be written down as part of a CONTRACT, and include a time scale and means of measuring success. Some counsellors argue that goal setting is central to counselling, since without it there is no focus in the counselling, nor any means of determining whether it has been successful. Goal setting may be contraindicated for clients who, for example, are obsessively inclined and who may benefit from a less focused model of counselling.

goals the objectives that clients bring to, or discover in, counselling. All counselling is implicitly *goal-directed*, the broadest possible goals being, for example, 'to be happy' or 'to understand myself better'. Some models of counselling are not explicitly goal-directed (e.g. the person-centred and psychodynamic) but have their own implicit objectives for clients (e.g. that they will be more in touch with their inner experiencing or that more of their unconscious will become conscious). Behavioural counselling is the most goal-directed model: 'to be able to go on escalators' is the kind of specific goal that behavioural counsellors prefer to work with. Goals begin with concrete, often limited aims (e.g. flying on a particular aeroplane at a particular time) and the attainment of successive goals is an implicit 'meta-goal' of counselling. Bordin (1979) regards the shared understanding of goals by client and counsellor as one of the cornerstones of all successful helping alliances.

good breast a Kleinian concept referring to the baby's psychological position in which he splits into two his understanding of good 'objects', such as the breast. The baby relates to a perceived good (nourishing, plentiful, accessible) breast and a bad (unreliable, frustrating) breast, before eventually understanding that they are one and the same object. This realisation leads to the more mature DEPRESSIVE POSITION.

good enough Winnicottian concept which refers to the ability of the mother to provide for the baby a 'facilitating environment' which is perceived as being reliable and containing enough to ward off anxiety and threat. People who suffer seriously inadequate mothering in the very earliest months of life may develop mistrustful personalities; where the suffering is severe enough, they may become psychotic or borderline in adult life. Originally the term 'good enough' referred to mothering. Now it is sometimes used more broadly to refer to any quality of therapeutic or nursing care that facilitates development; it also implies that perfect care may be neither possible nor desirable.

good moments term sometimes used in counselling research to denote perceived in-session 'high points' that can be identified by researchers listening to tape-recordings.

gratitude benevolent feeling, attitude or expression of appreciation towards others. Genuine gratitude is freely given and acknowledges that another person contributes positively to one's well-being. Kleinian thought locates the ability to feel and express gratitude in early infancy, in the relationship with the mother's breast and the experience of gratification. Contrast with ENVY. False gratitude manifests in over-polite behaviour and ingratiating manners. Simple gratitude (e.g. the client genuinely thanking the counsellor for her helpfulness) is a common occurrence in counselling.

grief the experience of loss and expression of emotional hurt following a profound, undesired change in circumstances. Grief is partly synonymous with BEREAVEMENT, but the word 'grief' often refers to the acute reaction immediately following a loss. It is thought that grief and grieving is a natural process and that when it is not experienced with due impact, but suppressed, the damming up of such emotion ('delayed grief') will lead to problems. It is recognised that grief reactions may be experienced very differently from one person to another. The phrase *grief work* is sometimes used of the need to face the loss, to share it, and to feel fully its emotional impact. Mourning refers to the way in which grief is expressed formally according to different cultures.

groundedness a term used in existentialist thinking to refer to a person's quality of equanimity, or solid rootedness in existence. The term is loosely equivalent to 'centredness' and loosely opposite to 'neurotic' or 'unbalanced'.

group counselling any counselling conducted in a group setting. Historically, counselling has not developed very well as a group activity, and therefore the term 'group counselling' has been used sparingly. (The terms 'group therapy', 'group analysis', 'encounter group', and so on, *are* well established.) *See*, however, Tudor (1999) and FORMING IN GROUPS.

group dynamics the study of typical phenomena in groups. Such phenomena include: cohesiveness, boundary testing, displacement, mirroring, scapegoating, leadership. Group dynamics occur in all kinds of groups (therapeutic or not). *Group process* is a term describing the ways in which members of therapeutic groups collectively interact within sessions over the life of the group (*see*, for example, FORMING IN GROUPS).

group supervision any SUPERVISION of counsellors in a group situation. Group supervision may take the form of peer supervision
or of a group being led or facilitated by an
experienced practitioner. Group supervision is often provided by counsellor training courses and by counselling agencies
for economic and accountability purposes. Typical group supervision sessions last
two hours and may have between three
and six members (although some are larger). In some, the time is divided evenly for
counsellors to present their work. Alternatively, common themes may be taken up,
people may bid for time, or await a turn
another week. The advantages of group
supervision are that there can be many perspectives on a given case, considerable
stimulation, and a chance to hear how others handle their work. Disadvantages
include a shortage of time, a possibly
unhelpful bombardment of opinions, and
potentially unhelpful group dynamics.
Beginning counsellors are advised not to
rely solely on group supervision.

group therapy any form of psychotherapy
practised in a group setting. Group therapy is practised by, among others, nursing
staff in psychiatric hospitals and day centres, and group workers in alcoholism
treatment centres. It is a psychotherapy in
its own right, requiring special training.
Distinctions are made between the therapy of individual clients in a group setting,
the therapy of the group-as-a-whole,
which is an exclusively psychoanalytically
derived treatment concept, and therapy
with and in the group as in group-analysis.
Group analytic treatment has an elaborate
theory of its own. Advantages of group
therapy include:

- it is economical with time and resources;
- clients can learn from each other (universality);
- clients can help each other (altruism);
- clients have access to a safe social situation in which to practise new behaviours.

Disadvantages include:

- it may not be an appropriate arena for
certain clients who need one-to-one
counselling;
- it may not always be possible to give each
group member the time and attention
she requires;
- it requires firm boundaries and sensitive
awareness of each person's progress.

See Aveline and Dryden (1988).

guidance helping by demonstrating, teaching or informing. While much counselling
contains an element of guidance (*see*
ADVICE) its central purpose is the empowerment of the client to find and use his own
resources. 'Guidance' is most frequently
used in the field of career information and
development and involves the passing on
of information.

guided discovery term used in COGNITIVE-
BEHAVIOURAL THERAPY for assisting the client
in recalling the steps in a given situation
which led to his feeling anxious or trou-
bled. The purpose of such a guided discovery is to convey a sense of enquiry rather
than confirm for the client that her anxious
feelings, for example, are inevitable or
causeless. By carefully tracing events and
the cognitive appraisals made of them, the
counsellor can help the client locate
changeable elements in her own thinking.

guided fantasy an exercise in which people are encouraged, often with the help of
relaxation techniques, music and other
aids, to enter worlds of experience other

than their own. Guided fantasy can be applied to clients' immediate concerns or to broader areas of PERSONAL GROWTH.

guided imagery an exercise in which the client is encouraged to recall past scenes, with their accompanying affect, in order to understand past patterns and to achieve catharsis. Alternatively, or in conjunction with this, guided imagery may be used to effect changes in the client's life by employing images of a desired future. Many schools of counselling use such exercises, although they are more commonly used by, for example, psychosynthesis counsellors. *See* IMAGINATION.

guilt the subjective experience of culpability and, frequently, self-chastisement. Objectively, someone may be said to be guilty of any action which has had negative consequences for others. As well as its strictly legal meaning, however, guilt has a long history of use theologically and psychologically. It is useful to register a degree of discomfort and penitence when one has in fact caused harm to others. However, many people experience exaggerated guilty feelings which lead to pathological anxieties and other symptoms, and serve no useful purpose. According to cognitive therapists, a more useful reaction than guilt is, often, one of regret, reassessment and learning. People who have had strong religious upbringings, however (e.g. Roman Catholics), may find it very hard to shake off feelings of guilt. The line between guilt and regret is often subjectively drawn. (In REBT, guilt is viewed as stemming from irrational thinking about the breaking of one's moral code while regret stems from rational thinking about the wrongdoing.) Freudians attribute the origins of guilt to early childhood sexual conflicts. It is sometimes claimed that many helping professionals harbour some sense of guilt, for which an altruistic lifestyle and profession acts as a form of REPARATION. Some people suffering from obsessive–compulsive disorder experience profound guilt for imaginary crimes. It is often crucial for counsellors to assist clients in distinguishing between functional guilt (which is vital to further development) and dysfunctional guilt (which impedes development).

gut feeling colloquial term for strong, immediate, non-intellectual experience of something or someone. Sometimes used synonymously with HUNCH, a counsellor's gut feeling (or gut reaction) about a client is a strong intuitive response to the client's material, and often occurs where there is no current evidence to support the feeling. A gut feeling implies an accurate intuitive judgement, but gut feelings about others can prove to be inaccurate. Models of counselling concentrating on feelings generally (e.g. gestalt and primal therapy) are more likely to rely on gut feeling, as are humanistic group therapies.

hallucination a sensory perception which is unrelated to any external stimuli and which frequently has a bizarre quality. Hallucinations are of many kinds, the most common being visual and auditory; people see things which are not there or hear things which are not said or emitted. Tactile, gustatory and olfactory kinds are also known. True hallucinations are associated with psychotic states (*see* PSYCHOSIS). (It is quite normal to experience 'pseudo-hallucinations' on falling asleep or waking up.) People who experience full-blown hallucinations are usually convinced of their reality; particularly menacing hallucinations cause great distress to those suffering from certain forms of SCHIZOPHRENIA. While some therapists argue that people suffering from such experiences can be helped by verbal therapies, anti-psychotic medication is much more reliable. Hallucinations can be caused by hallucinogenic drugs such as LSD; they can also be induced by the consumption of excessive amounts of alcohol.

harmful interventions any actions on the part of a counsellor which have a negative effect on the client. Such interventions may be foolhardy or simply ill judged, but lead to either short-term or long-term DETERIORA-

TION. Harmful interventions may include pushing a client overly hard to achieve goals; forcing a client to regress; confronting vulnerable clients beyond their capacity to withstand such confrontation; encouraging clients to withdraw too abruptly from medication; indulging in sexual activity with clients, etc.

hate an extreme loathing, wishing ill for another person. Hate is usually felt by people who have (or believe they have) been hurt or wronged by someone, and therefore hate has a quality of vengeance in it. While hatred may be enduring, it is also often fleeting or intermittent. Love–hate relationships seem to be based on intense and fluctuating positive and negative feelings. Psychoanalytic thinkers often trace love and hate back to the feelings of infants towards mothers. Hate can also be projected on to groups of people, as in RACISM. It is unlikely that feelings of hate will arise between client and counsellor but may do so in longer-term transference-based therapy. Counsellors are challenged to discern what nuances may be embedded in claims of hatred: is the client angry, frustrated, irritated, deeply hurt or filled with loathing and contempt?

healing literally, making whole and healthy. Methods and attempted methods of healing are as old as humankind. 'Healing' was and is used generally of physical pain and suffering more than of psychological ills, but it can encompass the treatment of all ills. Weatherhead (1951) traces the history of healing from illness and cure in primitive times, through religious miracles and scientific understanding, to present day psychological and PSYCHOSOMATIC insights. Certain humanistic and transpersonal counsellors regard their work as healing, and they may indeed combine mainstream counselling methods with the 'complementary medicines' of massage, homoeopathy, shamanism, etc. Because of its association with faith healing and healing by PLACEBO treatments, many counsellors avoid use of the term 'healing'. Interestingly, however, Aeschylus referred to iatroi logoi (healing words) as the earliest form of psychotherapy. Szasz (1988) proposes that counselling and psychotherapy be known as the art of offering 'healing words', rather than as a scientific profession.

hedonic calculus the practice, advocated in REBT, of basing personal decisions on a full understanding of the advantages and disadvantages of both short- and long-range considerations of salient options. This philosophy rests on the assumption that individuals are motivated by healthy self-interest, that the world frequently frustrates personal desires, and that people are therefore well-advised to devote their efforts to likely long-term gains rather than succumbing to LOW FRUSTRATION TOLERANCE.

helicoptering the act of imaginally hovering above oneself, watching one's own performance from above. It is thought by some that developing helicoptering skills (used in sessions) helps in counsellor development and self-supervision; others find this uncomfortably like SPECTATORING.

help any act of assisting another. Counselling is generally considered one of the *helping professions*, along with nursing, social work, etc. Most counsellors probably regard themselves as helping their clients to help themselves. The 'cry for help' expressed by some clients in the form of dramatic behaviour (e.g. attempted suicide) implies a difficulty in simply asking for help. There is some truth in the idea that in our culture it is still regarded as something of a personal weakness (particularly for men) to have to ask for (emotional) help. Partly for this reason, some therapies (e.g. primal) often urge clients openly to cry out for help (i.e. the help and understanding they did not receive as a child). Clients are sometimes referred to as 'helpees'. *See* Egan (2002).

helplessness the feeling of relative paralysis in the face of difficulty, and the belief that one is unable to find the resources to overcome it. 'Learned helplessness' is an important cognitive–behavioural concept, which broadly suggests that our early experiences of actual helplessness in inescapable situations are maladaptively ingrained in us as a fixed attitude to stress in adult life. Most people will have sufficient experiences as they grow up which will disconfirm their helplessness. For those who do not, coping skills and cognitive re-education can significantly alter their belief in their helplessness. Contrast with SELF-EFFICACY.

hemisphericity the brain's structure consisting of two halves (left and right hemisphere) with different functions. Referred to variously as left and right hemisphere/brain, cerebral dominance, asymmetry, and associated with cognitive style, the 'right brain' is considered an emotional processor (intuitive, artistic, lateral thinking, etc.) and the 'left brain' intellectual, planning-oriented, focused on language and maths, etc. Referred to in some NLP techniques and in MULTIPLE INTELLIGENCES.

here and now in this specific place at this specific time. Counselling often focuses on the immediate situation, the actual relationship between the client and the counsellor, temporarily suspending discussion of biography, chronic and urgent problems, and so on. The rationale for such a focus may be that the client is defensively engaging in FLIGHT INTO HISTORY or in avoidance of feelings about the counsellor. Clients' typical interpersonal styles are often replayed with the counsellor and may be usefully focused on and worked with therapeutically. Psychodynamic counsellors often purposefully elicit clients' thoughts and feelings about the interpersonal 'here and now' of the counselling session. Gestalt counsellors often aim for a heightened awareness of the here and now by drawing attention to the client's gestures, movements, tone of voice, and other behaviours. Encounter groups make use of the here and now in a powerful, challenging way. Most counsellors maintain a balance of attention to the here and now and the THERE AND THEN. 'Here and now' can also refer to the client's present life in general as opposed to her past.

heterosexuality that sexual orientation in which one is attracted to and involved with members of the opposite sex. Heterosexuality is the statistically prevalent sexual orientation in all cultures and in the animal world, and is overwhelmingly the main medium for the procreation of the species. Only in recent times has the assumption of universal heterosexuality (*heterosexism*) been seriously challenged. As the gay and lesbian movement has gathered strength and made its views known, this assumption has had to be modified. Counsellors need to be sensitive to the undisclosed sexual orientation of clients. Often the neutral words 'partner' and 'relationship' are used in preference to 'wife' or 'marriage', for example, when eliciting information.

hidden agenda *see* AGENDA.

hierarchy of needs the view that human beings are motivated by various needs, and that these needs can be clearly prioritised. Maslow suggested that the fundamental needs are satisfaction of hunger, thirst and related physical conditions. These are followed by the need for shelter and safety, and then by the affiliative need for acceptance and belonging. The next priority is the esteem needs: for competence, approval and recognition. Finally, human beings have the need for self-actualisation: the need to fulfil one's own potential. Nobody is likely to be able to strive further up the hierarchy who has not fulfilled the lower needs (hungry people are unlikely to be pursuing SELF-ACTUALISATION needs in the realms of aesthetics, for example). A schema such as Maslow's suggests that all human beings are innately inclined to strive ultimately for spiritual goals.

history taking the practice of formally eliciting biographical details from the client. In some settings this is standard practice, but for most counsellors it is optional. The advantages of taking a comprehensive personal history include:

- it gives a fuller picture of the client;
- it shows behaviour patterns over a period of time;
- it encourages exploration;
- it can act as a safeguard (in cases where the client may be dangerous or where his condition is too serious for counselling to deal with).

Disadvantages include:

- it may prevent the client from revealing the urgency of his concerns;
- it may be experienced as alienating by the client;
- it may be felt by some counsellors to affect adversely their relationship with the client.

Some approaches to counselling (e.g. experiential psychotherapy) eschew history taking altogether.

HIV counselling *see* AIDS COUNSELLING.

holding a metaphor for the psychologically containing attitude of the counsellor towards the client. Derived from psychodynamic therapy, the concept refers to the holding of an infant, especially where the infant is in distress. In counselling terms, holding implies that the counsellor understands the client's depth of suffering and patiently remains with the client and her confusion until she achieves greater understanding or maturation herself. Sometimes a counsellor will see her task as 'holding' a particularly difficult client until a residential facility becomes available, for example.

holistic concerned with the whole person (emotionally, intellectually, behaviourally, spiritually, environmentally, etc.). Holistic world views and holistic therapies became apparent in about the 1970s, placing emphasis on the idea that a person is a unity and that to regard him as less is disrespectful and countertherapeutic. The term does not have a precise meaning but lends itself to a host of fringe therapies. It is, however, clearly opposed to any form of counselling which does view human beings as collections of parts. Behaviourism would be a main opponent. GESTALT counselling is holistic in the sense that it addresses itself to the client's emotions, imagery, will, etc., but gestalt, like most forms of counselling, emphasises certain functions and de-emphasises others.

homework any assignment agreed with and carried out by a client between one counselling session and another. Many counsellors regard homework as an integral and indispensable part of the process of counselling and personal change, based on the view that client change does not come about purely by in-session work. A typical counselling session lasts for 1 hour out of 168 in a client's week. Homework helps the client to put her new learning to the test in everyday life and also establishes a pattern of self-change and autonomy. Counsellors negotiating homework with clients need to consider how challenging it is to be, and how specific, practical and measurable. It is important that counsellors check homework assignments each week and allow sufficient time for discussion of successes and failures.

homogamy the pairing of partners from the same or similar social group, as in 'like attracts like'; relevant to couple counselling.

homophobia literally, fear of people of the same gender. It is used more commonly to refer to a hateful anti-homosexual attitude. Homophobia is often characterised by an irrational, exaggerated dislike of, contempt for, and avoidance of gay people by particularly illiberal heterosexuals. Some gay critics might say that all non-acceptance of homosexuality is homophobic. It seems likely that the greater the ill feeling expressed by heterosexuals, the more this masks a fear about the security of their own sexuality. Certain quarters of society (e.g. some tabloid newspapers) deliberately pander to homophobia by promoting negative images of homosexuality. Recent gay writers have questioned the concept of homophobia on the grounds that it implies a disease for which the 'homophobic' person is not responsible.

homosexuality an attraction to and involvement with members of one's own sex, usually including sexual relations. Homosexuality (*see also* GAY ISSUES and BISEXUALITY) is a minority sexual orientation and gay people have suffered abuse and discrimination because of their orientation. Traditionally, homosexuality has been regarded by psychoanalysts as an aberration, a failure to achieve full, heterosexual maturity (*see* HETEROSEXUALITY); an avoidance of natural heterosexual genitality. Analyses of homosexuality suggested that these people had failed to identify with their same sex parent, and had possibly been sexually abused by a parent or other parental figure. Most gay people reject these analyses and insist that homosexual identity arises choicelessly within the person, often from a very early age. *Latent homosexuality* is a concept used by analytical thinkers to refer to a conflict within all or most people between the socially approved heterosexual part of themselves over the homosexual. Homosexuality is a complex subject, about which we are learning slowly. Counsellors of any orientation need to be thoughtful in their attitudes and response to people of different sexual orientations.

honesty truthfulness, genuineness. In accepting clients, counsellors make an assumption that their clients will be as factually and emotionally honest as they are able to be at that point in time. Some counsellors explicitly discuss a need or preference for honesty, and may include it in a contract. Many clients are able to be increasingly honest as they learn to trust their counsellors and their own experiencing. For some clients, honesty in close relationships is a major problem, which can be helped by practising honesty and learning its benefits in the counselling relationship. For some clients (e.g. certain offenders, alcoholics) compulsive dishonesty may be a central dynamic. It is assumed that counsellors have a high degree of honesty (integrity) in their professional dealings. *See* RADICAL HONESTY.

hope an attitude of positive expectancy. Hope is conspicuously absent or minimal in depressed clients but is implied in their coming for counselling. Genuine and total resignation or apathy is rare, although apparent in some clients at times. It is usually considered an ethical responsibility of counsellors to engender and/or keep alive hope for change in all clients. It is also clinical wisdom that client improvement is related in part to counsellor hopefulness. Hope must be tempered by honesty and realism. Emphasising hopefulness can be unproductive when a client needs to experience past or present trauma, and can amount to non-therapeutic denial. While advocates of complementary medicine are sometimes accused of offering false hope to clients with terminal diagnoses, others counter that transpersonal methods reinforcing positive beliefs have had demonstrable curative effects.

hopelessness the absence of hope. Hopelessness is a key symptom of DEPRESSION. The client is apparently unable to see any good change arising in the future; whatever he has suffered in the far or recent past, and however he construes events, a shadow is cast over the future so that (in extreme depression) the client really cannot conceive of any improvement in his fortunes. People who are in a state of agitated hopelessness are at risk of SUICIDE, but where the hopelessness is milder, counsellors may be able to effect gradual change.

hot cognitions according to cognitive therapy and REBT, these are extreme distorted or irrational beliefs, the intensity of which leads to or reinforces psychological disturbance. Clients are taught to hold and act on more realistic and healthy beliefs or 'warm cognitions'.

HOUND acronym for humble, old, unattractive, non-verbal and dumb. This is a little-used, humorous response to YAVIS and implies that there is an identifiable group of people who counsellors and therapists prefer not to work with.

hugging physically embracing another person, usually by wrapping one's arms around the other's body. Some counsellors, and some clients, find hugging normal and reassuring; others, however, find it threatening, pretentious or undesirable. Psychodynamic counsellors are unlikely to practise or approve of hugging clients. Humanistic counsellors, particularly those familiar with Californian-type growth centres, are likely to practise hugging freely and to regard it as having therapeutic properties of its own (*see* HUMANISTIC PSYCHOLOGY). Some counsellors use hugging and touching sparingly, at times of great emotion or in a calculated attempt to have a therapeutic impact. The tendency to hug or not is also related to cultural patterns.

human development the subject of how human beings grow psychologically and otherwise from birth (or before) to death (or after). Counselling training courses often include an element of human development, or 'lifespan development', which overlaps with concepts of developmental psychology, the life course, narrative, etc. It has special relevance for considerations of when and how clients acquired their PSYCHOLOGICAL DISTURBANCE but also refers to trainees' insights into their own personal development. Widely differing models exist, from Piaget to Freud, Klein, Erickson, Bowlby, et al. Originally the focus was on early childhood to adolescence but it has now shifted to the entire lifespan and to the likelihood that some combination of determinism and idiosyncratic freedom exists at all stages.

human nature the concept that there is something characteristic which all human beings have in common. 'It's only human nature' implies that one cannot expect too high a moral ideal for human beings. 'It is human nature to look out for oneself and one's family' is another such idea. 'It is human nature to hope against all odds' is a more positive conception of people. Every counselling theory has an explicit or implicit theory of human nature. Freudians tend to regard human nature with some pessimism: people are viewed as driven, as in inevitable conflict, and as capable of only so much change. Humanistic counsellors are likely to have more optimistic views (*see* HUMAN POTENTIAL). Some critics dislike the whole idea of the concept of human nature, arguing that there is obviously no fixed human nature, only tendencies or conditioned behavioural patterns, and that people are culturally and individually so different as to render the idea of a nature common to all human beings meaningless. (See Ashworth, 2000.)

human potential all that which it is yet possible for human beings to become. The 'human potential movement' is a network of people interested in exploring how alternative therapies, complementary medicine, spirituality, radical politics and communal living can realise human potential. Those involved are less interested in problem solution and remedial therapy than in personal growth. In character, this movement is forward-looking and imaginative, although critics suggest that much of it is fanciful, escapist nonsense. People involved in this movement are often interested in altered or higher states of CONSCIOUSNESS. *See* HUMANISTIC PSYCHOLOGY, SAFAA.

humanistic psychology that school of psychology which, in contrast to psychoanalytic and behavioural psychology, emphasises human goodness, potentiality and wholeness. Sometimes called 'third force psychology', humanistic psychology is made up of the approaches of Rogers, Perls, Reich, Moreno, Schutz, Assagioli and others. Humanistic psychology has been called 'abundance-orientated' (positive and forward-looking) rather than 'deficiency-orientated' (preoccupied with pathology). It is inclined towards experiment,

cooperation and the stretching of boundaries. It spans therapeutic work from the intrauterine to the spiritual. Humanistic psychology includes the areas of therapy, education and management, but *humanistic psychotherapy and counselling* is specifically focused on methods of personal change. There has been a lot of emphasis on work in groups, including psychodrama, encounter, primal and co-counselling. The terms humanistic and humanist (rational-atheist) are often confused.

humanity the core quality of individuals that marks them as human beings in contrast to animals. It can also imply a recognition of the value of other human beings, and a sense of compassion and willingness to help. It implies something caring and reasonable at the core of all human beings. *Humanitarian* suggests a special willingness to act 'charitably' towards others, and not to be motivated only by self-interest. *Dehumanising* refers to anything opposed to or likely to reduce our 'humanness', e.g. soul-destroying work, racism, etc. Postmodernism denies any *essential* humanity or humanness.

humour in counselling jokes, laughter, light-hearted banter within sessions. Counselling is characterised more by earnest dialogue than by merriment, and psychodynamic practitioners in particular may interpret humour as indicative of defensiveness. Many counsellors, however, regard humour as normal, innocuous or even beneficial in creating a working relationship. Complete absence of humour in clients may suggest severe affective problems. *See* LAUGHTER and JOY.

hunch a sudden and compelling intuition. Counsellors frequently have hunches about their clients, based on what clients say, how they say it, and on their paraverbal communications; counsellors may also experience more hunches as they become more experienced and able to compare the story of one client with another. Beginning counsellors are advised not to act on their hunches impulsively, because the task of beginners is to learn to track accurately what clients say. However, it is recognised that accurate hunches about clients are valuable tools in counselling, forming the basis of advanced EMPATHY. A hunch is not a wild guess but a strong feeling-based implicit idea about the client engendered by the client's particular statements and manner.

hyperventilation prolonged deep breathing, or 'overbreathing', often associated with panic attacks and leading to numbness, tingling, light-headedness, etc. It can be reduced and stopped by breathing into a paper bag or similar container.

hypnosis an altered state of consciousness, resembling shallow sleep, induced for therapeutic and other purposes. In hypnosis, normal alertness is suspended, the person is relaxed and suggestible. The person in a hypnotic trance is peculiarly open to the suggestions of a hypnotist or hypnotherapist, and these suggestions may often be implanted so as to take effect after the trance is ended (post-hypnotic suggestion). *Hypnotherapy* is the deliberate and ethical use of hypnosis to effect personal change in the lives of consenting clients. Hypnotherapy is often a directive method of therapy which can work well for people who wish to be treated by an 'expert'. However, there are indirect methods of hypnotherapy being increasingly practised which are based less on the 'expert' role of the therapist. People experiencing behavioural disorders including addiction to nicotine often seek hypnotherapy. It may well be contraindicated in instances where people are seeking total abdication of personal responsibility.

hypochondriasis a neurotic preoccupation with bodily functions, characterised by the conviction that one is ill when this is not the case. People suffering from hypochondriasis (*hypochondriacs*) may spend inordinate amounts of time studying their headaches, pulse, any instances of change in bodily performance, and so on; such people also frequently consult a doctor, sometimes several doctors. In extreme cases, people who are diagnosed schizophrenic are sometimes convinced that parts of their bodies are infected or absent; hypochondriasis in this context is symptomatic of psychosis. Some people with hypochondriasis feel driven to seek unnecessary surgery to cure imaginary illnesses (surgery is rarely helpful in such cases). This kind of behaviour is sometimes interpreted as a defensive somatising of more general anxieties. Some people have similar preoccupations with their mental health, becoming convinced that they are suffering from various psychological symptoms and spending inordinate amounts of time consulting psychotherapists, psychiatrists and counsellors and 'being in therapy'. *See* FACTITIOUS DISORDER.

hypomania psychiatric classification of people who exhibit signs of mild mania. Symptoms include impulsivity, overactivity, rapid speech, lability of mood, irritability and sleep disturbance. In a hypomanic state, people may make impulsive and self-defeating financial and sexual decisions. In the most severe forms, they rapidly become exhausted. The term is sometimes used in preference to MANIA.

hysteria a mood of unwarranted excitement; a condition in which the person reacts to events with inordinate emotion, appearing histrionic to others. Originally, hysteria was considered to be an exclusively female condition related to problems with the womb; psychoanalytically, it was usually considered due to sexual conflict. A condition known as conversion hysteria was common in Freud's time, in which neurotic symptoms were converted, for example, into paralysis of a limb or loss of speech: the conversion provides a solution for a psychological conflict (a paralysed person cannot raise their arm in anger, for example). Hysteria is characterised by the mental mechanism of dissociation, the client responding emotionally to a certain event or stimulus but being completely unaware of it. The caricature of the hysterical person who needs to be slapped in order to be 'calmed down' has some truth in it, but hysteria (in so far as it actually exists as a distinct entity) is more usually a mild form of excitability. Counsellors frequently encounter clients who have a predominantly emotional style of talking, and who may need help to modify their style. One category of personality disorder is said to be hysterical: the term is unreliable and much subject to sex bias in diagnosis.

'I' statement any statement which uses the first person form congruently. Clients may use phrases like 'You just feel so helpless' and 'One has always been highly strung'. Such usage has a defensive quality which serves to distance people from ownership of their feelings and thoughts. Counsellors in training are taught to recognise their own tendencies to deny responsibility for themselves in this way, and often counsellors explicitly teach clients the importance of using clear statements beginning with 'I'. 'I' is also encouraged in groups instead of the presumptuous 'we'.

I'm OK, you're OK slogan popularised by Harris (1967) and forming the basis of TRANSACTIONAL ANALYSIS philosophy: that people have 'worth, value and dignity' regardless of their individual circumstances and behaviour. 'I'm OK, you're OK' means the mutual acceptance of person by person, but does not mean that all human behaviour is acceptable. TA counsellors sometimes speak of OK and not-OK behaviour. They also point out that some people adopt positions of being 'one-up' or 'one-down' (e.g. 'I'm OK, you're not OK' and 'I'm not OK, you're OK'). Many TA counsellors have rejected the simplistic model purveyed by Harris and other popularisers.

I–Thou the kind or quality of relationship which is characterised by the full, open, non-exploitative, non-stereotyping meeting of one person with another. Buber (1937) distinguished between the I–It world of casual, exploitative, objectifying and demeaning relationships, and the I–Thou world of fully human relationships. Buber's 'I and Thou' has a mystical quality, and he viewed the human encounter as the primary avenue to religious experience. Buber's book has been enormously influential in the counselling world, yet it is apparent that Buber was far from convinced that therapeutic relationships offer genuine I–Thou encounters.

iatrogenic literally, a disease originated or caused by the physician, this term is used by critics of medicine who argue that many diseases are caused or worsened by medical intervention. In the counselling field, an iatrogenic condition might be a state of regressive helplessness induced in a client by a counsellor committed to confrontational and regressive techniques.

ICD-10 the *International Classification of Mental and Behavioural Disorders,*

107

10th Edition, which is produced by the World Health Organisation, setting out classifications of medical (including psychiatric and psychological) disorders and serving as an alternative system to the American DSM-IV TR. The *ICD-10*, issued in 1993, moved closer to the multiaxial form of the American classification system and contains descriptions of more than 300 disorders.

id part of the Freudian tripartite structure of the personality (id, *ego* and *superego*), the id is conceptualised as the deepest part of the unconscious, a well of libidinous, chaotic, amoral, uncivilised energy. Freud considered the id to be formed by both innate and learned aspects. Literally the 'it', the id is an instinctive, pleasure-driven psychic force which has to be contained and repressed by the mediating function of the ego. The id is sometimes wrongly understood as a kind of chamber in the mind, instead of a particular function.

idea of reference an acute form of PERSONALISATION in which someone firmly believes that certain gestures, however remote or innocent, are directly and usually maliciously referring to himself. Examples include the belief that every mention of the word 'red' is a coded form of persecution, or the belief that every time someone scratches his or her head, a message is intended. Such ideas of reference are a form of paranoid delusion and are unlikely to yield to counselling treatment, but may be ameliorated by appropriate medication.

ideal model technique a technique used by PSYCHOSYNTHESIS counsellors to enable clients to make progress by means of certain visualisations. Clients may be asked to create an image of a way out of their problem, an image of the opposite state to the one in which they are apparently trapped, an image of a generalised preferred future. It is emphasised that clients' negative experiences should be dealt with before entertaining the use of this technique.

idealisation defence mechanism whereby an object is invested with unrealistic positive attributes. Derived from psychoanalytic theory, the tendency of clients to idealise significant people in their lives is fairly common. Many people report having had 'a perfect childhood', for example, when it is clear from all objective accounts that their childhoods were anything but perfect. Also, it is common for people in love to idealise their partners, failing to notice any blemish or defect that is apparent to others. Persistent idealisation helps the person to ward off a reality (past or present) which may be painful. The greater the idealisation, the greater likelihood there is of SPLITTING good and bad feelings towards the same person, with bad feelings leading to denigration of others.

idée fixe a fixed idea held in defiance of any evidence to the contrary. Such pathologically held ideas vary in their severity, from everyday bigotry to psychotic DELUSIONS. In its most severe form, the person may live his entire life around the fixed idea, oblivious to the protests of others and even interpreting others' motivations in the light of the fixed idea.

identification the act of likening oneself to another (or vice versa). There is a crucial difference in counselling between *empathy* and the kind of sympathy that is associated with identifying with another person, her personality or predicament. It is a danger in counselling that the counsellor may, without realisation, identify with the struggles of her client to the point where she becomes over-involved and ineffective. Supervision should help with such problems. Identification also means the accurate classification of problems or conditions, as in 'problem identification'. *See also* PROJECTIVE IDENTIFICATION, TRIAL IDENTIFICATION.

identification with the aggressor the phenomenon occurring in certain intensely hostile situations (e.g. siege, kidnap) whereby victims are said to sometimes come to feel emotionally close to those being aggressive to them, as in 'Stockholm syndrome'.

identity crisis the experience of acute and distressing uncertainty about who one is, what one's values are, and where one's future lies. Identity crises are associated mainly with adolescence, a period when people are seeking to distinguish themselves from their parents and to carve a meaningful personal niche in the world. An identity crisis can be experienced by people whose circumstances change dramatically or painfully, forcing them to reconsider how they will relate to a new situation. Typical examples include sexual orientation, redundancy and rapid professional success. MIDLIFE CRISIS also challenges people to reconstruct their self-images and/or to view their past from a new perspective.

idiom a typical, recurring way in which the client presents behaviourally and attitudinally in the session, which offers clues to the counsellor (especially in short-term psychodynamic therapy) to the client's transference.

illness a malfunctioning of the body or mind; a marked departure from a state of normal healthy functioning. All cultures have an illness concept, although its nomenclature and classifications differ. In our culture physical illness has far less stigma attached to it than does MENTAL ILLNESS. There has always been a recognised overlap and causal link between physical and mental illness; many counsellors attribute considerable power to the mind to manifest its unease in physical illness. It is also recognised that acute or prolonged physical illness can have serious implications for a person's psychological health. People suffering from painful physical conditions often become depressed. Counselling may be able to help alleviate some of the secondary emotional consequences of illness.

illusion a form of deception. People speak of having their 'illusions shattered' when events disconfirm their habitually held beliefs. False predictions, MAGICAL THINKING, and FAULTY INFORMATION PROCESSING are all examples of illusions, or failures to live in reality. An *illusion of centrality* afflicts those who believe that a real disaster affecting many is happening only to them. Some critics of counselling argue that it encourages an illusion of change and personal power in a world that is unyielding and on which we actually exercise very little influence. Compare with DELUSION.

imagery mental pictures. Clients in counselling are often asked what spontaneous imagery they associate with their stories and problems. DREAMS are the purest source of involuntary imagery creation. Memories, treasured artefacts and daydreams are also examples of common imagery. Some systems of counselling and therapy request clients to construct imagery as part of a therapeutic strategy. Lazarus (1981) includes imagery as one of the fundamental modalities in which clients operate. The power of imagery resides in its preverbal and non-verbal nature; it can capture the essence of a client's feelings or subtle intimations where over-used words sometimes cannot. Visualisation techniques employ clients' idiosyncratic images, which may be auditory and olfactory as well as visual. The *imaginal world* is a subtle world that can be shared by counsellor and client.

imaginal characterised by the imagination. Imaginal flooding, for example, is an exposure therapy requiring clients to imagine the incident that triggered trauma in them.

imagination the ability to construct, mentally, images and scenarios which do not exist in reality. Imagination is a valuable skill, enabling people to 'see' beyond their circumstances and to test out possible futures. Imagination can also be painful, particularly when someone has an 'overdeveloped' imagination and is relatively unable to control the forms it takes. 'It's just in your imagination' is a typical response to someone who complains, for example, that everyone is talking about him. Unfortunately it is not always easy or even possible for such a person to throw off the creations of his imagination. *Active imagination* is the Jungian-inspired process of 'dreaming with open eyes', allowing images from the unconscious to arise and unfold therapeutically.

imago originally a Jungian term for the subjectively generated image of others as linked with archetypes (e.g. a mother imago); also used in dialogical psychotherapy and some couple counselling.

immediacy literally, without mediation. Immediacy in counselling is considered to be the key skill of focusing attention on the HERE AND NOW relationship of counsellor and client with helpful timing, in order to challenge defensiveness and/or heighten awareness. Immediacy is characterised by congruent 'I' STATEMENTS (e.g. 'I'm feeling angry at what you've just said'). Immediacy is *not* the same as simply saying whatever comes into one's head, but a rapidly calculated disclosure of the counsellor's present experience in relation to the client. Immediacy helps to make concrete what is discussed in counselling, serves to model the behaviour of trusting one's own experience, and conveys the sense that the counselling relationship is also a real relationship. Immediacy is important in supervision and training situations as well as in counselling.

impasse an obstacle to progress. Impasses in counselling are very common, from the initial RESISTANCE of clients to the counselling process, through almost inevitable patches of misunderstanding and reluctance in the middle phase of counselling to an unwillingness to do homework, accept responsibility for progress and to end counselling. Impasses may stem from clients' fears about counselling and personal change, or from the counsellor's countertransference or lack of skill. Different counselling approaches deal with impasses in their own ways: for example, psychodynamic counsellors interpret them; person-centred counsellors attempt to understand them from within clients' frames of reference; gestalt counsellors attempt to have the client experience how she is creating and maintaining the impasse. Such obstacles are not necessarily undesirable, but can be learned from and, if overcome, can enhance the therapeutic alliance. *See* Leiper and Kent (2001).

implosion the experience of being confronted suddenly and dramatically with a situation that one dreads. Implosion therapy (a term often used synonymously with FLOODING) aims to arouse anxiety initially by preventing avoidance, continuing exposure to the feared object. The purpose is to extinguish conditioned anxiety. Implosion can be very shocking to the client and its use requires careful scrutiny.

implosive therapy a form of therapy promoted by Stampfl, from a behavioural context, which advocates intensive emotional (or anxiety-arousing) experience as a means of desensitising the client to his fears. Also called 'implosion therapy'.

impotence powerlessness; inability to be effective. Its technical meaning is the inability of a male to achieve or maintain penile erection for the purpose of sexual intercourse. Impotence is not the same as sterility or INFERTILITY. Impotence may be due to organic or psychological factors. Careful analysis of the precipitating factors involved, combined with a possible variety of counselling techniques, sex therapy, and couple counselling, for example, can significantly help men with a problem of psychologically based impotence. Impotence also refers to any personal difficulty in being effective.

impulsivity unpremeditated behaviour which is often chaotic, immature and antisocial. Impulsive behaviour is characterised by tension before the behaviour and relief afterwards. Examples are pyromania (starting fires) and kleptomania (shoplifting or other impulsive stealing). Sometimes called *impulse control disorder*, it is ultimately self-defeating: it may be very difficult to treat using counselling.

in vivo desensitisation a behavioural technique usually employed to reduce or eliminate phobias. The client is asked to specify exactly what produces his anxiety, and from that a hierarchy of anxiety-invoking items relating to the phobia is drawn up. The client is taught PROGRESSIVE RELAXATION before being exposed first to the least anxiety-invoking item, then the next, and so on. The client moves on to the next most anxiety-invoking item only when he has successfully overcome the last. The ultimate goal is the removal of the phobia. In vivo desensitisation differs from SYSTEMATIC DESENSITISATION in being conducted in actual situations rather than by imaginal exercises. Critics complain that such methods ignore intrapsychic factors; and that gradual exposure methods cognitively reinforce clients' belief that feared situations are really fearful.

incest sexual activity between members of the same family, which is illegal in our culture. The most common form of incest is between father and daughter, although all other permutations occur. Incest is a form of SEXUAL ABUSE: it is a betrayal of trust, an abuse of power and a severe trauma that usually causes lasting psychological effects into adulthood. The illegal, furtive and often violent nature of incest can be understood as indicating a generally dysfunctional family system. Some incest perpetrators have been incest victims themselves in the past but many avoid repeating the cycle. The term 'incestuous' is sometimes used metaphorically to refer to any relationship which is too close and exclusive to be healthy. *See* CONFLUENCE.

incest survivors those who have been past victims of incest. As adults they are likely to have experienced difficulties in development: incest interferes with the process of moving successfully from childhood to separate adulthood through adolescence. The possible effects of incest on the adult survivor are many, but can include eating disorders, sexual and relationship difficulties, and self-destructive behaviour.

incongruence the opposite of CONGRUENCE; behaviour which reveals discrepancies between what is felt and what is said or enacted; behaviour which is experienced as inauthentic. A high degree of incongruence in counselling, particularly on the part of the counsellor, bodes poorly for the outcome, since congruence is considered a core condition for effective counselling. Almost all clients begin counselling with some degree of incongruence.

indecision a state of uncertainty; wavering; confusion. Many people present for counselling who find it difficult to make an important life decision (e.g. whether to get married, to change jobs or to emigrate). Counselling aims to help people in this position to clarify their values and to air any factors which impede their ability to choose particular options. A serious and chronic state of indecision may accompany depression. Although counselling is not conceived of as a process of making decisions for the client, the counsellor is faced with making ongoing microdecisions regarding his counselling interventions.

independence freedom from dependence or reliance on others or on particular circumstances. Independence often has a connotation of toughness, rationality and self-sufficiency. Some people are temperamentally more 'independent' than others, and it should not be thought that independence is necessarily a goal of all counselling. AUTONOMY implies an ability to think and act for oneself, whereas independence implies almost a need (for some) to be separate from others. The ability to choose to be healthily dependent and independent at different times might be considered optimal. *Interdependence* is a state of mutual need and/or mutual benefit.

individual differences that part of psychology which studies the many ways in which people differ in personality, performance, and so on, from others. The uniqueness of the individual is paramount in counselling and individuals react differentially to life stresses or to different forms of therapeutic intervention. Many individual differences may be innate. Counsellors must always gauge to what extent their interventions, and their chosen theoretical model, will suit the individual needs and learning style of each client.

individual psychology the personality theory and system of counselling and psychotherapy originated by Alfred Adler. Adler's individual psychology was a development away from psychoanalysis and Freud's emphasis on childhood sexuality as causative. Adler placed greater emphasis on infantile experiences of power and powerlessness, on contributing to society, on optimism and the goal-orientation of human behaviour. It was Adler who created the terms INFERIORITY COMPLEX and SUPERIORITY COMPLEX. He also drew attention to the significance of one's position in the family constellation and one's typical LIFE STYLE or outlook. Individual psychology has been influential in child guidance work and modern Adlerian counselling is one of the few approaches to engage in family counselling. Individual psychologists use interpretation and encouragement, and make unashamed use of common sense. Some cognitive therapists credit Adler with being one of the forerunners of cognitive therapy.

individuation a Jungian concept denoting the need in individuals to become themselves fully and to differentiate themselves psychologically from others. While Jung acknowledged the importance of the collective within the individual, he asserted that individuation was essential to optimal personal development. Individuation is a process continuing throughout life, but it has a particular poignancy or importance in the second half of life when people struggle to make their mark on the world. During the intensive phase of individuation, some people may be at risk of developing hypomania, depression or other pathological problems. Individuation can be roughly equated with SELF-ACTUALISATION.

infant observation the practice, in psychoanalytic forms of training, of spending some time in intensive, structured observation of an infant (usually in relation to its mother), sometimes from before birth towards the end of the first year of life, in order to understand this most crucial stage of development and one's own reactions to the emotions aroused. Barely used in counselling training.

infantile amnesia the inability to remember events from early childhood. Perceived by some psychoanalytic observers as an unconscious defence, many psychologists however argue that memory mechanisms are simply not in place before the age of about 4 or 5.

infantile feelings all those feelings and impressions formed in childhood which are both interpretations of the world and which may survive as adult views and feelings. Some writers prefer to speak of infantile feelings generally, rather than, for example, 'infantile sexuality', because this latter term is often misunderstood to mean actual physical sexuality instead of an attitude of curiosity and exploration. Infantile feelings can also include irrational but formative interpretations of rivalry, mastery, death, and so on. The word 'infantile' is often used pejoratively of immature behaviour.

infantile sexuality psychoanalytic theory claiming that humans from the earliest months of life gain a kind of sexual satisfaction from the sensations of sucking, from defecation, observation, masturbation, etc. This view of psychosexual development, stemming from Freud, has been contested by many, and argued to be simply metaphorical by others.

inference the drawing of a conclusion from empirical evidence. I may reasonably infer, if someone smiles at me a lot, that she likes me; or, conversely, that if she ignores me, she does not like me. These inferences may not be accurate, but they are made on the basis of circumstances and my reading of those circumstances (according to my pattern of construing events, according to my culture, family, etc.). Cognitive therapists make much use of identifying with clients their everyday inferences, and teaching them that alternative inferences exist for the same events. *Inference chaining* is a therapeutic process of persistently showing clients that the way in which they make inferences, and then make inferences from those inferences, is open to examination and is used in REBT to identify underlying irrational beliefs. An example would be: 'and if she did ignore you, what would that mean. . . ?' 'and if she didn't like you, what would that mean. . .?' and so on, until the client's irrational belief is identified (e.g. 'if she didn't like me, that would mean that I would never find a female partner and that would be terrible').

inferiority complex an Adlerian concept explaining how the sense of powerlessness commonly experienced in infancy may in certain circumstances become pronounced in adulthood and form the basis of neurotic symptoms. Originally the term referred to a cluster of experiences which the person attempted to compensate for by, for example, pretending greater prowess than was actually warranted. The term is now often used synonymously (but incorrectly) with 'inferiority feeling' for people who display obvious signs of LOW SELF-ESTEEM.

infertility the inability to conceive or to father babies. Causes of infertility vary but can cause great distress and feelings of loss. Infertility counselling is a growing field which is confronted with many special ethical issues. Key areas for counselling exploration include the effect of infertility on the sexual relationship, in vitro fertilisation (IVF), including full information on the possibility of multiple births, the couple's experience of grief, loss and expectation and the future rights and needs of the child. Donors also may benefit from counselling. Much useful counselling can be done on issues of guilt, shame and feelings of failure related to infertility.

influencing skills verbal and paraverbal communication which is deliberately used to produce a desired effect in other people. Many counsellors, taking the lead from Carl Rogers and the concept of non-directiveness (*see* NON-DIRECTIVE), regard any attempt to influence clients as countertherapeutic because it undermines the client's own autonomous processes. However, it has been shown that Rogers and other non-directive counsellors exert influence in very subtle ways (for example by differential nodding and other paraverbal cues). Some counsellors (e.g. Ivey, Ivey and Simek-Downing, 1980) suggest that counselling is a 'process of interpersonal influence' and that therefore counsellors would do well to study how this process works in order better to utilise it for clients' benefit.

information-giving the imparting of facts. In certain settings, it is indeed *part* of the counsellor's task to impart information, or the counsellor may have the dual role of personal counselling and information-giving (for example, EAPs often offer legal, financial and other information as well as counselling). People working in MEDICAL SETTINGS often have to give information, for example on genetics, cancer, HIV and AIDS. In such cases, the sensitive imparting of information and enabling the client to explore the impact of that information involves a high level of COUNSELLING SKILLS. Counsellors can legitimately give information to clients on the nature of counselling, on research, on alternative treatments, and so on. It becomes *advice* if the choice of how to respond to the information is asserted by the helper.

informed consent a term from medical ethics referring to the right of clients to receive treatment only after giving their permission based on full information about its rationale and implications. Counsellors vary in the extent to which they offer (or approve of offering) detailed information about themselves, their training and methods and the likely course and length of counselling.

inhibition the suppression or prevention of one psychological function by another. The concept has roots in both the Freudian and behavioural traditions. The ego or superego may inhibit instinctual processes. The word is commonly used of conditions like shyness, as in 'I felt inhibited', which could be said to mean that a wish to be extraverted was inhibited by a temporary need for self-protectiveness. *See also* RECIPROCAL INHIBITION.

injunction a command or direction. The concept of injunctions is an important part of TRANSACTIONAL ANALYSIS theory, where injunctions are viewed as negative messages which may be internalised in childhood. At least 12 typical injunctions have been identified: don't be (don't exist); don't be you; don't be a child; don't grow up; don't make it; don't (don't do anything); don't be important; don't belong; don't be close; don't be well (don't be sane); don't think; don't feel. A *counterinjunction* is a compensatory message the child receives from her parents' Parent ego states, generally later in development than the injunctions (e.g. 'work hard' as a verbal command following the non-verbal injunction 'don't exist').

inner child that part of oneself that is still the child one was. Some take this to be purely metaphorical, others believe in the emotional reality of an inner child. 'Inner child work' is a common feature of working with child sexual abuse, where the adult client comes to take a protective role towards the child they were and, perhaps, emotionally still are until liberated by therapy.

inner child advocacy a therapeutic approach which makes taking the side of the child (in the adult) central. Based on the work of Horney, Bowlby and Alice Miller, this approach stresses the vulnerability of the child, the reality of childhood trauma, the need to relive trauma (typically through the processes of crying, expressing anger, remembering, synthesising and 'moving on'). People often develop an internal figure, or internal advocate, but also usually need an external advocate, or therapist/counsellor in order to complete the healing journey.

inner dialogue the continuous or sporadic SELF-TALK or subvocalisation of the client. People often find themselves having conversations between two or more 'parts' of themselves. Prosaically, this may represent a rational debate aimed at making everyday decisions. It can also represent the tensions felt by people between warring parts of themselves, or between SUBPERSONALITIES. Some counsellors, particularly gestaltists and transpersonal counsellors, make deliberate use of inner dialogue by externalising and working through it.

inner skills also known as 'inside skills', these are about awareness of one's own in-session experiencing, ability to be an impartial witness, awareness of others' perceptions of oneself, etc. and are complementary to the outer or outside skills of greeting, interacting, assessment, etc. The terminology and intention relates to the National Vocational Qualifications (NVQs) framework.

inner world the internal, subjective experience of people. The terms 'inner world' and 'inner child' are often used to refer to those deep, often subtle and emotional experiences which it is hard for others to know. Even empathy may not always be enough to grasp the very personal nuances of others' experiencing. Therapists like Mahrer (1996) attempt to enter the inner worlds of their clients by avoiding the typical therapist–client role relationship and by aiming to re-create in their own bodies and feelings the deep feelings experienced by the client.

insanity a state of extreme mental disorder; mental illness; madness. Historically the term had a clear meaning; it refers roughly to schizophrenia, manic-depressive psychosis and other florid or potentially violent forms of mental disorder. The MENTAL HEALTH lobby has in recent years strenuously objected to the stigmatising impact of such language. Someone may be considered to be 'insane' or to have a 'serious mental health problem' if she is out of touch with reality, is a danger to herself or others, and cannot manage her everyday affairs. A counter-argument put particularly by the latter-day anti-psychiatry movement is that the behaviour of those called 'insane' may be understood as those individuals' only possible response to an 'insane world'. For some, such semantic play with words may deny the severity of their disorder. Legally, people may seek recognition as having 'diminished responsibility' because of their mental state at the time of a crime. The British Mental Health Act 1983 requires stringent assessment of people deemed to be in need of statutory care and control because of mental distress. The term 'insane' is sometimes used colloquially of someone whose behaviour is wild or antisocial (e.g. 'insane killer'); also, people are sometimes said to be 'insanely jealous', meaning extremely jealous and beyond the reach of reason.

insight the experience of looking inside oneself, of understanding the consequences of one's actions and the connections between one's thoughts, feelings and behaviour, past, present and future. Sudden insight is often known as an 'aha' experience. Lack of insight characterises people suffering from disorders of affect, in that they cannot utilise reason to make helpful personal interpretations. (In psychiatric terms, lack of insight into serious mental disorder is often considered a major reason for involuntary admission to hospital.) Insightfulness is sometimes considered synonymous with psychological-mindedness (*see* PSYCHOLOGICAL). Insight implies that the client is an active participant in counselling, with counsellor interpretations being of little use if not timed to coincide with the client's readiness to own them. Psychodynamic counsellors use the 'triangle of insight' model, which links counsellor–client experiences with client–parent ('there and then') experiences, and with present figures in the client's life. Some models of counselling advocate the sufficiency of insight as a means of personal change, others argue that insight must follow catharsis, and still others suggest that insight must include an understanding by the client of his current means of perpetuating problems and a commitment to self-changing actions.

instant gratification having one's wishes met without delay. The expectation or demand that one should have what one wants without waiting and even without effort, is a characteristic of some people with immature personality traits. LOW FRUS-

TRATION TOLERANCE is a characteristic of such people, and it may derive from experiences of being 'spoilt' as a child (or indeed from earlier infantile experiences of feeding) together with an irrational belief that being frustrated is intolerable. *Deferred gratification* is often considered a sign of psychological maturity, in that the person knows that things often take time to materialise, but critics rightly point out that an over-readiness to wait for pleasure can be seen as being as 'pathological' as an inability to wait.

instinct an innate tendency to respond to events in a particular manner; a biological drive. In Freudian thought, basic instincts were considered to be the LIBIDO (life instinct) and the DEATH INSTINCT. (The term 'instinct' is sometimes used mistakenly for DRIVE.) Psychoanalytic thinking has modified this emphasis on instincts, which imply a deterministic view of human nature. Much counselling theory questions the concept of innate instincts, regarding people as having a great deal of potential access to and control of their behaviour. A counsellor's clinical instinct is similar to the idea of hunches (*see* HUNCH).

insurance professional indemnity against possibilities of having legal suits brought against oneself as a counsellor, supervisor or trainer. It is not usually mandatory for counsellors to take out such insurance cover; nor is there a significant history of claims against counsellors in the UK. However, counsellors are advised to secure such cover against possible charges of MALPRACTICE, including sexual abuse and other unethical behaviour, as well as physical accidents within the counsellor's place of work. Some employers require counsellors to take out such cover as a matter of course.

intake interview a first meeting between client and counsellor (or intermediary) designed to determine the nature of the client's problems and the suitability of counselling. In some settings it is standard practice for senior staff to interview all applicants for counselling; they may take a history of the client (*see* HISTORY TAKING), form a tentative diagnosis, allocate the client to a particular counsellor, or decide to refer the client to another service. Many counsellors practise no such intake procedure; most devote the first session to a consideration of the client's presenting problems and to a mutual decision as to whether to proceed with counselling. One disadvantage of an intake interview where the interviewer is not subsequently the counsellor is that the client will have to retell his story to another counsellor. Also known as ASSESSMENT interview (AI).

integration wholeness, making whole, relating to a holistic view. In personality theory, integration is the ideal of a consciously accepted co-existence of traits including the 'shadow' aspects. In the field of counselling and psychotherapy, integration or *integrationism* specifically refers to a movement which seeks to promote the theoretical convergence of diverse schools of counselling and therapy. Unlike eclectic counsellors (*see* ECLECTICISM), integrationists emphasise the need for conceptual unity. Critics of integrationism (e.g. Arnold Lazarus) argue that there is probably too much conflict between various models of counselling to integrate them realistically, and that theoretical integration can only come about after the dismantling of the diverse schools and the rigorous testing of clinical strategies as applied to a wide range of client problems. In spite of this, many training courses in integrative counselling and psychotherapy now exist, usually based on the study and practice of at least two distinct models or aspects of them. Different models of integrative counselling and therapy developed through the 1990s, as well as competing definitions of integration, including Garfield's (1995) term 'eclectic-integrative'. Compare with ECLECTICISM.

integrity an ethical attitude of forthrightness and honesty in conducting one's affairs; wholeness of the personality; reliability of the counsellor in working ethically.

integrity therapy a form of therapy devised by O.H. Mowrer which emphasised the role of integrity versus dishonest and sinful behaviour. Often conducted in groups in which moral character and behaviour is modelled.

intellectualisation a defence mechanism whereby the client seeks to think his way around problems and provide theoretical explanations for them instead of facing them squarely and experientially or experiencing the feelings associated with specific events. Some critics of cognitive therapy wrongly perceive it as encouraging intellectualisation: there is an important distinction between rationally confronting and solving problems, and avoiding painful issues by intellectual escapism.

intensive short-term dynamic psychotherapy a form of brief psychotherapy developed by Davanloo (1990) which aims to challenge resistance vigorously, evoking transference feelings, exploring past-present connections and directly accessing the unconscious. Derived from psychoanalytic theory, intensive short-

term dynamic psychotherapy (ISTDP) claims to achieve 'massive de-repression' (breaking of defences) in a short time. Critics complain of its aggressive nature.

intention will, purpose. Counselling is an intentional activity on the part of the counsellor, and even when she claims to be working entirely intuitively, the counsellor exhibits intentions in each of her interventions. Transcripts of actual sessions can be and have been analysed in order to determine what counsellors' therapeutic intentions are throughout the session. Counselling is thus viewed as a process of continuous, if rapid, decision-making.

intentionality the purposeful element in human activity. Existentialist approaches to counselling (*see* EXISTENTIAL COUNSELLING) suggest that the will to create personal meaning is a basic human attribute and that counselling works best by helping clients to own their unique view of life and the ability and necessity to strive intentionally towards realisation of personal visions. Such views emphasise the role of volition in personal change. *See* WILL.

interaction any behaviour between two or more people. Interactions include gross physical exchanges, embraces, mutual inspection, silences, etc. Certain styles of counselling are more obviously interactive than others, and some require higher levels of activity from either the client or the counsellor. Counsellors have different *interactive styles* and many experienced counsellors recognise the advantage of being able to vary their interactive style to meet clients' individual anticipations and/ or preferences.

intermittent therapy through the life cycle a model of brief counselling/therapy promoted by Cummings, recognising that life events periodically tax our coping resources and that the most appropriate form of psychological help may be very brief, focused therapy for the problem presenting at the particular time, with further therapy available when necessary. This is in contrast to the notion of therapy as a 'once-and-for-all', intensive experience, and regards the practitioner as resembling a general practitioner.

internal supervisor that part of a counsellor's awareness within (and between) sessions which monitors his own work. Particularly in psychodynamic counselling, this process may involve analysis of the client's unconscious attempts to 'supervise' (alert or correct) the counsellor. The internal supervisor (that is, the counsellor's self-supervision) complements his actual supervisor's input and is not a substitute for it. The internal supervisor is *not an internalisation of the actual supervisor. See* SUPERVISION. *See* Casement, 1985.

internalisation the exposure to, and act of thoroughly accepting, ideas, images, values, etc., as one's own. Children internalise a great deal of what parents model to and teach them. Internalisation may occur unconsciously or after conscious effort. The concept of internalisation is often used in psychoanalytic thought in the same way as INTROJECTION, and identification, meaning the taking in of aspects of an external figure into the inner world. Counsellors in training are said to have internalised counselling concepts when their understanding and practice of them becomes congruent.

interpersonal that which is between people. (Compare with INTRAPSYCHIC.) Much of what is understood as 'interpersonal skills' is synonymous with COUNSELLING SKILLS, although interpersonal skills training is often conducted within management development programmes and may have very different goals from those of counselling. Some commentators regard counselling as an 'interpersonal influence process' (*see* INFLUENCING SKILLS).

interpersonal process recall a training method based on the use of audiotapes and videotapes to enable close examination of covert processes of both the (role-played) client and the counsellor. This method (Kagan and Kagan, 1990) complements other kinds of counselling skills training. It is also used to facilitate counsellor and client awareness of covert processes in actual counselling sessions. The same method is used in process research.

interpersonal psychotherapy an approach to therapy that derives from H.S. Sullivan and others who stressed the role of interpersonal relationships in the formation of personal strengths and neuroses; this has been developed into the idea that present dysfunctional interpersonal behaviour is largely responsible for the perpetuation of psychological disturbance.

interpretation adducing meaning from events, stories, dreams, etc., and offering this meaning to the client. While any construing of events (by people in general or by counsellors specifically) may be called an interpretation, the term has clear psychoanalytic roots (where it originally meant 'explanation' and 'clarification'). Interpretation renders latent meaning conscious. At its simplest level, interpretation is a linking response (*see* LINKING STATEMENTS) aimed at suggesting to the client important connections between his various utterances. Tentative interpretations offer clients the opportunity of finding their own INSIGHTS. Interpretations may relate to TRANSFERENCE phenomena, to defence mechanisms, to clients' use of symbolism in dreams, and other narratives. Correct and well-timed interpretations often help the client to achieve greater awareness. The main criticism of the use of interpretation is that it can often assume that the counsellor has greater knowledge of the client than the client himself has, or that the counsellor's fund of (psychoanalytic) knowledge will always apply to every client. Cognitive therapists are more interested in how clients interpret and misinterpret events themselves than in therapist-formulated interpretations.

intervening variable a psychological concept which posits the idea that a COVERT process or factor may be at work between certain observable behaviours and environmental stimuli (i.e. that the behaviours cannot automatically be held to be the result of known stimuli). Variables are an important critical and research concept which challenge simplistic psychological explanations. Intervening variables between a client's last counselling session and his subsequent experience of elation might include, for example, his belief that the counsellor had praised him, his meeting an old friend immediately after the session, his being promoted at work, and so on.

intervention any action on the part of the counsellor during a counselling session. Even minimal verbal or paraverbal gestures are interventions, because they may be perceived as the signal of an intention on the part of the counsellor to make some impact on the client. However, interventions are more commonly understood to be instances of counsellor strategy, implying that each statement the counsellor makes is part of a working hypothesis, moving towards therapeutic goals.

interview formal meeting with another person. The term 'interview' is not commonly used by counsellors, having its roots more in the fields of personnel management, social work, research, etc. It is considered good practice for counsellor training courses to interview personally all candidates for training and current BACP course accreditation criteria stipulate that this should be done by two interviewers.

intimacy emotional closeness. Counselling by its very nature often involves an intimate relationship requiring high levels of TRUST. Approaches like person-centred and psychodynamic counselling may cultivate intimacy more than others. There are dangers in becoming too intimate (over-involved) in counselling: the client may become too dependent and sacrifice autonomy; she may use the counsellor as a substitute confidante instead of learning to be intimate with others; in extreme cases, emotional intimacy in counselling may lead to professionally unethical behaviour. Some clients need to learn how to relate intimately to others, and counselling may be a starting point in this process. Erikson considered intimacy (versus isolation) to be an indicator of maturity. In person-centred counselling the establishing of intimacy is an important indicator of therapeutic progress.

intrapsychic events which occur primarily in a person's mind are said to be 'intrapsychic'. The term is in most cases synonymous with 'psychological' when used to refer to private, unobservable events. 'Intrapsychic conflict' is conflict between one part of the mind and another. The concept of intrapsychic events is used mainly by psychodynamic counsellors.

intrapsychic calendar memory and expectation of events, their meanings and recurrences, such as anniversaries of deaths of loved ones and fantasies (sometimes realities) of coincidental events.

intrauterine experience whatever may be experienced by the embryo or fetus within the womb. Some theorists claim that physical and emotional shocks, maternal depression and various other traumatic experiences (including BIRTH TRAUMA) are felt by the fetus and have lasting, damaging effects. Clients who exhibit great distress but who are unable to understand or describe it in concrete terms may be in touch with some deeply registered trauma stemming from intrauterine experience. Some clients may spontaneously adopt a fetal position or other postures relating to prebirth experience. Some accounts of intrauterine trauma have apparently been corroborated by evidence from the mother. There are claims that trauma can be experienced as far back as implantation. There are also counter-claims to the effect that all such hypotheses are unfounded, unprovable, fanciful and unhelpful.

introjection the process of taking representations of others, or parts of others, into one's inner world. Derived from psychoanalytic theory, introjection is specifically concerned with the way in which people absorb aspects of their parents' attitudes and values as *introjects*. Introjection forms the basis of the SUPEREGO but is also an important part of mourning, leading to the internalising of the lost person within the inner world of the bereaved person.

introvert a personality type characterised by introspection, withdrawal, melancholia, sensation and intuition. Originally a Jungian term, introversion was considered an 'inward-turning of libido' or heightened interest in internal events to the detriment of external reality. The terms *introversion* and EXTRAVERSION are used in psychological assessment (as refined by Hans Eysenck) and as general descriptions but are seldom used as diagnostic categories by counsellors or therapists *see* PSYCHOLOGICAL TYPE.

intuition a primary psychological function which serves as a subtle means of perception and/or judgement of circumstances and people; an 'instinctive apprehension' (Jung). Knowledge is considered intuitive when it is arrived at with no immediately observable evidence or thought process, and therefore resembles a psychic process. Jung considered intuition 'beyond reason' and many counsellors claim to have strong feelings about and insight into their clients based on intuition more than on clinical wisdom or counselling skills. It is probable that much 'intuition' is in reality a form of rapid SUBLIMINAL PERCEPTION and deduction, that can be analysed into ordinary thought processes, for example with the aid of supervised audiotapes. However, it seems likely that many counsellors do in fact work more intuitively than others (that is, less technically). All counsellors necessarily use intuition in deciding the timing of their interventions, and so need to study and develop it. So-called 'psychic counsellors' explain their work as being based largely on intuitive access to clients' inner worlds. Intuition has become the predominant mode of working in TRANSPERSONAL THERAPY. For Lomas (1993) it is the basis of all successful therapy.

invalidation a denial of the uniqueness, humanity or certain aspects of others' experience. Invalidation is the opposite of validation – the prizing of others. Many clients have had their experience invalidated by parents, teachers and others, as children, and continue to carry a sense of worthlessness. Counsellors need to be especially vigilant that they do not inadvertently worsen such invalidation by failing to respond to clients with the CORE CONDITIONS.

investigative counselling that focuses on a client's narrative, particularly in an attempt to piece together past events which may explain current problems, is said to be investigative. Certain clients, unaccustomed to thinking psychologically, gain understanding and relief simply from tracing the antecedents of their present problems.

investment emotional involvement. People are considered to have an investment in counselling and personal change when they are prepared to immerse themselves in the challenge of counselling and perhaps even (temporarily) to make sacrifices in other areas of life in order to reap the benefits of counselling. (It is also said that clients may have an investment in remaining the same.) Some counsellors (or, more particularly, some psychotherapists) argue that clients will not make significant progress unless they invest wholeheartedly in therapy. The counter-argument is that the greater the investment in counselling, the more disinclined will the client be to maintain an open-ended criticism of the process. This is also the case for counselling and psychotherapy trainees and practitioners who, having invested a great deal of their own time and money in their professional status, are unlikely to keep a radically critical eye on it. *See also* CATHEXIS.

irrationality a condition of unreason; an approach to life marked by FAULTY INFORMATION PROCESSING; being against or beyond reason. According to REBT beliefs that are dogmatic, illogical, inconsistent with reality and that lead to poor emotional and behavioural results are irrational. While Jung commended the positive value of irrationality in the sense of going beyond reason (into psychic exploration, for example), the cognitive therapists have focused attention on irrationality as a major contributor to psychological disturbance. It is argued that acceptance of the world as a less than ideal, intrinsically frustrating place, is rational, and that refusal to accept this and its implications for individuals leads to irrational beliefs and demands which serve only to exacerbate personal misery. *See* RATIONAL EMOTIVE BEHAVIOUR THERAPY.

isolation a state of alienation, removal from contact with others, psychological withdrawal. Deliberate isolation is a means of avoiding human contact because previous interpersonal experience has been painful. People also become isolated through bereavement, poverty, poor social skills, and so on. Psychoanalytically, isolation is a DEFENCE MECHANISM whereby a particularly painful experience is dissociated from meaningful affect and memory.

jargon the name sometimes given pejoratively to technical language used thoughtlessly and unhelpfully. Specialist counselling terms used between colleagues are usually readily understood by these colleagues, but can mystify or alienate clients. Jargon can also represent language which gains currency in certain subcultures of the counselling world (e.g. 'I hear what you're saying'; 'I gave him a stroke') but may sound like an insincere cliché to the uninitiated. *See* FRAME OF REFERENCE.

jealousy possessiveness; insecurity regarding loved objects. The most common form of jealousy is the attitude of anxious possessiveness exhibited by someone towards a romantic or sexual partner. People experiencing pathological (morbid) jealousy often become hypervigilant in relation to their partners, and not infrequently fantasise betrayals. Jealousy is a characteristic of some intense, symbiotic relationships (*see* SYMBIOSIS) and has, some argue, roots in infantile experiences, including sibling rivalry and competition for affection. It is a source of conflict between partners in committed relationships and can be alleviated within couple or individual coun-

selling. It is distinguished from ENVY (which requires only two parties) in that it involves at least three people.

Johari window a matrix, used in training, depicting the quadrants of public arena; blind spot; façade or hidden arena; and unknown arena. The Johari window is so-called because it is named after two psychologists, Joe (Luft) and Harry (Ingram).

jokes *see* HUMOUR IN COUNSELLING.

journal keeping the recording of observations of personal and professional growth by the trainee counsellor. Most counsellor trainees are required to keep a log of their personal experiences and professional observations as part of the training process. Most courses respect the privacy of such journals, but may ask for a separate 'professional log' for assessment purposes. Generally, written self-monitoring by clients is referred to as diary keeping but may also be referred to as journal keeping. The *intensive journal process* (Progoff, 1975) is a Jungian-based aid to personal and spiritual growth.

journey a commonly used metaphor in counselling training, whereby the trainee (or trained counsellor) sees himself or herself as in perpetual movement or on a quest for greater self-awareness. The term echoes the sentiment of 'to travel hopefully is a better thing than to arrive' (Robert Louis Stevenson). *See also* CONTINUING PROFESSIONAL DEVELOPMENT.

joy pleasure or elation. Joy can refer to the simple pleasure of absorption in work, recreation or relationships, or to the extreme positive passions engendered by, for example, sexual or religious ecstasy (*see* PEAK EXPERIENCES). Humanistic counselling often aims at, or produces incidentally, experiences of joy (Schutz, 1989). Since clients largely present for counselling in distress or with unhappy preoccupations, the potential for joy is easily overlooked. However, sensitive, open-minded counsellors will be aware of emotional nuances including potentials for joy.

judgementalism the consigning of clients to moral categories; an over-subjective attitude towards others. Counsellors are required to accept clients as unique individuals as a minimal condition for good counselling. They may note instances of client behaviours and attitudes of which they do not approve (e.g. procrastination, timidity, violence) but generally refrain from voicing such observations disapprovingly. Counsellor judgementalism undermines the trust that it is necessary for clients to feel in order to disclose their feelings and engage in risk-taking. Counsellors who are aware of often feeling judgemental towards clients are advised to monitor and work on such tendencies in supervision and in their own counselling. Judgementalism is not identical with instances of rational distaste for some client behaviours; nor is it the same as *clinical judgement*, which is the process of making diagnoses, formulating hypotheses, deciding on strategies, referrals, and so on. *See also* GENUINENESS.

Jungian refers to the ANALYTICAL PSYCHOLOGY of Carl Jung and to all theories and practices claiming an allegiance to Jung. Post-Jungian analytical psychology has developed into the classical, developmental and archetypal schools.

Karpman triangle otherwise known as the 'drama triangle' of transactional analysis. Psychological GAMES are characterised by people adopting the roles of Persecutor, Rescuer and Victim. The Persecutor denigrates and belittles others; the Rescuer sees others as inadequate and in need of help; the Victim regards himself as 'not-OK' and attracts the punishment or patronisation of the other roles. All these roles are drawn from past scripts, they are inauthentic and they discount self or others (*see* DISCOUNTING). People can switch dramatically between these three roles, which have been illustrated by reference to fairy tales (e.g. the Pied Piper).

Kleinian applying to the theory and practice of psychoanalysis as conceived or modified by Melanie Klein. With a special interest in child development and psychotherapy, Klein came to attribute great significance to developments in the early weeks and months of life. This led her to depart from (or, in the Kleinian view, develop) classical Freudian doctrine. She proposed two new aspects of development, the DEPRESSIVE POSITION and the PARANOID–SCHIZOID POSITION. She attached importance to PROJECTIVE IDENTIFICATION. Klein also drew attention to the baby's relation to the breast and to the action of phantasy. She made connections between guilt and reparation, and envy and gratitude. Her work contributed towards a better understanding of psychotic processes. Techniques associated with Kleinian therapy include interpretation of 'acting-in' and of destructiveness, and use of 'part-object' language and identification. *See* Bott Spillius (1988).

lability of mood psychiatric term referring to a state in which people experience fast-changing emotions or mood swings.

laddering a technique used in personal construct counselling (*see* PERSONAL CONSTRUCT PSYCHOLOGY) which requires the client to explore aspects of his self-image by answering a series of questions about constructs he himself has created. The client may be asked to consider a particular bipolar construct of himself (e.g. industrious versus lazy); he will then be asked *why* it is better to be described by one pole rather than by the other. He will then be further questioned on his reply, and each reply will be further questioned with the ultimate aim of arriving at superordinate constructs (or those fundamental and hard-to-shake beliefs that people have about themselves, other people and the world). Compare with PYRAMIDING.

latency a psychoanalytic concept describing the developmental period between childhood and adolescence. In this period there is some lessening of sexual interest. During the latency period children especially develop their cognitive and social skills and prepare for the tasks of adulthood.

latent content refers to that part of the client's material which has not yet been made conscious. An example is that by dream interpretation the MANIFEST CONTENT is used to uncover latent meaning.

latent homosexuality the Freudian concept of submissive behaviour by one person towards another of the same sex, echoing, for example, the boy's anxious fear of the father. Latent homosexuality has come to mean popularly the idea that heterosexuals have within them a homosexual potential.

laughter the involuntary expression of amusement, fun, hilarity. Laughter has many varieties in everyday human experience but is probably not a frequent behaviour within counselling or therapy sessions. *Congruent laughter* is a sign of good mental health. *Gallows laughter*, so called in transactional analysis, is unhealthy, defensive laughter at something which is actually distressing. Some forms of counselling may deliberately focus on and exaggerate laughter within some sessions as a means to greater access to feelings generally (e.g. EXPERIENTIAL PSYCHOTHERAPY, RE-EVALUATION COUNSELLING). *See* HUMOUR IN COUNSELLING.

learning difficulties developmental delays in cognitive functioning remaining relatively stable throughout life, sometimes associated with different syndromes, e.g. Down's syndrome. People with mild learning difficulties may function relatively independently and may self-refer for counselling without necessarily having sufficient insight to benefit. Sometimes known as 'learning disability'.

learning theory any systematic explanation of how human beings learn, but specifically it refers to the concepts underlying behaviourism and behaviour therapy. *Learning* implies a new response to stimuli, and may be adaptive or not. CLASSICAL CONDITIONING, OPERANT CONDITIONING and MODELLING are examples of learning and of the way an understanding of its processes can be utilised therapeutically. Learning theory suggests that because behaviour can be learned, it can also be unlearned by identifying precisely any problematic behaviour and the circumstances in which it arises, and applying relevant therapy. *Social learning theory* refers to certain developments of learning theory by Rotter and in particular Bandura (*see* Bandura, 1977). Key concepts include observational learning, 'self-efficacy' beliefs and other cognitive factors. Learning theory challenges the assumptions of depth psychology by arguing that many of our maladaptive habits are learned by imitation and association, and that specific de-conditioning rather than putative depth analysis is required to change them. The terms 'learning' and 'learnings' are often used by Rogers to refer to personal growth processes resulting from person-centred counselling and encounter groups.

legal issues any part of the law which impinges on the practice of counselling. Clear legal boundaries for counsellors in the UK are under-developed compared with those in many parts of the US. It is not at present (2004) illegal for anyone to profess to be a counsellor or psychotherapist, regardless of training. Anyone offering counselling, however, is vulnerable to law suits or professional complaints procedures regarding misrepresentation, malpractice, breach of confidentiality and breach of data protection legislation. Counsellors may in exceptional cases (e.g. child abuse and serious violence) be subpoenaed to appear in court. Few, if any, counsellors enter into legally binding contracts with clients. Counsellors are advised, however, to provide professional indemnity for their work (*see* INSURANCE). *See* Jenkins (1997).

lesbianism the sexual attraction of women for each other and the behaviour accompanying it (*see* GAY AND LESBIAN AFFIRMATIVE THERAPY, GAY ISSUES, HOMOSEXUALITY). Some women who have espoused radical (political) feminism have argued that lesbianism is a necessary move away from male interference in women's lives and, more specifically, a justified avoidance of sexual penetration (violence) by men.

levels of consciousness *see* CONSCIOUSNESS.

leverage a position from which it is possible to effect change. While substantial leverage may not be available to the counsellor in the earliest phase of counselling, Egan (2002) views the search for leverage as a crucial aspect of the counselling process. It is usually necessary for a certain amount of information to surface, and trust to build, before the counsellor can formulate a hypothesis and begin to put into practice a strategy. Crisis management, problem identification and prioritising can provide leverage for further change.

libido literally 'wish' or 'desire', this term has the original Freudian meaning of sexual energy and drive. In later usage, libido came to mean not only id-derived sexual energy, but also the function of the ego, which is synonymous with life energy. Jung used the term to mean psychological 'intensities or values'.

life events what happens to people in their lives that may be of special significance; life events may be expected aspects of the life cycle (e.g. becoming a parent) or unexpected (e.g. accidents). Particularly traumatic life events may tax people's coping resources much more than everyday frustrations. Those working in stress management recognise that clusters of stressful events within a short period can lead to a dangerous overload of pressure. Significant life events can occur during the course of counselling independently of the client's goals for herself (e.g. bereavement, illness, redundancy, promotion at work, etc.). While some counsellors may regard all life events as invariably meaningful, non-accidental manifestations of clients' inner dynamics, others believe that everyday life and significant life events are often beyond personal control and often effect much greater change (positive or negative) than counselling or therapy ever could.

life skills all those skills pertinent to everyday functioning and survival. Some counsellors, coaches and mentors (e.g. Nelson-Jones) have concentrated on identifying lifeskills deficits and explicitly teaching them to clients. These include how to make friends, perform well in interviews, etc. *See* SOCIAL SKILLS TRAINING.

life style an Adlerian concept referring to the sum total of a person's constructions about her life from infancy to adulthood. Also referred to as 'style of life', it embraces the person's view of herself and of the world. The life style includes the ways, both healthy and maladaptive, in which the individual develops in order to lead a satisfactory life. Adlerian counsellors conduct life-style investigations designed to trace the development of clients' life styles from their family constellation, relationships with siblings, early memories, parental role models, etc. Clients may also be asked for their favourite stories and heroes as a means of helping them gain insight into how they have developed their current strengths and weaknesses. The term 'lifestyle' also refers generally to the way in which clients live their lives, including their nutritional, occupational, recreational, relationship habits and circumstances.

linking statements observations voiced by the counsellor which make a connection between things expressed by the client at different times in counselling. Clients sometimes report their stories as meaningless or confusing narratives, and one of the counsellor's tasks is to remember statements, note significant themes, and reflect these back to clients for their consideration. INTERPRETATIONS are a kind of linking statement. The terms 'linking response' and 'bridging statement' are sometimes used. *See also* AFFECTIVE BRIDGE.

listening attending to what another says. Listening is the most basic activity in counselling, because the vast majority of clients come to talk about their concerns and often regard the counsellor as one of the few people, sometimes the only person, who is prepared to listen fully to them.

Counselling is often distinguished from everyday conversation by the fact that counsellors are trained to suspend their own internal preoccupations and conversational impulses. There are many levels of listening and hearing: non-selective listening means that the counsellor pays (or attempts to pay) equal attention to all the client says. Counsellors aim to listen to *what* clients say as well as to *how* they say it; they may listen *for* certain recurring themes and they may also 'listen to' what clients do *not* say. *Active listening* denotes a special alertness in the counsellor, coupled with the practices of PARAPHRASING, CLARIFYING, etc., which confirm for clients that they are being closely listened to. *Credulous listening* is an attitude of belief in what the client is saying. 'Listening with the third ear' (Reik) refers to a sensitivity to the possible deeper meanings of what clients say. 'Listening with the fourth ear' (Seidenberg) is a phrase that has been used to refer to the counsellor's sensitivity to the social context from which each client speaks (*see* SOCIAL CONTEXTS OF COUNSELLING). Levin (1989) argues that listening is, or can be, a radically new, non-patriarchal way of relating to others, and particularly to those who are oppressed or in pain. 'Listening' therefore has a particular poignancy for counsellors and clients with hearing disabilities, whose listening may be done more by observation, lip-reading, intuition, touch, sign language, and so on.

locus of control the position from which perceptions, ideas, values and decisions are formed. An internal locus of control refers to control from within the self, and the sense of mastery or ability that accompanies it. An external locus of control is characterised by the belief that 'things happen' to oneself and that there is little chance of affecting one's destiny.

locus of evaluation that to which people refer in order to make judgements about themselves, others and the world. An external locus of evaluation is characterised by people introjecting the values of parents and significant others, and apparently having little trust in their own ORGANISMIC VALUING PROCESS. Clients often begin counselling from an external locus of evaluation; as they progress, they often achieve a greater trust in their own decision-making processes (in their own GUT FEELING). The locus of evaluation is a ROGERIAN concept and therefore of particular importance in person-centred counselling.

logotherapy a form of existential therapy founded by Frankl (1971), concerned with personal responsibility, spiritual realities, and the meaning of life, love and work. Logotherapy addresses 'existential neurosis' ('despair over the meaning of life') and aims to provide both a specific clinical practice and a general 'medical ministry'. Frankl developed the technique of PARADOXICAL INTENTION for which he claimed extensive success. He also argues that God is for many people 'unconscious'.

loneliness the subjective feeling of being isolated from others. People may lead lives involving relatively little contact with others, and even spend much time alone, yet do not feel lonely. Conversely, some people have many friends or acquaintances, and yet feel lonely. Some forms of loneliness are a result of either pathological avoidance of people or of social skill deficits. Some people, however, due to life circumstances, are peculiarly vulnerable to loneliness (e.g. the bereaved, homeless and elderly people). Many disadvantaged and lonely people turn to counsellors, particularly in voluntary agency settings, hoping for companionship, and often treat the counselling session as an opportunity for longed-for social contact. BEFRIENDING is more appropriate for such people, although counsellors can sometimes help them through assertiveness training, and social skills training generally, to find ways out of their loneliness. Loneliness is often associated with DEPRESSION and a higher risk of suicide, and counsellors need to be aware of these possibilities.

loose construing one of the dimensions of Kelly's (1955) personal construct theory, characterised by a person's tendency to think and predict flexibly and openly. Clients who are problematically inclined towards TIGHT CONSTRUING (that is, whose predictions about their lives are invariable) are appropriately encouraged in personal construct therapy by relaxation, dream exploration, counsellor warmth and acceptance, to experiment with new, loose constructs. PCP counsellors aim to help clients progress within a creative cycle which includes both loose and tight construing.

loss the experience of (permanent or temporary) separation from loved or meaningful objects and people. Bowlby (1973) and others have suggested that ATTACHMENT is a fundamental need of babies and infants but is inevitably accompanied by experiences of separation, which form the basis of an attitude to all subsequent losses. Loss is a central concept in psychodynamic counselling: all bereavements are losses and even the temporary absences of the counsellor (e.g. through sickness or holiday) are deemed to arouse feelings associated with previous losses. The ending of counselling is itself viewed as a loss. Orientations such as REBT regard the client as far more robust and the issue of loss is not assumed to be important unless raised by the client. Also, in SOCIAL THERAPY (*see* Newman, 1991) linguistic and cultural assumptions about loss are questioned.

love affection, care, solicitude, warmth, desire. Love is probably one of the most potent, provocative and complex words in the English language. Its meanings are diverse and at times contradictory. Some counsellors consider their work to be motivated and characterised by love: this is particularly true of person-centred counsellors, by whom love is understood as a deep non-possessive concern for fellow human beings. Often such love has religious or spiritual underpinnings. The Christian concept of *agape* stresses a selfless concern for others. Love has long been understood as erotic love, or a sexual desire for others, which can include a concern for their welfare but also risks using others for one's own pleasure. Christianity, indeed, has been torn between the legitimacy of erotic enjoyment and its suppression. Most counselling theorists support the view that babies and infants have a need for love, although exactly what constitutes such love and how long it should last are questions that are debated. Many counsellors would assert that it is a human need to give and receive love, but this is disputed by REBT philosophy on the grounds that belief in a dire need for love is irrational and likely to lead to emotional disturbance. Humanistic psychologists like Maslow assert that an ability to love others, work and the environment is the pinnacle of human mental health.

low frustration tolerance (LFT) an intolerance towards frustration or obstacles to realisation of one's wishes, based on the idea that one cannot bear or tolerate such frustrations. The recognition and acceptance that we cannot always readily get what we want is considered by many counsellors to be a mark of maturity. Cognitive therapists focus particularly on the tendency of clients to refuse to accept such realities. REBT, which views low frustration tolerance as a form of DISCOMFORT ANXIETY, favours implosive or confrontational methods of teaching clients that they can in fact tolerate much more frustration than they suppose. *See* INSTANT GRATIFICATION.

low mood term often used as an alternative to DEPRESSION.

low self-esteem having a poor opinion of oneself; regarding oneself and one's attributes as worthless. Low self-esteem is a very common problem and often exacerbated by the cultural transmission (by parents) of the idea that it is wrong to think highly of oneself. It is also a feature of DEPRESSION. While many counsellors seek to analyse the roots of low self-esteem, or to offer a CORRECTIVE EMOTIONAL EXPERIENCE, others (particularly REBT practitioners) consider it counter-therapeutic to dwell on the activity of self-rating at all. In other words, both low and high self-esteem are seen as forms of global self-rating (*see* GLOBAL STATEMENTS) which inevitably leads to emotional disturbance or social maladaptation.

machismo a way of being that is based on a need to be perceived as invariably strong, powerful, independent and right. Men in general, certain men in particular, and men in certain cultures are often criticised for such an attitude, which denies vulnerability and respect for feelings. The word *macho* (the adjective from machismo) is more commonly used.

madness *see* INSANITY, MENTAL ILLNESS.

magical thinking the belief that people or events will automatically act or react according to one's wishes and preferences. Magical thinking is primarily associated with the early developmental stages in children but can also be observed in adults. It is sometimes expected that counsellors will provide a 'magical' cure.

magnification the cognitive error of exaggerating the personal significance and stressfulness of challenging events; blowing things out of all proportion in one's mind. In the field of alcoholism counselling, 'magnification' often has the reverse meaning of clients exaggerating the benefits and pleasures of drinking, their capacity to drink, etc.

maintenance the upkeep of therapeutic progress. If gains made in counselling are to be more than transient, it is good practice to assist clients in anticipating RELAPSE and implementing strategies for consistent progress. In reality counselling usually takes a non-linear course or follows a cycle such as Prochaska and DiClemente's (1984) STAGES OF CHANGE.

maladaptive behaviour that is self-defeating, which fails to serve the interests of the person. All models of counselling have a concept of maladaptiveness (*see* DYSFUNCTION). *See also* ADAPTIVE.

malpractice reprehensible actions or omissions on the part of a counsellor, considered serious enough by a client or colleague to lead to disciplinary and/or legal judgement. Malpractice usually refers to detected breaches in professional practice, and the most common examples are violation of confidentiality and sexual contact between client and counsellor. Malpractice suits are as yet rare in the UK, but are a source of concern in the US. *See* LEGAL ISSUES.

management of counselling the organisational structuring of a counselling service, or the way in which individual counsellors organise their caseloads and their clinical work. The smooth administration of counselling is an important part of the helping process. It can offer an element of CONTAIN-MENT for clients and also incorporates necessary elements of research, publicity, counsellor support and overall forward planning. 'Managed care' is an American term not readily used in the UK. *See* Lago and Kitchin (1998).

managerial supervision that form of supervision or direction provided generally by managers for staff. Managerial supervision differs from clinical supervision in having a broader remit and greater emphasis on performance, assessment and accountability. In some organisations the clinical and managerial supervisor is one and the same person; where this is so, it is vital that the supervisor and supervisee clarify BOUNDARIES. It is recommended by the BACP that as far as possible managerial and clinical supervision be provided by different people, and some counselling and other helping agencies provide funds for an external (clinical) supervisor.

mania irrational and dysfunctional elation, signifying a severe pathological state, in psychiatry. The term is rarely used separately from MANIC DEPRESSION, although it survives, for example, in terms such as *pyromania* (compulsive fire-setting). Historically the term *maniac* has referred to someone who is insane, and it is used popularly now to refer to someone who is dangerously psychopathic, a severe form of personality disorder (*see* PSYCHOPATH).

manic defence this can refer to any client's flight from painful reality and is characterised by denial, omnipotence and avoidant hyperactivity.

manic depression a bipolar emotional disturbance characterised by changes of mood from DEPRESSION to elation. Manic depression can be, but is not necessarily, cyclical, and sufferers may also experience periods of stable emotional adjustment. Mood changes may be extreme and involve irritability, impulsivity, incoherence, sleeplessness, despair and lethargy. Manic depression is a serious mental health problem (sometimes called *manic depressive psychosis*) and is frequently treated by medication (usually lithium carbonate). Counselling is unlikely to have a major impact on manic depression but can help clients to manage and understand their illness. Now also known commonly as bipolar disorder.

manifest content what the client presents in counselling, as opposed to LATENT CONTENT. Manifest content implies, also, that what the client speaks about is the 'tip of the iceberg' or a representation of unconscious problems. The manifest content of a dream is the dream as it is remembered and processed upon waking, as distinct from the latent content (thought to be the actual content of the dream).

manipulation the activity of covertly eliciting desired responses in others. While everyone manipulates their environment, pathological or self-defeating manipulation contains an element of inauthenticity and distasteful deceit. Some people learn early in life a necessity for and skill in using manipulation, and drug addicts, for example, are often adept at consciously or unconsciously manipulating the sympathy and rescuing behaviour of others. Some counsellors, however, strongly object to this concept's judgemental flavour.

marital counselling counselling for people who are married. Because of widespread changes in social groupings, the broader and more inclusive term COUPLE

133

COUNSELLING is favoured by many agencies, and 'relationship counselling' is also used. The term 'marriage guidance' is now less widely used.

masculine identity the self-concept of a man which confirms him as firmly rooted in his GENDER role. Such concepts have been challenged and modified by feminism, men's groups and changing social conditions generally, and many men experience confusion about their identity. There is a men's movement in the US and elsewhere which attends to such issues.

masochism the enjoyment of pain or humiliation of oneself. Masochism is both a loose concept referring to any kind and degree of the seeking out and enjoyment of pain, and also refers specifically to sexual masochism. The most common form of sexual masochism is being beaten, but some people practise elaborate forms of sexual violence and humiliation. Analysis of this attitude suggests that it often stems from unhealthy handling or sexual abuse in infancy. Masochism is frequently coupled with SADISM, and *sado-masochism* can mean that the same person enjoys alternately inflicting and suffering pain.

material all that the client brings for discussion in counselling; all the counsellor has to work with. The term can be used of presenting concerns only but is more often used of the totality of the client's content and feeling at conscious and unconscious levels. Supervision often helps to identify how the client's material differs from the counsellor's.

maternal deprivation a concept used by psychologists when studying the effects on infants of receiving less than adequate attention and nourishment from mothers. It is a controversial and much-debated topic. At one extreme it has been argued that even the most minor absences and inadequacies of the mother can adversely affect the development of infants in the short and long term. (It is implicit that no one can substitute for the mother.) The opposing view is that infants are robust and will flourish given GOOD ENOUGH care by any good enough caregivers.

maternal reverie a psychoanalytic concept referring both to the infant's experience of the security and enjoyment of the mother's presence and to the parallel experience of patients (or analysands) with their analysts. It is notable that some clients are stimulated by the very presence and care of the counsellor to enter into a dreamlike state.

meaning definition, symbolisation, value. The perception of events is given meaning by the individual according to inner assumptions, both conscious and unconscious. The experience of meaninglessness characterises certain forms of depression but in a milder form meaninglessness and the search for meaning is a common experience. Loss of personal meaning is often associated with identity crises, bereavements and perceived failure to develop in line with one's peers. Janov (1975) aligns loss of meaning with loss of affect and therefore views the restoration of the ability to experience strong feelings as remedying meaninglessness. EXISTENTIAL counsellors place great emphasis on the need for personal meaning, and seek to facilitate clients in discovering and creating their own meaning in their 'Dasein' or being-in-the-world. Most people derive meaning from relationships, work and ideologies, and therefore people who have poor, few or no relationships or occupation often experience life as having little meaning. The relative decline in religious affiliation in our age probably contributes to a common experience of lack of meaning in life. Many counselling theories, but especially the psychodynamic, hold that every act, thought and feeling has a particular individual meaning and that all acts are purposeful. *See* LOGOTHERAPY.

mediating goals client objectives which enable progress towards further, and often more ambitious, objectives. It is often necessary to help clients construct a series of GOALS which will take them realistically towards their major goal or goals. This is particularly the case where an ultimate goal is hard to attain or initially overwhelming. Working progressively from easier to harder goals is considered particularly useful with depressed clients.

mediation see CONCILIATION COUNSELLING.

medical model pejoratively, that view of personal functioning and change in which people are portrayed as somewhat mechanistic, as passive recipients (patients) of expert attention, biomedical diagnosis and (often chemical) treatment. However, more collaborative and less deterministic medical procedures exist. Most counselling is founded on concepts of client AUTONOMY and the internal LOCUS OF CONTROL, and is thus at odds with the passive, acted-upon position of the client in the medical model. Many counsellors prefer an egalitarian relationship with clients and eschew the role of expert. However, some of the more behavioural and psychoanalytic approaches are oriented towards the medical model, and there is evidence that some clients prefer a counsellor in whom they can invest a high degree of professional authority.

medical settings, counselling in the formal and informal use of counselling and counselling skills in hospitals, clinics, GPs' surgeries and health centres. 'Counselling' in this context is used in several different ways. Its use as a synonym for advice-giving is falling into disrepute. It is used as a generic term, or alternatively to refer to formal counselling provided by appropriately trained and supervised counsellors who may be doctors but are more likely to be nurses, psychologists, social workers or specially appointed staff. Such counselling is often involved with seeking valid consent for major decisions (e.g. those relating to HIV/AIDS, infertility, genetics and abortion; or terminal care). The more formal use of 'counselling' distinguishes this activity from the more widespread use of counselling skills, which are viewed as being helpful to anyone who has contact with patients.

medication the therapeutic use of prescribed drugs; the prescription of drugs in an attempt to make therapeutic impact; to tranquillise or stimulate temporarily or to modify the effects of other drugs. Medication which is specifically designed to reduce psychological distress includes antidepressants (*see* ANTIDEPRESSANT MEDICATION) and major and minor TRANQUILLISERS used in psychosis and hypomania. Such medication can only be prescribed in the UK by medically qualified practitioners. The use of such medication can be problematic. Psychiatrists and GPs are often criticised for too freely prescribing addictive and/or relatively unproven drugs, for

135

failing to advise patients on the side effects of drugs and for failing to explore alternatives like counselling. Antipsychotic drugs have improved the everyday quality of life of many people diagnosed as schizophrenic (*see* SCHIZOPHRENIA) but have also been used historically as a 'chemical cosh' to make hospitalised people easier to manage. Counsellors are advised to consider in certain cases (e.g. OBSESSIVE–COMPULSIVE DISORDER) whether clients would be better helped by medication than by counselling. They also need to consider whether counselling (or UNCOVERING therapies) will exacerbate the mental state of people already using medication, whether certain clients will be able to benefit from counselling if they are, for example, heavily tranquillised, and whether it is wise or timely to assist clients to withdraw from certain prescribed medication. Some clients ill advisedly practise *self-medication*, and alter dosages at will. Counsellors working in the field of addictions take care to monitor any use of mood-altering drugs (even if prescribed) and to watch for cross-addictions (the substituting of one drug for another). There is growing evidence that for certain conditions a combination of appropriate medication and counselling is the optimal treatment. *See* PSYCHOPHARMACOLOGY.

meditation the practice of mind control or relaxation. There are various methods of meditation, all based in some way on the suspension or modification of 'normal' psychophysiological processes. Meditation is designed to enhance everyday functioning by freeing the mind of unnecessary preoccupations. It is also used as a means of accessing higher levels of consciousness. While some counsellors regard meditation as a useful adjunct to counselling for certain clients, others argue that it is used to suppress rather than resolve conflict. (In much Japanese psychotherapy, meditation is an integral feature.) It is also argued that people need a strong ego before they begin attempts to achieve non-egoic consciousness (Wilber, Engler and Brown, 1986). *See* MINDFULNESS-BASED COGNITIVE THERAPY.

memory retention of and ability to recall information. The psychological and neurochemical processes involved in the functioning of memory are complex and still debated. The functioning of memory is a key item in psychiatric assessment and has a particular importance in working with older clients. Memory is often impaired in people who have suffered brain injuries (including lobotomies) and in those with serious alcoholic problems. (Alcoholics often suffer short-term memory 'blackouts' as well as long-term memory losses.) Memory is often categorised as long-term and short-term, and clients in those approaches to counselling which stress the influence of the past require the ability to remember events in childhood, or an awareness of feelings associated with certain past relationships. Some writers distinguish between autobiographical and more objective memory. According to some theorists, human beings have the capacity to remember intrauterine and neonatal events (by means of a kind of 'cellular memory') as well as events from previous incarnations. *Screen memory* is the psychoanalytic concept of one memory masking another, more traumatic memory. Counsellors need to be able to remember a lot of detail about their individual clients. *See* CHILDHOOD MEMORIES, FORGETTING.

mental health the healthy functioning of the person as in Freud's dictum that the mark of maturity is the 'ability to love and to work'; the unproblematic functioning of the mind. Optimal mental health might include the qualities of alertness, flexibility, creativity, joyfulness and equanimity. A mentally healthy person would perceive herself and others accurately and be able to engage with life without being crippled by anxiety. Positive mental health is not the subject of a great deal of scientific enquiry and has not attracted a consensual definition. 'Mental health problem' is considered by many to be a more acceptable term than MENTAL ILLNESS. The 'mental health field' is constituted largely by psychiatrists and other psychiatric staff, by community care workers, users of 'mental health services' and campaigners for better conditions for people with mental health problems. Much more attention is paid to attempting to ameliorate mental distress than to promoting positive mental health because disease processes are given higher priority and greater funding. That part of counselling which aims at psychological education can contribute to better mental health. *Mental health counselling* is a well-developed profession in the US.

Mental Health Act (1983) refers to mental illness, to mental impairment, severe mental impairment and to psychopathic disorder. It lays out the legal conditions under which someone can be involuntarily hospitalised on an emergency basis, following assessment by qualified professionals. The Act is in sections, and this term has been adopted colloquially, as in 'he is being sectioned' (which replaced the term 'committed'). Involuntary admissions (which account for less than 10% of all admissions to psychiatric hospitals) occur in cases where the person concerned becomes a serious danger to herself or others due to disturbed psychological functioning and will not give assent to voluntary admission, usually because of lack of insight into her state.

mental illness any form of serious mental disorder. Mental disorders include schizophrenia, manic-depressive psychosis, dementia, etc. Mental illness is a problematic term (*see* INSANITY) and its use is avoided by many people. The term 'mental disorder' is more specific, and the term 'severe mental illness' (SMI) is used commonly by CPNs and others.

mental state psychiatric and legal term referring to the quality of a person's psychological functioning and availability to reason, particularly at the time of psychiatric assessment or when a crime is committed.

mentoring *see* COACHING.

merging *see* CONFLUENCE.

meta-analysis *see* RESEARCH.

metaphor an image or narrative which communicates meaning in a coded form. Since much that clients discuss is either very painful or very elusive, they frequently resort to the use of metaphor, and counsellors too may deliberately use metaphor in attempting to capture the essence of the client's meaning. Metaphor has been called the 'language of the imagination'. Metaphors may be either interpreted or worked through, and the latter practice (entering into the spirit of the metaphor and delaying interpretation) is often advised when working with very defensive clients. Much psychological theory, attempting as it does to describe subtle inner, intangible aspects of the mind, also uses concepts which have the status of metaphor.

microcounselling skills those communication skills which build a helping relationship and which include attending, maintaining eye contact, appropriate vocal tone, and so on. Ivey (1971) used the terms 'microskills', 'microcounselling' and 'microtraining' to refer to the processes of learning and using such skills. Research suggests that explicit cognitive awareness of the presence and impact of such skills enhances their effective use; it also confirms that counsellors of different orientations tend to use certain of these skills more frequently than others.

middle phase of counselling those sessions between the beginning phase and termination of counselling. The middle phase is often characterised for the client by greater trust in the counsellor, deeper immersion in the complexities and pain of his or her concerns, and a willingness to confront doubts and impasses in the counselling process. It is clearer in time-limited counselling *when* the middle phase is than in open-ended counselling.

mid-life crisis a term used to describe the experience of distress, disillusionment or questioning of life purposes by many people in their forties or fifties. Many people are established (or 'stuck') in marriages and careers by this age, and mortality becomes a more obvious prospect; the finiteness of time reminds people of what they have not achieved, and are likely not to achieve. People start to think in terms of time left rather than time gone. Women experiencing the menopause and parents whose children are now adults may experi-

ence loss (the so-called 'empty nest' syndrome). Mid-life can precipitate various forms of escapism or depression (denial or resignation); alternatively, and particularly in the Jungian view, it may represent an opportunity for mature exploration of the self and of meaning in life. The term 'mid-life crisis' originated in the 1950s, with the writings of Jacques and others, but interestingly may have lost some meaning with increase in life expectancy.

mind set relatively fixed view of the world, oneself, others, the future. *See* ATTITUDE, WORLD VIEW.

mindfulness-based cognitive therapy (MBCT) an approach to therapy that integrates certain meditation practices with cognitive–behavioural techniques. Stemming from Jon Kabat-Zinn's mindfulness-based stress reduction practice, MBCT raises awareness of cognitive style, provides attentional control training, teaches acceptance of the flow of thoughts, breathing techniques, etc. and is often offered in an eight-session programme. Has been used specifically for depression (Segal et al., 2000).

minimal responses parsimonious use of verbal and paraverbal acknowledgements of what the client is saying and prompts for her to continue. The classic such responses are 'Uh-huh', 'Mmmm', 'Yes, I see', and the nodding of the head. American literature refers to these responses as 'minimal encouragers'. Counselling is sometimes caricatured as consisting mainly of such responses.

minimisation the cognitive error of ignoring or attributing little or no significance to evidence of one's positive achievements, of being liked by others, and so on. One can also have a minimising attitude to others (*see* DISCOUNTING). Counsellors working in the alcoholism field use the term to refer to the tendency of alcoholics to play down the enormity of their problem and of their abuses of other people. Compare MAGNIFICATION.

Minnesota method a particular approach to the treatment of alcoholics and addicts. The Minnesota method is an intensive, highly-structured, residential regime, which regards alcoholism as a disease. It uses the twelve steps of Alcoholics Anonymous (AA), regular and frequent sessions of group therapy, peer evaluation meetings, various assessment procedures, lectures and meditation sessions. It is committed to immediate confrontation of clients' denial of their problem, to complete and ongoing abstinence, and to appeal to the 'higher power' of AA. Residents are expected to attend AA (or Narcotics Anonymous) meetings and, if appropriate, be referred on to 'second-stage' or 'half-way' projects on completion of the Minnesota programme. It relies heavily on a group approach, on the use of 'recovering alcoholics' as counsellors (or group workers) and much of its ethos is alien to mainstream counsellors, whose emphasis is on individual autonomy. Academic critics suggest that it relies uncritically on AA folklore and 'spirituality', and on peer pressure.

miracle question a technique used in SOLUTION-FOCUSED BRIEF THERAPY whereby the client is asked to imagine that a miracle takes place tonight, their problems are solved and they report to the counsellor what minute changes are noticed in behaviour and demeanour by those who know them. The technique harnesses clients' imaginal abilities, renewed capacity for hope and ability to implement small changes towards progress. Similar to TA's 'outcome fantasy' technique.

mirroring the counsellor's skill of reflecting the BODY LANGUAGE of her client by adopting the movements and postures of the client. This skill tends to be practised unconsciously. The client also may mirror the counsellor's postures unconsciously. All such movements have the effect of positive bonding and assist the counsellor in gaining intuition into how the client feels. Mirroring and the 'mirror phase' have quite distinct meanings in the psychoanalytic thought of Kohut and Lacan respectively. Group psychotherapy is considered to produce a mirror phenomenon whereby each member unconsciously reflects aspects of all other members.

misattribution wrongly making inferences about the behaviour of others towards oneself or misinterpreting the causes of events generally. *See* FAULTY INFORMATION PROCESSING.

miscarriage counselling counselling of a woman who has experienced a 'spontaneous abortion' or stillbirth. There are no 'miscarriage counsellors' and most women are probably offered little or no counselling in these circumstances, but feelings about these experiences often surface later in any counselling the woman undertakes.

missed sessions scheduled counselling appointments which clients fail to attend. Also known as DNA (did not attend). A first missed session (particularly without warning) is often an indication of client resistance or dissatisfaction. A proportion of clients drop out of counselling after one or a few sessions. Frequent absences, even when notified, have to be taken seriously by counsellors as a sign that the client is ambivalent and perhaps acting-out. It is the usual arrangement that clients of private practitioners must pay for missed sessions if adequate prior notice has not been given.

mobilisation the client's becoming motivated, activated, and ready for increased effort. The term usually refers to the client's mobilisation of her own inner resources.

model a theoretical construct, approach or image. It can be thought of as a template or map which reflects aspects of the world regarded as important by its creators. It can be used to refer to a school of counselling or to particular aspects of the counselling process (e.g. models of the therapeutic relationship). Different counselling ORIENTATIONS or schools offer different models of counselling. Each model of counselling has a distinctive view of human development, psychological dysfunction, treatment strategies and techniques.

model of human beings any systematic view of and explanation for the ways in which people typically develop and function. All counsellors and counselling orientations have an implicit or explicit model of human beings. Such models are diverse and may include the views that people are, for example, innately good, innately self-actualising, driven to avoid pain, irrational, neurotic, creative, malleable, sexually motivated, spiritually motivated, self-centred. In general, Freudian and neo-Freudian models are often considered by critics to have a pessimistic, deterministic view, behaviourism to have a soulless and mechanistic view, and humanistic psychology to have an optimistic, holistic, but possibly naive view.

modelling the behavioural/social learning method of demonstrating procedures which the client wishes or needs to adopt. Deliberate modelling is a live enactment of a certain behaviour by the counsellor; modelling may be vicarious, for example by having the client discuss an admired person and describe his way of performing the targeted behaviour; also, video presentations may be used. Clients learn by observation and/or imitation, and learn gradually or from one demonstration. Inadvertent modelling refers to the behaviour exhibited by a counsellor, supervisor or trainer which is likely to be internalised by trainees or supervisees.

money financial currency; means of purchase. Clients whose problems are predominantly to do with (a shortage of) money are best helped by DEBT COUNSELLING from advice and welfare agencies. Where financial problems stem from a psychologically dysfunctional attitude to money (e.g. as in compulsive gambling) clients are likely to need practical, behavioural and confrontational interventions in the first instance. Where problems with managing money form a part of a client's concerns, counsellors may respond according to their orientation. It was part of original Freudian thinking to regard money as symbolising faeces (it can be stored and spent) and also as symbolising personal worth and love; it has also been linked symbolically with the (Kleinian) 'bountiful/withholding breast'. Explicit discussion of the client's feelings about having to pay for counselling is recommended by some counsellors. Counsellors and psychotherapists sometimes come under attack from political analysts for regarding people's 'money worries' as less serious than their psychological concerns.

mood the person's affective state at the time of clinical assessment or over some defined preceding period; in common usage it refers to any observable state of mind which differs from the person's habitual state.

mood disorder a generic psychiatric term for serious affective problems such as depression, mania, bipolar disorder, dysthymic disorder.

mood swings marked or abnormal alterations in mood/affect indicating a psychological disturbance (e.g. MANIC DEPRESSION) or, for example, a symptom of perimenopause.

morbidity morbid thoughts in which there are preoccupations with death or illness are a feature of some clients' depression. In medical terminology, morbidity refers to the presence of a disease process.

Morita therapy a Japanese therapy devised by Morita Shoma. It involves treatment in clinic or hospital for general neuroses with well motivated clients and includes intensive rest, followed by prescribed therapeutic activity, learning to accept symptoms and live in spite of them.

mother the female parent; the biological mother or adoptive mother. As a verb, 'to mother' means to nurture, care for in the most fundamental ways. Mothering is the activity of providing all that an infant needs, including food, cleaning, warmth and intuitive reassurance. Because of the powerful position of (or accorded to) the mother, much that subsequently goes wrong in child and adult development is attributed by many clients and counsellors to MATERNAL DEPRIVATION or inadequacy. The act of breastfeeding can be viewed as evidence of a vital biological and emotional tie between mother and child. These views are modified by those theorists who stress that it is the client's subjective (fallible) memory, and fantasies about her mother, which are of consequence, and not the (unknowable) reality. It is argued that infants require only *good enough* mothering for subsequent healthy development, and that fathers and other caregivers can be just as good 'mothers' (if not better than) as the biological mother. A *mother fixation* is a loose term describing anyone who is rigidly emotionally attached to his or her mother. *Motherhood* itself is an ongoing and absorbing experience and it is clear from mothers that pregnancy, birth, child-rearing and changes in reproductive functioning involve the whole gamut of emotions, encompassing a complexity of transitions, gains and losses that are not open to simple explanations and that continue throughout life.

motivation drive, arousal, readiness; having a reason for action. Motivation is a complex state made up of physiological, emotional, cognitive, behavioural and environmental factors. A feature of depression is lack of motivation, yet many depressed clients feel sufficiently impelled by their depression to seek counselling. Clients who are highly motivated when seeking counselling probably make most rapid progress and are often experienced by counsellors as 'more rewarding' to work with than those who are 'under motivated'; yet those who are under motivated represent more of a challenge to the counsellor's skills (*see* STAGES OF CHANGE). Motivation is both conscious and unconscious (*see* Davanloo, 1990). Behaviourists are inclined to link motivation with environmental stimuli and psychoanalysts to link it with innate instincts. The motivation of people to become counsellors is an important and under-researched subject, but the question of motivation is an important one for those interviewing candidates for counsellor training.

motivational interviewing the term given to an approach to helping people (often those addicted to drink and drugs) that draws on an understanding of STAGES OF CHANGE, that does not assume the person is currently ready to be helped, but aspires to motivate them at whatever stage they may be at. *See* Miller and Rollnick (1991).

mourning the term is often used of the identified conventions of grieving within a culture, following the fact of bereavement and emotion of spontaneous grief. It is also used psychoanalytically to refer to loss of any valued person, lifestyle or ideology.

movement action, changing of position, progress. Therapeutic movement refers to client PROGRESS (however slow) towards goals.

movement therapy refers to dance therapy and aspects of therapeutic dance and movement which are applied to certain clients or client groups. It can be particularly effective with some people who cannot easily verbalise or whose quality of life can be enhanced by using movement exercises to access other areas of vitality.

multimodal therapy an approach to counselling and therapy developed by Arnold Lazarus (1981). Originally called 'multimodal behaviour therapy', multimodal therapy is heavily based on a systematic assessment of the way in which clients function. Lazarus uses a BASIC ID 'structural profile' and 'modality profile', which yields information on the way clients typically react to events behaviourally, emotionally, and so on. Wherever possible, Lazarus aims to match each item of clients' dysfunctional behaviour with an intervention shown to be effective by research. Multimodal therapy relies, therefore, on TECHNICAL ECLECTICISM. Multimodal therapists aim to tune into clients' precise modalities and therapeutic needs, and are very willing to refer clients on to other counsellors if assessment suggests that it will be in the clients' best interests. *See also* TRACKING.

multiple abuse the past or present inflicting, by self or others, of diverse painful, addicting, degrading or traumatic experiences. A child may be multiply abused, for example, by being sexually abused by various family members and/or beaten, burned, starved, etc. People who are multiple abusers (who may themselves have been abused as children) may be addicted to alcohol, drugs and other substances, to promiscuous sexual behaviour, violent relationships. Such cycles of abuse are not, however, inevitable.

multiple intelligences the term used by Gardner (1993) to challenge the notion of singular and dominant intelligence (IQ) and to suggest that human beings are characterised by linguistic, musical, logical-mathematical, spatial, bodily-kinaesthetic and personal forms of intelligence.

multiple loss syndrome a term that can be applied to an individual who has experienced the deaths of several others in a relatively short space of time, in a disaster or otherwise, or the experience of a grieving population following a major traumatic incident.

multiple personality disorder a rare psychiatric condition in which the person manifests two or more distinct personalities. The existence of this condition has been the subject of much debate. Such personalities (not to be confused with non-pathological SUBPERSONALITIES) may name themselves, present themselves quite differently, and be unaware of each other's existence. While this condition may go undetected for some time, and people suffering from it may be able to function normally at times, they are more likely to be continuous users of psychiatric services. Inadvertently probing counselling in such cases may evoke aggressive and psychotic reactions (*see* PSYCHOSIS), but supportive counselling can be beneficial. There are indications that multiple personality disorder may often result from extreme forms of abuse (including sexual abuse) in childhood.

multiple problems general term for the common recognition that many clients do not present with a singular problem or goal but with several. *See also* COMORBIDITY.

music therapy treatment of certain problems utilising music. Often for rehabilitation or for use with autistic clients and those with learning difficulties and mental health problems, allowing for relaxation and expression in a non-verbal and non-threatening milieu.

musturbation a term coined by Albert Ellis which illustrates the common human tendency to believe that we *must* get what we want, *must* be perfect, *must* not be disappointed, etc., and also that others *must* conform to our preferences. It equates with the 'tyranny of the shoulds' (Horney) and the coined term of 'musturbation' is designed to challenge irrationality humorously and unforgettably.

mutuality reciprocity; involving both people in any dyad in responding to each other. All counselling and psychotherapy is based to some extent on the RELATIONSHIP between client and counsellor. CONGRUENCE, COUNTERTRANSFERENCE and USE OF SELF all imply that counsellors are deeply involved in an exercise of mutuality. Cox (1978) considers mutuality as one of the keys to therapy, along with time and depth. Mutuality is usually limited by the concentration on the client and his concerns. In person-centred counselling, however, mutuality which increasingly involves the counsellor's expression of self is seen as a common characteristic of the closing stages of counselling.

N

naming of feelings the ownership and accurate identification of complex or elusive feelings by the client. Clients are often tempted to describe feelings vaguely, to avoid articulating them altogether or to become confused instead of owning and expressing a feeling honestly. *See also* ACCURATE SYMBOLISATION.

narcissism excessive preoccupation with oneself; exaggerated self-love. In psychoanalytic thought, *primary narcissism* is the infant's self-interest or the adult's (usually neurotic) preoccupation with self; *secondary narcissism* refers to a kind of self-love reflected off or introjected from others. Infants who are not given an appropriate sense of self-respect may fail to achieve an adult interest in others and become dysfunctionally narcissistic. In extreme cases of *narcissistic personality disorder*, people are clinically incapacitated in engaging meaningfully with others. A *narcissistic wound* (or injury) is any perceived assault on the person's self-esteem. The term 'narcissistic' is sometimes popularly directed at counselling and psychotherapy clients who are thought to be indulging themselves in self-preoccupation instead of engaging fully in life.

narrative therapy a movement stemming from the 1980s that emphasises the role of stories and story-telling in understanding clients, ourselves and our approaches to counselling/therapy. Cultural and personal stories of identity and purpose are co-constructed, they are needed, and they are open to examination and change in therapy. Concepts include voice, habitual narrative, personal stories, chronicles, macronarratives, dominant narratives, being silenced, problem-saturated narratives, externalising the story, etc. (McLeod, 1997). Closely related to SOLUTION-FOCUSED BRIEF THERAPY.

naturalistic therapy any therapeutic gains following day to day encounters, friendly conversations, etc. *Naturalistic debriefing* refers to positive, therapeutic gains from talking with friends and colleagues following a traumatic or extreme event. Naturalistic enquiry refers to research relying on informal, everyday observation.

nature–nurture this term refers to the debate as to whether (or to what extent) human qualities and behaviour are innate, or genetically predetermined, on the one hand, or learned from (early) experience on the other. Also known as the 'heredity-environment controversy', the debate is ongoing and often centres on the issues of intelligence, temperament, gender, etc. While counsellors respect the uniqueness of individuals, counselling tends to accentuate the 'nurture' side of the debate, investing heavily in the idea that clients can change, relearn and overcome obstacles. Particularly controversial have been debates concerning, for example, homosexuality and mental illness.

necessary and/or sufficient conditions the indispensable requirements for effective therapeutic progress. Carl Rogers postulated that the core conditions of GENUINENESS, ACCEPTANCE and EMPATHY are necessary for positive progress in counselling, and also that (consistently) given these conditions alone, clients will flourish, provided that they have at least a minimal awareness of the presence of the conditions. PERSON-CENTRED COUNSELLING still holds broadly to this view, which places great faith in relationship factors and de-emphasises techniques. Others have suggested that the additional counsellor skills of confrontation, concreteness and immediacy are necessary for effective counselling. Most counsellors agree that the core conditions are indeed necessary, but many depart from the view that they are sufficient (or efficient, as reliance on them alone is considered by many to consign counselling to being a lengthy process). Research in this area is ongoing.

need a vital requirement. While certain human needs are universal and undisputed (e.g. food and a supportive physical environment) others are the subject of debate. Most theorists accept that human infants need warmth, food and various other kinds of attention and nourishment. There is no agreement, however, on what quality or quantity of maternal, parental or consistent care or love is *necessary*. In PRIMAL THERAPY, need is a central concept; in RATIONAL EMOTIVE BEHAVIOUR THERAPY, by contrast, humans are considered to have few actual needs but many irrational demands. Behaviourists argue that the concept of need is irrelevant as it cannot be linked to observed behaviour. Need can be distinguished from instinct, impulse, demand and preference. There is perhaps no essential need for adults to have love or sex, for example, but many people insist that these are emotional needs, deprivation of which results in psychopathology, illness or impaired self-actualisation (*see* Maslow's HIERARCHY OF NEEDS). Most counsellors will probably agree that clients whose basic needs (for food, housing and economic stability) are not being met are unlikely to be able to benefit from psychological help until they are.

negative outcome *see* OUTCOME.

negative transference *see* TRANSFERENCE.

negativity an attitude of refusal or apparent inability to consider the idea that life or parts of life may be positive, enriching and hopeful. Everyone has the capacity to be negative and it is probably an essential capacity; however, pathological negativity, which characterises DEPRESSION, for example, bars the way to significant therapeutic progress. Milder forms of negativity include cynicism and LOW SELF-ESTEEM (negativity towards the self). *Negative capability* (a term coined by Keats) denotes the ability to entertain doubt and ambiguity and is valued in particular by psychoanalytic practitioners.

neglect failure to give due attention and care to; to omit. Children who are seriously or chronically neglected (emotionally, intellectually or physically) may exhibit signs of 'failure to thrive' as a result. Memory of this kind of deprivation is sometimes difficult to gain access to as an adult in counselling, since recall of the absence of certain experiences (which has been called 'the trauma of eventlessness') is itself difficult.

nervous breakdown an imprecise term referring to a personal crisis, acute and (temporarily) incapacitating depression or similar disorder. This term has often been employed in cases where the person has no previous history of mental distress, and also where she has had a disintegrative reaction to unrecognised stress. *Nervous breakdown* reflects a popular view of the role of 'nerves' in psychological distress.

neurolinguistic programming a particular approach to counselling and many other fields. Neurolinguistic programming (NLP) resulted from Bandler and Grinder's study and synthesis of linguistics, innovative psychotherapy, hypnotherapy and examples of 'personal excellence' in general. NLP claims to explain how an understanding of information processing, combined with the idea of personal freedom to choose new behaviour, forms a new and effective tool for self-change. It places great emphasis on conceptualisations and their relation to bodily cues. While some counsellors regard NLP as a 'pseudo-scientific' collection of ideas from various fields including sales psychology and positive thinking, others value and integrate many of its catalytic methods into their work. *See* REFRAMING; *see* O'Connor and Seymour (1990).

neurology the medical discipline which deals with disorders of the central and peripheral nervous system. Sometimes applicants for counselling or clients in ongoing counselling exhibit signs of possible organic illness (e.g. frequent headaches, serious memory impairment). It is important that counsellors do not automatically view all somatic symptoms as psychological defences; concern for a client's welfare can indicate a need for a referral to a GP, who may call for a neurological assessment in some circumstances.

neurosis although literally a 'disease of the nerves', neurosis refers to 'psychoneurosis', or any psychological disturbance or maladjustment in which contact with reality is maintained but the person's reaction is disproportionate to their situation. The term has lost much of its meaning since its use by Freud (e.g. hysterical neurosis, anxiety neurosis) and can now be applied to almost any instance of psychological irregularity. *Neuroticism* is contrasted (or viewed as one end on a spectrum) with *psychoticism* and is defined thereby as a milder form of disturbance. Neurosis has been viewed as part of the human condition; Freud defined one successful outcome of psychoanalysis as the conversion of neurosis into ordinary unhappiness. It has been likened to a pervasive nervous disease resulting from 'excessive psychobiologic pain' (Janov). Traumatic (accidental) and character (innate) neuroses are sometimes contrasted. *Neurotic* is used loosely and sometimes abusively of people who react anxiously or exaggeratedly towards everyday events.

nightmares frightening DREAMS which often alarm and wake the dreamer. Nightmares are experienced by many children and are often associated with feelings of suffocation. They sometimes repeat themselves over the course of months or years. Nightmares may indicate the triggering of an underlying (repressed) TRAUMA seeking resolution (as in some post-traumatic conditions). *Night terrors* are more distressing experiences which may involve startled waking, sleepwalking and other bizarre behaviour.

nihilism personal or philosophical attitude which sees no intrinsic meaning in life. Nihilism may be passive or active, and pathological or well reasoned. Nietzsche is a primary example of a philosophical nihilist. Nihilism is frequently associated with depression and with angry denial of personal hurt (blaming the environment as a defence). It may be likened to global cynicism, and distinguished from healthy scepticism. *See* COMPASSIONATE NIHILISM.

nihilistic delusions are a feature of some schizophrenias or organic psychoses and are characterised by beliefs that one is dead or partially dead, or that others, or the entire world, have ceased to exist.

non-acceptance the counsellor's incapacity or unwillingness to offer a client unconditional acceptance. Counsellors may be aware of instantly or gradually disliking certain clients or of struggling to accept them fully. Premature negative judgement of clients can be offset by focusing on EMPATHY and also by referring any such difficulties to supervision.

non-compliance American term referring to the client's lack of cooperation with a therapeutic strategy deemed to be in the client's best interests.

non-directive intending to wield no direct influence; to be purely reflective. 'Non-directive counselling' was Rogers' original term for his non-interventionist approach to counselling. Although he subsequently changed to the terms 'client-centred' and 'person-centred', the concept of non-directiveness has remained highly influential in the counselling world. The rationale for non-directiveness is that clients make optimal progress by relying on their own ORGANISMIC VALUING PROCESS which can be hindered or obscured by directive counselling. In practice, it is doubtful whether any counselling can be entirely non-directive. Some counsellor training perpetuates a purist non-directive ideal which unfortunately inhibits some trainees' development.

non-judgementalism the quality of an attitude of acceptance and willingness to learn about, rather than entertain assumptions about, the client. JUDGEMENTALISM precludes the possibility of counsellor neutrality or objectivity and is highly likely to communicate itself to the client. A non-judgemental attitude allows the client to trust and to make necessary disclosures and allows the counsellor to empathise with the inner world of the client and gain a valuable picture of the client's frame of reference and the nature of his problems.

non-possessive warmth a friendly disposition towards clients which does not impose and makes no demands for reciprocal friendship. Warmth, or interest and liking, is considered a necessary condition by most (but not all) counsellors, since it fosters intimacy, revelation and freedom from fear and threat. Non-possessive warmth is a disciplined feeling towards the client, and the communication of that feeling in a manner that is therapeutic for each client.

non-sexist counselling counselling which integrates (or attempts to integrate) awareness and avoidance of sexist attitudes and behaviour in practice. Counsellors who are concerned to practise in a non-sexist manner avoid assumptions about gender roles, take care to avoid sexist language and are alert to the possibility of unconscious or non-verbal sexism in their behaviour. While some counsellors may be actively *anti-sexist* in their counselling (e.g. by challenging their clients' sexist statements) this is problematic because of the more primary requirement to remain in the client's frame of reference. Counselling agencies, and training courses, vary widely from active to passive commitment to non-sexist practice.

non-specific factors those therapeutic aspects of counselling which are not specific to the model being practised and may be common to all the psychotherapies. When researchers enquire into those technical factors which are supposed to effect change in counselling, such as interpretation, catharsis and cognitive restructuring, other change factors are present and stem from subtle and non-specific relationship factors. Counselling is sometimes criticised for being a non-specific approach to psychological disturbance whose main effect is that of a PLACEBO.

non-verbal communication any kind of information transmitted from one person to another without the use of spoken words. Non-verbal communication includes BODY LANGUAGE (which itself includes body position, interpersonal distance), EYE CONTACT (facial expression, etc.), paraverbal (or paralinguistic) communication (which is the *manner* in which things are said), clinical environment, attire. Counsellors need to be aware of what they (and their clients) may be communicating unconsciously, and what within such communication is therapeutic or otherwise; some counsellors make a point of asking clients for feedback on such communication. What counsellors model non-verbally and inadvertently may require particular attention. Trainers and supervisors also communicate a great deal non-verbally. Overt messages can be sabotaged if accompanying gestures conflict with the words being used. *See also* HUGGING, TOUCHING.

normal behaviour generally viewed as healthy, well-adjusted and culturally acceptable is considered 'normal'. The term also refers to everyday, universal experience, as in 'It is normal to feel sad sometimes'. When clients express doubts about their sanity, as an example, many counsellors offer 'normalising' feedback in the form of responsible reassurance (e.g. 'No, you're not mad'). Normality is also defined by its opposite: 'abnormal behaviour' suggests behaviour that is either personally out of character or beyond social norms; *abnormal psychology* is that branch of psychology devoted to the study of mental illness and abnormal behaviour. Normality is a problematic concept which can be viewed as in conflict with the concept of individual and cultural differences.

normative that which concerns norms, standards and regulatory functions. The normative function of supervision, for example, is to pay attention to professional issues, ethical boundaries, structuring of sessions, etc.

norming that part of group process which is concerned with establishing norms of behaviour within the group. *See* FORMING IN GROUPS.

nosology systematic (science of the) CLASSIFICATION OF DISORDERS. *See* DSM-IV TR, ICD-10.

'not knowing' a state or moment of confusion or difficulty in understanding the client; a willingness to suspend any personal need to know; a putting aside of knowledge in order to learn afresh from the client in each session. All counsellors experience instances of not knowing what to think, say or do in sessions. While these experiences may result from counsellor anxiety or inexperience, they can also reflect the simple reality that counsellors are not omniscient, or they can be COUNTERTRANSFERENCE reactions to client confusion or vulnerability (*see* Casement, 1990.) A client who reports that 'I don't know' what is happening (in his life or in the session, occasionally or frequently) may be avoiding responsibility, may be using CONFUSION as a defence, may be unconscious of certain factors, or may only have vague preconscious access to them.

note taking writing observations on clients. Most counsellors make notes after sessions but some make notes during sessions. The latter practice is considered by many to detract from the counselling relationship. All such notes are for the purpose of clinical recording, professional reflection and learning, and should be safeguarded to preserve confidentiality. Potentially all written accounts are subject to legal scrutiny. *See also* PROCESS.

nursing triad the term, derived from Winnicott, for the baby being cared for by the mother, who is in turn cared for by the father. The concept has also been applied to the parallel example of the client being cared for by the counsellor, who is in turn cared for by the supervisor.

Nurturing Parent the role of the PARENT EGO STATE, in the functional model of TA, which replays the caring and helping attitudes of parents. Such nurturance can be offered either positively or negatively as genuine helpfulness or as undermining 'doing for' or over-protectiveness. In contrast, the controlling or critical parent functions from within the parent ego state to direct and criticise.

obesity the condition of being significantly overweight. Exactly what constitutes 'overweight' or clinically obese is open to debate (some authorities use a figure of 20%+ of normal weight for age and sex), but some people are visibly obese, agree that they are, and suffer both physically and psychologically; some perceive themselves as obese in spite of the different and more objective view of others. Putative causes of obesity include genetic, dietary, physiological, viral, behavioural, psychological and cultural factors. Where obesity results from an EATING DISORDER, some form of counselling may assist the person to reduce food intake; where it is not of psychological origin, the person may still be helped to cope with their self-image and relationships with others by counselling. Obesity has been increasing in the US and UK in the 1990s and 2000s.

object relations this term refers to the relationships within a person's inner world and between this inner world of relationships and the external relationships with significant others, which are often then internalised. The word 'object' in psychoanalysis refers to a person or persons (as in 'the object of her affections') and is used quite distinctly from its 'objectifying' (dehumanising) sense. *Object relations theory* moved from Freud's early emphasis on the instinctual (inner) drives towards the significance of needing or seeking relationships with other people, and the developmental stages and disturbances pertaining to this. While Melanie Klein's concept of part objects (*see* PARTS) contributed to this theory, Fairbairn and others helped develop object relations theory to become a major force in the psychoanalytic theory of the structure of the personality.

observational skills abilities pertinent to watching and noting the manner of the client. Great emphasis is placed on listening skills in counselling but the significance of visual perception is often understated. Visual cues alert counsellors to clients' BODY LANGUAGE and especially to discrepancies between what is said and what is signalled non-verbally. Clients reveal much by the manner in which they enter the counselling room, where and how they sit or recline, their facial expressions, muscle tension, posture and so on. Gestalt counsellors attribute much significance to observation and often draw clients' attention to NON-VERBAL COMMUNICA-

TION. Psychoanalysts who sit behind their patients and experiential psychotherapists who work with their eyes closed de-emphasise observation and aim to attune themselves to clients' verbal and emotional nuances.

observing ego that ego function which reflects on the counselling process and cooperates rationally with the counsellor in psychodynamic counselling. The observing ego is distinguished from the *experiencing ego*, which may be immersed in the transference. The observing ego is an essential part of the THERAPEUTIC ALLIANCE.

obsession any preoccupation which is experienced as being beyond the person's control and which is frequently problematic and painful. An example of a 'simple' obsession is the romantic preoccupation which may often result in JEALOUSY.

obsessive–compulsive disorder (OCD) differs from mildly (and fairly common) obsessive behaviour in having no pleasure or profit in it. It has been called the 'morbid persistence of an idea'. Sufferers may have irrational fears of acting criminally; they may be fearful of dirt or sex; they may attribute special significance to colours, numbers, body parts, etc.: the form of the thinking is magical, belonging to the stage of development before the adult logic of cause and effect has developed. There are various explanations for OCD but treatment is problematic. It is claimed that behaviour therapy is more successful than other forms of therapy, and some (see Toates, 1990) commend appropriate medication, especially clomipramine, an antidepressant. Obsession is the thinking, ruminative aspect of OCD, with COMPULSION being the active component.

oceanic feeling Freudian description of ecstatic experiences, including mystical states. According to Freud, such experiences probably have more to do with dim memories of and longing for the security of the symbiotic relationship with the mother than with genuine religious phenomena, although other analysts (e.g. Erikson) see this as a legitimate return to a primary human experience.

Oedipus complex the Freudian concept of the child's ambivalence towards the parent of the same gender as himself or herself. According to Freud, between the ages of 3 and 5 years a boy experiences an intense desire for his mother and an accompanying rivalry with and hostility towards his father. For a girl the situation is more complex. This conflict, as well as a wish to identify with the father, is sometimes considered the foundation of all later relationship difficulties. The Oedipal feelings are thought to be repressed, leading to formation of the SUPEREGO. Both Jung and Klein were critical of, and suggested amendments to, Freud's concept. Jung suggested at one stage an Electra complex in girls (which Freud rejected) and Klein located the Oedipus complex much earlier in infancy.

offender counselling the counselling of people with criminal convictions. The term 'offender counselling' is not often used in the UK but many probation officers trained in (particularly, historically, psychodynamic and person-centred and increasingly in CBT) counselling. (The historical mission of probation officers was to 'advise, assist and befriend'.) Certain offenders (e.g. sex offenders, alcoholics and addicts) may be referred for specialist counselling and psychotherapy. Forensic psychiatry is that branch of psychiatry/ psychotherapy which addresses the assessment and treatment of serious criminal behaviour. *See also* CASEWORK, DEVIANCY.

offloading talking in order to achieve relief from tension. Many clients need to talk at length, and benefit from doing so, at the beginning of counselling. Some clients mistakenly perceive counselling as an opportunity simply to offload (or 'unload') aimlessly. While such offloading may effect short-term CATHARSIS it is unlikely to have long-term benefits. Some clients suffer from PRESSURE OF SPEECH, others have a conversational style which is rambling, and some counsellors experience difficulty in interrupting and assisting clients to structure their use of counselling.

older people, counselling of counselling people whose (advanced) age is a significant factor. In general, older people (the term 'the elderly' is rejected by many, because of the risk of losing the person behind the label) are likely to experience a greater incidence of bereavements, loneliness, economic hardship and illness. Retirement is an inevitable issue, and preparation for retirement, including counselling, is now provided and valued by many organisations. People who become physically and/or mentally impaired (e.g. by dementia) often require residential care. Certain models of counselling (e.g. the transpersonal and Jungian) have a more positive view of ageing than others. *See* REMINISCENCE.

omnipotence an attitude marked by the belief that one is all-powerful. In psychoanalytic theory omnipotence is considered a normal stage of development in which the infant expects her thoughts and wishes to be automatically fulfilled. Beyond its age-appropriate stage, omnipotence becomes dysfunctional. Here people believe either that events have conformed to their wishes or that they absolutely should. In extreme cases, people strive pathologically to manipulate their environment (including other people) to conform with their expectations. *See* MAGICAL THINKING.

one-to-one meetings between a single counsellor and a single client are called 'one-to-one' to distinguish them from contact in group work or in informal settings. Certain treatment regimes such as the Minnesota method, for example, discourage clients from having too many 'one-to-ones' in order to avoid dependency and manipulation. The term implies face-to-face meetings.

onset of disorder the time at which the client's problem manifested itself, its mode of beginning and the circumstances in which it occurred. 'Onset' is a medical term and the concept is used in assessment. Determining the date of onset and situational factors can help to trace significant antecedents (e.g. a bereavement) or to calculate how chronic and intractable a problem may be. Counsellors are more likely to ask 'Why has the client presented for counselling at this time?' than to use the term 'onset'. *See* Budman and Gurman (1988).

open question any question which encourages the client to explore and expand his understanding, as opposed to closed questions which can only be answered in a fixed and brief way. Open questions typically begin with 'how'. 'How do you feel about that?' is an example of an open question. *See* QUESTIONS.

open-ended contract agreement between client and counsellor which does not specify a desired outcome or fixed termination date. *See* CONTRACT.

openness an attitude or demeanour of receptivity and willingness to be known. In its most literal sense, openness is a complete lack of reservation or secrecy and a commitment to being totally transparent to the gaze and enquiry of others. Few clients or counsellors practise or endorse such total openness, but GENUINENESS implies high levels of therapeutic openness. Naive, boundary-less openness can be a sign of a social skill deficit or of acting-out. In general, humanistic practitioners endorse and aim at openness as part of personal growth in counselling and in group work.

operant conditioning the behavioural concept and technique which is based on the reinforcement of a person's actions when they conform to a desired response. Operant conditioning is contrasted with CLASSICAL CONDITIONING because the former depends on a volitional response or series of responses, and on reinforcement of those responses. *See also* SHAPING.

operating potential that part of a client's phenomenological (inner) world which, when contacted, contains the seeds of therapeutic change. Close experiential listening (*see* EXPERIENTIAL PSYCHOTHERAPY) brings the counsellor into contact with this part and enables him to help the client apply leverage.

operationalise to put into action a therapeutic procedure. Egan (2002) considers that many counsellors get stuck at the exploratory and problem-defining stages of counselling, and that a conscious action-orientation is necessary for real therapeutic movement.

oppression objectively, any form of social discrimination against relatively powerless groups; subjectively, the experience of such discrimination. Racism, heterosexism and the predominance of patriarchal values and institutions are examples of oppression. People who belong to relatively powerless minority groups may experience daily oppression, both implicitly and explicitly, which may either lead to or exacerbate acute personal problems. Women (not a minority group) also suffer oppression. *See* ANTIDISCRIMINATORY PRACTICE, SOCIAL THERAPY.

oral stage in psychoanalytic thought, the first stage of (psychosexual) development, from birth to weaning in which feeding, and the importance of the mouth and the breast is stressed. Sucking provides the basis of nourishment, satisfaction and pleasure, the excess of which in later life is sometimes called oral-dependence. When the baby begins to bite and chew, this is sometimes called the oral-sadistic phase of development.

organic illness any illness associated with the malfunctioning of the vital organs of the body secondary to structural or biochemical change. Organic illness is contrasted with psychological illness, where there is an underlying disease process. Organically produced symptoms are sometimes mistaken for signs of emotional disturbance. Striano (1988) refers to many cases of organic disease which have been wrongly diagnosed as depression, obsessive–compulsive disorder, and so on. *See* ILLNESS, NEUROLOGY.

organismic valuing process internal, reliable, psychophysiological indications of how one feels in relation to events, people and choices. The organismic valuing process is a concept from PERSON-CENTRED COUNSELLING and confirms the view that human beings are innately self-regulating and autonomous. It also implies an internal LOCUS OF EVALUATION. The terms *organismic self* and *organismic experiencing* are also used in the same sense.

orientation the adoption of a specific position. A counsellor's orientation is the MODEL of counselling she espouses and practises (e.g. psychodynamic, cognitive–behavioural, transactional analysis, eclectic). It can also relate to broad groupings (psychoanalytic, behavioural, humanistic or transpersonal). It is rare for a counsellor to have *no* orientation or theoretical persuasion. Many counsellors are trained in *one* orientation to which they remain faithful; others may be 'theoretically consistent eclectics' who base their understanding of clients on one main theory but call on a variety of techniques. The BACP requires training courses applying for course accreditation (*see* TRAINING) to teach a core theoretical model, and many commentators advise that counsellors ground themselves thoroughly in one model. In the early stages of practice counsellors are likely to be helped better by supervisors of a matching or similar orientation; later they may benefit from the challenge of a different orientation. Ideally, clients will find counsellors whose orientations match their needs, but in practice many clients are unaware of the variety and significance of counselling models. Lazarus, in Dryden (1991), is critical of the subjective and arbitrary way in which counsellors choose an orientation and practise without regard to individual client need or awareness of research on treatment of choice (*see*

TREATMENT). Orientation in psychiatric literature refers to the ability of people to locate themselves accurately in space and time and is part of standard assessment procedures. *See also* ECLECTICISM, INTEGRATION.

other-directedness the propensity to look outside of the self for meaning and validation. The term has the negative connotation of a lack of trust in one's own values and decision-making ability, but is also used to denote the ability of people to relate to others (rather than to retreat).

outcome the end result of counselling. Outcome usually refers to the result at the point when counselling terminates (although Mahrer refers to an 'in-session outcome'). While some counsellors place less emphasis than others on the achieving of results or meeting of goals, most would agree that it is desirable to have an identifiable outcome. Outcome is usually distinguished from PROCESS, especially by researchers, the latter term referring to how counselling works or what goes on within it, as opposed to whether it achieves clients' goals and how successfully it does this. *Negative outcome* refers to client dissatisfaction (including premature termination), DETERIORATION and failure to meet goals. *Successful outcome* refers to client satisfaction, removal of symptoms and achieving of targets. According to Eysenck (1992), it has never been satisfactorily demonstrated that counselling and psychotherapy have significant successful outcome (that is, any greater success than that 'achieved' by PLACEBO treatment or by the passing of time). Meta-analysis of pooled results from research across all therapies has shown that a decisive majority of clients is better off with therapy than without (Smith, Glass and Miller, 1980).

outer skills also known as outside skills; *see* INNER SKILLS.

outplacement counselling assisting people who are facing redundancy at work to come to terms with that loss and to search for alternative employment. Outplacement counselling is offered both in-house and by independent companies (*see* EMPLOYEE ASSISTANCE PROGRAMME, REDUNDANCY COUNSELLING). Outplacement counselling is provided in groups as well as individually, and may include a large element of help with job seeking, retraining and financial planning.

over-concern unnecessary and counterproductive worry and anxiety about something, as opposed to healthy concern. Over-concern often leads to anxiety and paralysis instead of optimal motivational states and constructive action.

over-generalisation a form of COGNITIVE ERROR in which inferences from certain experiences are extended well beyond their probable limits of application.

over-inclusion the cognitive error of failing to discern what is and what is not significant in any challenging situation. This may lead to a feeling of being overwhelmed.

over-involvement identification with clients' problems and an emotional investment in the outcome of their counselling that is counterproductive. Untrained counsellors may believe that a high degree of involvement is necessary or inevitable. Counsellors in general concur with the view that there is an optimal level of involvement or engagement, beyond which it is unwise to go. Chronic over-involvement is likely to lead to BURNOUT (but is likely to be identified by supervision). Some counsellors warn equally about the dangers of under-involvement.

overt behaviour visible, observable behaviour. Something which is overt is 'out in the open' or obvious. Overt behaviour is contrasted with COVERT behaviour or processes which are private thoughts or intentions and/or devious in nature.

pacing the clinical judgement and skill involved in delivering interventions at a rate at which the client will best benefit. The timing of interventions during each session is a form of pacing but the counsellor also seeks to be aware of the overall rate of progress appropriate and possible for the client. He does this by heeding signs that the client is highly motivated and receptive, for example, or particularly resistant, confused, or in need of a 'contemplative' approach, and by explicitly using the REFLECTION process (asking the client for her views on pacing). *See* TIMING.

pain the neurophysiological and psychological experience of hurt and suffering. Janov (1975) considers pain central to human experience and to the formation of neurosis and DEFENCE MECHANISMS against pain. According to Janov's account, all assaults on the human being which cannot be immediately avoided, discharged or integrated (from intrauterine life onwards) accumulate, rendering the person progressively more disturbed and unable to welcome new experiences. Only PRIMAL THERAPY, a form of radical detraumatising, can reverse the process, according to Janov. Most theorists agree that we seek to minimise painful encounters and experiences and to maximise pleasure. Pain is experienced both in acute reactions to injury or TRAUMA and in chronic conditions. 'Chronically endured pain' is the concept of inescapable, longstanding, soul-destroying suffering, which implies that the person has had no alternative but to endure it. According to Buddhism, 'all life is suffering'. Most world religions and philosophies have significant concepts relating to pain and suffering. Models of counselling offer different views on the inevitability of change being painful; some models use concepts such as frustration and difficulty instead.

pain management any method or programme aiming to help reduce unavoidable physical pain or the awareness of it. Counselling, particularly CBT, can help clients experiencing chronic physical pain (e.g. back pain and pelvic pain) to tolerate it better. Hypnotherapy is sometimes used temporarily to help suppress pain.

panic attack acute, distressing anxiety, often with dramatic physical symptoms such as hyperventilation, palpitations, fainting, 'pins and needles' or paralysis. The sufferer commonly thinks that he or she is going to die, have a stroke, experience loss of control or other catastrophic outcome. Panic attacks may come without warning, and in response to specific stimuli or apparently without cause. Also called ANXIETY attacks or panic disorder, such conditions are probably best helped by cognitive and/or behavioural therapy, using methods which carefully identify the severity, frequency and intensity of attacks, precipitating factors and accompanying catastrophic cognitive interpretations. Clients can often be helped to identify and change the ways in which their thinking causes or escalates the physiological components of their attacks. They may sometimes be helped by being instructed to breathe diaphragmatically in order to take in carbon dioxide and hence return to a state of calm. Panic attacks rarely last more than 5 or 10 minutes, although when in the midst of an attack the person may believe that it will go on forever. Contrast with GENERALISED ANXIETY DISORDER.

paradoxical intention a technique attributed to Frankl in which the counsellor instructs the client to engage in behaviour of which she is, for example, afraid or ashamed, with the intention of extinguishing that behaviour. For example, a woman who is afraid that she will become so anxious in a supermarket that she will faint, may be asked to go to the supermarket and faint deliberately. The rationale for this technique is that by bringing the feared, involuntary behaviour under voluntary control, it becomes unlikely or impossible that the person will subsequently experience such acute anxiety. Paradoxical intention may be most effective when carried out without any prior explanation, and for this reason some counsellors question how ethical it is. Also known as 'paradoxical injunction'.

parallel process the duplication in the counsellor of aspects of the client's material, which manifests in the supervisory relationship. The counsellor may unconsciously echo and mirror a client's hopelessness, for example, in discussing the case with his supervisor in an uncharacteristically hopeless way. The client's hopelessness may be further paralleled by the supervisor's feeling hopeless. Skilful identification and interpretation of such parallels is considered an important feature of (particularly psychodynamic) supervision. Such parallel dynamics may also manifest in group supervision and training settings. There is also some speculation that counsellors may unconsciously attract clients whose problematic processes parallel their own. The term 'isomorphic' is sometimes used in US literature. Compare COUNTERTRANSFERENCE.

paramedical professions which resemble, support or complement the medical profession are sometimes considered paramedical. These include occupational therapy, speech therapy, physiotherapy, social work and counselling. Counselling is sometimes included under the umbrella of alternative or complementary medicine. Some counsellors prefer to distance themselves from the medical profession. *See* COUNSELLING IN MEDICAL SETTINGS, MEDICAL MODEL.

paranoia a delusional disorder characterised by the unshakeable, irrational conviction that one is being persecuted. In its extreme form of *paranoid schizophrenia* people experience hallucinations, for example, of MI5 pursuing them or of being talked about by television celebrities. Paranoia, although a psychotic condition, does not necessarily prevent the person from functioning socially, and is often of a specific kind. Identifiable syndromes are associated with morbid jealousy, distorted views of one's own body, and beliefs that people are other than who they say they are. Counselling is unlikely to have any impact on such intransigent conditions. People are sometimes referred to as *paranoid* who are chronically or periodically apprehensive and suspicious of others' motives; this trait may be sufficiently severe to amount to a paranoid personality disorder. Adults who have often been physically beaten as children, for example, may continue to expect to be surprised and beaten by attackers. People who experience intense or chronic victimisation may develop hypervigilant habits which resemble paranoia. *Paranoiacs* often try to persuade others of the reality of their delusions, which makes for severe difficulties in creating non-collusive therapeutic alliances.

paranoid–schizoid position Kleinian concept referring to the developmental phase of the earliest months in which the baby frequently splits her experiences of a parent into categories of good and bad. She cannot perceive, initially, the whole mother, but precariously experiences parts of the mother's body and is often in a 'persecuted' state, not trusting that the ministrations of the mother will meet her needs. The paranoid–schizoid position is resolved by the DEPRESSIVE POSITION in normal development although in Kleinian thought no one ever negotiates the paranoid–schizoid position so successfully as to be free of it. Everyone experiences this position in the course of daily life, although some obviously are more permanently disturbed by it.

paraphrasing the counselling and communication skill of reflecting back to another what has been said in a slightly altered, although accurate form. By paraphrasing, counsellors demonstrate that they have heard the client, they offer their understanding of what they have heard (to be confirmed or otherwise), and their use of paraphrase casts a slightly different light on the original statements, allowing the client to hear their own statements in a way which itself can powerfully move her into new personal perspectives.

parapraxis slips in speech or writing, or momentary forgetfulness; in German, literally 'faulty function'. Parapraxes were attributed by Freud to the return to conscious expression of censored thoughts and feelings but in a disguised, or unsuccessfully disguised, form. Often known as the FREUDIAN SLIP.

parasuicide *see* SUICIDE.

parataxic distortion the cognitive error, identified by H.S. Sullivan, of attributing causal significance to probably unrelated events. Sullivan considered that people often transfer learning incorrectly from childhood and may mis-read events accordingly, as in TRANSFERENCE.

parent ego state the set of feelings, attitudes and behaviours which resemble those of significant past figures. The person is said to copy his parents' mannerisms and to act as they would have acted, when 'in parent'. A parent ego state can be functionally further subdivided into positive and negative nurturing and controlling parent.

parental injunction *see* INJUNCTION.

part objects refer to the Kleinian concept of an exaggerated preoccupation with certain body parts (e.g. breasts) or attributes of others and the resulting tendency not to relate to the whole person.

parts aspects of one's own consciousness; aspects of others which have special significance for us. People frequently say 'a part of me wants to do this, but another part wants to do that,' which refers to conflict, confusion or the process of decision-making. When those parts have some durable quality they can be thought of as SUBPERSONALITIES.

passive–aggressive a way of behaving characterised by indirect signs of aggression such as stubbornness, sullenness, together with denial that one is angry. Passive-aggressive behaviour may be seen in adults who as children were severely cowed by authoritarian or terrifying parents, or in adults whose social position is vulnerable (e.g. a prisoner, or an employee with no prospects of finding another job) and who therefore may exhibit their anger indirectly. It is a defensive position which may have once been necessary (or on occasion may still be necessary), but which in general fails to represent the person's interests. A mark of passive–aggressive behaviour is the irritation it may arouse in others.

passivity inactivity, lack of assertiveness, submissiveness. In contrast to rest or necessary temporary withdrawal, passivity implies that one fails to take appropriate action, either in a particular situation or chronically; one may take on a suffering role rather than a responsible, problem-solving adult attitude. Extreme passivity often denotes DEPRESSION (*see* HELPLESSNESS). In the area of sexuality, passivity has the connotation of an inability to engage fully in reciprocal lovemaking; or is associated with MASOCHISM.

past lives therapy therapy claiming to help clients make contact with previous incarnations of themselves, often with the use of regressive hypnotherapy. While the concept of reincarnation may lend support to this in principle, the subject is surrounded by suspicion and lack of evidence and credibility.

pastoral counselling counselling in the context of the Church or other religious groups (particularly Christians and Jews). Sometimes 'pastoral' is used in the context of primary and secondary education in 'pastoral care'. Pastoral counselling in the religious context draws on secular theories of psychology and psychotherapy as well as on some aspects of religious thought. It may include the functions of healing, support, guidance, reconciliation and nurturance. It is not a proselytising activity (i.e. inviting religious conversion) although it can be concerned with spiritual growth. Although frequently indistinguishable from secular counselling, its religious concerns may be apparent, and some Christian counsellors may use prayer or discussion of religious texts. *See* Jacobs (1982); *see* CLINICAL THEOLOGY.

patient one who suffers; one who seeks or needs the services of medical practitioners. Conventionally, people who use the services of doctors, psychiatrists, psychoanalysts and many psychotherapists are known as patients. The convention among counsellors is to refer to 'clients', which implies a free agent who chooses and purchases a service. *See* CLIENT.

patriarchy any social order governed by men, fathers or 'wise male elders'; the oppressive domination of male values and institutions. Many people agree (and feminists in particular assert) that most cultures, including that of the UK, have been thoroughly and detrimentally patriarchal for about the last 6000 years. The effect of this has been the promotion of aggressive, 'rational', technological values and the loss of 'female values' such as feeling, aesthetics and ecological awareness. Many feminists argue that patriarchal institutions are so pervasive and self-perpetuating that significant change is inevitably a long and difficult process.

patripsych is the concept of internalised patriarchal values (in men and women), which is a phenomenon to be taken seriously by radical therapists and counsellors. *See* FEMINIST COUNSELLING, NON-SEXIST COUNSELLING.

payoff a term from transactional analysis referring to the outcome of GAMES and SCRIPTS. It is the ulterior, hidden part of inauthentic transactions. People who want to confirm, for example, that they are unlovable, ensure either that they are rejected in their relationships or that they can interpret (twist) social interactions to confirm how unlovable they are. Counsellors may, therefore, ask clients who persistently fail to get what they say they want, what the payoff is for frustrating themselves. *See* SECONDARY GAIN.

peak experience elation or heightened awareness resulting from counselling, therapy, group work, or spontaneously. The term was coined by Maslow and is especially significant within the HUMANISTIC PSYCHOLOGY tradition. A peak experience may be, for example, a sudden breakthrough into a state of dramatically out-of-the-ordinary consciousness (such as the Buddhist 'satori'). Other examples may arise in the context of relationships, creativity or encounter groups. Peak experiences are characterised by the feeling, however momentary, of transcending one's normal limited awareness and at the same time

recognising a deeper potential within oneself that was always there. While some people engage in encounter groups, meditation and other activities of religions and cults specifically in the hope of having peak experiences, others consider such experiences as being either of no great importance, or of needing to be contextualised by the working through of other PERSONAL GROWTH processes.

peer counselling counselling members of one's own social or age group. The term is sometimes used synonymously with CO-COUNSELLING, and it is common in exercises on training courses, but its most usual use is now of school students engaging in structured, mutual support.

peer supervision the supervision by each other of counsellors of equal status. Peer supervision may be conducted on a one-to-one basis or in groups. Its rationale can be economic (it is cheaper than paying a supervisor), political (some counsellors are not in favour of a hierarchical professional model), pragmatic (some counsellors live in remote areas and have limited access to supervisors).

penalties negative consequences used as deterrents or incentives. Behavioural counsellors may agree with clients on suitable penalties for not completing a particular HOMEWORK assignment, or clients may propose their own penalties. Some clients find it helpful to arrange to reward themselves for completing certain assignments or taking certain risks, and conversely to penalise themselves for not carrying out such tasks. Such an intervention is contraindicated for people whose core problems concern failure, but is potent when addressing PROCRASTINATION, for example.

penis envy *see* ENVY.

perception the 'taking in', neuropsychological processing, and understanding of events by means of the senses. Some writers distinguish between perception as awareness of stimuli and conception as the means of understanding them. Perception is a complex discipline within psychology. It is recognised that although human beings perceive the world in a broadly similar way, perception is affected by cultural and individual differences. A person is said to be 'perceptive' when he accurately assesses situations or people. *See* SUBLIMINAL PERCEPTION.

perfectionism a character trait wherein the person constantly attempts to meet extremely (or impossibly) high standards, or expects others to meet them. Perfectionism is a form of obsessive behaviour. In its subclinical form it is fairly common and not necessarily distressing, but people who feel driven to 'be perfect' or perform perfectly, sooner or later disappoint themselves and/or irritate others. Perfectionism is marked by irrational thinking, particularly along the lines of 'If it isn't perfect, it's (I am) worth nothing'.

performance anxiety the specific form of anxiety which precedes participation in forthcoming theatrical, sporting and other public events. Many performing artists, for example, are physically sick before a performance, and some resort to the use of tranquillisers. Psychoanalytic theory has been used to suggest that musicians, for example, often seek to express *all* their feelings through their art, and hence make themselves unusually vulnerable to criticism. Surveys of musicians' families have shown their fathers to be (frequently) particularly influential, demanding and unfor-

giving. Cognitive approaches to performance anxiety examine clients' irrational self-talk, negative predictions, etc., and aim to encourage clients to separate their performance from their self-worth.

performing functioning. The word 'performing' has the connotations of functioning well or well enough; alternatively of putting on an act or insincere persona. *See also* FORMING IN GROUPS.

peritraumatic dissociation the dissociation occurring at the same time as the traumatic event. Feelings of unreality, confusion, tunnel vision, etc. may arise seemingly instantaneously as a means of self-protection.

permission allowing and encouraging. *Permission giving* by the counsellor to the client (e.g. 'It's OK for you to act this way') can be a powerful means of leverage; many clients may have never been told before (or not for a long time) that it is acceptable to be themselves or to have their own preferences. In transactional analysis, counsellors may give clients permission (or model permission) to contradict their script messages (e.g. 'You don't have to be perfect').

perpetuation of disturbance the maintenance of an unhealthy mode of functioning. Various intrapersonal, interpersonal and environmental mechanisms may be utilised by clients to keep their disturbances operative. According to cognitive therapy, for example, errors in thinking perpetuate disturbances, even when the origins of disturbance may have been a genuine trauma. *See* ACQUISITION OF DISTURBANCE, AETIOLOGY.

persecution pursuing, hunting, inflicting pain; deliberate OPPRESSION. Delusions of persecution, as experienced in PARANOIA, are characterised by the person believing that she is being followed, harassed or invaded when there is no such activity taking place in reality. *Persecution complex* loosely refers to this idea. According to Melanie Klein, we are all prone to persecutory feelings in infancy (*see* PARANOID–SCHIZOID POSITION) but most of us develop from this position. Interventions in counselling or therapy (or supervision) are said to have a persecutory quality when they seem to bombard or invade the client, for example in the form of a volley of questions.

Persecutor role a 'scripty role' in TA theory, according to which someone perceives others as being not-OK and therefore discounts them in a variety of ways. The Persecutor role alternates with the Rescuer and Victim roles in the KARPMAN TRIANGLE.

person human being; recognisable individual; one who experiences himself as a unique and consistent entity. The term implies a certain right to dignity. It is sometimes said that women are treated by men as sex objects rather than as persons; and that babies are considered to be 'feelingless blobs' instead of persons. People who object to abortion on religious grounds believe that the fetus is a person. *See* SELF.

person-centred counselling the counselling orientation developed by Carl Rogers and originally known as non-directive, then client-centred therapy/counselling. The term person-centred came to be preferred because Rogers applied his theories to contexts outside of therapy and desired a more generally applicable terminology. Person-centred counselling (which is identical to person-centred therapy and also known as the person-centred approach, or PCA) aims to remain faithful to the experiencing of the person who is in the role of the client, and requires that the counsellor establish a psychological climate characterised by empathy, congruence and unconditional positive regard (*see* CORE CONDITIONS). This approach views people as essentially forward-moving and innately self-actualising; their natural growth can be perverted, however, by adverse circumstances including destructive parental introjects; instead of relying on an internal locus of control, they depend on an external locus. In counselling, given the climate provided by the relationship with a counsellor, the person will gradually rediscover and nurture her self-actualising tendency (*see* SELF-ACTUALISATION) and will come to trust her own *organismic self*. Person-centred counsellors consider the core conditions to be NECESSARY AND SUFFICIENT for therapeutic change and generally avoid introducing other techniques into counselling. Critics claim that the approach is slow, aimless and only helpful during the initial exploratory phase of counselling. The person-centred approach is enormously influential within the British counselling world, and is considered by some to be synonymous with fundamental counselling skills (*see* ROGERIAN). *See* Mearns and Thorne (1999).

persona mask or face worn by people with which to confront and negotiate the world. Jung used the term as an archetype: all societies require such 'masks', but these need not be pathological or damaging. Examples of personas include gender identity and profession (whereby people may identify with and hide behind masculine stereotypes, for example, or business executive stereotypes) and people may project *one* aspect of their personality as a persona (*see* SUBPERSONALITY). A persona 'mediates between the ego and the external world' (Samuels, 1993).

personal construct psychology the 'total psychology of the person' developed by Kelly (1955). Based on the philosophy of CONSTRUCTIVE ALTERNATIVISM, personal construct theory concentrates on how people construe; it regards people as 'personal scientists' who build theories about their worlds and are capable of experimenting with these theories. In order to understand people's construing in personal construct therapy/counselling, the counsellor elicits constructs by various means, including credulous listening, LADDERING, PYRAMIDING, the use of SELF-CHARACTERISATION and the REPERTORY GRID TECHNIQUE. People are viewed as typically interpreting events in an overly controlled or undisciplined manner. By considering interpretations of behaviour which are slightly different from the interpretations they are used to, people can come to realise that by gradually experimenting with new interpretations and actions, a wider choice of potential behaviours are open to them.

personal counselling of the counsellor the counselling which trainee or qualified counsellors receive as clients. Most counsellor training courses require trainees to undergo a minimum period of counselling. This is intended to address trainees' current or underlying problems, thus reducing the likelihood of any pathological countertransference, and also to familiarise trainees with the experience of being the client. Some dissenters argue that such a requirement goes against the spirit of counselling as an autonomously desired activity. It is also debated whether

counsellors should be in counselling or therapy after qualifying. While the personal counselling requirement has an obvious appeal (and is paralleled in the training analysis of psychoanalytic psychotherapists) there is no research evidence to support the idea that it contributes decisively to higher standards of counselling practice. The BACP requires those applying for accreditation to demonstrate that they have had a minimum of 40 hours of purposeful personal development work, and this is sometimes taken to mean, narrowly, their own personal counselling or therapy.

personal development group a group experience provided by counsellor training courses to facilitate trainees' intrapersonal, interpersonal awareness and skills. Such groups are often led by external (non-assessing) facilitators and vary in length, frequency, content and style. They provide an opportunity for personal development, group bonding and counselling skills enhancement. They are complementary to, but not a substitute for, the trainee's own personal counselling.

personal growth the exploration and development of individuals' emotional, psychological and spiritual potential. Personal growth is a concept from HUMANISTIC PSYCHOLOGY which acknowledges the wish of many people to use counselling, therapy, group work and other exercises to explore and embrace parts of their personalities as yet under-developed. It stresses the view that counselling is not exclusively for people who have problems. Personal growth is roughly equivalent to *personality transformation* but in a humanistic context is often also associated with transpersonal and political awareness. It is

163

argued by some that counselling is not the best way of facilitating personal growth because of its short-term and problem-focused nature, but counselling can in fact address areas of personal growth that are reasonably well defined. Some have distinguished between personal growth and personal development, the latter being intentional and structured, the former possibly happening naturally (*see* Rowan, 1998).

personal science that view of people which stresses their capacity for rigorous empirical observation of their own behaviour. The 'personal science paradigm' of Mahoney focuses on personal data collection, identification of patterns and options, experimentation, data comparison and the revision of behaviour. *See also* PERSONAL CONSTRUCT PSYCHOLOGY.

personalisation the cognitive error of believing that events and remarks probably or necessarily refer to oneself. People who frequently or dysfunctionally personalise events fail to see the full context in which events occur and too readily assume that such events must be connected with or aimed at themselves. In its extreme forms, personalisation becomes a narcissistic condition, paranoia or a delusion of grandeur.

personality disorder psychiatric classification referring to a personally characteristic, enduring pattern of disturbed behaviour characterised by difficulty in maintaining relationships, by attention seeking, obsessiveness, and other traits. The DSM-IV TR lists paranoid, schizoid, schizotypal, antisocial, borderline, histrionic, narcissistic, avoidant, dependent, obsessive-compulsive personality disorders and 'personality disorders not otherwise specified'. It is regarded by many as a loose term to describe a wide range of people who experience difficulty in being cooperative, sociable, law-abiding or productive. Many people diagnosed as having a personality disorder have had highly unsatisfactory, abusive or disruptive childhoods, often including periods in institutional care, and many offenders, addicts and homeless people attract this diagnosis. They are unlikely to be helped markedly by counselling or therapy but will often be continuous or intermittent users of psychiatric and other helping services. Ryle (1990), however, claims some success with them using CAT. *See also* DIALECTICAL BEHAVIOUR THERAPY and BORDERLINE PERSONALITY DISORDER.

personality theory any theory purporting to explain in general terms how and why individuals differ from others and how they make unique adjustments to their environments. *Personality* refers to the unique combination of traits identifiable in any individual. Personality is sometimes considered synonymous with 'character'; alternatively, personality is sometimes considered to equate with temperament or inner qualities and character with external behaviour. The multiplicity of theories in counselling and psychotherapy have different implications for understanding individual development, functioning and psychopathology. There are also non-psychological personality theories, such as those suggested by astrology, which play a part in 'astrological counselling' and in the practice of some Jungians. Whatever the particular view on personality factors held by any counsellor, she must be aware of the ways in which individual differences from client to client (for example, in terms of extraversion and introversion) affect the counselling relationship. Counsellors need to be alert to what they (and clients) regard as valued personality traits and what may be regarded as undesirable, pathological traits. *See* DEVELOPMENTAL STAGES, INDIVIDUAL DIFFERENCES, MODEL OF HUMAN BEINGS, PSYCHOLOGICAL TYPE. *See* Storr (1963), Cramer (1992).

persuasion the act of influencing, inducing a desired response or belief in another. Most counsellors avoid attempting to persuade clients, valuing instead clients' own, autonomous decision-making processes. It has been argued, however (Frank, 1963), that counselling, like various systems of religious healing, inevitably contains an element, at least, of persuasion, both at the client-counsellor level and at the levels of training and professionalisation. *See also* INFLUENCING SKILLS.

perversion behaviour (usually sexual) which deviates from the cultural norm. Although certain behaviours (e.g. bulimia and self-mutilation) are *perverse* (i.e. not in the person's best interests) they are not categorised as perversions. In the classical psychoanalytic tradition, perversions include homosexuality, anal intercourse, and transvestism. There is no consensus as to where the boundaries lie between normal and perverted sexuality, although paedophilia (sex with children) and bestiality (sex with animals) are considered perverse, immoral (and properly illegal) by a majority of people. Freud postulated that perversion might stem from the *polymorphous perversity* of infancy (or tendency to enjoy sensual explorations without discrimination) before any awareness of genital sexuality; others theorise that perversions may stem from developmental failures and traumas.

phallic stage the developmental stage in Freudian theory which is characterised by preoccupation with the penis. Occurring at the age of 4 or 5 years, the phallic stage is said to represent a boy's awareness of the power of the penis and of his vulnerability to castration. Others claim that a girl's interest in her vagina at this age is equally significant, and that this aspect of Freudian theory is based on phallocentric myths.

phantasy *see* FANTASY.

phenomenology a philosophy arguing that events and objects are to be understood in terms of our immediate experience of them as they appear to us. (*Phenomena* are objects as they appear to us, while *noumena* are direct, intuitive awarenesses of objects.) Psychotherapy and counselling theory and practice derived from phenomenology dwell on the person's experience of events rather than on presuppositions, speculations or inferences. Thus, Mahrer (1996) stresses the importance of the counsellor 'entering the client's phenomenological world' and contrasts this with inference (or what it presumably must be like to have the other person's experience). Phenomenological counsellors generally attempt to see and hear the client's world as she sees and hears it, without, for example, negotiating to set goals or make interpretations. Spinelli has referred to a 'describe, don't explain' methodology. *Phenomenal field* refers to everything that is currently impinging on one (externally or internally).

philosophical counselling a relatively new movement attempting to shift counselling from reliance on the discipline of psychology towards philosophy. Proponents argue that philosophy is much older, deeper, and often better equipped to clarify problems in living. It may draw on any philosophical tradition and be delivered person-to-person or by email, for example. While it may share with REBT the likelihood that faulty logic creates and sustains our problems, it is not wedded to any one approach. *See* Howard (2000).

philosophical empathy *see* EMPATHY.

phobia persistent irrational fear and avoidance of certain situations. Some categorise phobias into simple/specific, social phobia and agoraphobia. A phobia is a form of anxiety disorder related to specific, dreaded stimuli. The best known is AGORAPHOBIA (fear of open and public spaces). Other phobias include fear of enclosed spaces (CLAUSTROPHOBIA), spiders (arachnophobia), birds (ornithophobia), madness (phrenophobia), dirt, blood, hair, flying, escalators. It is in the nature of phobias that they are specifically related to certain stimuli, and it has been suggested that the cause may lie in a conditioning experience in the client's past (e.g. witnessing a bloody accident). Various aetiologies are suggested but phobias are frequently very stubborn and chronic in nature. Phobic sufferers usually experience their conditions as stigmatic and therefore delay seeking help. Support groups for sufferers have been found beneficial, and there are claims that exposure methods (*see* FLOODING and SYSTEMATIC DESENSITISATION) are most successful in dealing with phobic disorders. Talking treatments alone are unlikely to alter the phobia.

phobia cure a term used in NEUROLINGUISTIC PROGRAMMING specifically for a method of eliminating a phobia. NLP claims to have removed certain phobias completely within a very short time, e.g. in minutes.

phototherapy use of a form of bright light to treat seasonal affective disorder and some other forms of depression. This intervention is thought to stimulate serotonin. Not to be confused with the use of the client's photographs in counselling, used to stimulate memory recall.

physical abuse hitting, beating, mutilating, torturing, starving. The physical abuse of babies and children is now generally considered to be intrinsically traumatic, to have long-standing effects and to result often (but by no means always) in the abused person behaving abusively to others as an adult (Miller, 1987). In this sense, physical abuse includes the corporal punishment administered by parents and teachers. Repeated physical violence between married or cohabiting partners is a recognised syndrome, usually stemming from the violence of the male partner and sometimes involving the adoption of a victim role by the female partner. Adults suffering serious accidental or criminal physical abuse are prone to POST-TRAUMATIC STRESS DISORDER.

placatory behaviour behaviour which is designed to please others or to avoid negative reactions from others. Ethological studies of submissive behaviour in animals and humans suggests that it is a universal phenomenon. People who habitually avoid confrontation, even at serious cost to themselves, and who go out of their way to be pleasant or innocuous, are sometimes referred to as 'pleasers'. Placatory behaviour usually ultimately fails to serve the best interests of the person concerned.

placebo a substance or procedure with no actual therapeutic properties which is administered in medical research to compare and determine the effects of other drugs. In psychological usage, the *placebo effect* refers to any change in clients which may be attributed to NON-SPECIFIC FACTORS (such as hope, attention, belief in the expert). Eysenck (1992) asserted that therapy generally is no more effective than placebo treatment and that any beneficial effects it does have are probably due to non-specific relationship factors. Others suggest up to 15% of outcome variance is due to placebo factors.

placement a period of practical, supervised counselling undertaken by counselling trainees, usually in counselling agencies other than their own workplace. Many counsellors-in-training offer their services voluntarily in return for client referrals (a figure of 100 required client hours over a period of a year or two is quite typical for training courses). Trainees are ethically obliged to inform clients of their status and, as Pitts (1992) underlines, trainers and supervisors should ensure that the clients of trainees in placements do not receive substandard treatment. A placement is known in North America as a 'practicum'.

plasticity neurological term for the brain's capacity to moderate its responses, to learn from experience in general and especially following accidents; sometimes contrasted with *canalisation*, or rigidity of learning pathways.

pleasure principle the Freudian concept according to which human infants primarily seek to avoid pain (or unpleasure) and to maximise satisfaction. Also known as the pleasure–pain principle, this concept includes the idea that tension is discharged by gratification. With the development of the ego comes the REALITY PRINCIPLE which tempers or alternates with the pleasure principle.

PLISSIT an acronym used in couple counselling for permission (for clients to experiment with what they may have perceived as immoral or wrong), limited information (the counsellor's judgement of what is useful), specific suggestions (e.g. for homework assignments) and intensive therapy.

pluralism any theory which acknowledges the multiplicity of stimuli and theories acting within and upon us. Psychological pluralism (akin to 'psychological polytheism') accepts, for example, that there are competing claims to therapeutic truth and potency and that these are not necessarily reducible to any 'grand universal theory': consciousness itself is pluralistic. Postmodernism supports such arguments. *See also* SUBPERSONALITIES.

political psyche the name given to the political content and concerns about power of the client's or counsellor's mind, sometimes the unconscious or pre-conscious aspects of the mind. Samuels (1993) relates depth psychology to politics and argues for greater awareness of the links as a balance to the individualistic focus of much therapy. *See also* Smail (1993).

Pollyannaish attitude an attitude towards life, obstacles and counselling characterised by a naïve positive thinking, seeing everything uncritically as wonderful. Associated with FLIGHT INTO HEALTH. After the novel by Eleanor H. Porter.

portrayal outward appearance, particularly in relation to trainee or beginning (person-centred) counsellors, of core conditions rather than a deeply internalised, congruent level of experiencing and relating; a SURFACE RELATIONAL COMPETENCE.

positive asset search an exercise requiring the client to think hard about and list his personal qualities, talents and achievements. This exercise may be particularly useful for depressed clients whose LOW SELF-ESTEEM includes an unrealistic global assessment of themselves as having no good qualities.

positive self-regard valuing oneself as one is; feeling good about oneself. Positive self-regard is not a POSITIVE THINKING attitude towards oneself but a discovered ability to value oneself unconditionally, as well as to value one's particular strengths. Positive self-regard often develops within the client as a result of engaging in counselling with a counsellor who offers UNCONDITIONAL POSITIVE REGARD. *See* UNCONDITIONAL SELF-ACCEPTANCE.

positive thinking an attitude towards life which is informed by optimistic self-talk. Mainly a self-help method, positive thinking has roots in religion, has little theoretical foundation and is often criticised as simplistic, as denying the reality of personal problems and pain, and as not having any enduring therapeutic potency. Cognitive–behavioural counselling is sometimes mistakenly caricatured as advocating positive thinking.

postmodernism an intellectual movement claiming that we now live in a time with no certainties, in which no 'metanarrative' is credible, and relativity reigns. Stemming from architectural criticism in the 1950s and with Lyotard as its chief exponent, postmodernism questions any attempt to set up grand systems. As such, some counsellors question core theoretical models, professionalisation, etc. and seek a postmodern therapy (*see* House, 2003).

postnatal depression a recognised form of depression which ensues from giving birth. Like DEPRESSION in general, the symptoms are despondency, emotionality and hopelessness, or may include anxiety and panic that can focus on the mother's feelings of inadequacy regarding caring for her child. The incidence of postnatal depression is reckoned to be one out of ten mothers. Also known as 'baby blues', postnatal depression can be helped by support and counselling, but sometimes antidepressants may be needed. *Puerperal psychosis*, a much more severe disturbance ('puerperal' means 'pertaining to childbirth'; *see* PSYCHOSIS), affects one or two new mothers in a thousand, manifests soon after birth and requires hospital treatment.

post-traumatic growth the phenomenon whereby, following traumatic or extreme negative events, individuals experience positive consequences such as greater emotional openness, perception of new life possibilities, profound and sometimes religious experiences, and greater personal strength. *See* Tedeschi and Calhoun (1995).

post-traumatic stress disorder a form of disturbance associated with involvement in or exposure to unavoidable, traumatic, life-threatening events (*see* TRAUMA). Technically, a condition may be known as PTSD (according to the DSM-IV TR) only if symptoms last for at least a month. People who experience personal or mass disasters (such as road traffic accidents, armed robbery, train crashes, war) often show similar PTSD symptoms: involuntary recall of the event; related dreams and nightmares; hallucinations, repetitive images and flashbacks. In an effort to avoid such after effects, sufferers may experience psychological numbing (a temporary inability to feel), and may feel compelled to avoid anything that will remind them of the trauma and may even have marked failure of memory. They may also experience symptoms of anxiety, such as sleep disturbance, hypervigilance and irritability. The shock of the event may unbalance the person's total world view (nothing seems secure any longer). As with other forms of bereavement, PTSD often follows a sequence of shock, disorientation, denial, searching (for lost loved ones), depression, guilt, anger, acceptance and return to relative normality. Treatment for PTSD depends on the nature of the event, the extent of its impact on individuals, and resources available. Typically, sufferers will need to confront the event again (particularly in imagery) and fully accept it as a fact in all its details; they need to talk about it and be given ample opportunity for CATHARSIS and WORKING THROUGH; medication, relaxation techniques, anger management and cognitive re-appraisal may be called for. People may be encouraged actively to let go of the dead and to immerse themselves in everyday routines when appropriate. Progress has been made on understanding the neurological mechanisms of PTSD. *Prolonged duress stress disorder* (PDSD) has been proposed for the kind of cumulative trauma (for example, in certain occupations such as police work) which can result in symptoms similar to those of PTSD, but which may have no single, dramatic, obvious cause. *See also* DISASTER COUNSELLING, SURVIVOR GUILT.

potency power or effectiveness. Therapeutic interventions are said to be potent when they can arouse and move the client sufficiently and helpfully towards change. In transactional analysis, potency has the following technical meaning: the self-evident power of the counsellor who, 'in parent', gives PERMISSION to the client to contradict messages received from her own parents.

potential the power to become. Potential can mean anything which is not, and therefore may yet be. Every counselling theory has some implicit concept of potentiality (*see* CHANGE). Humanistic counselling in particular invests much faith in HUMAN POTENTIAL. Mahrer (1996) identifies deeper and OPERATING POTENTIALS in clients' phenomenological worlds.

power ability to act or to effect change. Power is implied in the concepts of AUTONOMY and self-actualising tendency (*see* SELF-ACTU-ALISATION). There can be no therapeutic change without mobilising some minimal power within the client. Most counsellors see themselves as engaged in the empowerment of their clients. However, there is an important difference between personal and political power, because certain individuals and groups within society hold greater power than others. Those who claim that 'You have the power to become whatever you wish' are often criticised as politically naive. EMPOWERMENT is a central concept in counselling. Power is a significant issue between men and women, between adults and children and between classes and races. The power of the therapist or counsellor (in contradistinction to POTENCY) can be and has been abused (*see* MALPRACTICE), and Masson (1992) claims that all therapists are inevitably inclined to abuse their power over clients. In a quite different sense, the TWELVE STEPS approach argues that significant personal change cannot come about without recourse to a 'higher power' (God or the person's idiosyncratic concept of God). *See also* INDIVIDUAL PSYCHOLOGY.

powerlessness inability to act or to effect change; belief that one is unable to act effectively. Powerlessness is the converse of power. It can be said that one is as powerless as one believes oneself to be; it can also be said that certain individuals and groups are *relatively powerless*. (Many consider that the *disempowerment* of women and minority groups is a political fact.) According to re-evaluation counselling, 'powerlessness is a fraud'. According to the TWELVE STEPS approach to helping addicts and alcoholics, the first step towards recovery is for the person to *accept* his powerlessness (e.g. his addiction is stronger than he is, and he will be unable, by his own efforts alone, to overcome it). *See* HELPLESSNESS.

practice-based evidence a term that seeks to reverse the assumption that 'objective' evidence precedes practice, arguing that counselling practice – what actually transpires in counselling sessions – offers valid, qualitative evidence of how counselling works, what works best, how it might be improved, etc. *See* EVIDENCE-BASED PRACTICE.

prayer thoughts, sentiments, wishes directed towards God or other transcendent being. Some research suggests that an unexpectedly high proportion of counsellors engage in prayer, either outside sessions or in them (covertly, or overtly, with client permission). *See* SPIRITUALITY.

preconscious psychoanalytic concept referring to thoughts, images and feelings which, although accessible, are not currently in conscious awareness. The preconscious is quite distinct from the UNCONSCIOUS, the contents of which cannot be made conscious by an act of will or remembering alone. The preconscious is also called the 'descriptive unconscious'; it is not involved in censorship and is closely associated with the activities of the ego. The SUBCONSCIOUS is sometimes used as a synonym of 'preconscious' although it was only briefly used by Freud in this way.

pre-counselling factors the client's circumstances, anticipatory fantasies and fears about counselling before the first session. Pre-counselling factors include initial intentions to seek counselling, the influence of significant others in one's decision, knowledge about counselling and first contact with the counsellor or counselling agency. Awareness of and explicit discussion of such factors assist the formation of a THERAPEUTIC ALLIANCE.

pregnancy counselling counselling for women considering pregnancy, who are pregnant, or who are contemplating termination. This often includes information-giving. *See* ABORTION COUNSELLING and MISCARRIAGE COUNSELLING.

premature ejaculation this term refers to the ejaculation of semen during sexual activity which is regarded as occurring too soon to be satisfying to one or both partners. While there are many proffered explanations for its occurrence, probably the most reliable treatment is behavioural. The so-called 'squeeze technique' entails arousal to near ejaculation, which is interrupted repeatedly by applying pressure just below the coronal ridge of the penis, until the man learns that he can control ejaculation. Feelings of embarrassment and SELF-RATING may be addressed effectively by cognitive therapy. The role of the partner is crucial.

premature termination counselling which is ended before the client and/or the counsellor expected it to end. The term tends to refer to the termination of counselling by the client. Premature termination may refer to prematurity as measured by a contract (e.g. to work together for 6 weeks) or by the counsellor's assumption that the client was going to continue counselling. While some clients declare their intention to terminate, others simply fail to attend for their next appointment. Research efforts have been made to determine possible causes of premature termination (including client fears of dependence, ending itself and of destabilisation through uncovering more conflicts, and counsellor skill-deficits) but evidence suggests that a large number of counselling relationships are shorter than many counsellors expect or wish them to be. Sometimes referred to as 'attrition'. *See* ENDINGS.

premenstrual tension/syndrome the psychophysiological disturbance experienced by some women for some time each month before their periods are due. PMT ('premenstrual syndrome' is used more widely in the US, but is also in use in the UK) may begin from the time of ovulation, in mid-cycle. Symptoms may include irritability, depression, anxiety, mood swings, headaches, food cravings, fatigue. Possible causes include hormonal imbalance and stress. It may most affect those women in their thirties who have had one or two pregnancies. Regarded as a multifactorial condition, it can be relieved for some women by hormone replacement therapy, by the contraceptive pill, by pregnancy and to some extent by counselling. There is some debate as to the nature, extent and existence of this syndrome.

prescriptive counsellor interventions which seek to influence and direct the client are said to be prescriptive. Heron (2001) has suggested that prescriptive interventions have a place in counselling, but that care needs to be taken to consider whether to use them, when, at what level, etc. He outlines a variety of such interventions, including consultative, validating, paradoxical and quasi-hypnotic prescriptions. It has also been argued that all counselling is prescriptive, but many counsellors deny this. For example, if a counsellor asks a client 'How do you feel at this moment?', this prescribes that the client should have feelings, should know what those feelings are, should be able to put them into words, should trust the counsellor enough to reveal those feelings. *See* ACTIVE–DIRECTIVE METHODS.

prescriptive matching the attempt to identify and provide the best possible compatibility of client and client-problem with counsellor and treatment approach. Although more of an aim than a reality at present, prescriptive matching is implicit in Lazarus's (1981) MULTIMODAL THERAPY and in the integrative trend in counselling and psychotherapy generally. Prescriptive matching asks what the best choice of counselling approach is for this particular client's problem, with which counsellor, in which arena, and under which circumstances.

presence a state of alertness, availability and freedom from preoccupation. 'Presence of mind' is a heightened awareness and ability to respond creatively to immediate challenges. Rogers came close to suggesting that presence be considered a fourth core condition of counselling. 'Personal presence' implies the making of a significant impact on others. Sometimes counsellors-in-training fail to make their presence felt because they are anxiously preoccupied with their performance (*see* SPECTATORING). Personal presence or charisma is also considered by some to be a desirable quality for counsellor trainers. Rogers hypothesised that the counsellor's 'quality of presence' could sometimes be such that it could alone trigger a process of healing.

presenting concern the problem or issue to which the client attributes most importance in the first session or sessions. The concept of a presenting concern (or 'problem' or 'symptom') implies that there are other, deeper problems or dynamics below the surface of which the client may or may not be initially aware. This is an assumption in DEPTH PSYCHOLOGY. Most counsellors respect and work with the presenting concern until other concerns become apparent. Some counsellors and brief psychotherapists focus primarily or exclusively on the presenting concern (*see* Budman and Gurman, 1988).

presenting opacity the client's initial confusion and difficulty in telling the counsellor accurately or with due focus what their problem or concern is. There are often multiple worries or narrative threads that cause a sense of fogginess, and separating or prioritising these may take some time.

pressure of speech excessively, unnecessarily fast speech, in which ideas tumble out one after another. It is associated with some forms of anxiety, with manic defence (*see* MANIA) and is a feature of HYPOMANIA. Care needs to be taken by counsellors not to confuse this with a conversational style that is culturally determined.

pre-therapy a proposed theory and method within the person-centred approach addressing the difficulty of making psychological contact with certain clients (e.g. some with severe learning difficulties or psychoses).

preventive counselling any counselling that aims to help clients avoid future difficulties. Most counselling has a preventive or forward-looking aspect. Counsellors working with parents and young people (e.g. in schools or youthwork settings) have an opportunity to offer psychological education which can raise awareness of, and present strategies for dealing with, potential pitfalls. Counsellors working in the health education field (e.g. HIV and AIDS) transmit information on health risks and help clients to explore such issues. By their nature, counselling and psychotherapy attract clients who are usually already in difficulties and potential for preventive work is still underdeveloped. *See also* RELAPSE.

primal integration developed by Swartley, Lake and others (*see* Rowan and Dryden, 1988) primal integration is closely related to PRIMAL THERAPY but in addition to reliving primal pain it stresses the need to explore its implications: primal joy, love and spirituality are viewed as important aspects of therapy and personal growth, and cannot be reduced (as Janov suggests) to secondary or defensive behaviours. Primal integrationists also claim to bring some clients to re-experience INTRAUTERINE and implantation trauma.

primal scene the psychoanalytic concept of the child witnessing or imagining her parents engaging in sexual intercourse. Its importance lies in the anxiety it generates in the child, who is thought to view it as an act of aggression and/or sado-masochism.

primal therapy a form of psychotherapy developed by Janov (1975). Often caricatured as 'scream therapy', it is in fact characterised more by deep crying. Its aim is the sequential removal of clients' defences, therapeutic re-experiencing of repressed pain (not only psychic but also psychophysiological pain, and called by Janov *primal pain*) from the present back, if necessary, to traumatic birth, shedding along the way chronic tension, symptoms of arrested development and neuroses idiosyncratic to each client. It emphasises catharsis and authentic, spontaneous behaviour. It denies the claims of all other approaches to therapy and counselling, which Janov views as further neurotic escapes from pain (since the only valid and effective task for therapy is to restore the client as fully as possible to a pre-traumatised state of emotional and physical integrity). It is usually conducted in padded and soundproofed rooms. Some commentators consider primal therapy to be simply ABREACTION-based after the early Freud, or as neo-Reichian in its focus on bodily defences. (For variants of primal therapy, *see* CLINICAL THEOLOGY and PRIMAL INTEGRATION.)

primary care counsellor a counsellor employed to work in the primary care sector of the British National Health Service, chiefly in the surgeries of general practitioners (GPs), and thus acting as a generalist counsellor. A great deal of primary care counselling is time-limited, typically of 6 sessions.

primary process Freudian concept of the category of unconscious thinking or mental processes which are associated with the id: the pleasure principle, indifference to space and time, and the activities of displacement and condensation of thoughts and images. Dreams are the classical example of the primary process. *See* SECONDARY PROCESS.

prioritising ranking concerns or problems in order of personal importance or urgency. Clients with multiple problems often need help to prioritise their concerns in counselling. They may decide to work first on what is most urgent or what is easiest to change. Prioritising lends structure to counselling and implicitly teaches clients the importance of time and the management of personal resources.

private practice providing counselling on a freelance, commercial basis. Private practitioners may work alone or as part of a group practice, and either work from their own homes or from hired rooms. They are not salaried and charge clients an hourly fee. Since counselling is not universally available through the NHS or other free services, many people are prepared to pay for it. Many counsellors have a 'mixed portfolio' of work, which may include private practice and part-time employment in counselling or related positions. Private practitioners also call themselves 'freelance' and 'independent'. Private practice is probably the setting least affected by pressures for TIME-LIMITED COUNSELLING.

prizing valuing, appreciating another person. The term was often used by Rogers and conveys the counsellor's intention actively to accept the client, her uniqueness and struggle for self-actualisation.

problem difficulty, dilemma, preoccupation, or obstacle to happiness. Psychological problems are accompanied by degrees of distress or confusion, since the person's problem is within him or is experienced as pressing upon him. Counselling is often considered a problem-focused and problem-solving activity in contrast to the personality-transforming orientation of psychotherapy. Counsellors who do work in a problem-focused way seek first to agree on problem identification and definition; they may then help the client to prioritise her problems; this is followed by *problem-solving strategies*. Egan (2002) uses the concepts of *problem management* and 'opportunity development' in his model. Some counsellors prefer the terms 'concern' or 'issue' to 'problem'. *See* EGAN APPROACH, PRESENTING CONCERN, TARGET PROBLEM (*see* Feltham, 2004).

problem-in-living the term advanced by Szasz (1988) as an alternative to the concept of MENTAL ILLNESS. According to Szasz, whatever our inevitable problems-in-living are attributed to, they cannot properly be considered to be a form of mental illness. Common but distressing turmoil, heartache and desperation can be profoundly problematic. *See* SUBCLINICAL.

problem-saturated an influential term found in solution-focused literature suggesting that clients frequently tell their stories in a heavily negative mode that does not allow them to see the whole picture of non-problematic aspects of their lives, especially their positive capabilities.

process a movement, development or continuation; to effect or move towards finality. The term 'process' is used both broadly and precisely in counselling. The *counselling process* is all that goes on within counselling (as opposed to its OUTCOME) and *process research* looks at how counselling operates or is said to operate. Process is contrasted with CONTENT in that content denotes what is discussed, and process refers to how or why it is discussed. The term is used rather vacuously (*see* JARGON) by some people, as in 'It's my process'. As a verb, process (as in 'I need to process this experience') refers to a need for time to digest and assimilate. *See* PRIMARY PROCESS, SECONDARY PROCESS.

process-oriented psychotherapy (POP) a form of therapy created by Arnold Mindell, drawing from Jungian, Taoist and other approaches, which regards illness as a meaningful expression of the unconscious. POP has social as well as individual applications and is also known as process-oriented psychology and dreambody work.

procrastination postponing without good cause; delaying tasks and giving excuses to oneself and/or others to explain the delay. Procrastination often represents a problem of self-discipline and LOW FRUSTRATION TOLERANCE. It can also be the result of anxiety and the disguised expression of rebellion. Many people believe that they should not have to struggle to get what they want; others (perfectionists) put off important tasks because they worry that they may not complete them perfectly. Procrastination is irrational avoidance and is probably best treated by confrontative methods like REBT. It is indeed arguable that some clients seek out those very kinds of counselling which will encourage passivity, verbalisation and reflection instead of action and antiprocrastinatory attitudes.

profanity in counselling swearing by client or counsellor during counselling sessions. While many counsellors adopt a uniform stance of polite and expletive-free interaction, many clients prefer the freedom to swear and otherwise express anger and irritation. The therapeutic alliance can be consolidated by matching the client's conversational style, including the use of profanity. Some counsellors swear freely both because it is in their own nature and because it reflects part of their counselling philosophy (e.g. that there is no shame attached to swearing).

professional indemnity *see* INSURANCE.

professionalisation the movement of an activity towards recognised professional standards and status. Sociologists have identified stages of the professionalisation process and have offered critiques of it. Counselling in the UK is an emerging profession, as yet with relatively few full-time jobs and little career structure. (Much counselling is provided on a voluntary or sessional/part-time basis.) Professional standards for counsellors, supervisors and trainers are, however, well developed by the BACP. While increasing professionalism can be seen to serve and protect the public, critics of professionalisation argue that it often creates illusions of greater expertise than is warranted, that it fosters an entrenched rather than a self-critical attitude, that it creates a false division and competition between, for example, accredited and unaccredited counsellors and between counsellors and users of counselling skills. *See* STATUTORY REGULATION.

professionalism expertise and integrity in the practice of one's profession. Professionalism implies that counsellors conduct themselves and their work respectfully and ethically, observe appropriate boundaries, maintain professional skills and knowledge and represent the standards of the profession as a whole.

profession-centred therapy a term coined by House (2003) to combat the assertion that professionalisation is best, healthy and inevitable, and arguing that counselling/therapy has moved away dangerously from its genuinely client-centred values. House and others commend alternative means of 'regulating' counselling and draw attention to the importance of published accounts of clients'/consumers' experiences and views of counselling. House also uses the terms 'post-professional practice' and 'postmodern therapy'.

prognosis prediction of the outcome of a disease or disturbance with or without treatment. Although the term is rarely used by counsellors (and most counsellors probably avoid promises of particular outcomes) clients ask often enough 'Do you think counselling can help me?' or 'Do you think I'll get better?' While some counsellors will give broadly optimistic replies (e.g. 'Many people with your problem have been helped by counselling'), often a counsellor's responses will be to reflect the client's concern back to them and ask them for their own assessment.

progress change or improvement in counselling. Progress can be predicated upon clear baselines (problem definition) and GOALS; where these are clear, progress can be measured. Where there are no such baselines, either because the counsellor does not elicit them or the client is too confused to formulate them, then progress is usually evaluated by client and counsellor together. REVIEW of progress helps to mark changes experienced (or not) by the client. *See* CHANGE.

progressive relaxation   a procedure involving deep muscle relaxation which is used either for general stress reduction or as part of a programme of SYSTEMATIC DESENSITISATION. Progressive relaxation entails instructing the client to tense and then to relax small groups of muscles, often in the order of arms, face, neck, trunk, legs. The relaxing of eye muscles is also very powerful. This procedure has to be taught and reinforced, and counsellors sometimes suggest (or make) relaxation tapes for their clients. Progressive relaxation has been shown to be an important ingredient in the treatment of migraine, hypertension and insomnia.

projection   a defence mechanism attributing to others or to events qualities which properly belong within oneself. Originally a psychoanalytic concept, projection is now in universal usage. When someone finds something painful or conflictual within himself, he may first deny it, and then attempt to expel it, as it were, by attributing it to another. In the case of paranoia, for example, one's own hateful or suspicious feelings about others may unpalatably contradict one's self-image; they may then be projected, so that others are perceived as harbouring hate and mistrust towards oneself. The colloquial term 'dumping' is often used synonymously with projection. Jung considered projection to be the opposite of introjection (*see* SHADOW).

projective identification   the Kleinian concept that one may unconsciously project into others aspects of one's own psyche. (Jung's concept of 'participation mystique' is similar.) Unlike simple PROJECTION, projective identification involves the other then acting or becoming in some way like the projected figure. A counsellor may be made to feel, for example, persecutory towards the client when the client disowns, projects, and then suffers from the apparently hateful feelings of the counsellor. As part of the PARANOID–SCHIZOID POSITION, this is considered a normal developmental process.

projective tests   psychological tests which require the subject to declare what she 'sees' in an otherwise neutral stimulus (e.g. an ink blot) and thereby indicate inner conflicts and assumptions. *See* RORSCHACH TEST.

promiscuity   indiscriminate or disorderly thought and action. 'Promiscuity' is usually associated with sexual behaviour. In a climate of 'sexual permissiveness', the concept of promiscuity has less meaning than in some previous eras (in spite of the impact of AIDS on sexual behaviour). However, promiscuity denotes a tendency to think, feel and act sexually in ways which are either experienced as painful and incessant to the person, or which 'get him/her into trouble'. Typical promiscuous behaviour is characterised by frequent, unselective sexual activity; it may be experienced as outside of one's control (compulsive) or judged to be calculated risk-taking (e.g. cheating on one's monogamous partner). Possible causes include emotional deprivation in childhood or (blatant or subtle) sexual abuse; some people (e.g. Reich) argue that 'promiscuity' or free, pluralistic sexuality may be the biological norm, and monogamy the result of civilisation's suppression. The term *nymphomania* (female promiscuity) is now redundant, although women are still more likely to be judged to be promiscuous than are men.

prompting the counsellor's act of encouraging the client to begin or continue to speak or act in the session. Means of prompting include direct suggestion and invitation, offering linking statements, reminding the client where a sentence was broken off, and using expectant non-verbal gestures. Prompting should be used judiciously, with awareness of the client's interactional norms, her need for silent reflection, appropriate timing of interventions and specific client–counsellor relationship factors. While some counsellors avoid prompting clients, even the communicative approach allows for statements like 'Shall we see what thoughts that throws up?' There is also a specific behavioural technique known as prompting, which is used mainly in training settings.

prophylactic counselling interventions are said to be prophylactic which prevent further harm or the development of problems later on. *See* PREVENTIVE COUNSELLING.

protagonist the person who takes the central part in a PSYCHODRAMA, and whose problems and concerns inform the roles taken by others. The part of the protagonist is played until significant obstacles have been confronted and partially worked through.

protection caring for; defending against possible dangers. Counsellors take care not to be over-protective or patronising, but equally undertake to safeguard their clients against accidents or overwhelming distress in counselling. Counsellors are ethically obliged to protect the interests of their clients, both clinically (e.g. by referring on if necessary, or by deciding not to engage in emotionally threatening work) and professionally (e.g. by engaging in regular supervision and by remaining abreast of developments in the counselling profession). Transactional analysts undertake to protect their clients in sessions from the emotional consequences of resisting and altering their parental injunctions. Counsellors who work with children or with clients involved with children have a special ethical responsibility in relation to child protection legislation.

pseudo-competency behaviour characterised by individuals appearing to perform a task competently, but subjectively not experiencing the confidence that they will be able to perform it consistently well without severe anxiety or undue strain before or undue depletion afterwards. It may be observed in management, counselling, psychotherapy, supervision and other activities. Continuing anxiety experienced by practitioners may indicate a need for further personal counselling, further training in specific supervision and training skills, or a need to consider the limits of their competence. Good counsellors do not necessarily make good trainers (and vice versa). *See* Clarkson and Gilbert (1991).

psyche the mind, soul or spirit. Although used as the root of 'psychology', the term 'psyche' has come to represent the life of the mind, including its subtler, poetic qualities, which are overlooked by many approaches to counselling and therapy. *Psychic* refers to that which is of the mind or soul and can mean either psychological or spiritual. Hillman (*see* Moore, 1989) argues that modern psychology pathologises the expressions of the psyche; there are important distinctions to be made, he says, between soul and spirit. Freud used the term *psychic energy* of mental processes. Radical behaviourists argue that mental or psychic processes cannot be studied with any accuracy.

psychiatry the branch of medicine that treats disorders of the mind; the specialised medical study and practice of the assessment and treatment of mental disorders. Psychiatrists are medically qualified and have completed specialist training in psychiatry. Their work is done mainly in psychiatric hospitals or departments but increasingly in the community too (as 'liaison psychiatry'). Some psychiatrists also work privately. Psychiatry is concerned with assessment, treatment planning, prescription of medication, individual consultations and management of acute and chronic patients. As well as dealing with MENTAL ILLNESS psychiatrists are involved in the treatment and management of mental handicap, addictions, criminal behaviour, epilepsy, and so on. The largely humanistic ethos of counselling is at odds with a narrow MEDICAL MODEL of psychiatry which still prevails in some quarters, and some counsellors sympathise with the anti-psychiatric movement (Laing, Cooper and others) which opposes neurosurgery, ECT, excessive and counterproductive medication, labelling, institutionalisation and authoritarian attitudes. However, counsellors from time to time may need to liaise with and refer to psychiatrists (directly or via GPs) and vice versa. *Psychiatric debriefing*, as used of the help given to hostages

on their release, appears to be largely synonymous with counselling. Counsellor training courses often include a module on psychiatry. Some COMMUNITY PSYCHIATRIC NURSES provide counselling.

psychoanalysis the discipline, founded by Freud, of investigating unconscious processes and providing therapeutic interpretations for those (analysands) receiving analysis in its clinical form. Known also as 'analysis', psychoanalysis has evolved considerably since Freud's time. *Classical psychoanalysis* is characterised by the patient or analysand attending up to four or five analytic sessions every week for some years, lying on a couch, with the analyst behind her, observing the rule of ABSTINENCE, encouraging FREE ASSOCIATION and offering INTERPRETATION of TRANSFERENCE and other phenomena. *Psychoanalytically oriented psychotherapy* is the description given to a less intense form of analysis, with sessions held two or three times a week, in which the patient may be seated facing the therapist. Such psychotherapy is considered by some analysts to be a diluted form of analysis. Others regard psychoanalysis as a specialised form of psychotherapy; still others (e.g. Halmos) subsume both under the title of 'counselling'. PSYCHODYNAMIC COUNSELLING is based on psychoanalytic principles. *Psychoanalytic counselling* has also been used (Patton and Meara, 1992). Followers of Freud, Klein and the OBJECT RELATIONS tradition are usually known as psychoanalysts, but Jungians are known as analytical psychologists or Jungian analysts. Theories derived from psychoanalysis include INDIVIDUAL PSYCHOLOGY, TRANSACTIONAL ANALYSIS and micropsychoanalysis. Psychoanalysis is often criticised for being protracted, elitist, ineffective and dependency creating.

psychobabble derogatory term used by Rosen (and taken up by others) to describe the perceived, untenable proliferation of therapeutic models, claims and jargon.

psychocybernetics an approach to counselling and self-help based on principles of computing, communication systems and feedback mechanisms. It is criticised as being an elaborated form of POSITIVE THINKING and is not a significant influence in counselling. *See* NEUROLINGUISTIC PROGRAMMING.

psychodrama a method of group therapy developed by Moreno which emphasises dramatic enactment of participants' real-life concerns, using other participants as director, auxiliary egos, audience, etc. The director will cast people and suggest scenes which will bring the PROTAGONIST's concerns alive. People may be asked to change roles to bring new perspectives into the work. Moreno devised many techniques to be used within a psychodrama. Their purposes are to enable participants to re-experience events from their lives, to discover their suppressed emotions, to experience cathartic release (*see* CATHARSIS) and INSIGHT. Moreno considered psychodrama to be the 'theatre of truth' and many therapeutic approaches have been influenced by it, including gestalt, encounter and primal integration. Techniques include REHEARSAL, ROLE PLAY and ROLE REVERSAL, as well as modelling, doubling (having a group member mimic the protagonist) and future projection (enacting a feared or desired future scenario). Because psychodrama works with 'raw experience', encourages spontaneity and often cannot predict how sessions will end, leaders have to offer protection to participants. Thus, psychodrama is often conducted in the form of intensive, residential workshops to allow time for the build-up and resolution of powerful feelings.

psychodynamic counselling any counselling which makes primary use of DYNAMIC theories and practices. 'Psychodynamic' refers to the inner drives and conflicts of the mind and the term usually echoes the psychoanalytic tradition. Psychodynamic technique and theory may draw exclusively on Freud, Klein or Jung, or demonstrate its own eclecticism, learning from all three schools, as well as neo-Freudians, post-Freudians and others. Psychodynamic counselling employs the concepts of the UNCONSCIOUS, defences (*see* DEFENCE MECHANISMS) and RESISTANCE, TRANSFERENCE and COUNTERTRANSFERENCE, FREE ASSOCIATION and INTERPRETATION among others. Psychodynamic counsellors are particularly alert to client references to significant figures in their past and to the ways in which these may be linked with the client–counsellor relationship. Considerable emphasis is placed on reactions to boundaries, and to the meanings that clients attribute to holiday breaks, dreams, and so on. Most psychodynamic counsellors recognise a difference between their work and psychoanalysis, and tend to work more actively and less intensely in terms of length of treatment and frequency of the sessions. Although psychodynamic counselling, like other forms of therapy, aims at resolution of personal difficulties, it also values the client's development of insight and ongoing reflection on their personal dynamics. Critics claim that like psychoanalysis, it de-emphasises conscious, here-and-now reality issues, is based on unverifiable theories and can be very protracted. It is, however, one of the most widely practised orientations in Britain. *See* Jacobs (1999).

psychohistory a discipline seeking to inject into historical understanding an account of childhood suffering (from birth trauma to swaddling, circumcision, abandonment, physical, emotional and sexual abuse, etc.) and how it informs unconscious group fantasies, the compulsion to go to war, and the emotional life of nations generally. *See* deMause (1982).

psychological pertaining to psychology; emotional or mental; referring to matters which are broadly of the mind, rather than physical. 'Psychological' is often used synonymously with 'emotional', as in 'psychological/emotional problems'. (Behaviourists are unlikely to approve of this usage.)

psychological abuse refers to the many subtle forms of mental and emotional abuse inflicted primarily on children but also on adults (e.g. by husband on wife, by employer on employee).

psychological adjustment refers to a person's return to 'normal' behaviour or her ongoing ability to function well and within social norms.

psychological contact refers to the first of Carl Rogers' necessary and sufficient conditions of therapeutic personality change. It suggests that some minimal degree of relationship is necessary between client and counsellor for counselling to proceed successfully.

psychological debriefing an alternative term for CRITICAL INCIDENT DEBRIEFING.

psychological disturbance *see* ACQUISITION and PERPETUATION OF DISTURBANCE.

psychological education refers to any system of raising awareness of cognitive, emotional, behavioural and spiritual development, problems and prevention. Also known as the 'psychoeducational' approach.

psychological-mindedness refers to the ability or tendency a person has to reflect on her life and life problems insightfully, in psychological terms (as opposed, often, to naive, political, or astrological terms) and from an internal LOCUS OF EVALUATION; psychological-mindedness is often used as an indication of whether a client is likely to be able to benefit from counselling. People are said to (over)-*psychologise* when they habitually reduce human problems to supposed psychological causes and ignore, for example, socio-economic factors.

psychological therapy a term used to refer to counselling, psychotherapy, or any other therapy utilising non-medical and non-physical means of treatment for distress.

psychological type a Jungian-derived classification, used in the Myers-Briggs schema, of personality types into extraversion-introversion, sensing-intuition, thinking-feeling and judging-perceiving. People have *preferences* for acting in certain types, and counsellors may find it helpful to tune into clients (or recognise blocks to rapport) using such a system of guidance.

psychology the study of behaviour; the science of mental life; the 'laws of the psyche'. 'Psychology' is in such common use that the boundaries of its meaning have been stretched almost to the point of making it meaningless. Historically, psychology has developed from philosophy to a point where it claims to be a 'science' in its own right. Many psychologists argue that only behaviour which can be observed objectively is a legitimate subject for psychological study. Academic psychology includes the study of memory, perception, decision-making, child development, individual differences, personality theories, social interaction, abnormality and animal behaviour. *Psychologists* (all of whom must have at least a first degree in psychology, or equivalent) work in educational, health, occupational, commercial, forensic and other settings as specialists. *Clinical psychologists* often offer counselling and psychotherapy, as well as behaviour therapy and psychological assessments to their patients. A *chartered psychologist* has met certain assessment criteria of the British Psychological Society. Some psychologists have been harsh critics of their own discipline, arguing that it is often no more than elaborate common sense or that it has become an overly scientific activity alienated from its original subject – humanity and the human mind. *See* COUNSELLING PSYCHOLOGY, HUMANISTIC PSYCHOLOGY.

psychometry the measurement of psychological functions. Psychometricians devise, administer, score and interpret psychological tests intended to elucidate items relating to human intelligence, aptitude, competence, emotional problems and their alleviation. Much of the humanistic ethos of counselling is opposed to the psychometric tendency to 'put people in boxes'.

psychoneurosis synonymous with neurosis, but clearly separating that term from its biological associations. Although some writers prefer 'psychoneurosis' to 'neurosis' it now has no real additional meaning (in spite of its original classification into subtypes of conversion hysteria, anxiety hysteria and obsessional neurosis). *See* NEUROSIS.

psychopath *see* SOCIOPATH.

psychopathology sickness of the mind; the science of mental disorder. Psychopathology includes the aetiology, phenomenology and classification of mental disorder. It can be used to refer to psychological dysfunctions which are structurally deeper than current, presenting problems, and thereby imply a certain severity of disorder. Counsellors are more likely to speak of clients' real problem/s or underlying problem/s than of psychopathology, but the abbreviated term 'pathology' is used quite commonly. ('That's my pathology', for example, implies a recognised, but stubborn, typically self-defeating or unpleasant way of behaving.) *Pathological* behaviour characteristics are self-evidently dysfunctional or 'crazy'. Counselling and psychotherapy (or particular orientations within them) are sometimes criticised for *pathologising* clients (reading sickness or serious disturbance into their stories and behaviour where no such pathology may exist) or for de-emphasising human goodness, strength and integrity.

psychopharmacology the study of mind altering drugs. Counsellors need to be aware of some clients' need for medication, effects of current medication and of withdrawing from drugs. Most counsellors, unless psychiatrically trained, will have only a broad understanding of drug categories and indications for GP referrals. *See* Daines, Gask and Usherwood (1997); Sexton and Legg (1999).

psychosexual therapy psychotherapy that focuses on the sexual aspects of couples' problems, and usually the relationship between psychological and behavioural aspects.

psychosis a mental illness or aspect of mental illness in which the person is seriously out of touch with reality. At such times, the sufferer may not be able to exercise full responsibility for his own or others' safety. Psychosis is characterised by DEREALISATION, HALLUCINATION and other forms of distorted perception and thought processes. The two main forms of ('functional') psychosis are SCHIZOPHRENIA and manic-depressive psychosis (*see* MANIC DEPRESSION/ BIPOLAR AFFECTIVE DISORDER). There are many other identified variants. *Organic psychosis* is the result of physical disease and includes such conditions as dementia. People experiencing enduring psychosis or frequent psychotic episodes usually require hospital treatment, and almost always medication (*see* TRANQUILLISERS). Psychosis may result in progressive impairment in function. People sometimes experience a *psychotic episode* in relation to drug abuse, alcoholism and extreme bereavement reactions (e.g. post-traumatic psychosis, *puerperal psychosis* under POSTNATAL DEPRESSION). Subjectively, psychosis may feel all-absorbing, terrifying, or fascinating. Eysenck placed psychosis on one end of the neurotic–psychotic continuum. Some therapists work with people who are psychotic, attempting to follow them through and understand their mood swings and bizarre delusions, often in a residential setting. *See* REPARENTING.

psychosocial intervention 'psychosocial' has a variety of uses, all linking psychological with social concepts, but a common usage is to refer to work with the family of a given client as well as the client, e.g. helping a family to understand and cope with a schizophrenic member.

psychosomatic affecting body and mind simultaneously; physical illness caused by psychological factors. The most common usage is in the concept of psychological disturbances manifesting in physical ILLNESS, often because the nature of the intrapsychic conflict is repressed and seeks an outlet. One view, for example, is that people who chronically suppress their anger may develop headaches. Conditions such as asthma, migraine, colitis and cancer have been suggested as being (often) of psychological origin. Counsellors from the psychoanalytic and humanistic traditions in particular attribute much validity to psychosomatic theory and speculation (as signified in the phrases CONVERSION HYSTERIA and 'theatre of the body'). There are dangers in too readily assuming that physical symptoms are caused by and can be cured by counselling or therapy. 'Psychosomatic' is used *incorrectly* when it is said that a certain illness is 'only psychosomatic' (meaning imaginary).

psychosynthesis the approach to counselling, therapy, personal growth and global vision founded by Assagioli. Psychosynthesis is an optimistic, spiritually oriented theory and practice. Assagioli spoke of personal and transpersonal psychosynthesis, the former concerned with personality adjustment and transformation, the latter with the search for and realisation of higher meaning and purpose. Psychosynthesis aims to include attention to childhood-derived problems through psychodynamic understanding, but also explores the client's 'balance of will and awareness' through techniques such as inner dialogue, mental imagery, free drawing and the IDEAL MODEL TECHNIQUE. Encouraging the self-identification of the 'I' is a central concept. One of the main contributions of psychosynthesis is its unique model of the human psyche, from lower, middle and higher unconscious (or superconscious) to the conscious and higher selves, and finally the collective unconscious. According to Assagioli, we defend as much against the transpersonal (or spiritual) as against personal pain. *See* Whitmore (1991).

psychotherapy literally, the 'cure of souls' or 'attendance on the soul'. Modern psychotherapy is a form of talking treatment which addresses psychological problems. There are upwards of 400 variants of psychotherapy. Its theories and practices overlap significantly with COUNSELLING. Historically, psychoanalytic psychotherapy is derived from PSYCHOANALYSIS but it is characterised by, for example, less frequent sessions, the *choice* of chair or couch for the patient, therapist and patient being face to face, and greater interaction with the patient than is offered by classical psychoanalysis. Jung distinguished between minor and major psychotherapy (which corresponds roughly to supportive counselling/therapy and dynamic, uncovering therapy respectively); Jung referred to psychotherapy as 'a dialectical process between two psychic systems reacting and responding to one another'. Psychodynamic psychotherapy is often considered to differ from counselling in being more relationship based and taking greater account of transference, taking longer (years rather than weeks or months), involving longer and more rigorous training (requiring, for example, that trainees be in ongoing therapy of their own at least twice a week), addressing underlying dynamics (if not the entire psychological structure of the person) rather than symptoms, dealing with more serious categories of mental distress. Many of these claims are disputed and certainly there is overlap in practice. While different forms of psychotherapy and counselling can be distinguished, there is no evidence that one form produces a better outcome than another or that psychotherapy per se is better than counselling. However, certain approaches (treatments of choice), whether labelled 'counselling' or 'psychotherapy', are likely to be of special benefit for particular client problems. Many clients and referral agents, as well as counsellors and therapists, are confused about or indifferent to the distinctions. Psychotherapy is provided both within the NHS and privately, and training is conducted in independent, academic and medical institutions. The United Kingdom Council for Psychotherapy (UKCP) aims to represent the diverse schools of psychotherapy and the British Confederation of Psychotherapists (BCP) the rigorously psychoanalytic psychotherapists.

psychotropic drugs *see* ANTIPSYCHOTICS.

punctuality the prompt keeping of appointments. While it is of practical importance that clients are punctual for sessions, their *attitude* to time keeping is considered by many counsellors to be even more significant. Psychodynamic counsellors in particular attribute (unconscious) significance to clients arriving early, late, or at the wrong times, and so on. (A joke has it that clients who persistently arrive early are anxious, those who arrive late are resistant, and those who arrive on time are obsessive.)

put-down a statement which denigrates or discounts. Many clients with low self-esteem 'put themselves down', meaning that they habitually underestimate their strengths and speak negatively of themselves (or others). *See* DISCOUNTING.

pyramiding a technique used in personal construct counselling which begins with a client's superordinate (broad, inclusive) constructs and analyses them into concrete parts by means of questioning. A reversal of LADDERING.

qualities of counsellors personal and professional attributes, attitudes and skills considered to be common to good counsellors. Mearns and Dryden (1990) conclude on the basis of clients' reported experiences of counselling that transparency, commitment, engagement and a capacity for containment are especially valued qualities. The BACP's criteria for intending trainees on accredited training courses include self-awareness, maturity and stability, ability to make use of and reflect on life experience, capacity to cope with emotional demands, ability to form a helping relationship, ability to be self-critical, some awareness of the nature of prejudice and oppression of minority groups. An acceptable level of non-defensiveness or awareness of personal defences is also often cited as an important quality for candidates for training.

questionnaire a research tool offering the respondent a number of written questions which usually require answers in the form of a 'yes' or 'no' or checks on a rating scale. The kind of information gathered by questionnaires may easily be skewed or ambiguous, so researchers are cautious in their use of them and often employ a number of questions designed to compensate for possible bias. Simple questionnaires are sometimes used by individual counsellors or counselling agencies to assess the quality of counselling offered, the kinds of clients being seen, possible problems in delivery, etc. *See* RESEARCH.

questions requests for information. While questions naturally form part of any substantial conversation, there is general consensus in counselling training that the counsellor's asking too many questions of the client is to be avoided. Questions can be experienced as intrusive, they can easily interrupt or pre-empt clients' own thought processes and they can too easily be delivered in a bombarding manner. Multiple questions fired at the client are likely to be confusing. *Closed questions* limit the client to one answer, with no encouragement to explore further. 'Did you do your homework?' is a closed question requiring a 'yes' or 'no' answer. (Closed questions can also, used appropriately, be beneficially confrontative.) *Either-or* questions (e.g. 'Were you pleased about that, or not?') also tend to limit client responses and discourage exploration. *Open questions* are usually recommended by trainers. Examples include: 'How did you feel about that?' 'Can you say some more about that?' When questions are used, they should be clearly worded and, if necessary, accompanied by an explanation of why the counsellor wishes to have this particular information. Some counsellors deliberately disclose their own reactions to and interest in the client instead of asking direct questions (e.g. 'I felt very sad when you said that and wondered how you felt about it'). *'What if ...?' questions* encourage the client to explore scenarios beyond their current problems. Counselling orientations such as cognitive–behavioural and personal-construct therapy rely quite heavily on purposeful questioning, in contrast to the sparing use of questions in person-centred and psychodynamic counselling. Clients' questions to counsellors are met differently by practitioners of the various orientations. Many counsellors avoid answering personal or advice-soliciting questions; others are quite willing to give any pertinent and non-distracting replies; some interpret clients' questions as always referring to deeper anxieties. *See* ELICITING, SOCRATIC DIALOGUE.

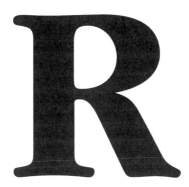

race awareness training training dedicated to exposing racism and encouraging those with racist attitudes to own and work on their racism. Now sometimes referred to as 'diversity training'.

racism individual and institutionalised negative attitudes and activity against groups of a different race. In the UK, racism refers mainly to the attitude of the white majority towards black people. The term 'black people' has been defined politically as *all* non-whites who are discriminated against on the basis of their ethnic difference; the term 'black and Asian' is now more common. Racism (or 'white racism') is considered to include covert and overt personal prejudices, racist harassment and violence, failure to implement equal opportunities policies, etc. Some assert that racism comprises of 'prejudice plus power'. Anti-racism implies individual and collective struggles and strategies to combat racism actively and to achieve genuine equal opportunities. Non-racist counselling implies that counsellors combat any personal prejudices they may have about race; anti-racist counselling may include the confrontation of all instances of racism (in clients and colleagues) and seeking actively to raise awareness of racism as a training issue for all counsellors. *See* CROSS-CULTURAL COUNSELLING, ANTIDISCRIMINATORY PRACTICE.

racket system the characteristic feelings, thoughts and behaviour generated and maintained by SCRIPT beliefs and feelings, 'rackety displays' and reinforcing memories. The racket system is a concept from TRANSACTIONAL ANALYSIS. Rackety displays are the observable behaviour patterns accompanying core script beliefs; such displays are instances of the acting-out, often, of deep-seated hurts from early childhood, and frequently achieve the PAYOFF of confirming script beliefs. People often remember selectively those events from their lives which confirm their scripts and their apparent need to resort to rackety displays. The racket system is a self-reinforcing loop, the therapeutic counterpart of which is the 'autonomy system', which seeks to identify and positively change elements of the racket system.

radical honesty an approach to living commended by Blanton (1996) calling for as total honesty as possible, in all situations, however difficult. Linked with certain principles of GESTALT THERAPY, radical honesty suggests that 'normal' levels of honesty, half-truths, dissembling, etc. contribute in a major way to stress, and freedom from these releases energy and facilitates far better relationships.

radical therapy any therapy or counselling which addresses deep-seated personal trauma (including birth and intrauterine trauma) and/or the roots of socio-political oppression in individuals. Radical therapy implies dissatisfaction with conventional methods of therapy. The British radical therapy movement of the 1960s and 1970s included experimental personal growth work stemming from the ideas of Reich, Jackins, Laing and others, often looking, for example, at introjected capitalist values, patriarchal assumptions and the embodied effects of social oppression (e.g. character armour). There is no current, cohesive radical therapy movement, but *see* FEMINIST COUNSELLING, RE-EVALUATION COUNSELLING, SOCIAL THERAPY.

rage extreme anger; historically, 'madness'. Melanie Klein highlighted the transitional tendency of infants to experience persecutory feelings and resultant 'murderous rage' towards supposed persecutory objects. Destructive impulses were considered by Klein to be expressions of the death instinct. Some child psychotherapists practise a form of 'rage reduction therapy', which rests on attachment theory and advocates confrontation of the rage and grief associated with problematic bonding processes. The 1990s saw the emergence of the concepts of 'road rage' (extreme anger and violence triggered by road traffic incidents) and 'desk rage' (marked anger and frustration at work) but these terms are journalistic coinages rather than formal diagnostic categories.

rape crisis counselling face-to-face and telephone counselling offered to the victims of rape. The effects of rape, which is a deeply traumatic violation of the woman's body and person, are considered to be similar to those of post-traumatic stress disorder generally. Women who have been raped report feelings of disbelief, numbness, anger, self-disgust and often chronic anxiety. Rape crisis counsellors recognise the importance of offering high levels of acceptance and support and, when called for, help with therapeutic re-experiencing of the trauma. For some women there is a delayed reaction to rape, and counsellors need to be aware that the surfacing of pain may be just as traumatic after a long delay as immediately following the rape. Most rape is of women by men, but there are instances of men being raped by men.

rapport a high level of interaction, bonding and understanding. Rapport is an important first step in counselling. Much rapport is established intuitively and fortuitously between people of closely matching or complementary personalities or backgrounds. Many counsellors aim for a helpful level of rapport by means of various relationship-building skills, but there are limits to the therapeutic effectiveness of spontaneous and genuine rapport. Some practitioners of neurolinguistic programming espouse the use of deliberate mirroring techniques to achieve rapport.

rational emotive behaviour therapy (REBT) a specialised form of cognitive–behavioural therapy formulated by Albert Ellis. REBT is based on the view that human beings appear to have an innate tendency often to think and act irrationally (for example, believing that the world must be a comfortable place for them). REBT is based on the ABC analysis of how each client upsets herself with irrational beliefs (B) which mediate between events in the world (A) and the emotional and behavioural consequences for the client (C): the therapist's task is to dispute the client's irrational beliefs (e.g. 'I must always be comfortable') and assist her in adopting, testing and thoroughly internalising rational beliefs (e.g. 'I would like never to feel uncomfortable but there is no reason why I must be comfortable and I can tolerate discomfort'). REBT is an active-directive, largely ahistorical method of counselling which advocates an anti-procrastinatory approach to change by means of a large variety of cognitive, imagery, emotive and behavioural tasks (for example, homework, shame-attacking exercises, and vigorous disputing of irrational beliefs). REBT is often criticised for allegedly minimising the role of feelings and exploration of childhood events. *See* AWFULISING, MUSTURBATION and OVER-CONCERN, *see* Dryden and Neenan (1997).

rational recovery an REBT model of treatment for alcohol problems that, in opposition to AA, argues that clients (or attenders at RR groups) would do better to accept responsibility for their condition rather than turning to a 'higher power', and learn to address their low frustration tolerance, etc.

rationalisation the defence mechanism, according to psychoanalytic thought, characterised by a person offering a plausible but essentially incomplete or intellectualised explanation of her behaviour. Rationalisation may disguise unconscious fears or wishes. Whereas rationalisation often comes easily to someone who is act-

ing defensively, *rational thinking* is usually hard won.

reactance the tendency to be very alert to others' attempts to influence oneself and to seek to regain a sense of autonomy often by reacting against the source of influence. Clients may be said to be highly reactant when they show signs of feeling threatened by directive counselling, for example. Counsellors sensitive to client reactance adjust their style of relating and intervening accordingly.

reaction formation a defence mechanism whereby a person's actions suggest the opposite of her real feelings. In sibling rivalry, for example, a girl who is envious of a younger sister to the point of wishing her dead, may ward off such a wish and its attendant guilty feelings by taking on an exaggeratedly solicitous role. The effort required constantly to deny underlying feelings may manifest itself, for example, in obsessive-compulsive symptoms. A common manifestation of reaction formation is the idealisation or idolising of another, which may conceal unconscious hostility.

reactive depression *see* DEPRESSION.

readiness preparedness; the client's state of motivation in relation to counselling. The counsellor will ideally assess and match the client's state of readiness for change with her own well-timed interventions. *See* STAGES OF CHANGE.

readiness to practise the point at which the counselling trainee is deemed by trainers and by him or herself to be sufficiently effective, safe and free of impediments to commence working with clients in a placement.

real self that part of one's identity felt or considered to be authentic, in contrast with the FALSE SELF. The term implies that there is a quality of authenticity beneath the persona, or habitual self, as presented to the world. Winnicott considered the 'true self' to be 'little more than the summation of sensori-motor aliveness'. Broadly speaking, nearly every model of counselling has a concept similar to 'real self' (e.g. the 'organismic self' of person-centred counselling). In transactional analysis, the real self equates with a person's experience of herself in an integrated ego state; this is contrasted with the *executive self*, or the ego state which dictates behaviour. *See* SELF.

reality principle the Freudian concept of that part of mental activity which parallels and checks the activity of the PLEASURE PRINCIPLE. Whereas the pleasure principle is innate and characterised by 'free energy', the reality principle is learned in childhood development and is characterised by 'bound energy', or the modification of instincts. The reality principle enables the ego to accommodate to everyday reality and its constraining factors.

reality testing the process whereby one assesses the external environment and the extent to which it is necessary to accommodate to it. Reality testing is a function that assists the ego in discriminating between internal constructs or phantasies, and external and consensual realities. An extreme example of faulty reality testing is a person whose psychotic delusions are so intransigent that they cannot be modified by reference to (consensual) reality.

reality therapy a model of psychotherapy and counselling founded by William Glasser. Reality therapy is sometimes likened to a common sense-based form of counselling. Glasser (1984) observes that all clients have dealt unsuccessfully with their problems, largely because they deny the realities of the world and refuse to accept responsibility for their own lives. Reality therapists help clients to identify what they *want*, assess the *direction* in which their actions are currently taking them, *evaluate* how realistic their desires are, *plan* for positive improvement. (This is known as the 'WDEP' system.) Glasser's CONTROL THEORY argues that we have control over our own lives and we can learn a 'positive addiction' to exercising that control. Reality therapy has often been used in alcoholism, addiction, probation and management settings in the US and to a slightly lesser extent is practised in the UK.

reassurance a comforting or anxiety-reducing statement. There is a view that any reassurance of the client by the counsellor (e.g. 'Don't worry, it will be all right') is bad practice because it robs the client of his own experience and his need to deal with it, and may be incorrect. However, there are instances when the use of normalising reassurance is therapeutic, particularly when important information is conveyed to the client within the reassuring statement (e.g. in cases of panic attack or in relation to serious fears of madness).

rebirthing a technique and a distinctive therapy which seeks to have the client re-experience the first breath after birth. Otto Rank first drew attention to the significance of birth as prototypic of all later anxiety experiences. Janov and many others conducting primal work view the re-experiencing of birth as a natural *part* of therapeutic regression. *Rebirthers* are practitioners who make the re-experiencing of birth the centre of therapy by using breathing techniques combined with affirmations, for example of the goodness and manageability of life. Rebirthers help their clients into powerful and often transpersonal (spiritual) states (*see* TRANSPERSONAL THERAPY). Critics of rebirthing suggest that the training is inadequate and that the method may induce a dissociative state of well-being but not true resolution of personal problems. *See* INTRAUTERINE EXPERIENCE.

reciprocal inhibition a method used in behaviour therapy to replace an undesired response with a desired response by counter-conditioning. Devised by Joseph Wolpe, this method relies on the gradual substitution of a response that is antagonistic to the original response and is potent enough to neutralise the anxiety-evoking power of the stimulus. A response that is incompatible with anxiety is relaxation.

reciprocity mutuality; give-and-take. There is probably a high level of consensus that reciprocity is a desirable human behaviour. Many family and couple therapists aim to help clients towards reciprocal interactions. In most counselling practice, however, the relationship has an unavoidable one-way character, the client seeking help and the counsellor endeavouring to be helpful, the client disclosing freely and the counsellor disclosing (if at all) much more discreetly. PERSON-CENTRED COUNSELLING probably seeks and endorses higher levels of emotional reciprocity between client and counsellor than most other models.

recognised course now defunct term for a BACP accredited course. *See* TRAINING.

record keeping opening and maintaining clinical notes on clients. Counsellors vary in the extent to, and the style in, which they keep records, but minimal factual information is necessary and some record of ongoing progress is widely accepted as advisable. Counsellor training courses often ask trainees to keep an ongoing professional log which includes details of cases, reactions to the work and general reflections. Some counselling agencies require detailed ongoing records to be kept. *See* CONFIDENTIALITY, NOTE TAKING.

recovered memory movement generic term referring to therapeutic approaches having a primary focus on childhood abuse and its treatment by invocation of early memories. It has been criticised for its insistence that an unwarrantedly wide range of presenting symptoms indicate repressed early (often sexual) abuse that can only be accessed and harnessed for 'cure' by the therapist's suggestions. Frequently associated with FALSE MEMORY SYNDROME.

recovery improvement of symptoms; overcoming of presenting concerns. As well as this general sense of progress, recovery has a specific meaning in the fields of alcoholism and addiction, where clients following a TWELVE STEPS method learn to describe themselves as being, for example, 'in recovery' or 'a recovering alcoholic', in perpetuity.

redecision the insight and new, responsible attitude of the person in an adult ego state, following a re-experience of feelings in the child ego state, and leading to new cognitions and behaviour; changing a script decision. The redecision school of TA combines the theory of TA with many of the techniques of gestalt therapy, seeking to free the client from early traumatic experiences and the impasse which wards them off from awareness. This is achieved by 'early scene work' (re-experiencing, for example, by CHAIRWORK) and by the client's committing herself to a specific new decision. Redecision therapy is often conducted in groups.

redundancy counselling any counselling addressing the needs of people made redundant from their jobs. Much redundancy counselling is heavily advice-based, the client being helped to compose a curriculum vitae, to consider retraining and adopt a proactive attitude to job seeking. It can include, when necessary, attention to the emotional impact of job loss and change of status; clients may experience feelings of disorientation, depression and anger. *See* OUTPLACEMENT COUNSELLING.

re-evaluation counselling (RC) an approach to co-counselling pioneered by Harvey Jackins. Re-evaluation co-counselling is the original model of co-counselling. People are taught the method in classes. Each person acts as counsellor to her partner, and then exchanges roles. RC teaches that people carry lifelong distress patterns which can be discharged through abreactive behaviour such as crying, shaking and laughing; people are helped into these behaviours by receiving the undivided attention of their partner/counsellor, who may encourage them to use affirmative self-statements, to repeat significant feelings, and so on. Jackins' (1965) RC is distinct from other CO-COUNSELLING models, having a very tight super-structure and radical political aspirations. Jackins' concept of distress patterns includes racism, ageism, classism, etc. as 'dischargeable'. Jackins had an idiosyncratic notion of (revolutionary) *thinking*, and hypothesised that death may not be inevitable.

re-experiencing remembering and vividly, emotionally and viscerally entering earlier states of personal experience for therapeutic purposes. *See* PRIMAL THERAPY.

referral directing someone to a counsellor or alternative source of treatment. People are described as being referred to a counsellor by their GP, for example, or self-referred if they seek counselling without an intermediary. Many counsellors will only accept clients who refer themselves. 'Referral' is also used in a personified sense, as in 'I have two new referrals' (applicants, or possible clients). Counsellors also refer on certain clients who may require a different client–counsellor match, or a psychiatric, medical or other assessment or service.

reflection contemplation; mirror image. The word 'reflection' has the specific meaning in counselling of a counsellor intervention which feeds back to the client his own material in a manner that is as faithful to his own presentation of it as possible. The skill of reflecting was largely developed by Rogers as part of NON-DIRECTIVE COUNSELLING: to reflect back is to offer a mirror-image which allows or encourages the client to see or hear himself clearly. (The auditory metaphor of 'echoing' is also sometimes used.) Reflection of CONTENT is the offering back to the client of his own phrases and meanings; reflection of FEELING is the empathic skill of understanding and offering back the emotional nuances in the client's speech and behaviour. 'Reflecting back' has sometimes been misunderstood and caricatured as a mechanical, parrot-like process; in essence it is about tracking, understanding, paraphrasing and facilitating. The *reflection process* is the counsellor-initiated practice of inviting feedback on how the client perceives his progress, the relationship with his counsellor, and so on, and its purpose is the strengthening of the therapeutic alliance.

reflective practitioner a term coined by Schön for any professional or dedicated practitioner who seeks to engage in ongoing monitoring and improvement of her or his work. It is an expectation that all counsellors are reflective practitioners and this is reinforced by SUPERVISION and CONTINUING PROFESSIONAL DEVELOPMENT.

reflexivity the practice of applying relevant concepts to oneself in one's work, testing the theory-into-practice assumption and pushing for authentic reciprocation between action and conceptualisation, thus heightening self-awareness.

reformulation any way of re-conceptualising a problem or constellation of problems. Reformulation is a central task in COGNITIVE ANALYTIC THERAPY (CAT). It is the aim of the first three or four sessions of CAT to arrive at an assessment of the client's problems which is written down and/or translated into diagram form, is agreed by the client, and which casts a new perspective on the problems. The reformulation acts as a psychological map to guide the focus of the therapy. This is achieved by means of the 'psychotherapy file' (a CAT questionnaire) and by active work by both client and counsellor. A significant part of reformulation is agreement on target problems.

reframing the concept and practice of imaginatively putting clients' concerns into alternative contexts which may helpfully challenge their one-dimensional view of them. Reframing is a major technique of NEUROLINGUISTIC PROGRAMMING. *Context reframing* aims to show how a reportedly bad experience may be viewed positively in another context. *Content reframing* involves the positive reinterpretation of a given situation. The counsellor's task is to consider the client's concern from a variety of perspectives and to provoke the client into similar considerations. The counsellor may encourage the client to view her concern not as a negative experience but as a valuable psychological part of herself, contributing towards overall vitality; he may elicit various PARTS and speak to them directly, using techniques including hypnotic induction to enhance future functioning. The solution-focused methods of brief therapy often utilise future-oriented reframing (e.g. 'How would your life look if a miracle occurred and all your symptoms disappeared?'). In a broad sense every counselling theory contains reframing concepts and skills (e.g. interpretation, cognitive restructuring, paraphrasing).

regression a process whereby the client re-experiences, to a greater or lesser extent, developmental stages earlier than her actual adult one. Therapeutic regression may be encouraged and achieved in small, controlled 'doses' (for example, in TA) or regularly and profoundly (for example, in primal therapy) or under hypnosis. Its purpose is the vivid recall and reintegration or reinterpretation of earlier, usually painful or particularly significant, events or clusters of events. Regression can also occur spontaneously, in or out of counselling sessions, and can occur in an uncontrolled and unhelpful manner. In psychoanalytic thought, regression is often considered a defence mechanism. Some critics argue that deliberate regression (e.g. hypnoregression) is unnecessary and counter-productive for clients, while proponents view it either as central or as sometimes necessary for therapeutic progress, for example when there are clear signs of blocked awareness.

rehearsal practice or preparation. Clients may be encouraged in some forms of counselling to rehearse situations with which they wish to cope better (e.g. job interviews, assertiveness with superiors). Such rehearsal may take the form of a ROLE PLAY between client and counsellor, preparing the client for a situation in 'real life'; it also takes the form of mental rehearsal, in which the client is encouraged to run through anticipated difficulties, picturing herself coping. Rehearsal also has the negative meaning of ruminative, non-spontaneous behaviour.

Reichian related to the theories and influence of Wilhelm Reich. Reich broke from classical Freudian theory in several ways. Instead of the id, he postulated a healthy inner core, closely linked to sexuality. He attempted to link Marxism and psychoanalysis, and was expelled by the Marxists and the psychoanalysts in the same year. He went on to originate his own theories of vegetotherapy and orgonomy. Vegetotherapy was based on the concept of stimulating the activities of the parasympathetic nervous system, which was pleasure-oriented (the autonomic nervous system was known in Reich's time as the vegetative nervous system). The concept of orgonomy was based on Reich's views about the direct positive connection between orgasm and mental health. Reich claimed to be able to store orgasmic 'bio-energy' in 'orgone boxes'. His enduring influence has been on the tradition of bodywork in humanistic therapy (*see* CHARACTER ARMOUR) and indirectly on sexology and sex therapy. Otherwise, many agree with Grant's (1981) view of Reich as a historical oddity. Some approaches dub themselves or are referred to as 'neo-Reichian'.

reinforcement support, endorsement, strengthening or confirmation. Reinforcement is used mainly in behaviour therapy approaches to counselling which are pschoeducational in nature. Reinforcement may involve the application of a positive stimulus after the performance of behaviour (positive reinforcement) or the cessation of a negative stimulus after the desired behaviour has been reached (negative reinforcement).

rejection turning someone away, making her aware that she is not wanted; the reality of not being (or the belief that one is not) wanted. Rejection takes many forms throughout life, from a parent subtly (emotionally) rejecting a baby, to a child 'feeling rejected' by peers; from not being successful in getting a specific job to being spurned by a longed-for sexual partner. Rejection can be real, imagined or exaggerated, but is frequently associated with subsequent depression, LOW SELF-ESTEEM, and even risk of suicide. People who have (or believe they have) often been rejected, may easily anticipate rejection and may unconsciously invite it (*see* SELF-FULFILLING PROPHECY). Some clients fear that their counsellor will reject them and this probably reflects a common human feeling of worthlessness and a belief that one is undeserving of another's time and care. People often say 'I feel rejected' even though rejection is not an emotional state.

relapse falling behind; failing to maintain therapeutic progress; reverting to previous symptomatology. The term is usually reserved for obvious, if not serious, instances of deterioration during or following counselling. Someone who has given up alcohol may be said to relapse if she takes a single drink; some would define relapse as a return to problematic drinking. Someone might achieve considerable progress in counselling, yet relapse shortly before the scheduled end of, or soon after, counselling. Psychodynamic psychotherapists frequently relate this type of relapse to SEPARATION ANXIETY.

relapse prevention planned strategies for minimising the likelihood of the client's therapeutic progress going into reverse. Many counsellors consider it good practice to incorporate systematic relapse prevention work into the middle or ending phases of counselling. This may be approached by mental rehearsal of future relapse and possible ways of dealing with such relapses and can be especially important in short-term work. A useful intervention can be to alert clients to the potential SECONDARY EMOTIONAL PROBLEMS associated with self-blame in relation to relapse: acceptance of fallibility is a good antidote to such self-blame. Prochaska and DiClemente (1984) consider relapse a part of the cycle of personal change. *See* ANTI-FUTURE SHOCK IMAGERY.

relapse signature the indications, whether conscious or unconscious, behavioural or otherwise, that one who has apparently recovered from a previous problem (usually an addiction) is beginning to succumb to that problem again. The 'signature', or cluster of changed behaviours, is idiosyncratic.

relational depth a term in use in person-centred counselling indicating that the counsellor has moved beyond, or is in any one relationship with a client moving beyond surface relational competence to a deeper, subtle level of genuine relationship.

relationship the meeting and quality of interaction between two or more people. While people are always 'in relationship' with each other, some relationships are more intense, helpful and deliberately undertaken than others. Most counselling has this latter character. The counselling relationship usually does not have the spontaneity, mutuality, encumbrances and permanency of friendships or sexually motivated relationships, but is a professional relationship, entered into by arrangement, conducted in a disciplined fashion and based on the goals of *one* of the parties. Of all counselling approaches, the person-centred places most emphasis on the client–counsellor relationship and its curative properties. Psychodynamic counselling is also highly relationship focused, but its views on expertise and interpretation remove it from the more 'egalitarian' climate of person-centred counselling. (Psychodynamic counselling distinguishes between the *real relationship* between client and counsellor, and the *transferential relationship*.) The early sessions of counselling, particularly with more apprehensive clients, are often devoted to 'relationship building'. Critics of approaches which are more relationship-based than goal-directed suggest that the former are unnecessarily protracted and dependency creating. The therapeutic relationship has come to be regarded by many as the central component of effective counselling. *See* COUNTERTRANSFERENCE, FIVE RELATIONSHIPS FRAMEWORK, THERAPEUTIC ALLIANCE and TRANSFERENCE; *see also* Clarkson (1993).

relaxation *see* PROGRESSIVE RELAXATION.

reluctance unwillingness, stubbornness, resistance to cooperation in counselling. Many writers consider reluctance to be identical with RESISTANCE, but Egan (2002) views reluctant clients as distinctly 'unsure of what they want' and as 'indirectly uncooperative'; they may experience a lack of trust and fear of change. Client reluctance may manifest in sullen silence, for example, or superficial cooperativeness. Resistant clients are more likely, in Egan's view, to have been coerced into counselling, for example as part of an offender rehabilitation programme. It has been suggested that special attention to interpretation of client silence, encouragement of client self-disclosure non-verbally (e.g. in writing, drawing and certain physical exercises) and helpful explanation of the counselling process, can all assist reluctant clients. *See* Manthei and Matthews (1989).

reminiscence therapy an approach to therapy with older adults (over 65 and often in the nursing home context), usually in groups, that encourages people to tell their stories and listen to others', thus increasing their self-respect, relationships and life satisfaction and reducing anxiety. Specialised approaches such as gestalt reminiscence therapy have been used and researched, demonstrating the potential emotional, social and spiritual advantages involved.

repair mending or improving the therapeutic relationship. In THERAPEUTIC ALLIANCE the-

ory, it is considered to be important that the counsellor consciously maintains an effective working alliance, and such maintenance may often include attention to rifts and misunderstandings; where these can be addressed and repaired the therapeutic alliance can often be strengthened.

reparation the making of amends or repairing (psychological) parts of oneself and/or others. According to Klein, the *reparative drive* is part of a normal developmental phase following the depressive position. In some psychoanalytic thought, reparation is considered a defence mechanism designed to ward off the guilt of having hurt others. It is suggested that many counsellors, and helpers generally, seek to help others both as a means of making reparation for hurt they feel they have caused and as a way of completing their own recovery. The making of amends is an integral part of the TWELVE STEPS approach.

reparenting any therapeutic technique which attempts consciously to offer (often very damaged) clients a consistent, benign and corrective experience of parenting. Reparenting is an intensive therapeutic method used by some TA practitioners (among others) under the name of 'regression therapy' or cathexis. Therapists may hold, bottle feed and clothe regressed clients. While certain successes are claimed, this method is controversial. *See also* CORRECTIVE EMOTIONAL EXPERIENCE, DEVELOPMENTALLY NEEDED RELATIONSHIP.

repertory grid systematic observation and charting of client constructs used in personal construct counselling. Methods such as LADDERING and PYRAMIDING may be used to elicit constructs. Kelly (1955) sought to analyse client self-perceptions in various ways. A numerical rating system is often used. For example, on a scale of 1–7, a client may be asked to rate how attractive she regards her father, her brother, herself and others. By using a variety of such constructs (e.g. intelligence, assertiveness) a comprehensive grid is built up. Often these grids are computerised. The externalising of personal constructs allows clients to study themselves with a certain objectivity and to consider gradual changes in how they begin to reconstrue themselves, others and the world.

repetition compulsion the psychoanalytic view that people commonly seek unconsciously to return to earlier behaviour, to replay it in everyday life and in counselling. Freud later related the repetition compulsion partly to the death instinct (people unconsciously 'remember' and are attracted to the state of non-being). The term is also used in reference to fixed and self-destructive behaviour patterns, which may represent an unconscious attempt to re-create original traumas in order to resolve them: some women, for example, repeatedly though unconsciously, seek out violent partners, perhaps because they have experienced violence in their childhood and either equate this with normality or have a SCRIPT which impels them to re-create the past again and again. Ritualistic behaviour, such as that exhibited in obsessive–compulsive disorder, is an extreme form of repetition compulsion.

repression the Freudian concept according to which painful and/or unacceptable memories, images, thoughts and feelings are consigned to the unconscious. At one point in Freud's thought 'the repressed' was considered synonymous with the unconscious. Repression has been considered the principal DEFENCE MECHANISM. Material that is repressed is so thoroughly censored by the ego or superego that it is 'as if it had never existed'. Initially, it is through dreams, slips of the tongue or symptoms that the repressed returns to consciousness. Psychoanalysis aims to help release such material by means of free association, the analysis of defences, and through dream interpretation. *Primary repression* refers to the censoring of the basic feelings or thoughts which are unacceptable; *secondary repression* refers to the censoring of any clues to this already repressed material. The term 'repression' is also used loosely, as in 'He is very repressed' to refer to lack of spontaneity and surplus self-control.

Rescuer role the TA concept of an inauthentic game role taken by someone when he believes or acts as if he has to help another from a position of superiority because she is incapable of helping herself. The Rescuer role alternates with the Persecutor and Victim roles. *See* KARPMAN TRIANGLE.

rescuing behaviour which consciously or unconsciously assists and/or undermines another. Psychological rescuing, as opposed to necessary physical rescue in an emergency, is considered to be of dubious value because it is based on a presupposition that the rescued person is unable to help herself; and because repeated rescuing reinforces the rescued in the role of inadequate victim (or 'learned helplessness'). In this context, empathy seeks to understand the client's plight, while sympathy involves a tendency on the part of the sympathiser towards rescuing the other person. Counsellors need to be alert to any compulsive inclination to rescue clients.

research study of or systematic enquiry into the nature of particular phenomena; scientific investigation into aetiology and how, and to what degree, counselling interventions work, and implicitly or explicitly into possible improvements or new discoveries; research frequently involves the testing of hypotheses. Much research in counselling and psychotherapy focuses on the PROCESSES and OUTCOMES involved (the 'how' and 'whether' they work). Many counsellors have been fairly indifferent to research, preferring anecdotal or subjective evidence of success, but the BACP and other professional bodies have promoted it. Research needs to be rigorous, replicable and relevant, but often fails in one or more of these areas. Research in counselling to date has claimed to demonstrate that the orientation of the counsellor is unrelated to client outcome (*see* Luborsky, Singer and Luborsky, 1975); that (untrained) paraprofessionals achieve results as good as trained counsellors (Durlak, 1979); that matching certain client and counsellor characteristics can increase successful outcomes (Howard, Orlinsky and Hill, 1970); that certain therapies appear to have a better evidence-base for their effectiveness than others (Roth and Fonagy, 1996). The research designs from which such results are taken are themselves criticised by Rowan (1998). While writers like Rowan argue for better humanistic research methods (e.g. action research, participatory research), others such as Kline (1992) call for even more elaborate, rigorous methodologies. Common research terminology includes:

control group – a group of people who are not exposed to a treatment condition and whose behaviour is monitored in order to provide comparison with the researched group, as in randomised control groups;

meta-analysis – the analysis of a significant number of existing research studies in the same area of concern, with a view to identifying common findings;

effect size – a complex measurement of the effectiveness of particular therapies;

variables – those contextual and complicating factors involved in any research which need to be taken into account when seeking to identify causal links between events;

qualitative research based on observation, participation, interviews, etc. seeks to find patterns in the information gained; it is usually presented descriptively and includes various methods such as grounded theory, discourse analysis, etc;

quantitative research based on rigorous, well-controlled designs which permit statistical analysis of the data obtained.

See also NECESSARY AND/OR SUFFICIENT CONDITIONS, PLACEBO, EVIDENCE-BASED PRACTICE. *See* McLeod (2001).

resentment undisclosed feelings of irritation or anger towards others. Resentment may take the form of an inwardly turned anger (sulking), fuelled by the belief that one has been slighted, hurt or unappreciated and that this absolutely should not have happened; such beliefs fester, become preoccupations and often take the form of UNFINISHED BUSINESS. Assertively stating one's feelings and preferences often obviates the need for resentful preoccupation.

residential treatment any form of therapy requiring the client to be in special accommodation for a period of time. People suffering from serious mental health problems often undergo voluntary or involuntary psychiatric treatment for the sake of safety, rest, assessment, and in order to monitor the effect of medication. Residential treatment is often necessary for people with serious problems of alcoholism and addiction because they are unlikely to be able to control their own behaviour unsupervised. Certain forms of therapy (e.g. the Japanese Morita therapy) may require an intensive period of rest and meditation in a therapeutic centre. Many humanistic counsellors and therapists make use of periodic intensive residential workshops to boost therapeutic progress. Certain projects offering alternatives to psychiatric treatment provide 24-hour access to 'residential psychotherapists'.

resilience psychological strength, especially in the face of challenging life events. Distinct from pseudo-resilience, or the pretence that one is unaffected by difficulties, resilience is the ability to remain unscathed and is probably related to certain personality types.

resistance the client's obstruction or opposition of the counsellor in her efforts to help; the client's self-obstruction in relation to change through discovery of painful or unconscious material. Psychodynamic counsellors recognise resistance as universal, although differing in degree and form from client to client. The counsellor's neutrality, awareness of transference and timely interpretations are designed to help the client work through resistance. Egan (2002) contrasts resistance with RELUCTANCE, viewing the former as the coerced client's 'fighting back' against treatment he did not ask

for. He cautions counsellors not to regard resistance automatically as an indication of client pathology, since it may well point to the client's justified dissatisfaction with the counsellor's work.

resolution the word has two distinct meanings: intention, and completion or solution. It is used in counselling primarily in the second sense. Problem resolution may mean that the client's target problem on presenting for counselling has been dealt with to his satisfaction (sometimes the most significant problem only emerges as the counselling develops). Where there is a cluster of problems or a general sense of confusion or distress, then resolution may be defined in terms of the client's subjective report that he feels significantly better, along with some assessment of actual behavioural improvements in his life.

respect positive regard; acceptance. The term 'respect' is often used synonymously with UNCONDITIONAL POSITIVE REGARD and refers to the counsellor's fundamental attitude of accepting the person of the client. Counsellors may not respect every aspect of their client's *behaviour*. This use of the word differs significantly from its use in the sense of coercion: parents who demand that their children 'respect' them, for example, often invite grudging compliance masquerading as respect. 'Respect' also carries the connotation of admiration, as in 'I respect her integrity and professionalism'.

response prevention a therapeutic intervention used mainly in the treatment of clients with obsessive–compulsive problems. Response prevention aims to expose the client to the object of her compulsion (e.g. dirt, untidiness, food) while simultaneously preventing the execution of her usual compulsive rituals. The precise manner in which this is done depends on the nature and severity of the problem and the ability of the client to co-operate. The central purpose of response prevention is to help clients deal with the anxiety that the compulsion seeks to keep at bay. Serious conditions (e.g. certain cases of bulimia) may require residential treatment with close supervision.

responsibility accountability. Responsibility is a complex concept. Radical personal responsibility means that each person is the author of his own life, responsible for how he uses the freedom of choice that is his. Certain counselling models regard the person as completely responsible for her life, including any illnesses or accidents she may suffer. Schutz (1979), for example, argues that we are responsible for everything that may happen to us, including cancer and rape. The more deterministic approaches, including psychoanalysis and primal therapy, regard humans as profoundly disturbed and effectively programmed, to a large extent, to act unaccountably (without extensive counselling or therapy). While approaches such as REBT, reality therapy and existential counselling place much emphasis on personal responsibility, they also accept that it is relative to one's social context. It should be noted that certain clients are 'pathologically' responsible, or inclined to over-estimate their part in others' lives, and they may experience guilt and obsessional symptoms. The *professional responsibility* of the counsellor embraces issues such as boundary keeping, maintenance of competency and clinical knowledge. The legal

responsibilities of counsellors are still ill defined in the UK (*see* LEGAL ISSUES). *See* CHOICE, DETERMINISM and FREE WILL.

restimulation a term used in re-evaluation counselling, which refers to the opening up or the triggering of old psychological wounds, distress patterns or traumas by new situations which recreate conditions similar to those in the person's past.

retroflection turning back against; a form of self-aggression; the concept, in gestalt therapy, which seeks to explain both how repression operates and how it can be reversed. Retroflection is the 'holding back' from life's challenges which becomes habitual and unaware, leading to chronic muscular tension, for example, or a severely limited lifestyle. Retroflection may be compared with primary REPRESSION. Gestalt counsellors work towards uncovering and redirecting retroflection, for example exposing resentment and encouraging the client gradually to convert it to a more healthy expression of annoyance or assertiveness.

revictimisation repeated experience of adverse circumstances, in particular abuse but also other kinds of traumas. For example, some individuals are unlucky enough to suffer childhood abuse, surgery in adolescence, and road traffic accidents in adulthood. One argument has it that such individuals may unconsciously invite repeated abuse or trauma but this is heatedly contested by many.

review reflection on the progress of counselling (or supervision), often in a prearranged, formal session. Many counsellors suggest to clients that counselling be mutually reviewed, for example, after six sessions; others schedule 3- or 6-monthly review sessions. Such an arrangement offers the opportunity for renegotiating contracts, for open feedback and for appreciating client progress and areas of difficulty.

rigidity psychological 'stiffness', unyieldingness, inflexibility. Rogers (1961) pointed out that clients often have very rigid self-concepts at the beginning of counselling, which soften or loosen as the therapeutic process takes hold. *See* AUTHORITARIAN PERSONALITY, TIGHT CONSTRUING.

risk assessment formally conducting an assessment of the client's vulnerability to danger. This applies to children considered 'at risk', and to adults deemed a potential danger to themselves or others, in cases involving serious mental health problems, drug and alcohol addiction, anorexia, aggression, life-threatening illness, etc. Systematic risk assessment is more likely in statutory agencies but many counselling agencies have their own procedures.

risk taking deliberately placing oneself in a situation likely to present some degree of threat or challenge to oneself. It is probable that many more clients defensively avoid risks than counterphobically confront them (although genetic research claims to be identifying high level risk-taking as a feature of certain individuals, e.g. gamblers, extreme sports enthusiasts). Some counsellors gently encourage sensible psychological risk taking while others may prefer to promote vigorous and undeferred confrontation of fears. Counsellors recognise that risk taking and personal growth are to some extent inseparable. Systematic desensitisation reflects a preference for gradual risk taking, while flooding and shame-attacking exercises reflect a belief in the potency of immediate and high-risk challenges, as well as confidence in the robustness of clients. REBT, gestalt, encounter groups and primal therapy groups largely reflect the latter practice. Psychoanalysts sometimes discourage clients (analysands) from undertaking any major risks in the early months or years of analysis. Therapeutic risk taking can take place both within and between sessions. Counsellors rarely take dramatic risks within counselling sessions but are frequently faced with decisions regarding risky interventions (e.g. confrontations, innovatory techniques and self-disclosure).

ritual abuse the sexual abuse, humiliation, mutilation and killing of children as part of 'satanic' or other ceremonies. There are many, often uncorroborated, testimonies of such abuse by individuals or groups. Individuals may practise idiosyncratic perverse rituals calling for the abuse of children. There are claims that babies have been deliberately conceived in order to be offered later as human sacrifices. This has as yet little proven evidence, and there is also speculation as to its reality and/or extent, but where it exists its traumatic results resemble those of CHILD SEXUAL ABUSE generally, with an additional overlay of secrecy, disbelief and horror. It is felt by some clinicians that there is a link between ritual abuse in childhood and the development of multiple personality disorder. *See* FALSE MEMORY SYNDROME.

rivalry competition. *Sibling rivalry* is the conscious or unconscious competition of children for their parents' affection and for other desired objects; such competitiveness may become generalised and carry over problematically into adult life. The

Oedipus complex is a particular form of rivalry and may be re-enacted unconsciously in the client's relationship with the counsellor. Counsellors-in-training and supervisees in the same supervision group may experience rivalry and exhibit signs of it.

road rage *see* RAGE.

Rogerian referring to the theory and practice of counselling and psychotherapy of Carl Rogers. 'Rogerian' is a term inappropriately but quite commonly applied to PERSON-CENTRED COUNSELLING and particularly to the non-directive nature of much counselling. It is in some ways paradoxical to speak of the 'enormous influence' of Rogers since he believed strongly in the individual's internal LOCUS OF EVALUATION and unique experiencing, and would not have encouraged an attitude of unthinking acceptance and compliance in relation to his views. In fact, he viewed the adjective 'Rogerian' with deep distaste.

role a position adopted temporarily and functionally. Even though one may be in a certain role over a considerable period of time (e.g. motherhood), this role is not identical with the whole of one's personality: everyone has a variety of roles, which correspond with the activities they undertake at any one time. It is important to remember that clients are in the *role* of clients and that their lives cannot be defined as wholly in the role of 'being helped'. Counsellors also take on a professional role that does not equate with their entire personalities. Mahrer (1996) criticises counsellors who fall into 'role relationships' in their work. A *role model* is someone whose successful lifestyle, mastery of particular skills or embodiment of

moral courage, for example, is found inspiring and/or useful (e.g. the counsellor's ability to tolerate uncertainty may teach the client similar skills).

role play a learning exercise in which clients, trainees or supervisees temporarily assume experiential positions other than their own. Counsellors-in-training are usually required to role-play the parts of clients, counsellors and observers as a means of developing counselling skills. Parts may be carefully prescribed or improvised. Clients are sometimes encouraged to role-play desired behaviour in certain scenarios (*see* REHEARSAL) or parts of themselves, or significant others (*see* CHAIRWORK). Supervisees can also access their clients' dynamics by role-playing them. Critics of role play suggest that it is less authentic and potent than direct personal learning and may encourage pretence and performance instead of genuineness. It is good practice to debrief (or de-role) people following any role play.

role reversal that aspect of role play in which the person takes the part of a person with whom he believes himself to be in conflict; or in which group or family members play the parts of each other. It also refers to the person playing parts of himself which may be in opposition to each other. *Rational role reversal* is an REBT exercise in which the client plays the part of the counsellor and disputes the irrational beliefs that underpin his dysfunctional behaviour, which are expressed by the counsellor in the role of client.

Rorschach test a means of psychological assessment using intrinsically meaningless designs (inkblots) to invite the projections of those being assessed. Devised by

Hermann Rorschach, this projective test has been refined by using colours supposedly to indicate emotional states, along with elaborate scoring systems. Critics argue that both its usefulness and its precision are spurious.

rumination severe and dysfunctional tendency to preoccupation. More than simply 'thinking too much', rumination is characteristic of obsessive personality types and of obsessive–compulsive disorder. In the latter, the person knows that their ruminations are illogical but has great difficulty in resisting ruminating. Ruminations of a pessimistic or nihilistic character may be a feature of depressive illness.

sabotage undermining a course of action. Sabotage on the part of the client is an indication of AMBIVALENCE towards change. Every counselling theory includes a concept of defences, resistance, discounting, flight, etc. Sabotage denotes a partial wish for change accompanied with a partial wish for STASIS. Transactional analysis counsellors often make an anti-sabotage contract with clients. *See* NON-COMPLIANCE.

sadism violent and/or sexual behaviour in which the person derives pleasure from another's pain. Sadism is characterised by deliberate cruelty towards and/or humiliation of others. It may have a general character of cruelty or be specifically sexual, as when the person must engage in sexual domination and humiliation of another in order to achieve pleasure. Sadism is often considered inseparable from MASOCHISM. Melanie Klein argued that sadism develops as part of 'persecutory anxiety' in the PARANOID–SCHIZOID POSITION. It has been argued that sadism is inherent in everyone: *Schadenfreude*, or pleasure at the misfortunes of others, may be considered a mild form of sadism.

sadness a mood of despondency, melancholia or sorrow, usually related to an experience or memory of loss. Sadness is considered a healthy, authentic emotional response following loss experiences. Failure to grieve adequately at such times can lead to depression. Sadness, and its expression through emotional vulnerability and crying, may be suppressed and masked by depression or anger. *See* FEELINGS.

SAFAA sufficient available functioning adult autonomy. This refers to the threshold at which individuals, on the basis of their 'average maturity', are suitable to undertake human potential work rather than needing medical or reparative therapeutic help.

sanctions actions taken by a professional body against a counsellor, following a complaint by a client that is upheld. It is common for a counsellor in this position to be required, for instance, to receive intensive supervision and/or submit a special report; in extreme circumstances, he or she may be compelled to cease practice.

sandplay therapy Jungian inspired form of therapy for various conditions including depression, anxiety, somatic disorders, ADD, etc. that uses sand as its main medium. It is tactile, non-verbal and non-intrusive and allows the client to use objects to construct a 'world' through which hard-to-access or hard-to-articulate experience can be surfaced and understood.

satisfaction   the experience of having enough; sufficiency. Gestalt counsellors use the term 'satisfaction' to refer to the experience following CONTACT. 'Deep organismic satisfaction' may ensue from completing particular pieces of gestalt work and it is important for both counsellor and client to savour, rather than take for granted, the effort expended in counselling and its results. Clients may be considered to be satisfied with the outcome of counselling if they have substantially reached their goals or modified their distress.

scaling questions   the technique, used in solution-focused therapy, of asking the client to rate their level of distress and satisfaction on a scale of 1 to 10, thus allowing them to recognise that their distress is not absolute and improvement is possible. SFT therapists use this information to identify with the client what will carry things forward positively, even fractionally; and congratulations on progress is also a feature.

scapegoating   the projection of bad feelings or disowned thoughts and behaviour on to one member of a group or family. It is common in group situations for one person to be identified as the main or exclusive source of 'the problem'. Group facilitators, alert to such dynamics, will interpret them and encourage every member to examine disowned parts of his or her own behaviour.

schema   an enduring construct, assumption or core belief about oneself, others and events generally. The concept of schemas was developed from Piaget's use by Aaron Beck in his COGNITIVE THERAPY. A dysfunctional schema is resistant to new and disconfirming information and faulty information processing is employed to protect the schema from change. Anxious and depressed clients are noted as having certain common dysfunctional schemas (e.g. 'The world is a dangerous place' or 'It is essential that others think well of me'). Cognitive therapists encourage clients to monitor such thinking and to develop more adaptive schemas. *Schema-focused* cognitive therapy differs from situation-focused therapy in its aims, depth and length. Compare DRIVERS, PERSONAL CONSTRUCTS and SCRIPT MESSAGES.

schizoid   refers to people who are cold, withdrawn and suspicious in character and/or whose cognitive and emotional functions are split from each other. The term 'schizoid' in Kleinian terminology is sometimes used of people who have not resolved problems associated with the PARANOID–SCHIZOID POSITION and have not progressed to the next stage, the 'depressive' position. 'Schizoid' has come to be used loosely of anyone detached from her true feelings, although its original meaning inclined towards 'schizophrenic' or 'psychotic'. People displaying eccentric behaviour are sometimes referred to as schizoid or as having a 'schizotypal personality'.

schizophrenia   a serious mental disorder characterised by disorders of thought and perception, particularly in the form of powerful and enduring delusions. Schizophrenia is an umbrella term for a number of psychotic conditions, all marked by decline in the person's functioning and by distorted perceptions. The most common feature of schizophrenia is AUDITORY HALLUCINATIONS (although other forms of delusional perception are known; for example, the belief that one is being controlled by others or having their thoughts inserted into one's brain – *paranoid schizophrenia*). Schizophrenia has often been understood wrongly as a 'split personality' comprising two distinct parts (*see* MULTIPLE PERSONALITY DISORDER). Originally known as 'dementia praecox', schizophrenia has historically been subdivided into the categories of simple, hebephrenic, catatonic and paranoid. Many critics are unhappy with all such terms, finding them imprecise and stigmatising. Schizophrenia usually has its onset before midlife and varies in intensity and manageability. The advent of psychotropic medication has enabled many sufferers to conduct reasonably normal lives, but hospitalisation or 'care in the community' is necessary for many. There is a substantial body of research which indicates that genetic and structural factors are important in aetiology. Research evidence to support the concept of the 'schizophrenogenic parent' has not been forthcoming. Certain kinds of counselling may help some people diagnosed as schizophrenic to accept and manage their condition better and family therapy can be useful in addition to appropriate medication. People diagnosed as schizophrenic may function quite normally if their condition is properly managed. *See* MENTAL ILLNESS, TRANQUILLISERS.

schoolism the tendency for practitioners to adhere uncritically and unhelpfully to a particular model or approach to counselling/psychotherapy (usually that in which they were 'schooled') and to avoid integrationism or even dialogue.

screening the assessment of clients, often in an intake or preliminary interview, with a view to deciding their suitability for counselling. Screening implies that on occasion it will be more appropriate for certain clients to have no counselling at all, because they may not need it or may not benefit from it (at this time).

script an 'unconscious life plan', according to TA theory. The script begins to be formulated at birth, is constantly reinforced both by oneself and parents, and by a process of SELF-FULFILLING PROPHECY. The script is decided on (preverbally) in childhood and has the character of a drama, including a preordained ending. Children are considered to make the best decisions they can, often in adverse circumstances, but they make these decisions with infantile logic, which can lead to chronic misinterpretations of reality. Berne referred to winning, losing and non-winning scripts (the last represented by a banal, compromising lifestyle, or what has also been called the 'psychopathology of the average'). The *script process* refers to the particular patterns of behaviour by which people live out their scripts (e.g. the 'never script' dictates that someone will never get what he really wants). *Script messages* are the influential, script-reinforcing messages, passed on by parents, about the child and people and the world in general. The *script matrix* analyses parents' script messages according to ego states. People are said to be 'in script' or to be engaging in 'scripty' behaviour when they repeat script options instead of acting autonomously. A *miniscript* is a condensed sequence of script feelings, beliefs and behaviours spanning seconds or minutes and initiated by DRIVERS.

sculpting a means of externalising one's feelings or constructs by placing them in meaningful three-dimensional configurations. In group settings, a client or trainee may be asked to place other group members physically in positions that represent their psychological relationship to each other; when completed, this exercise is explored and interpreted according to the 'sculptor's' imagination. Inanimate objects (stones, buttons, etc.) are also used for this exercise, in a three-dimensional, client-created configuration (a so-called 'mini-sculpt') that acts as a vehicle on which the person can project their unconscious feelings.

seasonal affective disorder a distinctive form of DEPRESSION, the onset of which is associated with winter. Also known as 'winter blues', SAD may be characterised by loss of energy, social withdrawal, sleep disturbance, overeating, increased alcohol consumption, and flattened affect. In one survey, 35% of people reported feeling more depressed and anxious in winter. Support groups offer help to sufferers, non-sedative drugs (e.g. Prozac) have been said to help, and it is claimed that special light equipment (phototherapy) provides effective relief for many people.

secondary emotional problem a problem experienced/caused by a client in relation to another, primary problem. The concept of secondary problems has been identified by cognitive–behavioural counsellors: someone who is depressed, for example, may become depressed or anxious about being depressed; in other words, he may disturb himself about his original (or primary) problem and perhaps blame himself for it. A recommended strategy for counsellors is to help the client overcome the secondary problem before working on the original problem, particu-

larly when the existence of the secondary problem interferes with work on the primary problem.

secondary gain the usefulness to someone of maintaining certain symptoms or problems. Secondary gains are in the interpersonal domain where, for example, a partner may be manipulated into a caregiving role by the depression of the other. Compare PAYOFF.

secondary process in contrast to the PRIMARY PROCESS, the secondary process (or 'secondary process thinking') is mental activity, according to Freudian thought, which is non-instinctual, logical, and governed by the REALITY PRINCIPLE. It checks and balances the excesses of primary process activity such as dreaming, wishing and distorting of ideas.

section to detain someone involuntarily for the purposes of assessment and treatment under the conditions of the Mental Health Act 1983. 'Section' is the colloquial term for such detention; there are various sections in the Act. *See* MENTAL ILLNESS.

seeding implanting ideas for future consideration. Seeding is a concept used mainly in brief therapy, and is an intervention on the part of the counsellor when, for example, she is aware that the client may be unable to contact part of her intrapsychic world or take certain risks at the moment; the counsellor may nevertheless offer an interpretation or suggest a course of action that may have meaning for the client after the termination of counselling.

selection choice; exclusion. Some therapists operate a selection procedure for clients who may benefit from brief or group therapy, for example, instead of long-term individual therapy. Candidates for rigorous counsellor training are selected on the basis of their suitability to work with others' intimate problems; their personal maturity, flexibility and capacity for further personal and professional development. It is also thought that people self-select for counsellor training and that those who drop out of such training are also self-selecting. *See* ASSESSMENT, QUALITIES OF COUNSELLORS.

selective abstraction the cognitive error of selecting from past or present experience data consistent with the cognitive set that is characteristic of a person's emotional problem. For example, a person who is anxious will tend to focus on aspects of a situation that are potentially threatening and will not process its benign or positive features.

self the 'I-that-I-know-myself-to-be'; the ego; the 'me' or sense of identity; personality; distinctness from others. The 'self' is philosophically problematic, since it cannot be located or proven to exist even though we are all intimately familiar with it. Some philosophers and mystics have argued that the self is an illusion or that it is more accurate to speak of many selves or attributes of a self. Psychodynamic counselling addresses the parts of the self known as ego, id and superego; transactional analysis addresses the parent, adult and child parts. Jung understood the self in a complex manner: 'an archetypal urge to co-ordinate, relativise and mediate the tension of the opposites' (Samuels, Shorter and Plaut, 1987). Some writers discuss the formation and the fragmentation of the self, in personality development and psychopathological development respectively. *Selflessness* implies altruism, and *selfishness* suggests

inadequate consideration for others. The advice 'to thine own self be true' implies that the self is a reality and that GENUINENESS 'adheres' to it. *See* EGO, FALSE SELF, REAL SELF, USE OF SELF, SUBPERSONALITIES (Rowan and Cooper, 1999).

self-acceptance ceasing to evaluate oneself. Acknowledging that one is, in essence, fallible, that one is too complex to be given a global rating and is in flux. Self-acceptance does not necessarily involve liking or disliking oneself; rather it involves acknowledging one's uniqueness. Achieving self-acceptance after years of self-torment is a positive change. Complacency (idle self-satisfaction), however, is not to be confused with self-acceptance.

self-actualisation realising one's potential; the continuing process of actualising or putting into practice one's aspirations, rather than ignoring, denying or suppressing them. Self-actualisation is a humanistic concept and implies both the possibility of personal growth and a natural tendency of humans to pursue it. *See* PERSON-CENTRED COUNSELLING.

self-aggrandisement exaggerated, unrealistic promotion of oneself. In contrast to positive self-regard, self-aggrandisement suggests an inauthentic, narcissistic presentation of the self based on anxiety about one's true worth.

self-analysis (psycho)analysis of oneself by means of free association, dream interpretation and other methods. Founders of movements, such as Freud, by necessity analyse or treat themselves (because no one has yet been trained to). Freud originally considered self-analysis a good alternative to 'psychoanalysis proper' but increasingly tempered this view. As a joke has it, 'the only problem with self-analysis is the counter-transference' – that is, there is enormous difficulty in being objective about oneself. Most analytic practitioners, including Karen Horney, who championed self-analysis, regard it as useful or essential *in addition to* analysis by an analyst.

self-awareness knowledge or consciousness of one's characteristic strengths and weaknesses; moment-by-moment alertness to one's subtle psychophysiological processes. Any exercise which assists people to reflect on their experience of themselves can be referred to as a self-awareness exercise. Much humanistic group work, for example, focuses on awareness of the self in interaction and on the possible expansion of awareness. Meditation often aims to raise awareness of the body, breathing, posture, etc. Most counsellor training courses require trainees to engage in self-awareness work. *See* AWARENESS.

self-change the effort, initiated by the person herself, to alter her own thoughts, feelings and/or behaviour without external or professional help. The distinction between self-change and SELF-HELP is sometimes made that the former is more proactive and can (and often does) occur naturally and effectively. The vast majority of the general population who encounter problems in living resolve them without recourse to a counsellor.

self-characterisation a description of oneself. As utilised in personal construct counselling, the self-characterisation exercise requires the client to describe herself in the third person, as if from the perspective of someone who knows her better than anyone can hope to know her and is willing to portray both her positive and negative attributes.

self-concept the image or beliefs one holds about oneself. I may, for example, consider myself to be humble, conscientious, insightful, unfulfilled, etc. Furthermore, my concept of myself may be that I am a dutiful husband, a bored housewife, or an unrecognised genius. Self-concepts, although usually of some persistence, may be modified by experience. Traumatic or fortuitous occurrences (e.g. losing a loved one in a road accident or winning the lottery) may dramatically challenge one's self-concept; or a changed self-concept may arise in the counselling process.

self-consciousness disabling form of self-awareness, often involving critical thoughts about oneself; over-concern for presentation of oneself and one's performance. Self-consciousness is a typical feature of shyness and social phobias. *See* SPECTATORING.

self-consistency the stability of the sense of self; the experience that one is the same self, regardless of place and time.

self-defeating behaviour any behaviour which is not in one's best interests, yet is engaged in, often repetitively, perhaps with the unconscious intention of punishing oneself, denying one's true needs, etc. *See*, for example, REACTION FORMATION.

self-destructive behaviour this term can refer to either SELF-DEFEATING BEHAVIOUR or SELF-HARM.

self-direction the client's choosing his own goals and meanings, 'away from pleasing others', which Rogers considered a central part of the therapeutic process.

self-discipline the practice of orderly behaviour established by oneself rather than by others. The term 'discipline' is unfashionable but denotes the ability to organise one's life sensibly and to internalise the lessons of experience. Wood (1983) argues that a 'morality therapy' based on self-discipline is of greater value than dubious systems of professional help.

self-disclosure sharing one's feelings, thoughts or aspects of one's personal history with another. Appropriate self-disclosure is recognised as an often valuable intervention on the part of counsellors since it can convey fellow-feeling, solidarity, normalising reassurance, understanding and a willingness to be known. Counsellors are advised to disclose their own experiences sparingly and judiciously, and for therapeutic impact rather than from any eagerness to talk about oneself. Self-help groups such as AA place considerable emphasis on the self-disclosures of fellow 'recovering alcoholics'. Self-disclosure is used extremely sparingly or not at all by more classical (psychoanalytic) psychotherapists, but is probably used with some freedom by more humanistic practitioners. HERE AND NOW disclosure is often more valuable than THERE AND THEN disclosure.

self-efficacy the belief that one is capable of producing desired change. It has been called 'a feeling of mastery and control'. It has been argued that the client's self-efficacy is an important key in all approaches to counselling. Those approaches (e.g. behavioural counselling, reality therapy) that emphasise the negotiation of appropriate tasks aim to affirm clients' coping and performing abilities and to build from small to larger experiences of success.

self-esteem the person's valuing herself. Absence (or relative absence) of self-esteem, known as LOW SELF-ESTEEM, is a common problem, particularly in depression. The opposite term, 'high self-esteem', is lit-

tle used, which may reflect a common human tendency to belittle rather than glorify oneself. In REBT, encouraging clients towards self-acceptance is a preferred goal to helping them to raise their self-esteem. This is because the latter involves making a global rating of one's self which is always dependent upon some variant. Thus, I may esteem myself if I am loved, achieve my goals, etc., but if I am not loved or if I do not achieve my goals I dis-esteem myself.

self-experience the way in which someone actually apprehends himself, his feelings and thoughts, from moment to moment. The term is used by Rogers (1961) of clients' realising that their experience of themselves in therapy often contradicts or deviates from their self-image. Rogers also used the term 'the experiencing of experience'. *See also* EXPERIENTIAL PSYCHOTHERAPY.

self-fulfilling prophecy the tendency for one's fears or expectations to become reality; or for the expectations that others have about us to become realities. Taken from social psychology, the expression 'self-fulfilling prophecy' suggests that our thinking dictates how we act, how we are perceived and what situations we create for ourselves, which reinforce our original expectations. *See* SCRIPT.

self-harm violence towards the self, usually of a physical nature. *See* DELIBERATE SELF-HARM.

self-help the practice of self-assessment and of initiating one's own significant life changes. Self-help can refer to self-improvement or change without the assistance of others or in addition to it. There is a large self-help literature encouraging individuals to initiate their own changes. There is also a large self-help movement consisting of voluntary self-help groups (e.g. AA) which rely on peer help rather than on professional help. There is much debate about the sufficiency or otherwise of self-help initiatives in the domain of mental health. *See* SELF-CHANGE.

self-holding an analytic concept referring to the client's behaviour when he is (or was as a child) forced to nurture, protect and stimulate himself in the absence of 'good enough' holding from parents or caretakers. According to Casement (1985) clients may sometimes complainingly allude to their having to hold or contain themselves when the therapist is failing to provide necessary HOLDING.

self-ideal the image one has of what one would like to be or what one considers oneself capable of becoming. Logically, there can be no self-actualisation without a sense of an ideal or improved self.

self-image the mental picture one has of one-self. The self-image may be relatively enduring or change according to circumstances. It may be confronted and changed when others present a contradictory picture. When I 'see' myself as a 'nice guy' and others in group therapy, for example, see me as passive–aggressive, I must either believe them to be wrong (and perhaps persecutory) or I must recreate my image of myself.

self-knowledge accumulated data and/or moment-by-moment awareness of oneself, one's abilities, characteristics, limitations, etc. There is some debate as to whether significant self-knowledge can be gained via others (including counsellors) or, perhaps more powerfully, by introspection, self-analysis and scrupulous honesty with oneself.

self-monitoring watching and noting one's own thoughts and feelings, usually with a specific purpose. Cognitive therapists encourage clients to monitor their behaviour, often as a homework assignment, in order to compare their self-schemas and irrational thoughts about themselves with carefully observed reality. Sometimes clients are asked to make written daily notes on their observations.

self-mutilation a severe form of self-harm in which the person may, in extreme cases, cut off parts of their bodies or gouge out an eye. Van Gogh's severing of part of his ear is one of the best-known examples, and demonstrates that self-mutilation is an extreme form of self-hatred and anguish, and signals a high risk of suicide. More frequently, people mutilate themselves by cutting or burning rather than severing parts of their bodies. As part of their sexual or lifestyle preference/perversion, some people practise (usually minor) forms of self-mutilation for pleasure, e.g. piercing, tattooing.

selfobject Kohutian term for the child's experience of people or objects used in the service of the self, 'when the object is cathected with narcissistic libido' (*see* St Clair, 2000).

self-organisation the manner in which people order their views of themselves and the world. *Self-reorganisation* is the process of change in such organisation resulting from counselling that stimulates self-reflection, insight and self-change.

self psychology a central concept in that school of psychoanalysis associated with Kohut that diverges from classical Freudian and OBJECT RELATIONS views of the self. Kohut regarded the self as best understood via introspection and empathy. This 'self' is experienced by the client in her transference towards the therapist. The 'Kohutian self' is focused on preoedipal development.

self-rating judgements made of oneself, by oneself. Self-rating may be considered distinct from self-assessment in that it has the quality of negativity and self-rejection. Self-rating is a term used by cognitive therapists; its opposite is self-acceptance. *See* GLOBAL STATEMENTS.

self-realisation synonymous with SELF-ACTUALISATION.

self-regard an ability to prize oneself as a person in such a way that even the dissonant or 'less desirable' parts of one's behaviour may be viewed from the perspective of self-liking.

self-reliance independence; a tendency not to look to others for help or encouragement but to depend primarily on one's own resources. Self-reliance may be interpreted either as an admirable character trait or as a mistrustful and defensive posture towards others; the latter is known as compulsive self-reliance.

self-sabotage the undermining of oneself or aspects of one's behaviour or aspirations. Self-sabotage may be effected unconsciously or preconsciously. *See* SABOTAGE.

self-schema an enduring view that one takes of oneself, in relation to particular situations. For example, someone who compulsively engages in self-harm may hold the self-schema 'I deserve to be punished'. *See* SCHEMA.

self-structure *see* self-organisation.

self-talk inaudible statements that a person makes to himself which influence how he will behave and construe events. Self-talk, also known as subvocalisation, is not necessarily 'words heard inside the head', but may be thoughts which are inferred from attitudes (that is, people are frequently unaware of their self-talk). Cognitive therapists aim to help clients identify their self-talk and to modify it. Certain approaches to personal change, including coaching and positive thinking, seek to replace negative self-talk with positive self-talk.

sensation bodily feeling; perception by means of the senses. Jung considered sensation a basic psychological function. It has been given prominent attention by Gendlin (*see* FELT SENSE) and Mahrer (*see* EXPERIENTIAL PSYCHOTHERAPY) and by many humanistic practitioners (*see* BODYWORK). Sensation is one of Lazarus' (1981) seven modalities in multimodal therapy. Sensations may include tension, dizziness, blushing and 'butterflies in the stomach', each of which may hold precise clues as to the client's typical responses to problem situations. Clients' attitudes to sex, dress, food, music and so on, can indicate the significance of sensation or its denial in their lives. Multimodal therapists may use focusing, catharsis, sensate focus, systematic desensitisation or other interventions as appropriate when working with clients in the sensory modality.

sensitivity training group a group convened for the purpose of examining and improving interpersonal relationships and skills. Sensitivity training groups evolved from the original T GROUPS of Kurt Lewin. Comprising up to 12 participants, they were usually held residentially and leaders often refrained from leading as such (instead taking the role of a convener/facilitator who also acts as a full group member). The groups attempted to be 'cultural islands' (as free from everyday expectations as possible), focusing on actual, unprescribed behaviour in the group. Key elements were the HERE AND NOW, self-disclosure and feedback. Certain organisations (e.g. the Group Relations Training Association) continue to run such group events.

sentence completion a counsellor intervention requiring the client to finish something she has begun to say. Certain clients, either characteristically or occasionally, speak in half-sentences, leaving significant meanings unsaid. The counsellor may intervene by using prompting statements or words to encourage the client to complete her meaning. As an example: client: 'I'm afraid to do it', counsellor: '... Because if I did, then ...'; or client: 'I was going to do it, but ...', counsellor: 'But ..?' Sentence completion can also refer to a questionnaire method that asks respondents to write the endings of provided sentences.

separate identity the experience of the developing infant and the mature adult that although he may have much in common with others, they and he are distinct beings. So-called 'primary identification' consists in the infant believing that others (particularly caregivers) and himself are merged; secondary identification is the ability to perceive and identify others as separate. *See* CONFLUENCE.

separation anxiety the experience of anxiety resulting from an interference of the infant's attachment to its mother/caregiver. Bowlby and others have argued that babies derive their principal sense of security from a primary caregiver, and that threats to this sense of security can lay the foundations for all later anxieties relating to separations. Others have suggested that insensitively managed birth procedures or birth itself provide the foundation for separation anxiety. Speculative connections are made between such early experiences and later symptoms such as agoraphobia; and with syndromes such as 'women who love too much' (anything is better/less anxiogenic than losing whatever security one has).

session a formal meeting between client and counsellor, usually scheduled in advance. The phrase 'within session' describes work done directly by client and/or counsellor; 'between-session work' refers to counselling-related tasks carried out outside the session time. *See* FIFTY-MINUTE HOUR, FREQUENCY OF SESSIONS.

seven-eyed supervisor model a specifically supervisory model attributed to Hawkins and Shohet (2000): focus on content of supervisory session; strategies and interventions; counselling/therapy relationship; counsellor's process; supervisory relationship; supervisor's own process; the wider context. These 'eyes' are referred to by these authors as modes, and their integration is the aim of effective supervision.

sex addiction an addiction to sex, most often applied to male promiscuous sex, which results in relationship problems. While TWELVE STEPS programmes and other specialist services exist for this condition, there is much debate about whether it should be regarded as a clinical problem rather than a moral one.

sex therapy any approach to the treatment of sexual dysfunction. Sex therapy may be practised in its own right or as part of couple counselling, its clients being individuals or couples. Diverse theorists including Freud, Reich, Kinsey, Kaplan, and Masters and Johnson have contributed to the range of methods offered. Sexual dysfunctions (e.g. difficulty in getting or maintaining an erection, premature ejaculation, vaginismus) may be regarded as symptoms of problems in the relationship, as stress related, as being physiologically caused or exacerbated, or as stemming from ignorance of sexual performance. Treatment approaches vary from the psychoanalytic interpretation of the presenting problem to educating partners in communication skills, identifying and modifying irrational beliefs, teaching relaxation and a range of behavioural techniques and sensate focus, to surrogate sex therapy. Where performance anxiety predominates, counsellors often instruct clients to follow a programme of gradual, non-threatening exercises designed to achieve incremental progress in verbal communication and physical and emotional intimacy.

sexism the attitudes and behaviours adopted by people on the basis of their assumptions about gender roles. Sexism manifests at various levels, from abusive behaviour including *sexual harassment* (which is based on the assumption that men have rights over women's bodies), through stereotyping and insensitivity, to institutionalised sexism, whereby women are denied equal opportunities in the job market, in political representation, and in many other ways. At the interpersonal level, sexist attitudes can be witnessed in both women and men and can include internalised sexism (e.g. a woman's judgement on herself or another woman that she or the other woman is a poor wife because she dislikes domestic tasks; or a man regarding another man, who shares

the child care with his wife, as 'unmanly'). *See* NON-SEXIST COUNSELLING.

sexual abuse violation of the sexual boundaries of another or of the norms of consenting sexual behaviour. While rape, for example, may literally be considered sexual abuse, in common usage the term 'sexual abuse' has come to refer to CHILD SEXUAL ABUSE, which includes a range of behaviours in addition to actual rape. The term 'sexual abuse' is also used to describe the action of a counsellor who engages in sex with a client (even where the client apparently consents).

sexual deviation departure from sexual behaviour considered to be normal. Sexual deviations may include bestiality (sex with animals), paedophilia (sex with children), voyeurism (vicarious sexual pleasure gained from watching others undress, engage in sexual intercourse, etc.), sado-masochism (giving and/or receiving pain in the course of sexual activity). While there is often a majority cultural view on what constitutes a deviation, those minorities with sexual preferences that offend others argue that any form of sexual practice between consenting adults constitutes a norm between them. A *paraphilia* is an *obsession* with (rather than a preference for) certain sexually deviant practices.

sexual differentiation the distinction between males and females, made on the basis of biological characteristics; the awareness which emerges in boys and girls of their sexual differences. *See* GENDER.

sexual orientation the predisposition one has for choice of sexual partners. Sexual orientations can be classified as heterosexual, homosexual, bisexual or transsexual. In a predominantly heterosexual culture, it is easily assumed that everyone is heterosexual, but counsellors need to guard against such assumptions, particularly (but not only) when counselling people who are in anguish over their sexual identity.

sexual orientation conversion therapy therapy claiming to alter a homosexual to a heterosexual orientation. An extremely contentious therapy (or variety of therapies), its practitioners usually have Christian commitments and/or psychoanalytic beliefs in the normality of heterosexuality. These 'reparative' therapies claim to work with clients who wish to change their homosexuality but critics argue that being gay or lesbian is not a pathological condition and such 'therapies' are likely to cause damage, as well as overstating their successes.

sexuality that part of human behaviour concerned with the experience and expression of sex. Enjoyment of sex is generally regarded as one index of mental health. Clients who do not appear comfortable with the subject of sex may have problems in relation to it. It may be the case, however, that clients do not wish to discuss sex with a particular counsellor; this is often so where women clients are allocated to male counsellors. Sexuality commonly refers to *genital sexuality*, but can also refer to behaviour preceding genital interaction, as well as to *sensuality*. The enjoyment of sensual experiences (especially touch) is sometimes considered synonymous with sexuality.

shadow a Jungian archetype which refers to the dark, disowned, threatening part of the self. Jung called it 'the thing a person has no wish to be'. It can be considered the repository of uncontrollable instincts, including destructive impulses, as well as personal qualities considered inferior and unwanted. As such, it is commonly observed that clients seek to deny their shadow and frequently project it, or aspects of it, on to others. Counsellors and clients may approach the shadow with an attitude that changes from judgement to acceptance and integration. It is sometimes speculated that the 'cleaner and brighter' people or institutions appear, the more likely it is that a shadow aspect is being concealed and/or projected on to others.

shadow syndrome a milder version of well-known severe clinical disorder. Term proposed by Ratey and Johnson (1997) for subclinical forms of distress with biological bases (e.g. mild versions of OCD, ADD, etc.) that may be ameliorated by appropriate medication, understanding and management.

shamanic counselling counselling which draws its philosophy and practice from shamanism, which originated from a Siberian context. Shamanism rests on a belief in being called by the spirits and may be characterised by trance and possession states. Shamans are sometimes perceived as wounded healers.

shame embarrassment; self-consciousness and judgement upon oneself for public displays of supposedly immoral or anti-social behaviour. Situational shame is often closely associated with GUILT but differs in that in shame there is a breach of a social code whereas in guilt there is a breach of a moral code. The distinction has been made between trait shame and state shame: the former is an enduring belief, and the latter a situational belief, that one is inferior for a public display of 'weakness'. In shame the individual believes that the audience has noticed the display and condemns one for it; the individual then condemns herself in line with the negative judgement of the audience. Considered an inevitable and sometimes useful part of human moral experience by religious adherents, shame is often highlighted by REBT practitioners as a dysfunctional result of irrational thinking: a better alternative would be, it is argued, concern about and willingness to learn from one's experience.

shame-attacking exercises exercises given to clients in REBT, designed to expose them to shame or embarrassment in order that they can learn to dispute their irrational thinking in such circumstances (e.g. 'Even if everyone does look at me and judge me negatively, I can still accept myself as a fallible human being who has acted foolishly').

shaping a behavioural method of effecting change by having the client undertake 'successive approximations' to the desired behaviour until the major goal is reached. Shaping is commonly based on small, manageable tasks which are systematically reinforced and gradually built upon to establish the desired, more complex behaviour pattern.

short-term counselling *see* BRIEF COUNSELLING, TIME-LIMITED COUNSELLING.

'should' statement any utterance which reveals the speaker's belief in absolute moral imperatives, as applied to herself, others or life conditions. Counsellors are particularly alert towards instances of the 'tyranny of the shoulds' (Horney) because they indicate clients' non-acceptance of themselves (and often of others). 'I should' implies 'I have been told that I should' or 'I believe that I should (if I am to be socially

accepted)' and points to an external LOCUS OF EVALUATION. Some counsellors explicitly teach clients to reword such statements in the form of, for example, 'I want', 'I prefer' or 'I had better (do X if I wish to achieve Y)'. Such statements are non-judgemental, and are rooted in self-experience and rationality. Most counsellors avoid the words 'should' and 'ought'. *See* INTROJECTION and MUSTURBATION.

shyness behaviour characterised by timidity, introversion, avoidance of social occasions, usually accompanied by subjective feelings of discomfort and irrational thinking. While a certain degree of shyness or reservation is extremely common in the population at large, acute shyness often constitutes a social PHOBIA which is severely incapacitating. Shyness may be a family trait, the result of experiences of childhood humiliation or other adverse circumstances, but there are also claims that it is genetically determined. Behavioural and cognitive–behavioural approaches are likely to be the most efficient means of helping shy clients, but a majority of people 'outgrow' it or are eventually successful in self-change.

sibling rivalry competition between brothers and/or sisters. *See* RIVALRY.

silence the temporary absence of any overt verbal or paraverbal communication between counsellor and client within sessions. This may be a time in which the client is digesting an experience, gathering her thoughts to speak or manifesting resistance to counselling. The lengths of silences and their possible meanings must be weighed against the client's unique experience of them. Clients, counsellors and schools of counselling differ in their approaches to, use or tolerance of silence, with more active and time-limited counsellors discouraging long silences. Communicative therapists regard silence as one of the few legitimate *techniques* for therapists. Complete and prolonged silence on the part of the client may indicate severe pathology. It has also been pointed out that secrets within families often constitute a kind of silencing of an abused person, and the job of subsequent counselling is to help them tell the story that has been silenced or censored.

single session therapy therapy or counselling which by design or default lasts no longer than one session. Single session therapy by design (SST), taking seriously research findings that a high proportion of clients claim to be helped significantly and sufficiently by one session, aims to maximise the gains that can be made in that session. Talmon (1990) advocates pre-session preparation (e.g. expectancy conveyed in telephone contact), identification of 'pivotal chords' (especially meaningful, repeated statements or refrains) in what the client says and reinforcement of positive attitudes.

six category intervention the analysis into six distinct kinds of practical therapeutic action suggested by Heron (2001). Heron claims that there are three main authoritative interventions – prescriptive, informative and confronting; and three facilitative kinds of intervention – cathartic, catalytic and supportive. While this model is used by many helping professionals (e.g. psychiatric nurses) it has not had the popular success with counsellors that the EGAN APPROACH, for example, has.

skilful neglect the short-term counsellor's intentional and competent avoidance of certain aspects of the client's material, and focus on the most fruitful aspects.

skilfulness competence, artistry, dexterity. All counsellors learn the use of counselling skills but do not necessarily apply their learning skilfully in all counselling situations. The extent to which a counsellor translates her conceptualisations into specific interventions with a client in a potent and elegant manner is a measure of her skilfulness.

skills development the teaching/learning and refining of COUNSELLING SKILLS. Skills development is considered an essential component of any counsellor training course. Such skills are usually demonstrated and developed in experiential exercises, including role play. Skills development complements theoretical work, personal development and counselling practice.

sleep disorder difficulties in getting to sleep or remaining asleep. The most common sleep disorder or disturbance is insomnia, which is an apparent inability to sleep. Some counsellors suggest that insomnia betrays an inability to surrender, which in turn suggests deep intrapsychic conflict. It seems likely, however, that there is no *one* explanation or solution for insomnia. Sleep patterns are disturbed in a variety of emotional disorders, e.g. in clinical depression, when the person may experience early morning waking.

sliding scale a means of charging fees to clients on a differential basis. Many counsellors, motivated by humanitarian and political sentiments, prefer to negotiate fees that a client can afford to pay. A common sliding scale is based on a fee of £1 for each £1000 of the client's income (per counselling hour). Some counsellors have fee 'bands' for clients to choose from (e.g. £20, £30 or £40). Such negotiations rely on trust, but some counsellors prefer a flat-rate charge because it is clear and does not intrude into clients' private economic affairs; others believe that a firm and constant charge is an analytic necessity (i.e. part of good frame management – see COMMUNICATIVE APPROACH).

smoking cessation individual attempts or programmes designed to end cigarette smoking and nicotine addiction. The NHS runs many such services, sometimes staffed by trained counsellors, under the name of 'Quit' programmes, and the term 'smoking cessation counsellor' has some currency. The aim of reduction and cessation is linked with health targets, and methods include education, analysis of use, diaries, groups, nicotine patches, CBT, motivational interviewing, etc.

snags the name given in cognitive–analytic therapy to the reasons clients offer for their ambivalence towards change. Snags may be synonymous with the 'YES, BUT' response and may apply to present or past behaviour (e.g. 'I would like to train to become a teacher, but...' or 'If only I had had better parents, then...'). They may also be manifestations of unconscious self-sabotage (e.g. 'forgetting' to attend an important appointment). *See* DILEMMAS and TRAPS.

social anxiety any anxiety experienced in relation to social interaction. Embarrassment, shyness, and 'being afraid of people' are examples of social anxiety. In its extreme form it becomes a *social phobia*, characterised by extreme fear and avoidance of other people. *See* ANXIETY.

social contexts of counselling consideration of the place that counselling occupies in society and how it interrelates with social factors, known in the US as *contextualism*. The (largely) one-to-one activity of counselling often ignores or de-emphasises wider social questions. How does counselling relate to issues of class, unemployment, poverty, homelessness, mental illness, feminism, race, disability and political and socio-economic matters generally? From which class, gender, race, etc., are counsellors drawn, and which do they represent? What values does counselling (consciously or unconsciously) promulgate? Which groups of people are offered, or can afford, counselling and psychotherapy? Does it address people's real needs or rather attempt to convert people to therapeutic values? Counsellor training which ignores or marginalises these issues fails to engender 'critical intelligence' (Kovel) in trainees. The BACP's Course Accreditation criteria ask for attention to be paid to social contexts. *See* Smail (1993).

social learning theory *see* LEARNING THEORY.

social skills training training which is intended to address deficits in life and communication skills and to enhance such skills as exist. Associated with LEARNING THEORY, social skills theory argues that certain problematic behaviours are not psychopathological in kind, but result simply from the person never having gained competence in certain social interactions. (Other explanations include the concepts of conditioned anxiety and faulty discrimination.) It is also sometimes argued that certain clients (those who are not psychologically minded, for example) benefit more from 'concrete' social skills training than from verbal therapy and intrapsychic exploration. Typical social skill deficits include lack of assertiveness, lack of awareness of body language, insensitivity to others' relevant cues regarding interpersonal distance, failing to maintain socially expected eye contact, etc. Training methods include instruction and modelling by a teacher or video demonstrations, role play with feedback, and practice in homework assignments. Some critics of this approach argue that it easily overlooks subtle psychopathological factors and that it often does not take into consideration cultural and subcultural differences in communicative competence.

social therapy a form of therapy for individuals and groups, practised by Newman (1991). Social therapy derives from Marxist socio-economic theory and Vygotskian linguistic analysis. It argues that profound individual and collective change can only come about when people liberate themselves from oppressive social conditions and received (uncreative) language. Newman challenges traditional analyses of depression and drug addiction, for example, and also seeks to redefine transference (and other therapeutic phenomena) in terms of social alienation. Much of social therapy is addressed to ethnic minorities and other disadvantaged social groups. The term 'social therapy' is also used more broadly of group therapy in certain residential treatment centres and is sometimes known in North America as 'milieu therapy'.

sociogram a diagrammatic representation of the relationships within groups, first devised by Moreno. Arrows may be used to indicate, for example, attraction and antagonism between group members.

sociopath a personality type characterised by antisocial behaviour, callousness, absence of guilt and remoteness from the feelings and views of others. 'Sociopath' was intended to replace the term 'psychopath', but has not become popular in the UK. In psychiatric parlance, the correct term is *sociopathic personality disorder*.

Socratic dialogue that form of purposeful conversation which is characterised by questions and answers, by reasoning and deduction, and is aimed at discovering the truth. In counselling, Socratic dialogue is used to a considerable extent by cognitive–behavioural counsellors, particularly practitioners of RATIONAL EMOTIVE BEHAVIOUR THERAPY. Most counsellor training discourages the posing of many questions and therefore many counsellors avoid this kind of dialogue. Its use in REBT is based on sound therapeutic hypotheses and it requires special skills in order to be effective.

solution-focused brief therapy an approach to counselling and psychotherapy developed by Steve de Shazer (1985) and others, originally from a family therapy model. This therapy concentrates on the present and future, on clients' existing problem-solving competencies and future goals, and on identifying occasions on which clients are not beset by their problems. Indeed clients may be discouraged from dwelling on problems. Its ethos is one of empowerment and reframing generally. Solution-focused (brief) therapy is promoted as a creative, collaborative approach and successes with particularly challenging client groups are claimed.

somatise to express through the body, and particularly through illness or transient physical disturbances. Someone unable to deal emotionally with a traumatic experience, for example, may suffer from post-traumatic headaches. *See* PSYCHOSOMATIC.

space in the counselling context, 'space' refers to freedom and safety to reflect, in having protected time (free from everyday pressures) and a place that is private and free from intrusion. It has connotations of physical sanctuary but also respect for the need to exercise one's thoughts, imagination and feelings in ways that are often denied in daily routines and commitments. It can also be used as empty jargon.

specialist counsellor a counsellor who works with a particular CLIENT GROUP using specialised knowledge, or who practises a particular counselling orientation in which he has in-depth training. *See* GENERALIST COUNSELLOR.

specificity the precise identification of detail in the recounting of past events, present problems or future goals. Lack of specificity is commonly noted in clients' accounts of themselves and can stem from defensive vagueness, a tendency to make GLOBAL STATEMENTS or simply a habitual pattern of conversation. In order to help clients focus better on exactly where their problems are located and how they can be remedied (and how both counsellors and clients can measure improvement) counsellors encourage specificity.

spectatoring the self-conscious and dysfunctional act of watching oneself perform, as if divorced from the performance. Spectatoring is similar to 'egotism' in gestalt writings. Beginning counsellors, especially in the early sessions of actual counselling, and also when first using audiotapes, sometimes experience themselves as spectators: the anxiety to counsel well (or train or supervise well) can escalate into spectatoring, and can be diminished by acceptance of self as fallible.

spiritual emergency a concept associated with Grof, according to which people experience spontaneous life crises that cause, or are caused by, spiritual awakening. These may either resemble or overlap with serious mental health problems. There are resemblances to the ideas of shamanic counselling, that there is 'no gain without pain', etc. May involve rebirth and near-death experiences.

spirituality concern for a quality or domain of life beyond the self-centred, the materialistic and the culture-bound; the experience or pursuit of wholeness; a lifestyle dedicated to a god/goddess or religious or mystical tradition; the transpersonal. Certain approaches to counselling are explicitly concerned with some aspects of spirituality (e.g. psychosynthesis, logotherapy, clinical theology, TRANSPERSONAL THERAPY); person-centred counselling may be said to have an implicit spirituality. Meaning, literally, the 'vital principle in human beings', *spirit* is sometimes understood as being akin to human energy and courage or alternatively as distinctly transcendent (derived from God or a superhuman domain). Some feminist counsellors wish to see exerted on counselling and human affairs generally the influence of *Goddess spirituality*. Self-help groups such as AA and the MINNESOTA METHOD based on it (*see* TWELVE STEPS) make spirituality a central part of the change process. Critics of spiritual attitudes in the counselling field sometimes suggest that it can represent a flight from difficult or painful realities (*see* OCEANIC FEELING). The slogan 'Religion is for people who are afraid of hell; spirituality is for people who have been there' seeks to make a radical distinction between spirituality and religion. *See* West (2000).

splitting a defence mechanism, in psycho-analytic theory, in which a person perceives or construes certain significant objects (e.g. a mother, a lover) or herself as being divided into parts. Splitting is primarily related to early childhood: the infant cannot accept that her mother, for example, acts differently on different occasions and that the same person may engender feelings of trust and mistrust, love and hate; the infant splits mother into two images: a good mother and a bad mother (the witch in fairly tales). Clients also split when they try to see two or more helpers at once. Splitting may take subtle forms and in the extreme may be associated with schizophrenia. An everyday example of splitting is DICHOTOMOUS THINKING, or inaccurate polarisation of views (e.g. 'I'm OK, you're not OK'). *See* PROJECTIVE IDENTIFICATION, PROJECTION.

spontaneity uninhibited, unpremeditated behaviour; a genuine, unsolicited response. Spontaneity is associated with the behaviour of children prior to the effect of social conditioning or prior to a certain age where the onset of self-consciousness becomes inevitable. Spontaneity, unlike IMPULSIVITY, is not pathologically motivated. All approaches to counselling recognise the positive value of spontaneity and generally endorse the view that an inability to be spontaneous indicates an impoverished level of mental health. However, humanistic approaches in particular honour and foster spontaneity. GESTALT THERAPY, psychodrama and encounter groups are particularly oriented towards spontaneity. *See also* FREE CHILD.

spontaneous remission the lifting or disappearance of a problem with no apparent explanation. 'Spontaneous remission of symptoms' refers to the phenomenon of improvement in clients' conditions without therapeutic intervention. It has been argued by Hans Eysenck that at least one-third of all personal or emotional problems remit spontaneously. He suggests that this explains many of the success claims of counselling and therapy and probably invalidates much counselling theory.

stable under stress the ability to function relatively normally under abnormal pressure. SUS is an index of personality adjustment which suggests that accurate assessment of individual stability should take environmental factors into account.

stages of change the marked phases which clients (or people attempting self-change) pass through. Prochaska and DiClemente's (1984) model of stages of change includes the *pre-contemplative* (not yet aware of any problem or need for change), the *contemplative* (aware of having problems and considering taking action, but with some ambivalence), *action* (readiness for change and commitment to counselling), *maintenance* (awareness of the possibility of relapse and willingness to work at consolidating therapeutic gains). Prochaska and DiClemente do not consider change to be linear; they allow that relapse is a likely component of any cycle of change. It is also important to observe that people may be in different stages of change in relation to different personal problems. Rogers' (1961) 'stages of process' runs from 1 ('remoteness from experiencing') to 7 ('experiencing effective choice of new ways of being').

standards of practice guidelines for counsellors on issues of responsibility, contracting, competence, professional development, legal, ethical and other matters. The former BAC Codes of Ethics and Practice gave examples that set out acceptable levels of practice. *See* ETHICAL FRAMEWORK.

stasis a condition of stability or unchanging-ness. Stasis may be regarded as either a state of equilibrium, poise and rest, or as resistance to change and a preference for non-growth, avoidance of risk and effort. In actuality, everyone needs and experiences both stasis and change. By implication, counsellors are more change oriented than stasis oriented.

statutory regulation formal governmental endorsement of professions. Since the late 1990s and early 2000s moves have been afoot in the UK to decide whether, and in what form, counselling (and psychotherapy and psychology) should be regulated: voluntary self-regulation (via the BACP); voluntary state regulation (via the Health Professions Council); professional statutory self-regulation (professional body and regulatory council as identical); or professional statutory regulation by council (e.g. the Health Professions Council). BACP accreditation is the likely standard for regulation in counselling. Statutory regulation is likely to lead to 'protection of title', i.e. only those registered may be able to use the title 'counsellor'.

staying with listening, attending to, containing, remaining available to the client particularly at times when it is unclear what the client is experiencing. The ability to stay with the client emotionally through periods of confusion, acting-out and pain (which may also deeply affect the counsellor) is an important quality. 'Staying with' is intimately related to 'BEING WITH' and (periodic) 'NOT KNOWING' and implies a need for persistence and faith.

stereotyping regarding and acting towards others as if they have a distinctly identifiable and unchanging kind of behaviour. Many stereotypes have a racist or sexist nature (e.g. 'all black people are good dancers', 'all women are emotional/good homemakers', 'all men like sport'). Stereotyping dehumanises others and prevents the stereotyper from knowing or having accurate information about others. Counsellors are, ideally, aware both of the UNIQUENESS of individuals, and of genuine social commonalities (e.g. many women are paid less than men). There are also problematically subtle stereotypes (e.g. that all counsellors are non-directive listeners).

stigma something perceived as marking a person out as unacceptably different or socially deviant. Mental illness, extreme poverty, pregnancy outside marriage, cancer and AIDS, for example, have all been considered stigmatic by many of those experiencing such conditions. Recent critiques of psychiatric labelling have pointed out the negatively stigmatising power of language, and non-stigmatising substitutes (e.g. 'mental health problem') have been suggested. The stigma of being known to be in therapy or counselling (with the inference that one must be 'mad' or 'unable to cope without help') has lessened considerably in recent years. Certain commentators suggest that no so-called stigma can be operative without the person concerned subjectively acceding to it. *See* SHAME.

stimulant a drug which acts on the central nervous system and has the power and intention of arousing, stimulating and heightening awareness. Amphetamines are the best known stimulants (known colloquially as 'speed' or as 'uppers'). These are not now in common medical use, because, although they were found to have short-term beneficial effects, they frequently caused or exacerbated depression, agitation, paranoia and led to dependence. Stimulants may be abused in anorexia nervosa.

stimulus–response a primary behavioural concept concerned with the relationship between the environment and the person (or any organism). A *stimulus* may be considered to be anything which acts or exerts some influence on the organism. A *response* is any (internal or external) behaviour aroused by a stimulus. A repeated stimulus is likely to be associated with a repeated response – this is the foundation of the concept of conditioning. *See* CLASSICAL CONDITIONING.

Stockholm syndrome named after the emotional phenomenon following a 5-days long bank raid in Stockholm in which captives came to feel close to and grateful to their captors for not harming or killing them. Also referred to as 'traumatic bonding'. *See* IDENTIFICATION WITH THE AGGRESSOR.

stocktaking reviewing the client's achievements in counselling and/or in life. Stocktaking is synonymous with what happens in any REVIEW in counselling and applies to progress, self-image, client–counsellor relationship and anything deemed significant by the client. A systematic form of personal stocktaking is practised by people using the TWELVE STEPS approach.

storming that stage in group dynamics characterised by conflict between members, following the initial forming stage. *See* FORMING IN GROUPS.

story telling the client's narrative, referring to the story of his life or to the sequence of events leading up to his perceived presenting concern. Many counsellors regard the client's story as central to counselling; most recognise the inevitable subjectivity with which it is constructed and told. Some counsellors, particularly those practising brief counselling or ahistorical approaches, discourage story telling which is not related productively to the client's present and urgent concerns. Egan (2002) regards it as a central (but not sufficient) part of the counsellor's task to help clients tell their stories. Exhaustive story telling may represent a FLIGHT INTO HISTORY; alternatively, refusal to consider antecedents to present problems may signify a defensive strategy. Story telling can also refer to the use of didactic stories or fables to illustrate certain points to clients. *See* NARRATIVE THERAPY.

strategy the laying down, or tentative construction of plans for therapeutic treatment; intended procedure. Strategy may refer either to the counsellor's 'grand strategy' for a client (i.e. the entire treatment plan) or to particular in-session or session-to-session plans. A clinical strategy implies judgement and forethought rather than hit-or-miss or habitual approaches to clients' problems, but strategies should always be flexible. *See* INTENTION, TREATMENT.

strengths-based approach any method of counselling (e.g. solution-focused therapy) emphasising positive aspects of clients' functioning or potential, as opposed to problem-centred or deficit-focused approaches.

stress psychological pressure. While some writers distinguish between external *stressors*, the internal experience (or appraisal) of stress and stress responses, the word 'stress' has come to signify the whole subject of pressure and/or stimulation and how people cope with it. An optimal amount of pressure is considered necessary for healthy adaptation: people are motivated to negotiate, anticipate, avoid or enjoy certain stressors. Too little pressure may foster boredom and depression. Too much pressure (heavy workload, trauma, divorce, financial hardship, etc.) can test coping resources severely. The experience of chronically high stress levels can create anxiety and psychosomatic illness. It has been suggested that certain positive life events (e.g. promotion at work, holidays) also challenge individuals' equilibrium. Some distinguish between 'ambient stress' associated with everyday pressures and life event stress associated with extraordinary levels of unexpected stress. *See* Sapolsky (1998).

stress counselling refers to any counselling addressing problems of stress, is likely to be short term, and often emphasises the benefits of talking and catharsis as well as multimodal, cognitive–behavioural and problem-focused strategies.

stress inoculation training an approach to the understanding, anticipation, prevention or reduction of problems related to stress. It has been called a 'multicomponent coping-skills approach'. Using the principle of immunisation, Meichenbaum suggested that people need small, manageable experiences of stress to prepare for later, larger stressful experiences. Stress inoculation training comprises an educational stage (conceptualising stress problems), a skills-building stage (e.g. relaxation exercises, coping self-statements), an application stage (exposure to a variety of stressors in order to test out skills).

stress management any programmes or methods addressing the problems of stress. These have evolved out of the concern within organisations to address occupational stress (which has both human and organisational costs). Methods of stress management include reorganising one's workload, assertively declaring one's boundaries, challenging one's irrational beliefs, and finding a healthy balance between work, home life, recreation, etc.

stroke a TA concept referring to a demonstrated recognition of someone's need for contact. Strokes have been called 'units of recognition'. Berne postulated that just as infants appear to need physical contact, so humans throughout life need (or have a 'recognition hunger' for) others to acknowledge them. Strokes may be positive or negative and conditional or unconditional, but it is argued that we elicit (approving or disapproving) strokes rather than no strokes at all. We may also, however, discount strokes by means of a *stroke filter*. The *stroke economy* is made up of the internalised rules, learned in childhood, by which we give, take, discount or distort strokes.

structure the frame within which counselling operates. The structure is an agreement between counsellor and client as to the practicalities (e.g. times, fees) and boundaries (e.g. ethical and professional contract, therapeutic procedure) of counselling. The structure or frame allows the client to know, to an extent, what to expect, and the clarity with which it is established and adhered to serves a containing and facilitating function. *Structuring* is the mutual activity of negotiation by which the structure is decided upon, maintained and modified. Because such structuring demands open communication, assertiveness and self-reflection, it is in itself of therapeutic value.

stuckness the experience of impasse. *See* IMPASSE.

student counselling the counselling of people enrolled in courses of further and higher education. Most large institutions of higher education provide student counselling services in recognition of the peculiar stresses encountered by students, including the transition from parental home to independence and from adolescence to adulthood, coping with parental and societal expectations of educational achievement, adjusting to new social and academic challenges, examination anxiety, aspects of career choice. However, much of the work of student counsellors is not specific to the academic context (involving, for example, depression and eating disorders). Student counselling services commonly work with mature students and the staff of the institution as well as with younger students. Some services also provide separate welfare and advisory services dealing with financial, housing and other matters. Student counselling is one of the longest established sectors of the counselling profession in the UK. Much student counselling is of a brief nature (around 5 sessions), but some students require ongoing counselling and student counsellors are well equipped to undertake longer-term work.

style the characteristic manner in which one presents or conducts oneself or one's work. Counsellors' styles differ according to their personalities, theoretical orientations and other factors. Even when counsellors practise a near-identical therapeutic approach, its delivery will be modified by personal style. Adjustment of counsellor style to meet the apparent preferences or needs of clients, and to help overcome resistance, is advocated by some counsellors.

subclinical problems are said to be subclinical when they are below the threshold for diagnosing traditional serious mental health disorders. Some would say that counselling addresses mainly subclinical, or mild to moderate, problems. *See* PROBLEM-IN-LIVING, SHADOW SYNDROME.

subconscious below the level of immediate awareness; 'at the back of one's mind'. What is UNCONSCIOUS is completely (under normal circumstances) outside of awareness; the psychoanalytic concept of the PRECONSCIOUS closely resembles the idea of subconscious processes (and is used in preference to 'subconscious' by many counsellors and therapists). What is subconscious, then, is not currently within one's attentional field, but may be summoned to awareness.

subjective units of distress a means of assessing how severe a client's distress or discomfort is in his own judgement. A subjective units of distress scale (SUDS) is typically a 1–10 scale. The client is told that 1 equals a very low, and 10 a very high, level of distress, and is asked to rate subjectively how distressed he feels within this scale. This serves as a useful baseline for measuring progress and may be used in self-monitoring as well as in counselling sessions.

subjectivity the individual's personal, private, idiosyncratic views, constructs, feelings, experiences. Our own subjective world is more real and significant to us than the experiences of others, or the published knowledge-claims of others. However, subjective judgements can be mistaken: I may feel or believe that 'everyone hates me', for example, even though this is objectively untrue or unverifiable. I may feel 'wonderful' even though I am ill or dying, if I have ingested certain drugs. Subjectivity is contrasted unfavourably with objectivity by proponents of 'scientific method' as if only what is objectively proven is trustworthy. Subjective reports about benefits derived from counselling may be dismissed by researchers demanding 'hard evidence'. Existentialist thinkers promote acceptance of our subjective worlds, and Buber (*see* I–THOU) extolled the values of deep, genuine *intersubjectivity* (the owning and honest dialoguing of subjective selves).

sublimation suppression of supposedly base instincts and their apparent replacement by nobler behaviour. Sublimation is a psychologically inexact term, but has popular currency. The most common example is 'He has sublimated his sexual desires in hard work'.

subliminal perception awareness and processing of environmental data that takes place below the level of conscious intention. We are said to be *subliminally aware* of something that is beyond our normal or current field of attention. Similarly, subliminal learning takes place outside of our conscious effort to learn.

subpersonality an intrapsychic part of the person which appears, at least at times, to have an identity of its own, and which may form part of a system of other such identifiable subpersonalities. Rowan (1990) defines a subpersonality as 'a semi-permanent and semi-autonomous region of the personality capable of acting as a person'. Subpersonalities can be understood on different levels; they may be identified as similar to Jungian archetypes, psychodramatic doubles, parts of the psychoanalytic psychic apparatus or TA ego states, for example. The idea of subpersonalities or plural selves challenges that of the unitary self and is a promising field for clinical and research work. Note that subpersonalities are quite different from multiple personalities and do not in themselves indicate psychopathology.

substance misuse abuse of drugs, alcohol, solvents (e.g. aerosols, glue, butane gas refills, typewriter correcting fluid) and other addictive or damaging substances. *See* ADDICTION, CHEMICAL DEPENDENCY.

subtle body a term used in transpersonal therapy whereby the body is regarded as a spiritual entity.

subtle level a level of consciousness suitable for TRANSPERSONAL THERAPY. This is a realm of archetypes, images, symbols, deity figures, etc. Originating from Ken Wilber.

subvocalisation *see* SELF-TALK.

successful outcome *see* OUTCOME.

suffering the experience of hurt and pain; the enduring of pain or adversity; the passive acceptance of circumstances. The word is frequently used as a synonym for psychological PAIN, although Janov (1975) argues that suffering results when pain is denied or suppressed. Suffering (*dukkha*) is regarded in Buddhism as universal. Writers such as Bourdieu (1999) and Kleinman (1997) discuss the reality of 'social suffering'. Some writers avoid the term 'sufferer' in relation, for example, to AIDS or mental illness, because it suggests passivity and hopelessness.

suggestion the proffering of information and advice; recommendation. Suggestion is a subtle form of advice giving, is not overtly coercive, and may overlap with probing and other interventions. *Post-hypnotic suggestion* is a suggestion given to the client during a hypnotic state which is intended to be enacted afterwards (e.g. 'You will feel no desire to smoke'). *Autosuggestion* is the practice of self-talk and/or self-hypnotic suggestion. *Suggestibility* is a vulnerability to the influential ideas of others.

suicide killing oneself. Durkheim distinguished between altruistic suicide (sacrificing self for others, as in war), anomic suicide (suicide resulting from feelings of loneliness, anomie, alienation), and egoistic suicide (resulting from feelings of personal failure). In our culture suicide is most often associated with severe hopelessness and depression. Clients representing a suicide risk can include the severely depressed, those recently traumatised or whose memories of trauma have been re-stimulated, those who have been suddenly rejected, who have lost jobs or partners, who are in 'hopeless' situations, etc. Single alcoholic men in their 50s and living alone are particularly at risk. Suicide is the ultimate ESCAPE HATCH, and particular care, contracting and appropriate liaison with medical and informal supports should be mobilised where it is suspected to be a real possibility. The main British agency addressing the needs of people who feel suicidal is The Samaritans, much of whose work is telephone befriending and support. Attempted suicide (or *parasuicide*) is deliberate and life-threatening self-harm which may be either genuine failure to execute suicide or a 'cry for help' (*see* ATTENTION-SEEKING). *Suicidal ideation* or *suicidality* (thoughts of wanting to die, of wanting to 'give up the struggle', etc.) should be investigated seriously but do not always signify suicidal intentions. Violent forms of suicide (hanging, shooting, throwing oneself in front of a train) are associated more with men than with women, who characteristically choose drug overdoses, poisoning and inhaling gas. 'I should never have been born', 'I can't see any way out' are some of the typically hopeless thoughts associated with suicide. *Suicidology* is the academic specialism focusing on all matters relating to suicide. *Rational suicide* implies that one decides to kill oneself not out of depression but quite rationally, usually in circumstances of, for example, terminal illness. *Assisted suicide,* illegal in the UK, involves help from another.

summarising accurately and succinctly reflecting back to the client, from time to time within and across sessions, the substance of what she has expressed. Summarising enables the counsellor to gather the various strands of the client's material together and to offer it back to her so that both client and counsellor can check whether understanding has been achieved; it enables the client to hear what she has expressed from a slightly different perspective. It also offers an opportunity for structuring counselling, especially with clients who have difficulty in focusing on specific topics and goals. Summarising at the end of a session can provide a useful orientation towards homework and future sessions. Gilmore (1973) regards summarising as especially useful for 'forming a choice point' and 'gaining a figure–ground perspective'.

superconscious the 'higher unconscious' of PSYCHOSYNTHESIS. Part of Assagioli's model of the human psyche, the superconscious is associated with spiritual, artistic, noble aspirations and states of ecstasy.

superego that part of Freudian personality theory which is concerned with self-criticism, self-observation and idealism. The superego is formed by introjection of parental values and restrictions; it has the functions of conscience and censorship but differs from conscience as such in being a psychological, not an ethical category, and being partly unconscious in operation. While Freud considered the superego to emerge during the Oedipal stage, Melanie Klein and others argued for its development from the earliest months of life. The PARENT EGO STATE of TA resembles the superego, but is a directly observable, conscious state.

superiority complex derived from Adlerian theory, the superiority complex is constituted from thoughts, feelings and behaviour which attempt to compensate for underlying low self-esteem. A person may believe herself to be superior to others, and act in a superior manner, although unconsciously feeling quite the contrary. *See* INFERIORITY COMPLEX.

superordinate construct the concept, in personal construct psychology, according to which people have a characteristic hierarchy of (polarised) ways of construing the world. Overarching or central constructs in personal construct psychology are known as 'superordinate'. Good versus evil, for example, is a superordinate construct. *See* LADDERING and PYRAMIDING.

supervision literally, the overseeing of counsellors' work, supervision aims to protect the client and support the counsellor. Regarded by the BACP as a professional and ethical necessity for practising counsellors, supervision takes various forms but all address key elements of a counsellor's work: its professional and ethical boundaries; the competence and continuing professional and personal development of counsellors; the skilful and purposeful use of therapeutic techniques; client material and client–counsellor interaction; the well-being of counsellors themselves. Counselling itself being an emerging profession, supervision is a parallel discipline within counselling. Models of supervision differ according to the orientations of counsellor and supervisor; while the psychodynamic model places a certain emphasis on client–counsellor and counsellor–supervisor dynamics, the cognitive–behavioural model is likely to place greater emphasis on the skilful use of particular techniques as applied to client goals. The supervision of trainees and beginning counsellors is likely to have a greater tutorial element than the more facilitative, consultative and collegial styles suited to the supervision of experienced counsellors. The issues of necessary minimal frequency of supervision, the use (or not) of tape recording, etc. are debated. Supervision is considered distinct from the personal counselling of the counsellor and from any managerial supervision he may require. Forms of supervision include one-to-one, peer, group, and permutations thereon. *See* Hawkins and Shohet (2000**).**

support assistance; backing; sustenance; reinforcement. People are considered to need social support when, for example, they are going through a crisis such as divorce, bereavement or mental illness.

Counsellors may ask whether certain clients have sufficient support networks in addition to counselling. A *support group* is usually a self-help group offering peer support for others suffering crises or chronic difficulties. *Supportive psychotherapy* is considered suitable for certain patients with long-term psychiatric problems; its aim is the person's 'best possible adjustment' in his circumstances and its methods include reassurance, guidance, suggestion and encouragement. *Supportive interventions* (*see* Heron, 2001) include caring, loving, concern, validation, greeting, and encouragement of self-celebration.

suppression the 'pushing down' or banishing from consciousness of certain unwanted thoughts and feelings. Suppression differs from REPRESSION in being a conscious activity that temporarily removes unnecessary and/or uncomfortable ideas from one's mind; repression is an entirely unconscious defence mechanism. Critics of certain therapeutic approaches (e.g. REBT and behaviour therapy) sometimes claim that these approaches 'work' only by superficially suppressing underlying pain, which will still have to be worked through at a later date.

surface relational competence the concept mooted to describe superficial or partial mastery of certain skills, e.g. communication of understanding, rather than finely honed, deeply internalised and flexibly delivered skills and attitudes; the latter in contrast with measurable skills such as those named by National Vocational Qualifications.

survivor guilt the particular kind of anguished guilt felt by people who have either been in, but survived, a traumatic accident or disaster, or have known intimately someone who was so involved. Those involved in disasters, for example, may have witnessed others dying around them, and they may or may not have tried or been able to help; the experience is often felt to be 'haunting' and some survivors have been known to commit suicide because of the intensity of such feelings. Survivor guilt is a form of POST-TRAUMATIC STRESS DISORDER which may be treated by means of working through memories, enabling catharsis, challenging irrational thinking, and so on.

switching the activity of a client who consciously or unconsciously alters the direction of conversation or the intensity of feelings. Switching may be either defensive or risk-taking in nature. It may also be used purposefully, and with skilful timing, by the counsellor.

symbiosis a TA concept resembling collusion or co-dependency, in which two or more people act as if they are one. Symbiosis is effected by each of the parties excluding at least one ego state, which is 'supplied' by the actions of the other/s. There are both healthy and unhealthy forms of symbiosis. A typical symbiotic transaction involves one person using exclusively adult and parent ego states to rescue another; such transactions are fuelled by each person's SCRIPT.

symbolism the disguised expression of repressed material. According to psychoanalytic thought, unconscious conflict gives rise to images (especially in dreams), which safely convey repressed meanings and feelings. Knives, pens and swords, for example, may symbolise the penis, and contextually tell a story that encapsulates a conflict or wish. The Jungian, and particularly the post-Jungian archetypal–psychological understanding of symbolic imagery (*see* Moore, 1989) regards symbolism as being much more fundamental and collective than the Freudian, individualised and conflict-created view has it. Because of such different uses, the term 'symbolisation' has sometimes been used to represent the exclusively psychoanalytic understanding. *See* DISPLACEMENT.

sympathy the ordinary human feeling for someone in distress; 'feeling the same as'; pity. Sympathy can be a genuine expression of concern for another; a polite but not deeply felt expression of condolence for another who has suffered a particular personal loss; an unhelpful attempt to reassure by identifying with another (as in 'I know exactly how you feel'). Sympathy is different from EMPATHY, the latter being a disciplined attempt to grasp another's feelings as if from their own, internal frame of reference. Sympathy tends to be bestowed or projected upon people, while empathy is felt from alongside. 'Tea and sympathy' is one of the critics' most commonly used misrepresentations of counselling.

symptom a problem or disturbance which occurs as a result of an underlying malady; an observable sign from which illness can be inferred. The term symptom is sometimes used interchangeably with 'problem' or 'presenting problem', but has medical origins. Frequent headaches may be regarded as a symptom of chronically suppressed anger; depression may be considered a symptom of unresolved grief; self-harm may be considered symptomatic of childhood sexual abuse. In medical practice symptoms are distinguished from *signs*, which are observable clues to illness.

symptom formation the process whereby an original trauma or conflict is neurotically converted into symptoms that may be quite removed in kind from the underlying distress.

symptom substitution the concept whereby one symptom may be converted into another; therapeutic approaches which, allegedly, simply suppress symptoms rather than uncovering their origins, are sometimes said to lead only to symptom-substitution.

syndrome a recognised constellation of symptoms or features which can be ascribed (provisionally or with certainty) to a unitary disease or disturbance. Examples include seasonal affective disorder and pre-menstrual syndrome.

systematic desensitisation the gradual elimination of anxiety or phobic states by the behavioural method of graded exposure of the client to the object of her fear or avoidance. Systematic desensitisation is usually carried out in imaginal exercises in the consulting room (but *see* IN VIVO DESENSITISATION). The most common method begins with an exercise in deep muscle relaxation; mildly anxiety-inducing stimuli are introduced to the person and, as each 'dose' of exposure loses its impact, successively stronger stimuli are introduced until the goal of anxiety or phobia elimination is reached. Systematic desensitisation utilises relaxation techniques, the construction of anxiety hierarchies and the SUBJECTIVE UNITS OF DISTRESS scale (SUDS). While some critics find it overly mechanical, others believe it to be unnecessarily circuitous.

systemic therapy any therapy or counselling resting on the principles of SYSTEMS THEORY.

systems theory systems or systemic theory is based on the view that the 'presenting client' (or 'identified patient') represents problems in the interactions of group, family or organisational members. Systems theory is derived from cybernetics and is applied in social psychiatry, group and family therapy. It takes as its subject not the individual but the system of which she is a part. In treatment, when problematic interactions or attitudes in the system can be resolved, the individual's problems are, it is thought, likely to be resolved. Systems thinking informs the understanding of some counsellors who work primarily with individuals as well as many who work with families.

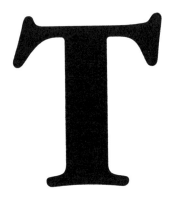

T group training group. *See* SENSITIVITY TRAIN-ING GROUP.

taboo a prohibited subject. Its original meaning related to 'sacred' and 'forbidden' and carried much more weight than 'embarrassing'. Psychoanalytic theory stresses the importance of the taboo on incest and its supposed effects on oedipal dynamics. The sexual taboos of Freud's time have given way to others. Terminal illness and death have been taboo subjects in recent times; expressions of vulnerability may be taboo in particularly macho cultures. Our own, contemporary taboos are more difficult to identify: perhaps open discussion of money, wealth differentials and envy are taboo areas. Indeed, Hillman argues *(see* Moore, 1989) that such discussion between client and therapist is more taboo than even the subject of sex between them.

talking treatment a term used to distinguish between verbally based treatments of psychological problems and treatments which employ drugs or other physical methods (e.g. ECT). Counselling and psychotherapy are often referred to as talking treatments and can also be distinguished from approaches which primarily use bodywork, movement, drama and art therapy.

tape recording the use of audio technology for recording counselling sessions and training exercises. Tape recording is increasingly recognised by trainers as a valuable, if not indispensable, part of counsellor training. (Some counsellors object to its use on theoretical and ethical grounds.) Actual counselling work is made available for study, analysis and assessment. Many trainers and supervisors believe that tape recording is superior to process recordings or verbal reports because it is not selective. The study of tapes allows trainees to consider what their intentions were in the session and how they might improve on them. Permission is needed to tape record, and confidentiality must be assured. Some counsellors give clients the tapes for them to study their own material, and specific relaxation tapes, for example, may be made as an aid to the counselling process.

target problem the concern which is the client's explicit current priority. Cognitive analytic therapists work with the client to identify key problems which are then targeted as the focus of therapy. They then work together on defining the *target problem procedures (TPPs)* which underpin and sustain the target problems. TPPs include the client's habitual coping strategies, and homework assignments may be set to encourage monitoring of these and attempts at new strategies.

task any activity conducted in the furtherance of counselling. Tasks are purposeful activities carried out by counsellor and client. Counsellor tasks may include explaining the nature of counselling, reflecting feelings, ensuring that the session ends on time, interpretation, disputation, homework setting; client tasks may include goal setting, free association, dream recall, learning TA theory, generalising learning from counselling to everyday life, etc. Tasks should be clearly explained, meaningful to the client, within her ability to carry out and potent enough to effect therapeutic change; the client should understand the counsellor's tasks and their rationale. Tasks should preferably be mutually agreed, flexible and skilfully executed by counsellors. *See* THERAPEUTIC ALLIANCE.

technical eclecticism an approach to counselling based on the informed, systematic and judicious use of techniques from diverse schools of counselling. Technical eclectics (see Lazarus, 1981) often have a preferred theoretical base (and therefore the term 'theoretically consistent eclecticism' is sometimes used) but recognise the complexity of human beings, the fallibility of preferred orientations and the usefulness of a variety of techniques in addressing unique clients. Lazarus suggests that far from being a hit-or-miss affair, technical eclecticism is based on awareness of research indications regarding treatment of choice *(see* TREATMENT), individual learning styles, etc.; also, whilst emphasising techniques, this approach recognises the importance of the client–counsellor relationship and particularly that different clients require different types of relationship with their counsellors.

technique a therapeutic tool; any deliberately employed, distinct means of attempting to help the client. Most counselling orientations have a number of recognised therapeutic techniques (e.g. interpretation, chairwork, systematic desensitisation, hypnotic induction) which are distinct from common counselling skills and core conditions, and are intended to help shift the client from her current state. Person-centred counsellors and communicative therapists believe that techniques tend to distort the counselling relationship and undermine client autonomy. Practitioners of technical eclecticism select techniques from various orientations as part of a comprehensive therapeutic strategy.

technophobia anxiety related to technology. While broadly related to *any* technology, the term is often used to refer to computer-related anxiety, i.e. fear and avoidance of computers, more properly known as computerphobia. Regarded by many writers as an entirely irrational, unnecessary anxiety that can be overcome by CBT-like staged learning, others regard it as an important indicator of different aptitudes, perhaps akin to dyslexia (and hence 'dystechnia' has been suggested as an alternative term). Interestingly, the term *technomania* is used far less, although terms like computer-addict, 'nerd', etc. imply something like it. Technophobia is not yet a classified diagnostic condition.

telephone counselling any counselling by telephone. One of the major providers of telephone counselling in the UK is Child-line, an organisation offering help to abused children. Various 'helplines' offer confidential information, advice and counselling (in relation to AIDS, drug abuse, etc.). The Samaritans offer befriending or 'listening therapy' by telephone. Some EAPs offer telephone counselling, sometimes on a nationwide basis. Some individual counsellors offer telephone counselling in crises or in other exceptional circumstances. Telephone counselling relies on non-visual cues, is unlikely to include many silences, and demands a particular presence of mind from the counsellor for what is often a 'one-off' distress call. *See* Rosenfield (1997).

tenderness a warm emotional quality; affective gentleness; a particularly caring response, often evoked by clients in unavoidable distress or during moments of painful struggle or self-disclosure. An extension of generalised, non-possessive warmth, tenderness has the compelling quality of humanly reaching out towards another who suffers with loving gentleness.

tension strain, tautness, restlessness. Chronic muscular tension is frequently a somatic defence against perceived threat (perhaps originally a real threat, for example a violent and/or alcoholic father). Freud regarded 'instinctual tension' as a basic human motivator. Janov (1975) claims that most people have high levels of chronic tension which can only be discharged by systematic (primal) therapy; therapies which do not radically affect somatic tension provide only symptomatic relief, he argues *(see* also CHARACTER ARMOUR). 'Tension' is also used in the interpersonal sense: 'There is a tension between us', for example.

termination the end of counselling. Termination may be planned or unannounced. It is regarded as highly significant by some (particularly psychodynamic counsellors) and as natural and unspectacular by others, but most counsellors recognise a need for sensitive management of termination. Termination should preferably be accompanied by evaluation of progress towards goals. Planned endings may depend on the client's readiness to end, may be achieved by a mutually agreed date for ending, by a tapering-down process (e.g. from weekly to fortnightly or monthly meetings) or by arranging a follow-up meeting after termination. In practice, many terminations are not mutually agreed upon. *See* ENDINGS, LOSS, PREMATURE TERMINATION.

testing the giving of various tests designed to aid the counselling process (e.g. occupational stress tests); behaviour which is intended to ascertain another's trustworthiness. Clients may test trust by acting out in various ways (e.g. arriving late, being sullen, being abusive). They may anxiously request information, disclose a secret or question the counsellor's motives as ways of deciding whether this is a person they can trust. *See also* PROJECTIVE TESTS.

Thanatos adopted synonym for the Freudian death drive or instinct, opposed to the life instinct (Eros). *Thanatophobia* is a morbid fear of death.

theory conceptualisation of and explanation for the ways in which people function and malfunction, and in which counselling helps or cannot help. 'There is nothing so practical as a good theory' (Lewin) challenges the view that theory is useless, remote or 'academic'. According to some research, however, many counsellors have found their personal development and supervised practice more useful than theory. BACP course accreditation requirements stipulate that courses should offer a *core theoretical model* (e.g. person-centred counselling, gestalt). The kind of theory counsellors are exposed to includes: models of human beings, human development, institutional functioning in relation to counselling psychology, psychiatry and sociology, among other disciplines. Counsellors-in-training are required to demonstrate an ability to link theory with practice. Integrationism (*see* INTEGRATION) seeks to create overarching theoretical unity in the field of counselling, which is currently characterised by theoretical pluralism. *Transtheoretical* approaches (*see* Prochaska and DiClemente, 1984) describe approaches to counselling which can span or transcend different models. *Theory of mind* refers to one's implicit understanding that others have minds and are different, an understanding that is deficient in AUTISM.

therapeutic alliance the helping relationship and those factors within it which implicitly or explicitly maximise its therapeutic effectiveness. Bordin (1979) extended the concept of the psychoanalytic working alliance to therapeutic, helping and caring relationships generally. Therapeutic alliance comprises the domains of bonds, goals and tasks: bonds are constituted by the core conditions, the client's attitudes towards the counsellor, and the counsellor's style of relating to the client; goals are the mutually negotiated, understood, agreed upon and regularly reviewed aims of counselling; tasks are the activities carried out by both client and counsellor in the pursuit of goals. These three domains are interrelated, but attention paid to them by counsellors, especially at the very beginning of counselling, is likely to enhance the ultimate outcome of counselling. *Helping alliance, working alliance* and *collaborative alliance* are sometimes used synonymously.

therapeutic factors those precisely identifiable aspects of counselling which can be shown to be causative in the change process. Whilst every model of counselling and therapy tends to argue for its specific efficacy, in broad terms research has not validated any one approach more than others. Because of this, many have concluded that NON-SPECIFIC FACTORS (e.g. relationship factors) may be responsible for therapeutic change. Frank (1963) suggested that the six most influential factors in therapy are a therapeutic rationale, exploration of traumas and conflicts, the social stature of the therapist, encouragement of hope, experiences of success, and a confiding relationship. However, there are findings that certain psychological problems are more reliably eliminated or reduced with specific methods (*see* EVIDENCE BASED PRACTICE).

therapeutic writing any use of writing by the client to help effect therapeutic change. The late 1990s in the UK saw some growth in the strategic use of diary writing, poetry, etc. in the service of therapeutic exploration and movement. Research by Pennebaker and others underlines the cathartic value of writing, as well as its being preferred by some clients for the control they have over it alongside or within counselling, or as an alternative.

therapist/counsellor intention the moment-to-moment purposes behind the therapist's or counsellor's interventions in each session. Every counsellor statement, gesture or silence may be regarded as purposive. Examples of intentions include setting limits, building rapport, clarifying client statements, instilling hope, promoting relief, identifying maladaptive cognitions, reinforcing change attempts, and resolving problems in the therapeutic relationship. *See* Hill and O'Grady (1985).

therapist giftedness refers to the therapist's or counsellor's personal qualities that make them better practitioners regardless of or in addition to training. Intuition, imagination, warmth, creativity, etc. may all result from individual therapist giftedness. This is still a poorly understood aspect of counsellor selection and training.

therapy literally, 'attendance on', and etymologically derived from 'servant' and 'minister to', its modern meaning is 'treatment'. The word 'therapy' can be attached to many others (e.g. beauty therapy, physiotherapy, occupational therapy, psychotherapy). Many people use the word to refer to counselling and psychotherapy, as in 'I am having therapy' and 'I am in therapy'. Also, *therapist* is commonly used of counsellors, clinical psychologists and others. *See* PSYCHOTHERAPY.

therapy junkie derogatory colloquial term for one who has become unhealthily dependent on therapy or counselling and its culture, probably spending a great deal of money on it but with nothing of note to show for it.

there and then referring to events and people in the past and in other places (e.g. childhood, parents, parental home). 'There and then' is contrasted with HERE AND NOW. Whilst certain clients apparently resist any discussion of the there and then, many dwell on it excessively and may try to avoid acknowledging the presence of the counsellor or the significance of any feelings they may have in the present. *See* FLIGHT INTO HISTORY.

thinking mental activity, usually associated with unvoiced verbal constructions; analysing, contemplating, planning; ideation; cognition. People think at many levels, from concrete to abstract, and with varying degrees of logic, purpose and effectiveness. Thinking is a distinctively human characteristic. Thinking is often contrasted with feeling in counselling; cognitive therapy, for example, concentrates mainly on thinking processes, and primal therapy on feeling. In general, cognitive-behavioural models of counselling reflect a belief in the primacy of thinking, and humanistic models the primacy of feelings. Although thinking, feeling and acting are intimately interrelated, cognitive behavioural counsellors consider cognitive and behavioural interventions to be frequently more potent and effective than, for example, interventions promoting catharsis or transference. In multimodal therapy, cognition is considered one of seven modalities in which clients manifest problems and clues as to how they may best be helped. Forms of dysfunctional thinking include rumination, intellectualisation, magical thinking, irrational thinking and thought disorders. Distinctive models of therapeutic and creative thinking are found in REBT, cognitive therapy, re-evaluation counselling, positive thinking and lateral thinking (de Bono). *See* Nelson-Jones (1989) and Jacobs (2000).

third ear, listening with the *see* LISTENING.

third force psychology humanistic psychology, designated as 'third force' in relation to the 'forces' of behaviourism and psychoanalysis.

thought cognition; mental activity. 'Thought' and 'thinking' are often used interchangeably. Certain mystical traditions, however, depart radically from the view that there are helpful and unhelpful kinds of thinking/thought, and suggest that thought itself, which arises from the human condition of suffering, dissatisfaction, restlessness and desire, is responsible for perpetuating unhappiness and distorted perception: a state of 'no-mind' or 'no-thingness' is often advocated. This may be counter-intuitive to westerners in particular whose associations to 'thoughtful' and 'thought-through' are positive.

thought disorder is a symptom, in psychiatric terms, of psychotic or schizophrenic ideation (e.g. the belief that aliens are controlling one's brain).

thought-stopping a behavioural technique designed to arrest or reduce dysfunctional, negative, compulsive self-talk; the technique requires the therapist to encourage the client to engage in his dysfunctional thought processes and to shout 'Stop!' in order to interrupt this process. Variations on this exercise (e.g. the client shouting 'Stop' when in the midst of obsessive thinking) are introduced until the client internalises the ability to stop his own unwanted thoughts.

threat menace; internal assessment or external possibility of danger or harm. The belief that one is threatened when this is not the case is a characteristic of paranoia, but is also commonly a feature of any anxiety. *Non-threatening* is sometimes used of people with warm, accepting personalities. The therapeutic alliance in counselling may be considered to be threatened when bonds, goals or tasks are seriously undermined or mismatched. *See also* WORST SCENARIO.

tight construing the tendency observed in some people to think and consequently act in rigid ways, to make predictions about life which are severely constrained. Such people may be characterised by lack of spontaneity, anxiety, authoritarianism, etc. Tight construing is the polar opposite of LOOSE CONSTRUING and personal construct counsellors seek to help clients who use dysfunctionally tight construing to become aware of alternative possibilities of construing.

time the dimension of human experience associated with the distance between one moment and another, one day/week/year and another, one event and another; with ageing, remembering, anticipation. (This latter definition is sometimes known as 'psychological time', as opposed to 'objective time' as measured by the clock or calendar.) Most contemporary models of counselling and therapy are by convention non-specific about time: therapy is expected to take 'some weeks, months or years'. (A rule of thumb used by some is that time needed in counselling is in proportion to the client's age, how psychologically damaged she is and how hard she is prepared to work in therapy to deal with her problems.) Certain models of long-term psychoanalytically oriented therapy have been criticised for fostering a sense of timelessness; the functions of the unconscious are considered to be timeless. Practitioners of brief or time-limited counselling tend to be more conscious of, and explicit about, the use of time. Certain (particularly existentialist) approaches to counselling make time an explicit consideration, because it is considered to relate to mortality and the anxiety generated by avoidance of facing death. The uninterrupted, dedicated time available to clients in each session is recognised by all counsellors as one of the most significant factors in counselling. *See* BRIEF COUNSELLING, PUNCTUALITY, TIME-CONSCIOUS PSYCHOLOGICAL THERAPY, TIME-LIMITED COUNSELLING/THERAPY.

time-conscious psychological therapy psychotherapy or counselling that takes into account temporal realities and constraints. *Not* always time-limited, but concerned with assessment of very brief contact needs, crisis needs, short-term focal work and longer-term therapeutic work.

time-limited counselling/therapy any counselling or therapy which is designed to last for a specified period, which is clearly announced at its commencement. Six sessions is a common parameter. Cognitive analytic therapy is an example of time-limited therapy within 16 sessions. The purposes of such a time limit are the economic use of resources, the discouragement of dependence, the mirroring of real life, the encouragement of focus on problems and their resolution. There is some research evidence that fewer clients drop out from time-limited therapy than from therapies where no ending date is set, possibly because they find the structure of time-limited work containing. See Feltham (1997). *See* BRIEF THERAPY, SINGLE SESSION THERAPY.

timeline (a) an NLP concept referring to the organisation of memories in the mind; (b) the counselling technique – also known as 'lifeline' – of asking clients (or trainees) to construct a linear model of their life from birth onwards, marking on it significant events and relationships.

time structuring a TA concept affirming the need people have for structure ('structure-hunger' in Berne's terms) and which can include withdrawal, ritual, past-time, activity, rackets/games and intimacy.

timing the counsellor skill of delivering interventions at the right moment for optimal impact. Timing applies both to small in-session interventions and to strategies and interventions over the course of time in counselling. Rarely is timing a precise art, but critical moments can be lost, or the client may be thrown on the defensive when timing is poor. It is recognised that interpretations, for example, may have no impact or be anxiety provoking if delivered prematurely.

token economy a treatment regime based on behavioural principles which assert that desired behaviour *will* be reinforced by rewarding instances of desirable behaviour with tokens which may be accumulated and traded in later for money or other goods which are valued by the patient. Token economies operate in some psychiatric, penal and other institutions. *See* SHAPING.

tool any technical means the counsellor has at his disposal. 'Tool' is an inexact term which can refer to skills, techniques, questionnaires, use of self, or even an entire theoretical and clinical orientation. (Note that questionnaires and other research tools are usually known as 'instruments'.) Counsellors sometimes refer to their 'toolkit' of techniques.

top dog a concept used in gestalt therapy which represents the critical, persecutory, judgemental observer within the person. The top dog approximates to the CRITICAL

PARENT of TA, and is characterised by negative self-statements. Its counterpart, the *underdog,* is the submissive, placatory, victimised part of the person. Gestalt counsellors often suggest that clients engage these two parts of themselves in dialogue by means of CHAIRWORK.

touching physical, intentional contact between client and counsellor. Attitudes to the wisdom and permissibility of touching vary considerably from the completely 'hands off' practice of classical psychoanalysis to the free and frequent hugging of some humanistic counsellors, and the purposeful and integral contact of counsellors incorporating bioenergetic massage, Alexander technique and other tactile methods in their work. Touching is more or less powerful and meaningful to different clients and transferential seduction and countertransferential abuse are salient considerations. Many counsellors adhere to a policy of discretionary touching based on sensitive awareness of the strength and history of each counselling relationship and of critical moments in counselling.

tracking the counsellor skill of listening intently and empathically to the moment-by-moment explorations of the client, with an ability to reflect back and/or summarise what is said; close attention to and comprehension of content. A counsellor's preoccupation, including personal and theoretical preoccupations during the session, can lead him 'off track'. However, no counsellor practises tracking *only.* Lazarus (1981) discusses the importance of tracking the client's 'firing order' of modalities *(see* BASIC ID). He suggests that each client has a characteristic chain of reactions to problematic events (e.g. tension, anxious thoughts, frightening images, etc.) which give clues as to the best order of therapeutic interventions.

trainee see COUNSELLOR IN TRAINING.

training the teaching and facilitating of counselling skills, acquisition of theory and knowledge and all aspects of counsellors' professional development. Counsellor training courses can vary considerably in their quality, content, duration and ethos, but typically include counselling theory (at least one orientation is usually covered in depth), supervised counselling practice, skills, professional and personal development. While there is evidence that some untrained people have been perceived as offering counselling that is as helpful as that given by trained counsellors, there is also evidence to the contrary. Clinical wisdom suggests that certain issues are of critical significance in practice (e.g. professional ethics and the establishing of the core conditions). Because counselling is predominantly a skill or craft, counsellors are best trained by means of experiential exercises (e.g. role-play), supervised clinical work, the personal experience of counselling and participation in a learning community where interpersonal issues are constantly monitored. A BACP *accredited* (previously *recognised*) *training course* is one that has voluntarily sought accreditation and met certain stringent criteria laid down by the BACP. Such courses are 1 year (full time) or 2–3 years (part time) in length. An accredited *trainer or supervisor* has also voluntarily sought and achieved such status through the BACP. Counsellors are ethically committed to ongoing professional development (or 'continuing professional education') and therefore frequently attend workshops and short courses. *See also* COUNSELLOR IN TRAINING, PERSONAL COUNSELLING OF THE COUNSELLOR and SUPERVISION.

tranquillisers *minor tranquillisers* are those prescribed drugs whose function is the reduction of anxiety, insomnia, epileptic fits and certain other conditions; *major tranquillisers* are drugs prescribed as ANTIPSYCHOTIC agents for people suffering from psychotic symptoms, including schizophrenia. The best known minor tranquillisers are the benzodiazepines (such as diazepam, e.g. Valium). Minor tranquillisers are often known as *anxiolytics* and hypnotics. Although they can have short-term beneficial effects, they can have problematic side-effects and addictive properties; they are also abused by some addicts, and by those using them as lethal overdoses. People wishing to withdraw from tranquilliser use should do so gradually and in consultation with their GP. Major tranquillisers (which are often not tranquillising, but a cause of agitation) have enabled many people to live better lives, but can also be problematic.

transactional analysis the theory of personality and approach to psychological therapy devised by Eric Berne and subsequently refined by others. Its main contributions are in the areas of interpersonal functioning, child development and individual psychopathology. TA has as its centrepiece the PARENT, ADULT and CHILD EGO STATES, which are relatively simple to teach to clients or students and to use in self-understanding. The original TA model, popularised by Harris (1967), has been extensively elaborated in working concepts and terminology. In counselling, the use of the PAC model is referred to as structural analysis. Key concepts in TA include DISCOUNTING, ESCAPE HATCHES, GAMES, KARPMAN TRIANGLE, RACKETS, SCRIPTS, STROKES and REDICISION. The process of counselling in TA rests on clear contracting, open communication and adult responsibility. There are three schools of TA:

- the classical, which follows Berne's model closely;
- the redecision school, which links TA theory with gestalt methodology (*see* REDECISION);
- the cathexis school, which acknowledges developmental deficits and employs techniques of REPARENTING and 'consistent confronting of discounts'.

Many TA counsellors are technically eclectic, rather than bound to one of the above schools. *See* Stewart and Joines (1987); Tilney (1998).

transcendental going beyond or rising above. Transcendental experiences imply that the person steps out of or is transported out of her everyday, egoic consciousness. The word is best known in the context of *transcendental meditation*, which seeks to bestow a radically new perspective on personal problems. However, periodically any client or counsellor may, through the intensity of the counselling relationship, embrace aspects of transcendental experience. *(See* ANOMALOUS EXPERIENCE, CONSCIOUSNESS, MEDITATION, SPIRITUALITY, TRANSPERSONAL.) In Jungian terms, the transcendental function is that which enables us to stand between the ego and the unconscious, and do justice to both. Its main mode of operation is through active imagination.

transcript a written account of a counselling session, using actual (verbatim) dialogue. Transcripts of tape recordings are requested on some training courses for assessment; the actual dialogue may be accompanied by a commentary on the counsellor's intentions, his views on how well he intervened and what alternative interventions he might have made. For an example of the extensive use of transcripts of a therapy see Dryden and Yankura (1992).

transcultural counselling *see* CROSS-CUL-TURAL COUNSELLING, COUNSELLING.

transference the phenomenon in counselling and therapy whereby the client unconsciously relates to the counsellor/therapist as if to a significant person (or persons or aspects of persons) from the past. It is recognised that everyone carries forward and inadvertently transfers on to others images of and feelings about other people (particularly parents). Transference is not confined to the client–counsellor relationship, but infantile feelings, fears and expectations may be displaced on to the counsellor or therapist with a compelling sense of reality and immediacy. The counsellor may be experienced, for example, as exaggeratedly wise, nurturing, frustrating or insignificant. *Positive transference* represents good feelings towards the therapist and forms the basis for the working alliance. NEGATIVE TRANSFERENCE consists of feelings which may get in the way of therapy and the therapeutic relationship; although they are seen as significant signs of previous relationship difficulties. Transference is fostered by the intensity of the analytic situation and by the relative neutrality of the counsellor: intense, problematic feelings from the past repeat themselves in a bid for resolution. *Erotic transference* is particularly exagger-ated transference which takes the form of the client (apparently) harbouring sexual desires for and/or falling in love with the counsellor. The *transference-countertransference relationship* is the unconscious interaction between counsellor and client. Transference, and its INTERPRETATION and WORKING THROUGH, is central to psychoanalysis and its variants. Other counselling orientations place less emphasis on transference. Some recognise its presence and occasional dangers, but do not consider work with it the most efficient vehicle for therapeutic change.

transformational object any object, event or person sought out by the child or adult as a means of altering self-experience. This concept derives from the Winnicottian concept of the facilitating environment: the mother acts upon the child, giving meaning from outside the child which modifies its experience. Memory traces of such interactions may be responsible for much searching behaviour; people seek material goods, and aesthetic and sexual experiences which provide momentary, subjective transformation. The transformational object is distinguished from the transitional object in that the latter is associated with attachment, the former with process and searching. *See* Bollas (1986).

transgenerational psychotherapy a form of therapy making links between the client's narrative and relevant, accessible elements of his or her ancestors' lives. This 'psychogenealogical' therapy posits the notion that unfinished business, reverberating traumas, injunctions, etc. pass down the generations to become problems for successive generations. Alluding to Freud's concept of the 'uncanny' and certain family therapy themes, Ancelin (1998) argues for the reality of traumatic anniversaries, coincidences of birth date, family secrets, 'invisible family loyalties', etc. Genograms and genosociograms are a central component of the method.

transitional object Winnicottian concept suggesting that the infant develops an attachment to certain favourite objects (e.g. dolls, teddy bears, comfort blankets) as a way of coping gradually with the separation from mother to a way of being able to 'control' the loved object. Initially the attachment takes place in the ORAL STAGE enabling a transition from the breast to greater independence. In a wider sense, any personal talisman or cherished possession, as well as non-material 'possessions' such as personal ideologies, religious or other affiliations, may function as a transitional object or transitional phenomenon.

transitive diagnosis *see* DIAGNOSIS.

transmutation counsellor intervention which seeks to help the client therapeutically change or redirect her distress instead of its being expressed cathartically. Various cognitive and imagery techniques, for example, can channel distress constructively or cast a new, positive light on it. Heron (2001) argues that transmutation is an important alternative strategy to what can become a 'cathartic treadmill'.

transpersonal therapy any form of counselling or therapy which places emphasis on spirituality, human potential or heightened consciousness. The 'transpersonal' is concerned with what is beyond purely individual, problematic everyday experience. The transpersonal is often known as 'fourth force psychology' (after the psychoanalytic, behavioural and humanistic)

and is considered by many to represent a higher stage of human evolution. Clients in transpersonal therapy will often engage in 'disidentification' with the 'lower' aspects of the psyche. Counsellors working in the transpersonal field are concerned with the cosmic context in which clients live; they may use visualisation, meditation, dream work and breathing techniques to access and explore this wider domain. Psychosynthesis, analytical psychology and psychological astrology are part of the transpersonal movement (*see* Rowan, 2002).

transvestism the sexual preference, or 'perversion', requiring the person (usually a man) to wear the clothes appropriate to members of the opposite sex. Transvestites who 'cross-dress' for sexual pleasure are fetishistic; the practice is not necessarily a homosexual one, however. Some psychoanalytic theorists suggest that its source may lie in intense infantile identification with the mother or female siblings and failure to mature beyond this position. Many transvestites, however, regard their behaviour as a harmless sexual preference. Transsexuals, by contrast, are people who feel biologically uncomfortable ('gender dysphoric') in their gender-consigned bodies and may seek complete surgical transformation to change gender, for which they must usually receive counselling.

traps maladaptive patterns of thinking and behaving, from which there appears to be no way of escaping. Traps are like vicious circles. An example of a depressed thinking trap is 'I'm bound to mess up any new relationship I get into'. The term is used (along with DILEMMAS and SNAGS) in COGNITIVE ANALYTIC THERAPY (CAT) and identification of such patterns is part of CAT's basic treatment sequence. Compare SCHEMA and SCRIPT.

trauma a painful or threatening event in a person's life, the suddenness of which cannot be readily integrated psychologically. The psychological effect of trauma is sometimes called *psychotrauma*. Examples can include birth complications, sexual abuse, rape and other physical violence, surgery, traffic accidents and profound losses. The key characteristic of trauma is that it is usually unexpected, unavoidable and overwhelming. Because of these factors it is commonly defended against psychologically and somatically by being blocked off from conscious awareness, temporarily or chronically. Some theorists argue that since the greater vulnerability of babies and infants leaves them more open to traumatic events than adults, trauma and *cumulative trauma* is experientially universal, and no counselling can avoid addressing it. Early psychoanalysis placed much weight on trauma as a causative factor in neurosis and on the ventilation of feelings related to repressed traumatic memories. Others minimise the emphasis given to traumatic aetiology, arguing that it is our interpretations and evaluations of events rather than the events themselves which cause distress. *See* POST-TRAUMATIC STRESS DISORDER.

traumatic incident reduction a form of therapy for PTSD symptoms and other traumatic experiences using a simple, brief method for helping the client safely put traumatic memories into perspective.

treatment chosen method of addressing an illness or psychological problem; cure. The term 'treatment' is associated with the medical model and is avoided by many counsellors. A *treatment plan* is the overall counselling strategy decided upon by the counsellor (usually in consultation with the client) following initial ASSESSMENT. Many counsellors are, however, ideologically opposed to assessment and treatment planning; those who do use such an approach usually negotiate it openly and adjust or abandon it in the light of its observable success or otherwise. *Treatment of choice* is the concept (based on research evidence) suggesting that certain identifiable psychological problems, symptoms or syndromes are best met with or treated by specific techniques (e.g. compulsive behaviour by response prevention). *Treatment* role is the term used by insurers to refer to the legal vulnerability of counsellors and other helping professionals to lawsuits being brought by clients for malpractice, accidents, etc. *See* INSURANCE, LEGAL ISSUES.

triad any constellation of three people. Counsellor training makes much use of experiential exercises in twos (dyads) and threes, often requiring a role-play of counsellor, client and observer. There are triadic or triangular themes referring to interpersonal dynamics throughout counselling and therapy (e.g. the oedipal triangle, nursing triad, Karpman triangle).

trial identification a skill used by the psychodynamic counsellor who seeks to understand his client's inner world by empathic attempts to identify with her and/or with the significant people in her story. Casement (1985) suggests that the analyst/counsellor utilises a former (pre-analysed) part of his own experience in order to 'monitor what it may feel like to be the patient'. In the 'listening reverie' the counsellor moves between his observing and experiencing ego, or between clinical attention to and human identification with the client. *See* INTERNAL SUPERVISOR.

trial interpretation the counsellor's offer to the client of a tentative interpretation which is open to rejection or amendment. The counsellor, heeding the client's verbal or non-verbal reaction to interpretations, may adjust or withdraw them and/or note their impact for future reference. Trial interpretation can also refer to the counsellor's offering interpretations to a client, early in the counselling process, to ascertain whether the client is likely to be responsive to such interventions at all.

trial therapy counselling or therapy offered in the first session or sessions as a means of assessing the client's suitability or readiness for a particular form of therapy; and as a sample of therapy for the client to consider whether she wishes to proceed. In intensive short-term dynamic psychotherapy, trial therapy is usually characterised by direct confrontation of defences, coupled with psychiatric assessment.

triangle of challenge the client's challenging circumstances as presented in counselling (e.g. being overwhelmed by demands), which may call for a specific challenging response from the counsellor (e.g. suggesting the client expresses anger and experiments with assertiveness); and the counsellor's awareness of internal challenge (e.g. she knows that she herself has some difficulty expressing anger and being assertive, and must either do some work on herself or respond in spite of her own limitations). This can feel uncomfortably like hypocrisy for the counsellor.

triangle of conflict the client's problemat-ic *impulses*, which are checked by identifiable *defences*, which themselves have arisen (or been mobilised) in order to ward off deep-seated *anxiety*. This is a central concept in intensive short-term dynamic psychotherapy (ISTDP).

triangle of insight *see* INSIGHT.

triangulation a key concept in family therapy (and systems therapy generally), denoting a process in which two family members (or two parties in any system) who are in conflict draw another person into their conflict in a bid to divert it. The third person is said to be 'triangulated' when he is coerced or invited, for example, to side with one of the other two; or he may become part of a 'detouring coalition', in which case the other two side against him. A family or systemic therapist may also become triangulated. Triangulation is also a key term in RESEARCH.

trust confidence in another; willingness to be intimate and vulnerable with another. Trust is shown in relying on another and believing that one will come to no harm from the other in doing so. The capacity for trust is probably established in childhood experience; the more reliable one's caregivers and psychological environment, the more likely one is to develop with a sense of inner safety and perception of the world and of people as trustworthy ('basic trust'). Conversely, damaging early experiences are likely to predispose one to suspicion and anxiety. The modern, urban, alienated lifestyle may also contribute generally to the undermining of trust. Clinical experience suggests that many clients need to test the trustworthiness of counsellors repeatedly in the initial stages of counselling. *See* TESTING.

twelve steps a self-help/group approach to the treatment of addictions pioneered by AA (and now used also in the treatment of addictions, overeating, sexual dependency, etc.). The steps begin with the alcoholic's acceptance that she is powerless in the face of alcoholism. The steps then require: acceptance into one's life of a 'higher power' (however so defined), making a 'moral inventory, of one's life (including one's 'character defects'), sharing or confession of that inventory, appeal to God/one's higher power to 'remove shortcomings', the systematic making of amends, prayer, meditation and the propagation of the 'message'. Ongoing abstinence from drinking or drug taking (or other addictions) is expected. *See* MINNESOTA METHOD.

two plus one approach an experimental therapy pioneered by Shapiro et al. structured as three sessions, the first two being close in time, the last one at some distance in time. This allowed researchers to study the effects of waiting list expectations; helpfulness of brief therapy for mild to moderate depression, anxiety and stress; effects of elapsed time (the gap between second and third sessions); and usefulness of such brief work within limited NHS resources.

unconditional positive regard acceptance of the client without reservation. Unconditional positive regard is a core condition associated particularly with person-centred counselling. It is characterised by a consistently non-judgemental attitude which allows the client to relax, trust and disclose. It denotes acceptance of the person, but not necessarily all the person's behaviours. The terms acceptance, non-possessive warmth, respect and prizing are often used synonymously with unconditional positive regard. Most counsellors acknowledge that this attitude constitutes a desirable foundation for counselling which it is not always possible to achieve or maintain. *Unconditional positive self-regard is* often difficult for clients to achieve but is greatly facilitated by the counsellor's non-judgemental attitude.

unconditional self-acceptance a concept from REBT denoting the attitude of non-judgmentalism towards oneself. Regardless of performance and failures, clients can be taught to accept themselves wholly and thus not succumb to feelings of worthlessness and low-self esteem.

unconscious the most fundamental of concepts in the depth psychologies, the unconscious is understood primarily as that domain or system of mental life which embraces the instincts, primary processes, infantile conflict and repression and which is well beyond the conscious apprehension of the client. The term is used both as a noun (the unconscious) and adjective (e.g. unconscious conflicts). It is sometimes used to mean 'unaware' and 'not currently in the field of awareness' *(see* PRECONSCIOUS) but its main identity is the Freudian unconscious. *Dynamic unconscious* is sometimes used to distinguish the repressing function from the latter, preconscious operation (which is sometimes known as the *descriptive unconscious).* It is a central tenet of psychoanalysis that clients (and people generally) are unaware of their unconscious motivations, that one of the functions of the unconscious is to hide painful and/or dissonant material from us, some of which emerges in dreams, slips of the tongue and symptoms. Only thoroughgoing clinical analysis can significantly alter this state of affairs. (Making the unconscious conscious is one of the analytic objectives.) While recognising the reality of *relative* unconsciousness (or aspects of our mental life that are non-conscious), some counsellors and therapists consider the concept of the unconscious problematic and/or unhelpful and believe that clients have more conscious control and responsibility than they are credited with by the depth psychologies.

uncovering models of counselling are said to demonstrate uncovering interventions when they focus on analysis of symptoms, progressive stripping of defences and baring of the 'real self, either aggressively or gently.

underdog the opposite of TOP DOG.

understanding grasping the intended meaning of another's words and expressions; perceiving and summarising accurately the nuances of deeper meaning in clients' communications, including nonverbal behaviour. True understanding of another is inseparable from EMPATHY. The assumption that one understands, or the (often shallow) assurance of the statement 'I understand', may not match the client's reality. Although it may be possible to understand someone who does not understand himself or his own behaviour, such understanding is likely to be of little therapeutic use if it cannot be communicated.

unfinished business any incomplete process, but in counselling terms the phrase refers to personal experiences which have been blocked from being fully expressed. 'Unfinished business' is a gestalt concept resting on the view that humans have an 'urge to complete' in order to achieve satisfaction and peace. A child who suffers parental cruelty, for example, but who lives under a threat of violence, will probably be forced to suppress his rage and hurt; this may lead to chronic muscular tension and/or avoidance of confrontation in adult life. This tension and/or avoidance points to unfinished business. Counselling can identify and address such unfinished business, allowing it to be discharged cathartically. Unfinished business may refer to single or multiple events from the past or in the present (e.g. in relationships or in group work).

unilateral couple counselling the counselling of one partner on her or his specific relationship problems. Even when only one of the partners wishes to receive counselling, the focus remains on the relationship. A high proportion of couple counselling is in fact unilateral, although some counsellors will only undertake couple work when both parties are involved.

unipolar affective disorder psychiatric term for a serious mental illness characterised by episodes of mood disturbance of only one kind (e.g. depression without a manic component).

uniqueness singularity, individuality or specialness. Uniqueness has both psychological and spiritual connotations. Counsellors recognise and value each of their clients in his or her own right, respecting individuals' particular qualities, character traits and idiosyncrasies. Paradoxically, all models of counselling contain certain presuppositions about *general* human functioning. However, while many counsellors may bring the same theoretical orientation to bear on every client, they (ideally) intuitively adapt their model to the unique characteristics, needs and learning style of each client. *See* INDIVIDUAL DIFFERENCES. Compare UNIVERSALITY.

universality the experience that one's private concerns and travails resemble those of others, if not of the entire human race. The universality of personal problems is witnessed particularly in group therapy, and clients report this as one of its most helpful factors. Defensive universality is observable in clients who may claim that their problems are unimportant because they are common to everyone.

unsent letters letters written by clients – but not actually sent – to significant people in their lives. This practice is sometimes suggested or encouraged by counsellors as a means of externalising feelings, directing them to the person concerned, completing unfinished business and effecting catharsis.

use of self the conscious employment by the counsellor of all that may be therapeutically beneficial in her repertoire of personal characteristics. The term has been extended from its original association with the Alexander technique. Counselling calls on the intuition, openness and involvement of the counsellor in a way that few occupations do. Counsellors are affected, often deeply, by the struggles and emotions of their clients; they may make themselves available to intense transference, for example, as an intrinsic part of the work. Counsellors frequently encourage clients to 'test out' with them unfamiliar ways of relating (or degrees of openness). They may also render themselves vulnerable and disclose themselves in emotionally demanding ways. For these reasons, regular supervision of the counsellor, and access to personal therapy when needed, are considered essential by the BACP. *See* Wosket (1999).

user this term has various meanings:

1. Anyone who uses a service as a consumer (e.g. a counselling service, a day centre, NHS facilities).
2. Someone who is addicted to and actively uses certain damaging drugs (e.g. heroin).
3. Colloquially, anyone who primarily manipulates or exploits others instead of relating to them as valued fellow human beings.

vaginismus painful spasms of the muscles surrounding the entrance to the vagina, experienced by some women when intercourse is attempted, making it difficult or impossible. Vaginismus is sometimes successfully treated by combinations of individual and couple counselling, focusing on it as a symptom of problems in the relationship or as an expression of the woman's intrapsychic conflicts. Its most effective treatment is behavioural, involving the gradual insertion into the vagina of dilators of increasing size, together with relaxation techniques. Support groups have been established for women experiencing this distressing problem, and many women regard it as always symptomatic of deeper issues.

values strongly and enduringly held views about desirable behaviour, including views on personal conduct, politics, religion, etc. Examples of strongly held personal values might include: sex before marriage is wrong; people should work hard; racism is wrong and should invariably be challenged; it is right to respect everyone's personal choice of sexual orientation. It is not unusual for counsellor and client (or any other pair of people) to have different values, but this becomes problematic if either party expects the other automatically to agree with or change their value system. Most counsellors seek to clarify and work within the frame of the personal values of each client, except where the client's values may be offensive or unacceptable to the counsellor (e.g. paedophile views and practices) or therapeutically counterproductive (e.g. the self-punishing internalisation of certain rigid religious values). Central to counselling ethics is the value placed on AUTONOMY. *See* Holmes and Lindley (1989).

valuing prizing or appreciating another person; explicitly appreciating that progress has been made in counselling. Valuing is not without problems because it implies that while you apparently accept and prize the humanity or 'personhood' of another or of yourself, you may well be capable of degrees of judgementalism. Valuing can also be considered the opposite of DISCOUNTING.

ventilation of feelings the expressive release of emotions. Feelings may be aired and discharged at many levels, the simplest of which may be 'just getting things off my chest' by talking to a sympathetic listener. More deeply, they may be expressions of anger, fear, pain and so on, through shouting, trembling, sobbing, etc. This is equivalent to abreaction. Mere ventilation of feelings is not necessarily therapeutic, whereas catharsis usually is. Primal therapy, primal integration and co-counselling make use of catharsis a good deal, and most therapies which allow deep feelings to be expressed do use it from time to time.

verbatim recording any record of a counselling session which represents the dialogue that has taken place in a word-for-word manner. *See* TRANSCRIPT.

vicarious modelling *see* MODELLING.

vicarious traumatisation traumatic feelings experienced by anyone associated with a direct victim of a traumatic or extreme event. Counsellors working closely with trauma victims, hearing their accounts of events, etc., may after many or even one occasion develop symptoms of their own. Also known as secondary traumatic stress.

victim one who suffers any form of abuse, accident or adversity. Most people accept that someone who has been raped or burgled is a genuine victim of something beyond their control, and *victim support* schemes attest to this. Beyond this point, however, there is some debate about who is a victim as opposed to who invites victimisation or places and maintains himself in the role of victim. (The Victim role described in the KARPMAN TRIANGLE of TA attests to this.) A typical example of someone who often finds herself in the role of victim (or who unconsciously seeks *revictimisation*) is the 'battered wife' who repeatedly returns to her violent husband. People suffering from psychotic delusions may believe themselves to be victimised when they are not.

Use of the term 'victim', like 'sufferer', is rejected by certain groups (e.g. people with AIDS, people with mental health problems) on the grounds that it promotes inaccurate, unhelpful and undermining stereotypes of passivity and fatalism, and 'survivor' may be preferred.

vignette a small story or excerpt from experience which illustrates a point. The writings of counsellors and therapists make ample use of clinical vignettes to demonstrate, for example, the success of certain interventions.

violence uncontrolled or controlled attack on others or on things. While AGGRESSION can have both negative and positive connotations, violence is always associated with the negative pole (e.g. violence against women, racist violence, football violence). It implies the violation of someone who does not wish or deserve this. Victims of violence (e.g. people who have been involved in bank raids) can benefit from counselling which is offered promptly and sensitively (*see* POST-TRAUMATIC STRESS DISORDER). Actual violence within counselling is rare, but its possibility is taken seriously by many agencies, for example by ensuring that counsellors do not work alone in a building. Violence is more likely to occur in certain settings (e.g. acute psychiatric, probation and addiction projects) than in others. *Violent thoughts* and fantasies are not unusual and counsellors need to be comfortable enough with these to help clients explore, interpret or release them appropriately.

visiting clients the counsellor's meeting his or her clients in a place other than the usual designated counselling/consultation room (often on the client's 'home ground').

Some counsellors will never agree to such arrangements on the grounds that boundaries are seriously compromised. Some, however, are quite flexible and will consider the circumstances (e.g. when a client is hospitalised, is physically disabled, has ME or is agoraphobic). It is recognised, for example, by probation officers on 'home visits' or community psychiatric nurses on 'domiciliary visits', that much useful information and insight can be gained from such visits.

visualisation the deliberately undertaken exercise of imagining scenes designed to have therapeutic impact. Visualisation can be used as an attempted self-change technique or within formal counselling sessions. Clients whose favoured modality is imagery, or clients for whom other, verbally oriented techniques are not working well, may benefit from such a counsellor-initiated exercise. Often the client is asked to picture a memory of a place associated with peaceful feelings, or a series of images with symbolic potency. Visualisation has many possible uses: for relaxation; as part of a programme of cancer counselling or 'wealth creation'; for mental rehearsal of imminent challenges, or for accessing difficult feelings. *See* GUIDED IMAGERY.

voice quality the characteristics of the counsellor's voice. It is recognised, particularly in live training situations or in the supervision of counsellors' audiotapes, that counsellors' responses to clients may be strengthened or weakened by the tone in which they are delivered. Mehrabian's (1971) research on interpersonal communication found that 38% of what was communicated was by tone of voice, compared with 7% by verbal content and 55% by facial cues. Ideally, the counsellor's voice quality will appropriately reflect (or echo) the tone in which the client speaks or will congruently express the counsellor's periodic need to confront the client. Counsellor incongruence may be conveyed when, for example, she overtly conveys one message, yet covertly (e.g. by a withholding flatness in her voice) conveys a contradictory message.

voice therapy this has at least two distinct meanings: (1) any therapy utilising a focus on the voice to improve confidence, assertiveness, etc.; (2) a distinct form of psychotherapy working with the 'inner voice' in suicidal clients. The latter is a cognitive-affective-behavioural approach (Firestone, 1997) addressing negative thought patterns, discussing insights and counteracting self-destructive behaviour.

volunteer counsellor a counsellor or allied professional who offers counselling without receiving payment. Volunteer counsellors are used by many voluntary organisations such as Relate, Cruse, MIND, etc. Often counsellors receive training in return for their work, and many counsellors-in-training are volunteer counsellors in such settings. Volunteer counsellors may either have substantial prior training, or very little experience. Some trained and qualified counsellors volunteer in order to accumulate the hours of practice (450) necessary to apply for BACP accreditation.

voyeurism sexual 'perversion' in which the person gains pleasure from watching (furtively or otherwise) others engaged in sexual activity or simply in a naked state. The degree to which the person feels compelled to engage in voyeuristic activity in order to derive sexual satisfaction suggests the degree of pathology involved. EXHIBITIONISM is the paired opposite of voyeurism. Dogging – organized, promiscuous sex in secluded public places, watched by others – increased as a phenomenon in the 2000s.

vulnerability openness; an emotionally undefended state. Vulnerability may be regarded either as a desirable quality and sign of healthy adjustment (where the person 'has nothing to hide' and therefore lives without 'normal' social barriers and roles) or as unnecessarily risky behaviour (for example in the case of someone who naively insists on confronting an unfair boss or an armed robber). It also has the meaning of being exposed to risk or harm without a sense of being able to cope with such dangers; this meaning is associated with the person's relationship with a powerful other who may be damaging. Also, young people may be considered in law to be vulnerable or 'at risk' if they have an abusing parent and/or live in insecure conditions not suitable for their age.

waiting list a written or computerised record of people who have applied for counselling or other treatment but who cannot be seen immediately because of limited resources. While some counsellors in private practice maintain such lists, they are more commonly found in statutory or voluntary organisations (e.g. NHS psychotherapy, counselling or clinical psychology clinics, Relate). Some research suggests that the sooner clients who are in crisis can be seen for counselling, the better the prognosis for a good outcome. Some evidence also exists supporting the idea that a significant number of 'wait list' applicants for counselling subsequently consider themselves (or their situations) sufficiently improved without counselling, due to either their situation having improved or their mood and self-image having improved as a concomitant feature of having motivated themselves to seek help.

ward off to keep certain thoughts or images at bay; to prevent painfully meaningful mental connections from coalescing into conscious awareness. The term is used frequently in psychoanalytic literature, confirming the dynamic nature of unconscious conflict and defence mechanisms.

warmth caring, interested attitude towards clients. The place of warmth in counselling is usually discussed in terms of NON-POSSESSIVE WARMTH. Warmth conveyed without awareness of its possible impact and misunderstanding may be mentally converted by clients (perhaps otherwise starved of such attention) into sexual interest, the offer of friendship or an invitation to dependency. Sociological critics of Rogerian 'warmth' regard it as naive and superficial, and as ignoring the 'real problem' of clients' alienated lives. Ellis has argued that undue counsellor warmth can reinforce clients' dire needs for love and approval.

welfare any or all aspects of a person's mental, physical, financial, occupational and environmental health. Many organisations appoint welfare officers whose diverse duties may include personal counselling, debt counselling, liaison with legal, medical and immigration authorities, pensions departments, etc. 'Welfare' can also have the negative association of dependence on charity or social security benefit systems.

well-being the subjective experience of health, security and peace of mind. Well-being or 'wellness' is used both of acceptable minimal levels of personal functioning and survival, and also of potentially profound levels of optimal functioning. In the US, and to some extent in the UK, there are 'wellness clinics' and 'well-woman' centres concerned with holistic health assessment, counselling and treatment.

Weltanschauung world view; philosophy of life. Thanks to the influence of German existentialists on philosophy and psychotherapy, this word has established itself in its German form. *See* WORLD VIEW.

wholeness integrity, non-fragmentedness. The term 'wholeness' is used in the same sense as 'holistic' and implies a view of the ecological interdependence of life forms. It also refers to the interdependence, within individuals, of their body, thinking, feeling, spirituality and behaviour. Wholeness also implies a sense of deep well-being, as in 'I feel whole for the first time in my life'.

whole object from object relations theory, refers to a person's capacity to regard others in an unfragmented manner (*see* PARTS).

wild analysis the practice of using arbitrary, impulsive and/or inappropriate psychoanalytic interventions, especially interpretation. Wild analysis may be seen either in untrained (or incompletely trained) therapists, or in trained but impulsive, 'omniscient' therapists who show insufficient regard for clients' readiness to benefit from their 'pearls of wisdom'.

will desire, determination, choosing, effort; volition; conation. Will has the connotation of taking action and being prepared and able to surmount obstacles. Rank, Assagioli, Frankl, Rollo May and others have considered will a vital component of personal change. Others de-emphasise

will, perhaps recognising the almost universal observation that if people only had to will themselves to feel better, for example, the world would be a happy place and have no need for counsellors. Willpower implies a fund of personal strength upon which one can call and employ heroically against all odds. (To advocates of the MINNESOTA METHOD such ideas are anathema, because they appear to deny a need for outside, and particularly spiritual, help.) Rank espoused 'Will therapy' but this is not now a common approach. People are popularly said to be *weak willed* when they show no resistance to obstacles and no commitment to effort; they are considered *strong willed* when they are prepared to confront obstacles; or *wilful* when they fail to compromise when it is helpful to do so. People are said to have 'lost the will to live' when they surrender the fight against highly adverse circumstances or terminal illness. *See* DETERMINISM, FREE WILL.

winning succeeding. The (largely American) focus on winning or 'being a winner' has influenced psychological training approaches (e.g. neurolinguistic programming and *est*) which are more concerned with personal growth and self-actualisation than with understanding psychopathology. Management training, for example, is often concerned with the psychology of success, positive thinking, assertiveness and 'getting what you want from life'.

wisdom perceptiveness, mature judgement, intelligent disposition. This term is used rarely in counselling literature because it is thought to imply some sort of superior insight or ability to act in a guru-like manner but mature practice as a counsellor undoubtedly demands a degree of wisdom.

wish fulfilment the symbolic realisation of (frustrated or forbidden) desires, usually in the form of dreams. Freud postulated that a major function of dreaming was the (illusory but powerful) satisfaction of unconscious instincts. *Wishful thinking,* while similar to the wish fulfilment process, is conscious and anchored in reality.

withdrawal removing oneself from engagement in social life or from difficult life circumstances. Withdrawal is often a symptom of depression, the person feeling uninterested in socialising or believing herself to be of no interest to others. Withdrawal is defined in TA as a mode of time structuring in which the individual does not transact with others. Withdrawal also has the particular meaning in the context of addiction, of someone suffering psychologically and physiologically from the effects of abstinence from their drug or other habit.

womb envy *see* ENVY.

word association originally a Jungian technique, now little used, of eliciting from clients their characteristic thought processes and possible unconscious conflicts, relying on their making uncensored responses to key words presented by the therapist.

work purposeful activity and/or paid employment. Freud considered the ability to engage in work and love to be key indices of mental health. Clients' inability to function at work is still a guiding assessment criterion for counsellors and therapists, since an inability to 'face the day' or to order one's thoughts, for example, may indicate severe depression or anxiety. Contemporary western societies value work highly and the so-called *workaholic* (one who works compulsively, often ignoring the stress he places on himself, is currently unlikely to be considered to have pathological problems. Many employing organisations, recognising the contribution that counselling at work can make, initiate EMPLOYEE ASSISTANCE PROGRAMMES. A high correlation between chronic *unemployment* and compromised mental health has been demonstrated. The term 'work' is often used to underline the effort and commitment required of clients in counselling. 'Work on self' is sometimes used synonymously with personal development and is considered essential in counsellor training.

working alliance 'the relatively non-neurotic, rational relationship between patient and analyst which makes it possible for the patient to work purposefully in the analytic situation' (Greenson, 1967). Such an alliance is considered to be between the 'reasonable ego' of the client and the 'analysing ego' of the analyst or (psychodynamic) counsellor. The more commonly used term is now THERAPEUTIC ALLIANCE.

working hypothesis the tentative conceptualisation of the client's problems formulated by the counsellor, used to guide the choice of interventions, and open to appropriate modification throughout the counselling process.

working through a psychoanalytic concept arguing that catharsis and insight are not sufficient for change, but that client and counsellor need to go on working over and over again on the client's reactions and responses. Working through implies that therapeutic change takes time, and that it cannot be condensed. The term is also used more generally of the learning effort required of clients seeking change (e.g. REBT asks clients to engage in homework assignments and repeated disputing of irrational beliefs).

workplace counselling any counselling dedicated to issues raised by employees. Workplace counselling may be in-house or supplied by an external provider (*see* EMPLOYEE ASSISTANCE PROGRAMME). Also known as employee counselling.

workshop an educational or training event, usually experiential in nature and of relatively short duration (anything from hours to days). There is no real distinction between 'workshop' and 'short course'. The workshop format is particularly suitable for the kind of continuing professional education to which counsellors are committed.

world view the prevailing way in which people mentally construct or interpret the world (the 'world' meaning existence, history, society and values generally). Existentialist counsellors (*see* van Deurzen, 2001) often refer to the dimensions of *Umwelt, Mitwelt, Eigenwelt* and *Uberwelt.* These correspond respectively to the natural environment, the social and public sphere, the private, psychological world, and the transpersonal domain. Individuals develop unique views of their relationship to each of these dimensions and a central task for existentialist counsellors is to help clients elucidate their views in order to effect meaningful personal change. More prosaically, any general outlook ('Life is nasty, brutish and short' or 'Life is what you make it') may be said to be a world view. Compare SCHEMA, SCRIPT, MODEL OF HUMAN BEINGS.

worried well somewhat derogatory term for clients or helpseekers whose problems are not perceived, by busy healthcare providers in particular, as serious enough to warrant protracted attention, even though they may be technically entitled to help. This group of clients probably suffer from various subclinical problems that appear mild relative to those suffering from more acute and easily diagnosable problems.

worry non-clinical term for dysfunctional preoccupation, anxiety and rumination. Worry is dysfunctional because it is characterised by circular thinking, avoidance, inaction, guilt and disengagement: from reality-testing. Appropriate concern, by contrast, is a mental orientation to the problems of the past, present or future which is in proportion to the nature of those problems and is likely to lead to problem-solving attitudes and action.

worst scenario the most unpleasant, distressing or anxiety-provoking situation that the client is capable of imagining. Cognitive–behavioural counsellors may ask anxious clients 'What is the worst possible thing that you fear could happen to you (for example if you stood up in front of a class to give a speech)?' Such an intervention confronts the client concretely, forcing her to consider that feared events are not in themselves 'the end of the world' (or 'awful') but rather undesirable, uncomfortable, finite, survivable and perhaps even instructive.

worth value; estimation of how important one may be to others, to oneself, or in general. The person-centred concept of CONDITIONS OF WORTH highlights the common tendency of humans to think that they fall short of parental and other expectations, and to consider themselves less worthy if they do so. Hence, many clients report feeling 'worthless', which is often a global, inaccurate allusion to being less attractive, intelligent, athletic, empathic (or whatever) than they believe they 'must' be. Such attitudes are implicitly challenged by the counsellor's consistent respect for the client. Strictly speaking, phrases such as 'I am worth more than that' (spoken by a woman, for example, whose husband denigrates her) incorrectly reinforce judgements of self worth; 'I want/think I deserve better treatment than that' might be better. *See* LOW SELF-ESTEEM.

wounded healer an archetypal image suggesting that the counsellor/therapist (or other helper) is simultaneously one who suffers and/or has suffered deeply. The concept, derived from classical mythology and Jungian psychology, also suggests that the 'inner healer' in the client identifies with the healing persona of the counsellor. There is thought to be a conscious and unconscious interplay between the forces of sickness and health in client and counsellor. The term 'wounded healer' suggests, further, that counsellors and therapists are drawn to become helpers or healers because of their own emotional wounds (*see* REPARATION) and that their own knowledge of suffering is likely to make them more effective helpers; this last suggestion is not, however, borne out by research. *See* PERSONAL COUNSELLING OF THE COUNSELLOR.

writing, use of in counselling self descriptions, client diaries, assessments, force field analysis, letters between client and counsellor, etc. Although the predominant mode of therapeutic interaction is the spoken word, certain approaches utilise written exercises or material when appropriate. Cognitive–behavioural counselling, cognitive-analytic therapy and personal construct counselling are probably the main proponents of the uses of writing in counselling. Rationales include encouraging clients to focus on specific thoughts and behaviour, to engage in activity, to provide concrete, visible markers of goals and progress, and to maximise the possibilities of change in brief counselling contracts. For a Jungian-based example of the therapeutic use of writing, *see* Progoff (1975). *See also* THERAPEUTIC WRITING.

written contract any contract between counsellor and client which sets out the terms of what the counsellor is offering, what the client's goals are and what she intends to do to reach them. The strength of making written contracts (which are not popular with a majority of counsellors) is that they can be referred to concretely in order to reinforce client commitment. *See* CONTRACT.

YAVIS an acronym – young, attractive, verbal, intelligent, successful – for that group of clients found by some counsellors to be easier, more exciting or more rewarding to work with. Critics of counselling and therapy point out that it is often this less damaged group of people who have easier access to psychological help, rather than people of lower socio-economic status. Compare HOUND.

'yes, but' a common expression of client ambivalence, signifying apparent assent to the need for change and effort, along with reservations about it. It is a classic 'game' in TA theory. *See* AMBIVALENCE, SNAGS.

yes-saying that attitude towards life which is hopeful, risk-taking, responsibility-accepting and generally forward-looking. Yes-saying stands in contrast to fear of and retreat from life and its challenges.

'you' statement speech which directly and honestly refers to another person, avoiding oblique or defensive coded statements; a statement by which the speaker avoids direct ownership of what he has said. Phrases like 'It's stuffy in this room' or 'Some people have no consideration for others' are often coded and evasive ways of saying 'You (and your smoking) are really annoying me'. Clients often say 'You' when they mean 'I', as in 'You just feel so helpless'. You statements may be either positive or negative and form part of true (I-Thou) dialogue. Having the client address absent people in sessions (primarily parents) as 'you' instead of talking *about* them, has a recognised enlivening effect, and is used, for example, in gestalt and primal therapies.

youth counselling counselling provided specifically for young people. Certain counselling agencies are funded to offer counselling for people up to the age, sometimes, of about 20 or 25 years, in recognition of their social vulnerability. The problems of very young children are likely to come to the attention of social workers, educational psychologists and child guidance workers (and some counsellors based in schools). Teenagers often experience developmental crises, conflicts with parents, peer pressure and so on. They may be particularly vulnerable to substance misuse, unwanted pregnancy, etc. Youth counselling may contain elements of parenting and information giving. Much youth counselling is offered by youth and community workers in youth clubs and similar settings.

Zen therapy an integration of Zen Buddhist psychology with western therapeutic aims. Zen therapy focuses on here and now awareness, tranquillity, mindfulness, compassion, wisdom, letting go (Brazier, 1995).

References

AMERICAN COUNSELING ASSOCIATION (1992). *What is Counseling and Human Development?* Alexandria, VA: ACA.

AMERICAN PSYCHIATRIC ASSOCIATION (2000). *Diagnostic and Statistical Manual of Mental Disorders,* 4th edition, Text revised. Washington, DC: American Psychiatric Press.

ANCELIN, A. SCHUTZENBERGER (1998). *The Ancestor Syndrome: Transgenerational Psychotherapy and the Hidden Links in the Family Tree.* London: Routledge.

ASHWORTH, P. (2000). *Psychology and 'Human Nature'.* Hove: Psychology Press.

AVELINE, M. and DRYDEN, W. (eds) (1988). *Group Therapy in Britain.* Milton Keynes: Open University Press.

BALINT, M. (1968). *The Basic Fault.* London: Tavistock.

BANDURA, A. (1977). *Social Learning Theory.* Englewood Cliffs, NJ: Prentice-Hall.

BECK, A.T. (1979). *Cognitive Therapy and the Emotional Disorders.* New York: Meridian.

BELLACK, A. S. and HERSEN, M. (eds) (1987). *Dictionary of Behavior Therapy Techniques.* New York: Pergamon.

BLANTON, B. (1996). *Radical Honesty.* New York: Dell.

BOLLAS, C. (1986). The transformational object. In: Kohon, G (ed.), *The British School of Psychoanalysis,* pp.83-100. London: Free Association Books.

BORDIN, E. S. (1979). The generalizability of the psychoanalytic concept of the working alliance. *Psychotherapy: Theory, Research and Practice* **16**, 252-60.

BOTT SPILLIUS, E. (ed.) (1988). *Melanie Klein Today,* Volumes 1 and 2. London: Routledge.

BOURDIEU, P. (ed.) (1999). *The Weight of the World.* Cambridge: Polity.

BOWLBY, J. (1973). *Attachment and Loss. Vol. 2: Separation.* Harmondsworth: Penguin.

BRAZIER, D. (1995). *Zen Therapy.* London: Constable.

BRITISH ASSOCIATION FOR COUNSELLING (1985). *Counselling: Definition of Terms in Use with Expansion and Rationale.* Rugby: BAC.

BRITISH ASSOCIATION FOR COUNSELLING (1990). *Code of Ethics and Practice for Counsellors.* Rugby: BAC.

BRITISH ASSOCIATION FOR COUNSELLING AND PSYCHOTHERAPY (2002). *Ethical Framework for Good Practice in Counselling and Psychotherapy.* Rugby: BACP.

BUBER, M. (1937). *I and Thou.* Edinburgh: T. and T. Clark.

BUDMAN, S. H. and GURMAN, A. S. (1988). *Theory and Practice of Brief Therapy.* New York: Guilford Press.

CASEMENT, P. (1985). *On Learning from the Patient.* London: Tavistock.

CASEMENT, P. (1990). *Further Learning from the Patient.* London: Routledge.

CHAMBERLAIN, L. L. and BUTZ, M. R. (eds) (1998). *Clinical Chaos: A Therapist's Guide to Nonlinear Dynamics and Therapeutic Change.* Philadelphia, PA: Brunner-Mazel.

CLARKSON, P. (1989). *Gestalt Counselling in Action.* London: Sage.

CLARKSON, P. (1993). *On Psychotherapy.* London: Whurr.

CLARKSON, P. and GILBERT, M. (1991) The training of counsellor trainers and supervisors. In: Dryden, W. and Thorne, B. (eds), *Training and Supervision for Counselling in Action,* pp. 143–169. London: Sage.

COX, M. (1978). *Structuring the Therapeutic Process.* Oxford: Pergamon.

CRAMER, D. (1992). *Personality and Psychotherapy.* Buckingham: Open University Press.

DAINES, B., GASK, L. and USHERWOOD, T. (1997). *Medical and Psychiatric Issues for Counsellors.* London: Sage.

DAVANLOO, H. (1990). *Unlocking the Unconscious.* New York: Wiley.

DEMAUSE, L. (1982). *Foundations of Psychohistory.* New York: Creative Roots.

DE SHAZER, S. (1985). *Keys to Solution in Brief Therapy.* New York: Norton.

DEURZEN, E. VAN *(2001). Existential Counselling and Psychotherapy in Practice*, 2nd edition. London: Sage.

DRYDEN, W. (ed.) (1991). *The Essential Arnold Lazarus.* London: Whurr.

DRYDEN, W. and FELTHAM, C. (eds) (1992a). *Psychotherapy and its Discontents.* Buckingham: Open University Press.

DRYDEN, W. and FELTHAM, C. (1992b). *Brief Counselling.* Buckingham: Open University Press.

DRYDEN, W. and YANKURA, J. (1992). *Daring to be Myself.* Buckingham: Open University Press.

DRYDEN, W. and NEENAN, M. (1997). *Dictionary of Rational Emotive Behaviour Therapy.* London: Whurr.

DURLAK, J. A. (1979). Comparative effectiveness of paraprofessional and professional helpers. *Psychological Bulletin* **86**, 80–92.

EGAN, G. (2002). *The Skilled Helper,* 7th edition. Pacific Grove, CA: Brooks/Cole.

ERIKSON, E. (1959). *Identity and the Life Cycle.* New York: International Universities Press.

EYSENCK, H. J. (1992). The outcome problem in psychotherapy. In: Dryden, W. and Feltham, C. (eds), *Psychotherapy and its Discontents,* pp. 100–123. Buckingham: Open University Press.

FELTHAM, C. (1995). *What is Counselling?* London: Sage.

FELTHAM, C. (1997). *Time-Limited Counselling.* London: Sage.

FELTHAM, C. (2001). Counselling studies: a personal view. *British Journal of Guidance and Counselling* **29**(1), 111–119.

FELTHAM, C. (2004). Problems Are Us. Felixstowe: Braiswick.

FELTHAM, C. and HORTON, I. (eds) (2000). *Handbook of Counselling and Psychotherapy.* London: Sage.

FIRESTONE, R. W. (1997). *Suicide and the Inner Voice.* Thousand Oaks, CA: Sage.

FRANK, J. D. (1963). *Persuasion and Healing.* New York: Schocken.

FRANKL, V. E. (1971). *The Will to Meaning. Foundations and Applications of Logotherapy.* London: Souvenir Press.

FROMM, E. (1973). *The Anatomy of Destructiveness.* New York: Holt, Rinehart & Winston.

GARDNER, H. (1993). *Frames of Mind*, 2nd edition. London: Fontana.

GARFIELD, S. L. (1995). *Psychotherapy: An Eclectic-Integrative Approach,* 2nd edition. New York: Wiley.

GARFIELD, S. L. and BERGIN, A. E. (eds) (1986). *Handbook of Psychotherapy and Behavior Change*, 3rd edition. New York: Wiley.

GENDLIN, E. T. (1978). *Focusing.* New York: Everest House.

GILMORE, S. K. (1973). *The Counselor-in-Training.* Englewood-Cliffs, NJ: Prentice-Hall.

GLASSER, W. (1984). *Control Theory.* London: Harper and Row.

GOLEMAN, D. (1995). *Emotional Intelligence: Why it can matter more than IQ.* London: Bloomsbury.

GRANT, J. (1981). *A Directory of Discarded Ideas.* Sevenoaks: Ashgrove Press.

GREENSON, R. R. (1967). *The Technique and Practice of Psychoanalysis.* London: Hogarth.

GREENWALD, H. (1974). *Active Psychotherapy.* New York: Aronson.

GROF, C. and GROF, S. (1990). *The Stormy Search for the Self.* Los Angeles, CA: Tarcher.

GUINAGH, B. (1987). *Cognition and Catharsis in Psychotherapy.* London: Springer.

HALMOS, P. (1981). *The Faith of the Counsellors.* London: Constable.

HARRIS, T. (1967). *I'm OK, You're OK.* New York: Grove Press.

HAWKINS, P. and SHOHET, R. (2000). *Supervision in the Helping Professions*, 2nd edition. Buckingham: Open University Press.

HERON, J. (2001). *Helping the Client,* 5th edition. London: Sage.

HILL, C. E. and O'GRADY, K. E. (1985). List of therapist intentions illustrated in a case study and with therapists of varying theoretical orientations. *Journal of Counseling Psychol*ogy 3(2), 3–22.

HOBSON, R. F. (1985). *Forms of Feeling.* London: Tavistock.

HOLMES, J. and LINDLEY, R. (1989). *The Values of Psychotherapy.* Oxford: Oxford University Press.

HOUSE, R. (2003). *Therapy Beyond Modernity: Deconstructing and Transcending Profession-Centred Therapy.* London: Karnac.

HOWARD, A. (2000). *Philosophy for Counselling and Psychotherapy: Pythagoras to Postmodernism.* Basingstoke: Macmillan.

HOWARD, K. I., ORLINSKY, D. E. and HILL, J. A. (1970). Patients' satisfactions as a function of patient-therapist pairing. *Psychotherapy: Theory, Research and Practice* 7, 130–134.

IVEY, A. (1971). *Microcounseling: Innovations in Interviewing Training.* Springfield, IL: Charles. C. Thomas.

IVEY, A. E., IVEY, M. B. and SIMEK-DOWNING, L. (1980). *Counseling and Psychotherapy.* Englewood Cliffs, NJ: Prentice-Hall International.

JACKINS, H. (1965). *The Human Side of Human Beings.* Seattle: Rational Island Press.

JACOBS, M. (1982). *Still Small Voice: An Introduction to Pastoral Counselling.* London: SPCK.

JACOBS, M. (1999). *Psychodynamic Counselling in Action*, 2nd edition. London: Sage.

JACOBS, M. (2000). *Illusion: a Psychodynamic Interpretation of Thinking and Belief.* London: Whurr.

JAMES, O. (1998). *Britain on the Couch.* London: Arrow.

JANOV, A. (1975). *Primal Man: The New Consciousness.* New York: Crowell.

JENKINS, P. (1997). *Counselling, Psychotherapy and the Law.* London: Sage.

KAGAN, N. and KAGAN, H. (1990). IPR: A validated model for the 1990s and beyond. *The Counseling Psychologist* **18**, 436–440.

KELLY, G. A. (1955). *The Psychology of Personal Constructs.* New York: Norton.

KLEINMAN, A. (1997). *Social Suffering.* Berkeley, CA: University of California Press.

KLINE, P. (1992). Problems of methodology in studies of psychotherapy. In: Dryden W. and Feltham, C. (eds), *Psychotherapy and its Discontents,* pp.64–85. Buckingham: Open University Press.

LAGO, C. and KITCHIN, D. (1998). *The Management of Counselling and Psychotherapy Agencies.* London: Sage.

LAGO, C. and SMITH, B. (eds) (2003). *Antidiscriminatory Counselling Practice.* London: Sage.

LAKE, F. (1966). *Clinical Theology.* London: Darton, Longman and Todd.

LAPLANCHE, J. and PONTALIS, J. B. (1988). *The Language of Psychoanalysis.* London: Karnac.

LAZARUS, A. A. (1981). *The Practice of Multimodal Therapy.* New York: McGraw-Hill.

LEIPER, R. with KENT, R. (2001). *Working Through Setbacks in Psychotherapy.* London: Sage.

LEVIN, D. (1989). *The Listening Self.* London: Routledge.

LOMAS, P. (1993). *Cultivating Intuition: An Introduction to Psychotherapy.* Northvale, NJ: Aronson.

LOWEN, A. (1976). *Bioenergetics.* London: Coventure.

LUBORSKY, L., SINGER, B. and LUBORSKY, L. (1975). Comparative studies of psychotherapies: Is it true that 'everyone has won and all must have prizes'? *Archives of General Psychiatry* **32**, 995–1008.

MAHRER, A. R. (1996). *The Complete Guide to Experiential Psychotherapy.* New York: Wiley.

MANTHEI, R. J. and MATTHEWS, D A. (1989). Helping the reluctant client to engage in counselling. In: Dryden, W. (ed.), *Key Issues for Counselling in Action,* pp. 37–44. London: Sage.

MASSON, J. M. (1992). The tyranny of psychotherapy. In: Dryden, W. and Feltham, C. (eds), *Psychotherapy and its Discontents,* pp. 7–28. Buckingham: Open University Press.

MAYS, D. T. and FRANKS, C. M. (1985). *Negative Outcome in Psychotherapy.* New York: Springer.

McLEOD, J. (1997). *Narrative and Psychotherapy.* London: Sage.

McLEOD, J. (2001). *Qualitative Research in Counselling and Psychotherapy.* London: Sage.

MEARNS, D. and DRYDEN, W. (eds) (1990). *Experiences of Counselling in Action.* London: Sage.

MEARNS, D. and THORNE, B. (1999). *Person-Centred Counselling in Action,* 2nd edition. London: Sage.

MEHRABIAN, A. (1971). *Silent Messages.* Belmont, CA: Wadsworth.

MILLER, A. (1987). *For Your Own Good.* London: Virago.

MILLER, W. R. and ROLLNICK, S. (1991). *Motivational Interviewing: Preparing People to Change Addictive Behavior.* New York: Guilford.

MINDELL, A. (1995). *Metaskills: The Spiritual Art of Therapy.* Tempe: New Falcon.

MOORE, T. (ed.) (1989). *The Essential James Hillman: A Blue Fire.* London: Routledge.

NELSON-JONES, R. (1989). *Effective Thinking Skills.* London: Cassell.

NEWMAN, F. (1991). *The Myth of Psychology.* New York: Castillo.

O'CONNOR, J. and SEYMOUR, J. (1990). *Introducing Neurolinguistic Programming.* London: Mandala.

PALMER, S. (ed.) (2002). *Multicultural Counselling: A Reader.* London: Sage.

PALMER, S. and McMAHON, G. (eds) (1997). *Client Assessment.* London: Sage.

PATTON, M. J. and MEARA, N. M. (1992). *Practice of Psychoanalytic Counseling,* Chichester: Wiley.

PITTS, J. H. (1992). Organising a practicum and internship program in counselor education. *Counselor Education and Supervision* **3(1)**, 196–207.

PROCHASKA, J. O. and DICLEMENTE, C. C. (1984). *The Transtheoretical Approach.* Homewood, IL: Dowjones-Irwin.

PROGOFF, I. (1975). *At a Journal Workshop.* New York: Dialogue House.

RATEY, J. J. and JOHNSON, C. (1997). *Shadow Syndromes.* London: Bantam.

ROGERS, C. R. (1961). *On Becoming A Person.* Boston, MA: Houghton-Mifflin.

ROSENFIELD, M. (1997). *Counselling by Telephone.* London: Sage.

ROTH, A. and FONAGY, P. (1996). *What Works For Whom? A Critical Review of Psychotherapy Research.* New York: Guilford.

ROWAN, J. (1990). *Subpersonalities.* London: Routledge.

ROWAN, J. (1998). *The Reality Game,* 2nd edition. London: Routledge.

ROWAN, J. (2002). *The Transpersonal in Psychotherapy and Counselling,* revised edition. London: Routledge.

ROWAN, J. and COOPER, M. (1998). *The Plural Self: Multiplicity in Everyday Life.* London: Sage.

ROWAN, J. and DRYDEN, W. (eds) (1988). *Innovative Therapy in Britain.* Milton Keynes: Open University Press.

ROWLAND, N. and GOSS, S. (eds) (2000). *Evidence-based Practice and Psychological Therapies: Research and Applications.* London: Routledge.

RUSSELL, D. E. H. (1983). The incidence and prevalence of intrafamilial and extrafamilial sexual abuse of female children. *Child Abuse* 7, 133-146.

RYCROFT, C. (1988). *A Critical Dictionary of Psychoanalysis.* Harmondsworth: Penguin.

RYLE, A. (1990). *Cognitive-Analytic Therapy: Active Participation in Change.* Chichester: Wiley.

SAMUELS, A. (1985). *Jung and the Postjungians.* London: Routledge and Kegan Paul.

SAMUELS, A. (1993). *The Political Psyche.* London: Routledge.

SAMUELS, A., SHORTER, B. and PLAUT, F. (1987). *A Critical Dictionary of Jungian Analysis.* London: Routledge and Kegan Paul.

SAPOLSKY, R. M. (1998). *Why Zebras Don't Get Ulcers.* New York: Freeman.

SCHUTZ, W. C. (1979). *Profound Simplicity.* London: Turnstone.

SCHUTZ, W. C. (1989). *Joy: Twenty Years Later.* Berkeley, CA: Ten Speed Press.

SEGAL, J. (1985). *Phantasy in Everyday Life.* Harmondsworth: Penguin.

SEGAL, Z. V., WILLIAMS, J. M. G. and TEASDALE, J. D. (2000). *Mindfulness-based Cognitive Therapy for Depression.* New York: Guilford.

SEXTON, J. and LEGG, C. (1999). Psychopharmacology: A Primer. In: Bor, R. and Watts, M. (eds) *The Trainee Handbook: A Guide for Counselling and Psychotherapy Trainees.* London: Sage.

SILLS, C. (ed.) (1998). *Contracts in Counselling.* London: Sage.

SMAIL, D. (1993). *The Origins of Unhappiness.* London: Harper Collins.

SMITH, D. L. (1991). *Hidden Conversations: An Introduction to Communicative Psychoanalysis.* London: Routledge.

SMITH, M. L., GLASS, G. V. and MILLER, G. I. (1980). *The Benefits of Psychotherapy.* Baltimore, MA: Johns Hopkins University Press.

ST. CLAIR, M. (2000). *Object Relations and Self Psychology*, 3rd edition. Belmont: Brooks/Cole.

STEVENS, A. and PRICE, J. (2000). *Evolutionary Psychiatry: A New Beginning*, 2nd edition. London: Routledge.

STEWART, I. (1989). *Transactional Analysis Counselling in Action.* London: Sage.

STEWART, I. and JOINES, V. (1987). *TA Today: A New Introduction to Transactional Analysis.* Nottingham: Lifespace.

STORR, A. (1963). *The Integrity of the Personality.* Harmondsworth: Penguin.

STREET, E. and DRYDEN, W. (eds) (1988). *Family Therapy in Britain.* Milton Keynes: Open University Press.

STRIANO, J. (1988). *Can Psychotherapists Hurt You?* Santa Barbara: Professional Press.

SUTHERLAND, S. (1991). *Macmillan Dictionary of Psychology.* London: Macmillan.

SZASZ, T. (1988). *The Myth of Psychotherapy.* New York: Syracuse University Press.

TALMON, M. (1990). *Single Session Therapy.* San Francisco, CA: Jossey-Bass.

TEDESCHI, R. G. and CALHOUN, L.G. (1995). *Trauma and Transformation.* Thousand Oaks, CA: Sage.

TILNEY, T. (1998). *Dictionary of Transactional Analysis.* London: Whurr.

TIMMS, N. and TIMMS, T. (1982). *Dictionary of Social Welfare.* London: Routledge and Kegan Paul.

TOATES, F. (1990). *Obsessional Thoughts and Behaviour.* Wellingborough: Thorsons.

TRUAX, C. B. and CARKHUFF, R. R. (1965). *Toward Effective Counseling and Psychotherapy: Training and Practice.* Chicago, IL: Aldine.

TUDOR, K. (1999). *Group Counselling.* London: Sage.

WALKER, M. (1990). *Women in Therapy and Counselling.* Buckingham: Open University Press.

WALROND-SKINNER, S. (1986). *Dictionary of Psychotherapy.* London: Routledge and Kegan Paul.

WEATHERHEAD, L. D. (1951). *Psychology, Religion and Healing.* London: Hodder and Stoughton.

WEST, W. (2000). *Psychotherapy and Spirituality.* London: Sage.

WHITMORE, D. (1991). *Psychosynthesis Counselling in Action* . London: Sage.

WILBER, K., ENGLER, J. and BROWN, D. P. (1986). *Transformations of Consciousness.* Boston, MA: New Science Library.

WOLFF, S. (1990). Child psychotherapy. In: Bloch, S. (ed.), *An Introduction to the Psychotherapies,* pp. 222–251. Oxford: Oxford University Press.

WOOD, G. (1983). *The Myth of Neurosis.* London: Macmillan.

WORDEN, J. W. (2003). *Grief Counselling and Grief Therapy*, 3rd edition. London: Routledge.

WORLD HEALTH ORGANIZATION (1993). *International Classification of Mental and Behavioural Disorders,* 10th edition. Geneva: WHO.

WOSKET, V. (1999). *The Therapeutic Use of Self.* London: Routledge.